Introducing
Sociolinguistics

MIRIAM MEYERHOFF

Routledge
Taylor & Francis Group

LONDON AND NEW YORK

First published
by Routledge
2 Park Square, Milton Park, Abingdon, Oxon OX14 4RN

Simultaneously published in the USA and Canada
by Routledge
270 Madison Ave, New York, NY 10016

Routledge is an imprint of the Taylor & Francis Group, an informa business

© 2006, Miriam Meyerhoff
Typeset in Akzindenz Grotesk and Eurostile by
Keystroke, Jacaranda Lodge, Wolverhampton
Printed and bound in Great Britain by Bell & Bain Ltd, Glasgow

British Library Cataloguing in Publication Data
A catalogue record for this book is available from the British Library

Library of Congress Cataloging in Publication Data
Meyerhoff, Miriam.
    Introducing sociolinguistics / Miriam Meyerhoff.
        p. cm.
    Includes bibliographical references and index.
    1. Sociolinguistics. I. Title.
    P40.M498 2006
    306.44–dc22   2006002748

ISBN 10: 0–415–39947–5 (hbk)
ISBN 10: 0–415–39948–3 (pbk)
ISBN 10: 0–203–45649–1 (ebk)

ISBN 13: 978–0–415–39947–0 (hbk)
ISBN 13: 978–0–415–39948–7 (pbk)
ISBN 13: 978–0–203–45649–1 (ebk)

Intr

'H   eld.
Us

                                                                          SA

'M   ne
of   ing
an   ed
an   es
all   io-
lin

                                                                          UK

Introdu   ary
nature   es,
present   sh
example   rns
and syste   ns
between d   ity.

Individ

- Social d
- Languag
- Politeness
- Multilingualism and language choice
- Real time and apparent time change in language
- Social class, social networks and communities of practice
- Gender
- Language and dialect contact

Most chapters include: exercises that enable readers to engage critically with the text; break-out boxes making connections between sociolinguistics and linguistic or social theory; and brief, lively add-ons guaranteed to make the book a memorable and enjoyable read. With a full glossary of terms and suggestions for further reading, this text gives students all the tools they need for an excellent command of sociolinguistics.

Miriam Meyerhoff has lived and taught sociolinguistics in places as diverse as New Zealand, Hawai'i, the mainland United States, Vanuatu and Scotland. She has consulted on sociolinguistic issues for the print and broadcast media and published books and articles on language variation, language and gender, and language contact. She is currently Professor of Sociolinguistics at the University of Edinburgh.

For Gillian and Janet –
because apples don't fall far from the tree

Contents

Figures

Tables

Sounds and symbols used in the text

The symbols that are used to represent speech sounds in this text are generally the symbols used in the IPA (International Phonetic Alphabet). The main vowel symbols used in this text are shown in the vowel chart over. The main consonant symbols are as follows:

Symbol	Example
p	pen
b	bit
t	tell
d	die
k	ca<u>k</u>e
g	goat
ʔ	[glottal stops, replaces final stops in many varieties of English, e.g. *hat* as [**hæʔ**]
tʃ	<u>ch</u>ur<u>ch</u>
dʒ	<u>j</u>ud<u>g</u>e
f	fan
v	view
θ	<u>th</u>irteen<u>th</u>
ð	<u>th</u>en
s	sick
z	zoo
ʃ	<u>sh</u>ip
ʒ	mea<u>s</u>ure
h	hat
m	moon
n	nine
ŋ	si<u>ng</u>
l	love
r	run
j	<u>y</u>ellow
w	wine

VOWELS

Where symbols appear in pairs, the one to the right
represents a rounded vowel

Sometimes the text uses the keywords from Wells's (1982) lexical sets to identify sounds in English. Wells's lexical sets are quite useful for identifying sounds across varieties of English. They were chosen so as to be able to refer concisely to groups of words that generally share the same vowel in varieties of southern British English and what is known as General American. The phonetic realisation of the vowel may be rather different in Received Pronunciation (RP) and General American (GenAm), but the set of words identified by the keyword generally will be the same. A list of Wells's keywords and the phonetic realisation of the vowel in those words in RP and GenAm follows:

RP	GenAm		Keyword	Examples
ɪ	ɪ	1	KIT	ship, sick, bridge, milk, myth, busy
e	ɛ	2	DRESS	step, neck, edge, shelf, friend, ready
æ	æ	3	TRAP	tap, back, badge, scalp, hand, cancel
ɒ	ɑ	4	LOT	stop, sock, dodge, romp, possible, quality
ʌ	ʌ	5	STRUT	cup, suck, budge, pulse, trunk, blood
ʊ	ʊ	6	FOOT	put, bush, full, good, look, wolf
ɑː	æ	7	BATH	staff, brass, ask, dance, sample, calf
ɒ	ɔ	8	CLOTH	cough, broth, cross, long, Boston
ɜː	ɜr	9	NURSE	hurt, lurk, urge, burst, jerk, term
iː	i	10	FLEECE	creep, speak, leave, feel, key, people
eɪ	eɪ	11	FACE	tape, cake, raid, veil, steak, day
ɑː	ɑ	12	PALM	psalm, father, bra, spa, lager
ɔː	ɔ	13	THOUGHT	taught, sauce, hawk, jaw, broad
əʊ	o	14	GOAT	soap, joke, home, know, so, roll
uː	u	15	GOOSE	loop, shoot, tomb, mute, huge, view
aɪ	aɪ	16	PRICE	ripe, write, arrive, high, try, buy
ɔɪ	ɔɪ	17	CHOICE	noise, join, toy, royal
aʊ	aʊ	18	MOUTH	out, house, loud, count, crowd, cow

ɪə	ɪ(r	19 NEAR	beer, sin<u>cere</u>, fear, beard, <u>se</u>rum
ɛə	ɛ(r	20 SQUARE	care, fair, pear, where, scarce, <u>va</u>ry
ɑː	ɑ(r	21 START	far, sharp, bark, carve, farm, heart
ɔː	ɔ(r	22 NORTH	for, war, short, scorch, born, warm
ɔː	o(r	23 FORCE	four, wore, sport, porch, borne, <u>sto</u>ry
ʊə	ʊ(r	24 CURE	poor, <u>tou</u>rist, pure, <u>plu</u>ral, <u>ju</u>ry

In some varieties of English Wells's keywords are not unique sets (e.g. many speakers of English do not distinguish FOOT and STRUT), or there may be splits within a set (e.g. the BATH set may subdivide, and speakers may have different vowels for *dance* and *grass*). So the keyword system is in no way a substitute for the detail of the IPA. Nevertheless, it is a very useful system, especially for readers who may not be 100 per cent fluent in the IPA.

Acknowledgements

This book is the product of a strong team that has stood beside me, giving me help as I worked on it. My thanks go to the many people who generously answered my questions, shared useful teaching materials, discussed theory and helped with specific linguistic examples that have informed the final product. These include: Peter Austin, Loreen Bani, Vanua Bani, Andrew Beach, T.G. Beekarry, Emily Bender, Hélène Blondeau, Dave Britain, Isa Buchstaller, Debbie Cameron, Abby Cohn, Mary Cresswell, Terry Crowley, Alexandre François, Howard Giles, Alice Greenwood, Zakaris Hansen, Jake Harwood, Jennifer Hay, David Heap, Mie Hiramoto, Catriona Hyslop, Janet Holmes, Stefanie Jannedy, William Labov, Bob Ladd, Lamont Lindstrom, John Lynch, Miki Makihara, Julian Mason, Norma Mendoza-Denton, Sam Meyerhoff, Amanda Minks, Naomi Nagy, Terttu Nevalainen, Nancy Niedzielski, Shigeko Okamoto, Mitsuhiko Ota, Robert Podesva, Dennis Preston, Aaliya Rajah-Carrim, Suzanne Romaine, Gillian Sankoff, Guy Sibilla, John Singler, Oliver Stegen, Karin Sode, Sumittra Suraratdecha, Sharon Morrie Tabi, Sandra Thompson, Graeme Trousdale, Peter Trudgill, Kaori Ueki, Linda Van Bergen. The exercises on how people address each other are based on those devised by Sally McConnell-Ginet and William Labov for their sociolinguistics classes. Used with permission and thanks. The students in L102 Fall 1999 at the University of Hawai'i provided the input on the decision trees in Chapter 6. The generosity and insights of all these people have enriched my understanding of sociolinguistics and language in use, and I thank them for that.

Conversations over the years with David Adger, Emily Bender, Jenny Cheshire, Chris Collins, Dave Embick, Kirk Hazen, Nancy Niedzielski (and through her, Robert Englebretson), Mark Steedman, and Sandy Thompson have fostered and reinforced my belief that sociolinguistics can and should always strive to make connections with other fields.

I perhaps owe my interest in sociolinguistics most of all to someone who works entirely outside the profession. For more than thirty years, Madeline Smith has been sharing with me her tips and observations on incipient language change and the role of language in society. Without a doubt, she is one of the most gifted and natural sociolinguists I have ever known, and it is a privilege and a joy to me that after all these years we are still mucking around with language together.

The map in Figure 4.3 is courtesy of Land Information New Zealand/Toitu te Whenua, free download available from <www.linz.govt.nz/rcs/linz/pub/web/root/core/Topography/ TopographicMaps/mapdownloads/juliuspetroterrainmap/index.jsp>, sampled 29 May 2003. The Vanuatu and South African Constitutions (Chapter 4) can be viewed online at <http://www.vanuatu.gov.vu/government/library/constitution.html> (sampled August 2004, June 2005) and the Constitutional Court of South Africa <http://www.concourt.gov. za/constitution/> (sampled May 2005).

Figure 3.6 from A. Bell, 'Language style as audience design' in *Language and Society* 13, 1984, p.160, reprinted by permission of Cambridge University Press.

Figure 5.2 from Penelope Brown, Stephen C. Levinson and John L. Gumperz, *Politeness*, 1987, p.69, reprinted by permission of Cambridge University Press.

Figure 7.1 from Van de Velde *et al.*, 'The devoicing of fricatives in Standard Dutch' in *Language Variation and Change*, 1996, p.165, reprinted by permission of Cambridge University Press.

Figure 7.2 from Sali Tagliamonte, '*Was/were* variation across the generations' in *Language Variation and Change*, 1998, p.182, reprinted by permission of Cambridge University Press.

Figure 7.3 from Sali Tagliamonte, '*Was/were* variation across the generations' in *Language Variation and Change*, 1998, p.179, reprinted by permission of Cambridge University Press.

Figure 8.2 from Shana Poplack and Douglas Walker, 'Going through (1) in Canadian French' in David Sankoff (ed.) *Diversity and Diachrony*, 1986, p.189, reprinted by permission of John Benjamins Company, Amsterdam/Philadelphia <www.benjamins.com>.

Figure 8.4 from Labov, *Sociolinguistic Patterns*, 1972, p.127, reprinted by permission of the University of Pennsylvania Press.

Figure 8.11 from William Labov, *Sociolinguistic Patterns*, 1972, p.129, reprinted by permission of the University of Pennsylvania Press.

Figure 8.13 from Terttu Nevalainen, 'Making the best use of "bad" data' in *Neuphilologische Mitteilungen*, 1999, p.523, reprinted by kind permission of the author.

Figure 10.7 from Sali Tagliamonte, '*Was/were* variation across the generations' in *Language Variation and Change*, 1998, p.178, reprinted by permission of Cambridge University Press.

Table 11.1 from Gillian Sankoff, 'Focus in Tok Pisin' in Francis Byrne and Donald Winford (eds) *Focus and Grammatical Relations in Creole Languages*, 1993, p.131, reprinted by permission of John Benjamins Company, Amsterdam/Philadelphia <www.benjamins.com>.

Figure 11.3 from Gillian Sankoff, 'Focus in Tok Pisin' in Francis Byrne and Donald Winford (eds) *Focus and Grammatical Relations in Creole Languages*, 1993, p.133, reprinted by permission of John Benjamins Company, Amsterdam/Philadelphia <www.benjamins.com>.

Example 6 in Chapter 11 is courtesy of Isabelle Buchstaller and the Stanford University research project studying *be all*.

Every effort has been made to trace and contact copyright holders. The publishers would be pleased to hear from any copyright holders not acknowledged here so that this section may be amended at the earliest opportunity.

The following people volunteered to read sometimes very rough drafts of this work as it was in progress: Debbie Cameron, Kirk Hazen, Sally McConnell-Ginet, Naomi Nagy, Nancy Niedzielski, Jack Sidnell, Jennifer Smith, Graeme Trousdale, and (with very special thanks) James Walker.

I would like to also express my gratitude to two anonymous reviewers and Aaliya Rajah-Carrim who read the entire manuscript in final draft and provided me with challenging and supportive commentary on content and structure. Readers have a special reason to be grateful to Evelyn Reid and Laura Robson who so generously made time to give the manuscript a close reading and provide me with exhaustive comments from a student's-eye view – even as they were finishing their own undergraduate dissertations and fourth-year final assignments.

For financial support in fieldwork, which I hope makes this a more lively read, and for administrative assistance, I thank: the Wenner-Gren Foundation; the University of Edinburgh Alumni Development Trust; the University of Edinburgh School of Philosophy, Psychology and Language Sciences; the British Academy; and the Carnegie Trust for the Universities of Scotland.

My thanks as well to the team at Routledge for the genial and speedy handling of the book's production, especially Kate Ahl and Alan Fidler.

Maps

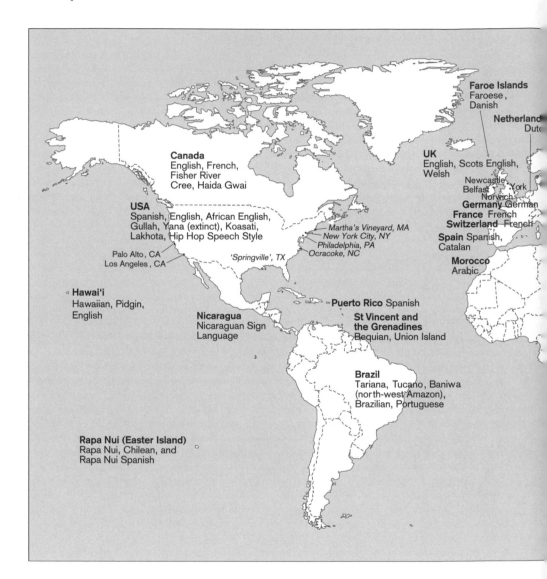

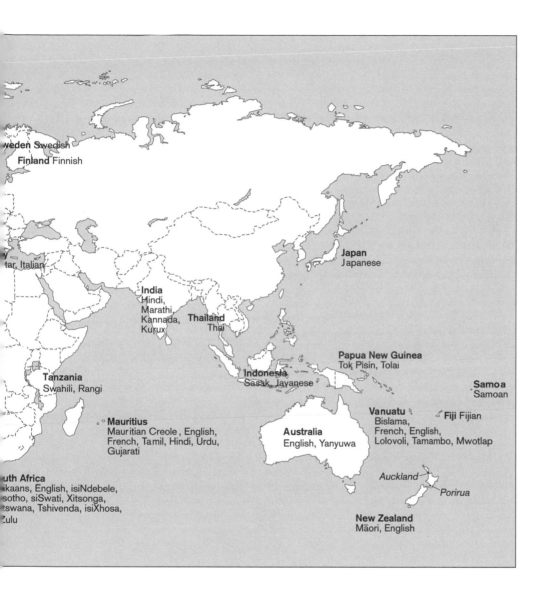

This textbook draws its examples from many languages and many different countries or locales. Some of them you will be familiar with; some of them you may not. This map shows where the languages mentioned in the text are spoken. Note that there are more languages spoken and used on a daily basis, in every country identified here. Also note that some of the language labels (such as *Fijian*) lump together a number of different varieties.

CHAPTER 1

Introduction

WHAT IS SOCIOLINGUISTICS?

If I had a penny for every time I have tried to answer the question, 'So what *is* sociolinguistics?', I would be writing this book in the comfort of an early retirement. And if there was a way of defining it in one simple, yet comprehensive, sentence, there might not be a need for weighty introductory textbooks.

Sociolinguistics is a very broad field, and it can be used to describe many different ways of studying language. A lot of linguists might describe themselves as sociolinguists, but the people who call themselves sociolinguists may have rather different interests from each other and they may use very different methods for collecting and analysing data. This can be confusing if you are coming new to the field. Is sociolinguistics about how individual speakers use language? Is it about how people use language differently in different towns or regions? Is it about how a nation decides what languages will be recognised in courts or education?

The answer is: yes, yes, and yes. Sociolinguists conduct research on any of those topics. For example, if a speaker describes a funny or amusing situation as 'kicksin', I know they are from, or have spent a good deal of time in, the English-speaking Caribbean. I am drawing on sociolinguistic (social and linguistic) knowledge to draw this inference.

Or take the case of Jennifer, who grew up in a small traditionally fishing village in the north-east of Scotland, but spent many years teaching English in Greece. Jennifer can draw on a number of different styles or ways of speaking, depending on who she is talking to. If her interlocutor is a member of her family, she still uses a variety of Scots which is virtually incomprehensible to other native speakers of English. She says 'fit' instead of 'what'; 'na' instead of 'don't'; 'doon' instead of 'down'; 'be'er' instead of 'better', and so forth. But in Greece she quickly learnt that she needed to adopt a less regionally marked way of speaking if her students were going to understand her, and when she later began attending professional conferences with an international audience, she had the same experience. Everyone can modify the way they speak depending on who they are with or what the situation is. When they do this, they are drawing on their sociolinguistic knowledge. And every time they change the way they speak, depending on their interlocutor or situation, they provide more sociolinguistic information that builds up the sociolinguistic knowledge in the community.

HOW DO SOCIOLINGUISTS STUDY SOCIOLINGUISTICS?

Sociolinguists use a range of methods to analyse patterns of language in use and attitudes towards language in use. Some sociolinguistic patterns can only be observed systematically through close examination of lots of recorded speech and a good understanding about the speaker's background or place in a community.

On the other hand, sociolinguists who are interested in investigating national language policies might never need to use any audio or video recordings at all. A lot of relevant information on language planning can be gleaned from library and archive materials, or from more free-form discussions with members of the communities being studied. For example, official newspaper reports and letters to the editor provide the researcher with a range of perspectives just in one medium.

A major challenge that sociolinguists face is that a lot of the time speakers are completely unaware of the ways in which language is used differently in different contexts. Or if they are aware, they can only talk about it in very general terms. For example, when dialectologists want to find out where one traditional local dialect begins and ends, they can often ask people directly. It's not unheard of for people to be able to identify (correctly) the village – or even the house! – where people stop using one pronunciation of the word for 'child' and start using another pronunciation. But when sociolinguists try to get people to discuss the different ways they use language, the answers they get are typically more vague: 'Of course I change the way I speak. How? I don't know, lots of ways . . .' So sociolinguists have devised a number of different methods for getting at these semi-conscious or subconscious norms. We will examine a number of such methods in this book.

MAKING BROADER CONNECTIONS

As well as differing in the kinds of methods they use, different kinds of sociolinguists may have different goals – what they want their research to shed light on, or how they hope it might change the field. This book also tries to make these kinds of issues clear to readers. In order to do this, it stops at various points to comment explicitly on relevant theoretical issues raised by the data or methods being discussed at that point. I feel this is very important for a number of reasons. The first is that students often have the opportunity to take only one sociolinguistics course in an undergraduate linguistics degree. This means it is particularly helpful if they can see quickly – as the subject unfolds – where and how sociolinguists might have something to contribute to or learn from descriptive or theoretical linguists.

The second reason is that many people take sociolinguistics as an 'outside' subject while they are pursuing a degree in another field, e.g. languages, social anthropology, sociology, media studies, or communication. For these students, it is even more imperative that an introduction to sociolinguistics provides them with both the basic findings and linguistic insights of the field, and also an immediate sense of how and where sociolinguistic research intersects with and can inform research in their major subject.

A third reason is even more pragmatic. In a sense, each of the boxes in the text that offer a 'Connection with Theory' represents one attempt to answer the question I started out with: 'So what *is* sociolinguistics?'

SOCIOLINGUISTIC QUESTIONS

Even though sociolinguistics wears many caps, one thing linking all of the practitioners in the field is that they are all interested in how people use language and what they use it for. In other words, sociolinguists are not only interested in documenting the different form of language – what it looks like and how it is structured – but also want to answer questions like:

- Who uses those different forms or language varieties?
- Who do they use them with?
- Are they aware of their choice?
- Why do some forms or languages 'win out' over others? (And is it always the same ones?)
- Is there any relationship between the forms in flux in a community of speakers?
- What kind of social information do we ascribe to different forms in a language or different language varieties?
- How much can we change or control the language we use?

This is what we mean when we say that sociolinguists are interested in both 'social' questions and 'linguistic' questions. Inevitably, some sociolinguistics research has more to say about social issues, and some sociolinguistic research has more to say about linguistic matters, but what makes someone's work distinctively sociolinguistic will be the fact that, regardless of its emphasis, it has something to say about both linguistic structure and social structure.

STRUCTURE OF THIS BOOK

This book introduces some of the different ways in which sociolinguists research language in use. It looks at the ways in which people use language and how these are related to larger issues of social structure. You will find that it is structured rather differently from other introductions to sociolinguistics, and sometimes discusses 'classic' sociolinguistic studies from a novel perspective. However, its structure reflects what I have found works best after nearly twenty years of involvement in teaching sociolinguistics to undergraduate and (post-)graduate classes. It also directly reflects the extremely helpful feedback and advice about structuring a one-semester course in sociolinguistics that I have received from students themselves over the last five years.

One of its more radical departures from most sociolinguistics texts is that it starts by providing the reader with a very firm grounding in research showing how speakers use language to present themselves to others and to identify or differentiate themselves from others. This includes variation in the form of an individual's choice of language as well as their use of different styles, or repertoires, in a language. In my experience, starting with the individual, and then working through other sociolinguistic topics, has a number of teaching advantages. First, it makes the subject matter directly accessible and relevant to students. As I have noted, people are generally aware of their potential to use language differently in different social contexts, but they lack the means of articulating this sociolinguistic knowledge. The first half of this book provides them with the means to articulate what they already know through personal experience.

Second, I feel that by gradually expanding the focus from the way individuals use language to the way groups of individuals use language enables students to see more clearly what the connections are between sociolinguistics and contact between dialects and languages. Most introductory sociolinguistics texts either finesse this link or add it in as a chapter that is only minimally connected to the larger picture of language in use. The goal of this book is to provide readers with a sense of the seamless connections between individual speakers and varieties of languages. When readers subsequently choose to specialise or focus their attention on one part of the continuum (as we all must), they will nevertheless do so with a clear sense of how their work fits into a broader social and/or linguistic picture.

In addition to the connections with theory, readers will find two other forms of 'digression' in this text. Exercises are provided in order to consolidate through practice the information that has just been discussed in the text. These are not intended as test questions; I have interleaved them with the text because they are designed to take the reader a little further (sometimes anticipating material which follows later).

Finally, the text also includes what newspaper journalists call 'brights'. These are short, sometimes quirky, comments which (I hope) remind us that, when all is said and done, we study sociolinguistics because it is fun.

The chapters

Chapter 2 starts with a historical perspective and discusses how both the methodological and theoretical roots of sociolinguistics lie in traditional regional dialect studies. It discusses how researchers were able to show that there are social dialects, just as there are regional dialects, and how the methods associated with traditional regional dialectology have been adapted to sociolinguists' interests. The kinds of differences between the ways different speakers use language can be used to define not only regional but also social dialects.

These methods continue to be very influential in the study of language in society so they provide an important backdrop to interpreting the research that is discussed in subsequent chapters. This is especially true for the kinds of research identified as variationist sociolinguistics. However, I believe it is just as true for any study of the relationship between society and language use and that is why I devote a good deal of space to establishing some of these principles and theoretical tools early in the book. Even qualitative studies, and even studies of language and politics, are improved if researchers understand that their work is concerned with (i) establishing social patterns and (ii) understanding the systematicity or social beliefs underlying apparently unconstrained variation.

Chapter 3 then looks at how we all alter the way we speak depending on where we are, who we are talking to, and what our attitude is towards the people we are talking with. In other words, this chapter focuses on the speech of individual speakers. This kind of variability in language use is highly salient, which means that if you ask the average person to think about the way people use language in their community, one of the first things they talk about are the changes that people make to their speech in different situations or with different addressees. This can be called style-shifting, and we will see how you can objectively identify features of different speaking styles. Chapter 3 also considers some of the different explanations that have been proposed for how and why people alter their speaking style in different contexts.

Chapter 4 builds on the style-shifting discussed in Chapter 3 and looks more generally at how speakers use language as a scaffold for formulating and expressing attitudes about others. It begins with a discussion of how this relates to sexist language. We return to the dialectology roots of sociolinguistics, but with a new perspective. This chapter explores how people's attitudes to language and language users can be used to complement traditional maps of regional dialects. Also, it introduces and defines the important notion of speaker accommodation or attunement to others. It considers some interesting case studies that indicate that speakers may sometimes believe they are saying one thing, or intend to say one thing, but what they in fact produce is very different.

Chapter 5 develops another strand of research that was implicit in Chapters 3 and 4. It discusses politeness – a feature of language which is clearly very heavily affected by cultural and societal norms or expectations, but which is generally expressed and realised between individuals. Politeness strategies in different languages provide an interesting case study of how macro-social, or societal, factors interact with and are mediated by considerations that are essentially micro-social, or inter-speaker.

In Chapter 6, we draw back from the very personal perspective on style-shifting and language attitudes that have been the basis for Chapters 3–5. Here, we consider issues such as how speakers within multilingual communities decide which language to use and when. We consider some of the ways in which institutions and nation-states have engaged with the politics and emotions surrounding the recognition and validation of different language varieties. Here, too, we introduce the idea that languages have different levels of vitality. This refers to how widely used a language is within a community and how good a chance it has of continuing to be used by successive generations. All these matters are of particular importance now, given the very real concern that many languages today are dying out or being abandoned by their speakers in large numbers. This concern is shared by linguists and the speakers of such lesser-spoken languages. Measures to maintain and enhance the vitality of languages are also a challenge for large institutions like the European Union as more states are admitted to the Union and more language varieties officially and unofficially become part of the cultural and communicative repertoire of the EU.

At this point, there is a shift in focus. In Chapters 7–10 we examine some of the social factors that have often been found to delineate different social dialects. Chapter 7 looks at time. Time has been a hugely important topic throughout the history of philosophy, and sociolinguists are among the few linguists to grapple with some of the problems associated with exploring time. We know that languages change over time, and in this chapter we look at how interspeaker variation can be observed by comparing the speech of a community at different periods. But we also see that traces of the passage of time can be detected even in samples of speech at a single moment in time. We will see that speakers of different ages can provide a window on how languages change over time. We will also look at cases where speakers change the way they speak over time and see how such examples of intraspeaker variation can be used as diagnostics of different kinds of sociolinguistic variation.

Chapters 8 and 9 examine the effects that social class or speakers' social networks have on the variation that exists in the community at large. Perhaps unsurprisingly, we will see that who you associate with through work or friendship networks can have a significant impact on how you talk. We will consider the possibility that it is within very tightly knit friendship networks that the changes which become associated with a particular social class are negotiated and first emerge.

Chapter 10 looks at the effect of gender on speech and distinguishes 'gender' from 'sex'. This chapter is somewhat longer than most others, but this is because of the tremendous interest this topic usually generates in sociolinguistics courses and because research in language and gender has been particularly lively since the early 1990s. The chapter focuses largely on research that has been concerned with the details of linguistic performance and how these details are related to details of social organisation between and among groups of male and female speakers. It links very closely with the discussion of networks and the intimate relationship between social and linguistic practices that is introduced in Chapter 9.

In effect we move from a discussion of the outcomes of contact between individuals in Chapters 2–6, to contact between and within social groups in Chapters 7–10. Finally, in Chapter 11, we broaden the lens even further. In Chapter 11 we consider contact at an even more abstract level, and examine several case studies of the outcomes of contact between different varieties of English and the contact between quite different languages that leads to the creation and development of creole languages. These examples raise timely issues like the question of whether increasing globalisation and cross-linguistic contact is having an effect on the structure of languages and the vitality of languages in a multilingual world. There are links here with Chapters 4 and 6.

ON QUANTITATIVE AND QUALITATIVE METHODS

The content of the book is intended to circle round on itself, examining aspects of how people use language and the social meaning of variation from a number of different perspectives – broad and narrow views of variation, idiosyncratic and personal meanings of language in use, as well as more conventionalised, social meanings ascribed to language in use. These different perspectives provide complementary views of what language does in a social world, and this book provides a number of complementary means by which we can analyse the different social functions that language serves. As we will see, quantitative data is complemented by what researchers call qualitative data. In practice, this means that in order to interpret what the distribution of forms means across different groups or in different contexts we need solid data on the distribution of forms; but we also have to know when and how to move beyond the numbers in order to evaluate the way in which those distributional patterns are being used by speakers in a particular social or interactional context.

A note for instructors on the quantitative skills required

Generally, this book doesn't require the reader to be able to handle anything much more complicated than percentages in order to understand the points being discussed. Percentages are OK as a first pass over quantitative data (they make a small adjustment for the relative frequency with which a form is used by, say, different groups of speakers). However, in some places, I will be reporting the results of studies that have made more sensitive, statistical adjustments.

> Readers don't need to be able to do these tests themselves in order to understand what's going on.

Students in sociolinguistics classes have often convinced themselves that they are the kind of people who 'can't do' numbers, and they get very nervous when numbers start to appear. Even these students can handle the quantitative data in this book. The text always demystifies and explains what the tests show (and sometimes explains what the tests are doing). Aside from percentages, the kind of quantitative adjustment you are most likely to encounter in this book is one that provides a **weighting** for the frequency of a form. Very simply, this means that it restates how often a form occurs in the speech of a particular group of speakers, or in a particular style, or in a particular linguistic environment, *given how common that group, or style or environment is in the entire corpus*. So it is a further adjustment, over and above the kind of frequency adjustment a percentage makes.

Although weightings don't actually represent a frequency count like percentages, but since most university students feel competent enough to handle percentages, I have found that, for the purposes of an introductory class in sociolinguistics, it works quite well to gloss weightings as 'adjusted percentages'. Other instructors may find better terms for their audience of students.

CHAPTER 2

Variation and language

Key terms in this chapter:

- **variable**
- **variants**
- **constrain/constraints**
- **free variation**
- **determinism**
- **regional dialectology**
- **reallocation**
- **intermediate forms**

- **social dialectology**
- **interspeaker/intraspeaker variation**
- **synchronic variation**
- **diachronic change**
- **stereotypes**
- **markers**
- **indicators**

VARIABLES AND VARIANTS

Variable

In this text, principally an abstract representation of the source of variation. Realised by two or more *variants*.

Some friends were sitting outside one evening in Bequia (an island in St Vincent and the Grenadines) where they were about to watch a video and have a drink. One person lifted their glass and said 'Cheers!', to which their neighbour replied 'Chairs and tables'. This is a play on the way *cheer* and *chair* are often pronounced the same way on Bequia. The **variable** (i.e. the feature that varies) is the vowel – in this case a centring diphthong – and the different variants at play in the community at large are realisations of the diphthong with a closer starting point [tʃiəz] that sounds like Standard English *cheers* or a more open starting point [tʃeəz] that sounds more like Standard English *chairs*.

When you are studying variation, whether it is from a quantitative or qualitative perspective, it is important to define as precisely as possible what the object of your investigation is. The general or abstract feature that you are investigating is what is called the **variable**. The actual instantiations of the variable in speech are known as the **variants**.

Variant

The actual realisation of a *variable*. Analogous to the phonetic realisations of a phoneme.

There are two ways we can identify a variable. One convention is to write a variable in parentheses, i.e., (ear) in this case. A second convention is to refer to vowel variables by using the system of key words in Wells (1982). In this particular case, we would talk about the NEAR vowel or the NEAR lexical set. I will often use Wells's key words in this text, because they have been chosen carefully to pick out classes of words which are reasonably robust across different varieties of English. (A full list of Wells's key words is provided on pp. xvi–xvii.)

The relationship between variables and variants is shown in Figure 2.1. On the left, I have tried to illustrate the general relationship between an abstract linguistic form and the variants that actually realise that form in speech. On the right, I have replaced the general terms with the variable discussed above, and shown the two most common variants: one with an open onset to the diphthong; the other with a more close onset.

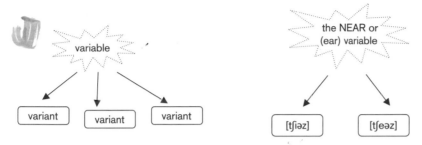

Figure 2.1   The relationship between a sociolinguistic variable and its realisation as different variants. Illustrated with an example from the English spoken on Bequia (St Vincent and the Grenadines).

Identifying variables and variants

- How do you express the concept *die* or *dead*? How many different ways can you think of expressing the idea that someone has died? What determines your use of these different ways of phrasing the same idea?
- Now try and think of at least one word (or set of words) that you sometimes pronounce in different ways (like the example of 'cheers/chairs' in Bequian given above). What determines your use of these different pronunciations? Is it the same kinds of factors that you identified in the *die* example?
- Do social factors enter into your account of pronunciation more or less than they do into your account of vocabulary differences? Why do you think that might be?
- For both the examples above, say what you would consider to be the **variable** and say what the **variants** are.

exercise

Regular vs probabilistic alternations between variants

So the relationship between the abstract concept of a variable and the actual variants that realise it is very similar to the relationship between the abstract notion of a phoneme and the actual phonetic realisations of that phoneme. The sound represented orthographically as *p* in English has very different realisations, depending on where it occurs in a word. When it occurs by itself at the start of a word, as in *pinch*, it is pronounced with quite clear aspiration (i.e., an extra burst of air that is very clear if the speaker is standing too close to a microphone). But when it occurs at the end of a word, as in *rap*, or when it follows an *s* at the start of a word, as in *speak*, it is pronounced without the aspiration.

This variation is quite predictable and depends entirely on the immediate linguistic context in which the *p* occurs. Phonologists distinguish what they call the phoneme, which is represented as /p/, from the phonetic variants, one of which is aspirated and one of which is not aspirated (together these are called the allophones of /p/). The phonetic realisations of /p/ can be distinguished in print by using the conventions of the International Phonetic Alphabet (IPA), i.e., [pʰ] for the aspirated variant and [p] for the unaspirated one. (A full list of the symbols in the IPA is provided on pp. xv–xvi.) Because syllable position determines which variant of /p/ is used, we can say that the realisations of the phoneme are **constrained** by where it occurs in a syllable.

However, there is an important difference between the alternation between [pʰ] and [p] in English and the alternation between [tʃiəz] and [tʃeəz] in Bequian. The constraints on /p/ are completely regular and predictable so you always know which variant will surface when. With the NEAR class of words in Bequian, the situation is less precise. The same person will sometimes use one variant and sometimes the other variant. The same speaker may even alternate in different sentences. For instance, a woman on Bequia was heard calling to her grandson at dusk one evening. The exchange went like this:

> (1)   Jed! Come here! [heə]
>   (silence from Jed)
>   Jed!! Come here!! [hiər]

The first time she said *here* she pronounced it with the open variant, and the second time she pronounced it with the more close variant (the appearance of the 'r' sound at the end is a separate phenomenon in Bequian; what is of interest is the realisation of the vowel).

For a long time, linguists described variables like this as examples of **free variation**. By *free* they meant that there were no clear linguistic constraints which would predict when you got one variant rather than another. So *free* essentially meant *unconstrained*. You will still hear linguists use the phrase *free variation*, but it is a bit sloppy to employ it now. This is because since the 1960s sociolinguists have amassed considerable evidence showing that speaker variability can be constrained by non-linguistic factors (things external to the linguistic system) as well as by linguistic factors. The effects of social factors are seldom categorical; that is, all speakers generally alternate at some time. No social or contextual constraint determines where you will hear one form rather than another 100 per cent of the time. However, they will tell you how likely you are to hear different forms in different contexts and with different speakers. The difference is probabilistic. This is why it is so helpful to take the trouble to quantify forms for different speakers or in different contexts. (The notion of **determinism** recurs in Chapter 4 when we discuss sexist language. The theoretical importance of distinguishing between forms which occur 100 per cent of the time or just most of the time in some people's speech is discussed further in Chapter 10 where we look at the question of whether women and men speak the same or differently.)

Arguably, though, the only thing that is free about free variation is that it frees the linguist up to dust their hands and say 'OK, we've analysed that!' Sociolinguists' studies of language in use have shown that variation is always more or less constrained by some factor relevant to the context in which a speaker is using their language. Assuming that a linguist's job is to account for as much of the diversity of human language as possible, then they can be seen as abdicating a lot of their responsibility if they consign aspects of the linguistic to a black box called 'free variation'. Sociolinguists have shown that a lot of what appears to be free variation can be accounted for if linguists take social factors into account as well as linguistic factors.

Linguistics has a great deal to gain by distancing itself from a notion like free variation. Sociolinguists argue that even though sociolinguistic analyses don't enable us to predict with

Constrain/ constraints

If the distribution of *variants* is neither random nor *free*, and instead shows systematic correlations with *independent factors*, those factors can be said to constrain the variation, or to be the constraints on the *variable*.

Free variation

The idea that some *variants* alternate with each other without any reliable *constraints* on their occurrence in a particular context or by particular speakers.

Determinism/ deterministic

The idea that there is a strong causal relationship between two factors (i.e., one determines how the other will be). The idea that if you know the value for one factor, you can automatically and reliably predict the value for another. (See also *Linguistic relativism*.)

100 per cent certainty which variant will surface, where, and when, sociolinguistic studies reveal an additional layer of systematic structure that justifies the limited indeterminacy that remains.

In sum, a sociolinguistic variable can be defined as a linguistic variable that is constrained by social or non-linguistic factors, and the concept of a variable constrained by non-linguistic factors emerges straightforwardly from the traditions of dialectology.

In the next section, we briefly look at the methods that are used by dialectologists who are interested in documenting the way speakers use language differently and why language varies depending on what village, town or region speakers come from. Following this, we move on to examine how a more comprehensively *social* dialectology emerged from **regional dialectology**.

REGIONAL DIALECTOLOGY: MAPPING SPEAKERS AND PLACES

The nineteenth century was a particularly good time in the history of the study of regional variation in language. Some very large projects were initiated in Europe, some of which continued to run well into the twentieth century. An early and ambitious example of these was the *Altas Linguistique de la France* or 'Alf', as it is commonly called. This project was begun by Jules Gilliéron and the data collection was carried out by a fieldworker, Edmond Edmont, who bicycled all around France stopping in small villages where he interviewed older speakers and asked them what the local word was for a number of vocabulary items and then carefully noted the local pronunciation of different words. Edmont was trained to use a consistent system for transcribing regional pronunciations, and at every point in his fieldwork he administered the same questionnaire. This standardisation of methods was an important breakthrough as it allowed thorough and reliable comparisons to be made between different localities.

The results of dialect surveys are often plotted on maps, thus providing an atlas which, instead of showing topographical features like mountains and plains, shows how speakers' pronunciation of words changes as you move across physical space. The distribution of different forms – pronunciations or sentence patterns – can be shown with different symbols superimposed on a map of the region which plots every point surveyed.

> In 2000, three sociolinguists celebrated the 100th anniversary of the completion of Edmont's fieldwork. David Heap, Naomi Nagy and Jeff Tennant cycled from point 797 to point 798 (the towns of Rivesaltes and Collioure).

A number of detailed atlas projects were undertaken across Europe at about the same time – for example, in Switzerland, Germany, Italy and Spain. (More recently, dialect atlases of North America have been undertaken.) One of the last to be completed was the dialect atlas for the Iberian peninsula (*Linguistic Atlas of the Iberian Peninsula*, or *ALPI*), because work on this was interrupted by the Spanish Civil War in the first half of the twentieth century. However, regional dialectology is by no means a historical exercise. For example, there are ongoing projects involving the comparison of structures across Germanic languages.

Regional dialectology

The identification and mapping of boundaries between different varieties on the basis of clusters of similar and different features in particular regions, towns or villages.

No, really?

One of the *ALPI* fieldworkers found out firsthand how badly people can mis-understand linguistic research. Following the military coup in Spain in 1936, Aníbal Otero (1911–1974) was arrested while undertaking fieldwork in northern Portugal. He had sent a letter back to his family in Galicia commenting on the legitimacy of the Republican government. On the basis of 'evidence' that he was a spy – which included, especially, his suspicious notebooks full of incomprehensible notes in 'code' – Otero was convicted of treason and sentenced to death by firing squad. The testimony of scholars that Otero's notebooks were not in fact a spy's code, but rather linguistic transcriptions, enabled him to have his sentence commuted to life imprisonment. Otero somehow managed to continue his research during his years in various military prisons: he surveyed different fellow prisoners' speech, carefully noting each subject's place of birth and other characteristics. After being released, Otero's health never recovered and he returned to live a private life in his home village, Lugo.

Our awareness of the different linguistic forms we use

One problem with the methods used by dialectologists is that they depend almost entirely on speakers' reports of what they *think* they say. People may not be very accurate in reporting what they actually *do* say. For example, we may believe that we use one form because school has drummed it into us that this is the 'correct' way to speak. Or we may be subconsciously influenced by the spelling of a word when we report on how we pronounce it.

What would **you** say if someone asked you:

'Do you say *The problem is, is that we need more time* or *The problem is that we need more time*?

What would **you** say if someone asked you:

'Do you say *fas' cars and dangerous livin'* or *fast cars and dangerous living*?'
'Do you say *libry* or *library*?'

Try asking some other people and see what they say.

USING REGIONAL DIALECT DATA TO INFORM THEORY

The maps that Gilliéron and Edmont produced from their fieldwork display how language intersects with geographical space, but regional dialectology can be used to do more than simply document where people use one form or another. Quite early on some linguists realised that the level of detail in many of the regional dialect atlases could be used to inform linguistic theory. For instance, William Moulton used the dialect maps for parts of Switzerland and Italy to argue in favour of the principle of maximum differentiation. Moulton noticed that in varieties of Swiss there was a consistent relationship between whether or not a dialect centralised its low, short-*a* vowel and the number of other low vowels in that variety. He noticed that if the variety had a central [a], then it would have both a low front and a low back vowel. But if speakers of one variety had fronted the short-*a*, then that variety generally did not have another low front vowel. Conversely, if speakers had backed the short-*a* in any particular variety, then that variety generally did not have another low back vowel, it would only have a *mid* back vowel. Moulton suggested that the reason for this was that if the short-*a* vowel fronted there might not be a big enough difference between the way it sounded and the way the other low front vowel might sound, and this would lead to speakers confusing words with different meanings. He suggested that speakers prefer to maintain a safe level of differentiation between the phonemes in their language, so if there is change in part of the system they will reorganise the rest of the system so as to keep the distinctions between different words clear. He was able to induce this principle solely from the data on regional dialect maps.

In addition, linguists have found that regional variation can highlight the importance of non-linguistic factors. Work by the sociolinguist Dave Britain shows how the features of different regional varieties intersect with a range of non-linguistic features. One of his more important studies involved studying the English spoken throughout the Fens, a low-lying part of England, north-east of London. For a long time, the Fens were largely covered in swamps, and this made them very difficult to cross. These swamps formed a barrier to movement and contact between people in many of the region's villages. In particular, they divided areas to the north and west, where speakers used the same vowel in the STRUT and BOOK classes of words (i.e., /ʊ/) from areas in the south where the STRUT class had developed a different vowel (i.e., /ʌ/). The Fens also divided into two major regions with respect to the PRICE vowel. Speakers in the eastern part of the region started the diphthong from a more central position (e.g., *night* /nəit/ and *tide* /təid/), while speakers in the western part of the region used a more open onset (e.g., /nait/ and /taid/). However, starting in the eighteenth century, the swampy areas of the Fens began to be drained, and communication between villages in the north-west and the south-east parts of the region became much easier and increasingly frequent.

Britain recorded the casual speech of a large number of people in the central Fens in the late 1980s. He was also able to compare this with earlier records from regional dialect surveys of what speakers sounded like in the villages he studied. He found there was a clear reduction in the amount of regional variation in the central Fens in the 1980s compared to previous records. Once the Fens ceased to be such a big barrier to the movement of peoples and communication, some of the regional differences began to disappear. But they disappeared in rather different ways for the STRUT/FOOT words and the PRICE words.

Britain found that in the central Fens where the eastern and western varieties had met, the pronunciation of PRICE words had absorbed the pronunciations used in both the western and eastern varieties. Typically, speakers used a raised pronunciation of words like *night* or *ice* (i.e., words that have a voiceless consonant after the diphthong), and they had a very open vowel as the main part of the diphthong when the following vowel was voiced (as in *tide* and *rise*). This makes a lot of linguistic sense, and many varieties of English have somewhat raised forms of the diphthong before voiceless consonants. In other words, speakers had **reallocated** the regional forms according to regular linguistic principles. Britain, like Moulton, was able to use regional dialect data to better understand how linguistic and non-linguistic factors are interrelated.

However, when Britain examined the STRUT and FOOT classes of words, he found the situation was less clear-cut. Within a single village, and even in the speech of a single person, he found a lot of variability. That is, unlike the PRICE words, there was no evidence that speakers had developed a single new set of norms for the STRUT and FOOT words. Some people were still using the same vowel in both sets of words (the northern pattern); some people had different vowels in the two sets (so they sounded more like speakers in London); and some people were doing something completely new, and pronouncing the words with a vowel that was different from the standard southern pronunciations *and* the standard northern pronunciations. These **intermediate forms** seemed to be emerging as the preferred local norm in the Fens, but in the 1980s it was still very hard to see which regional pattern would win out.

Britain points out that the regional dialectologist wants to go beyond simply describing the different ways in which contact between different regional varieties is being resolved in the Fens. He notes, for instance, that the regional dialect records show that speakers resolved the PRICE diphthong quickly and they did so on neat linguistic grounds. But they are still struggling with STRUT and FOOT after more than 200 years. The reason for this is both linguistic and non-linguistic.

The reallocation of the PRICE forms was actually quite simple. As noted, it follows a widely attested and phonetically motivated pattern that has emerged spontaneously in other varieties of English, and this was probably why it was resolved so quickly. Separating the STRUT and FOOT classes, though, is a more complicated task, because there are no natural linguistic principles differentiating the two classes. It is notoriously difficult to learn which words fall into the FOOT class and which fall into the STRUT class, and it is often a shibboleth that can be used to identify a speaker of northern English English even if they have lost most of the other regional markers of their accent.

Reallocate/ reallocation

Reassignment or reanalysis of forms in contact in a systematic way, e.g., as allophonically distributed *variants* of a phoneme.

Intermediate forms

Forms emerging following contact between closely related varieties that fall in between the various input forms.

No, really?

Shibboleth

A shibboleth is a linguistic variable that can be used as a diagnostic of where someone comes from. The story goes that the Ephraimites lost to the Gileadites in a battle. They tried to flee, but the Gileadites were able to unmask them because they pronounced the word *shibboleth* with an /s/ and not an /ʃ/. Wucker (1999) tells a similar modern story from Hispaniola, where during a pogrom Haitians in the Dominican Republic were identified partly by their pronunciation of <r>. Dominican soldiers would hold up some parsley, *perejil* in Spanish, and ask people to name it. If they could not produce the trilled Spanish /r/, the person was killed.

In addition to the purely linguistic difficulties involved in resolving the contact between different pronunciations of the STRUT/FOOT classes of words, there were social factors slowing down and increasing the complexity of the task. The difference between the northern and southern variants of the STRUT vowel have almost no salience for speakers from the Fens. None of the speakers Britain recorded mentioned this variable as a feature of local speech at all. Britain suggests that the fact that most speakers in the Fens are unaware of this variable has also impeded the speed with which they have resolved this particular variable. Their linguistic and social difficulties can be seen in the patterns of regional variation.

Britain's study is an important one for several reasons. He reaffirms the usefulness of regional dialect data as a resource for inducing linguistic principles and constraints on variation and change. He also illustrates very nicely the way in which sociolinguists have to think about a whole range of different issues when analysing data. They have to be sensitive to aspects of linguistic structure, aspects of social structure and aspects of how speakers conceive of themselves and relate to others. As such, his study provides an excellent entry point for exploring more closely how regional dialectology expanded into **social dialectology**. In the next section, we look at the study of a small island in Massachusetts, in which methods and principles were established that have proved to be essential to the field known as sociolinguistics.

Social dialectology

The study of linguistic variation in relation to speakers' participation or membership in social groups, or in relation to other *non-linguistic factors*.

Connections with theory

Many factors influence the diffusion of linguistic innovations through a community: communication networks, distance, time and social structure (Bailey *et al.* 1993; Rogers 1995). We could add *imagination* to Rogers's list of factors: LePage and Tabouret-Keller (1985) argue that a lot of the differences in how speakers use language depends on what kind of person we perceive ourselves to be, or how we want to be perceived by others. For them, differences between speakers (or even in the speech of a single speaker) can be thought of as *acts of identity* (more on this in Chapter 11). The idea that different ways of using language (i) constitute social actions, and (ii) involve expressing social and personal identities, will recur in a number of later chapters.

STANDARDS, NORMS AND ALTERNATIONS FROM THE NORMS

Amidst all this regional variation, where are the standards and norms? It is important to remember that when we consider how people use language, one of the things we are trying to do is to understand better what the norms are underlying some of the alternations we observe in practice. This intersects in interesting and complicated ways with what we understand 'Standard English' to be. There can be typical (and in that sense, standard) ways of expressing something that are particular to a very specific locality. But what we mean when we talk about Standard English is a set of norms that are shared across many localities and which have acquired their own social meaning. In general, they are the norms that are associated with education, and they may function as gatekeeping norms, establishing who will and who will not be able to exercise authority or power. They may be deployed as signs of upward mobility (or aspirations for upward mobility).

Some sociolinguists argue that 'Standard English' can only be used properly to refer to features of grammar and vocabulary; Trudgill and Hannah (2002), for example, point out that the features that make up Standard English can be spoken in many different local accents.

On the other hand, other sociolinguists (Milroy 1992; Mugglestone 2003) find the term 'standard' useful for discussing attitudes to different accents. In particular, they discuss the way in which standardisation works as a social and historical process. The process of standardisation involves a community of speakers converging on a shared sense that some forms (spoken or written) are valued more than others and are therefore more appropriate in situations where people are speaking carefully and the exercise of social power is relevant – for example, in law courts, schools, funeral services, and so forth.

Milroy (1992) discusses the overlap and also the divergence in what the terms 'prestige' and 'standard' refer to (and we return to this in Chapter 3). For now it will be helpful to understand 'standard' as referring to norms which represent an intersection of other sociolinguistically interesting phenomena such as carefulness, education, and social status. As we progress through the book we can start to unpick the web that they form. One of the principal tools we will use to unpick them is by looking closely at the way speakers use different languages or different variants in a language in different social contexts and with apparently different motivations.

MARTHA'S VINEYARD: A STUDY OF SOCIAL DIALECTS

The first social dialect study was conducted in the summer of 1961 on Martha's Vineyard, an island off the coast of Massachusetts in the north-eastern United States. Martha's Vineyard was then already something of a summer playground for people who live most of the year on the mainland US – in the 1960s, the number of residents during the summer increased nearly seven times over the winter population. This has only increased in the years since; in the year 2000, the year-round population on the Vineyard was 14,000, but during the summer the population of the island ballooned to 100,000. Moreover, there is a big discrepancy between the circumstances of the summer-only people and the year-rounders. The cost of housing on the Vineyard is fabulously expensive, driven up by the intense demand of summer residents, yet the island has the second-lowest per capita income in the entire state of Massachusetts. Many year-rounders on the Vineyard struggle quite hard to get by and increasingly have to do so by providing services for the summer visitors.

In 1961, William Labov was one of those summer visitors. A student of Uriel Weinreich's at Columbia University, Labov was well acquainted with Weinreich's work on language and dialect contact and he was therefore well placed to extend this work in new directions. Weinreich's work built on the descriptive tradition of the European regional dialectologists; however, he was interested not just in variation as a linguistic phenomenon. He was also interested in the relationship between different linguistic variants and the local social order. This approach (which Labov has always considered to simply be sound *linguistics*) has come to be known as sociolinguistics.

Although the island lies not far off shore from the mainland United States, the pronunciation of certain key variables on Martha's Vineyard differs markedly from the neighbouring parts of the mainland, and it appears that it has done so for some time. The specific variable that Labov became aware of was the realisation of the diphthong in words like *ice* and *time*. In Wells's (1982) standard lexical sets we would call these the PRICE words. Of course, in 1966 Labov didn't have access to Wells's sets. Instead he introduced a new convention: he used parentheses to represent the sociolinguistic variable; that is, he talks about the (ay) variable which is realised by different phonetic variants.

On the Vineyard, the PRICE words were very often pronounced with a more raised, centralised onset (i.e., [əi]), which is not typical of the island's mainland neighbours. The centralised variant is recorded as characteristic of the Vineyard in the 1951 *Linguistic Atlas of New England*. However, Labov noticed that not all the year-round residents of the Vineyard used the centralised pronunciation. Some of them used a lower, fronted onset, more like the mainland norm (i.e., [ai]). The same variability occurred in words with the back-gliding diphthong such as *south* and *loud*; that is, the MOUTH set or what Labov called the (aw) variable.

Even more importantly, he noticed that speakers who used the centralised variants didn't always do so. Sometimes a speaker would use a centralised variant and then in the next sentence use something more like the mainland variant. In other words, not only was there variation *between* individual speakers (**interspeaker variation**) on the Vineyard, there was also variation *within* individual speakers (**intraspeaker variation**).

The extent of this variation piqued Labov's interest. Was the variation a very subtle pattern of regional differentiation? Or was there more to it? He set out to find out by gathering data on these two variables from as many people as he could find.

Ideally, Labov hoped to capture the way people talked when they were talking with one another at home or with their friends. He realised that as an outsider to the Vineyard, and, moreover, as an outsider with a mike and tape-recorder, it wasn't going to be easy to get the kind of speech he was after. He decided first to record people engaged in fairly formal, language-oriented tasks like reading lists of words out loud. However, once this was completed he would shift to a more informal frame of conversation in which he asked them about their life on the Vineyard. This method for collecting data represented a significant departure from the brief question-and-answer format of regional dialect surveys, and it has subsequently formed the basis for numerous other studies.

Labov conducted these sociolinguistic interviews in a number of different parts of the island. In some places, the inhabitants were mainly of Anglo-British descent, in some they were mainly of Portuguese descent, and in some they were mainly of Native American descent. He also sampled speakers from different walks of life. Some of the people he talked to worked on farms, some worked in the fishing industry, and some worked in service occupations. Some were older, some were in their thirties and some were younger. In the end, he interviewed 69 people, more than 1 per cent of the year-round population on the island. Although some ages or groups of speakers were better represented than others in the final sample, the survey provided a much better cross-section of the Martha's Vineyard community than regional dialect surveys had in the past. What Labov saw in his interviews fundamentally challenged the notion of **free variation**.

Interspeaker variation

Differences and variation that is measured between different speakers (individuals or social groups).

Intraspeaker variation

Differences in the way a single person speaks at different times, or with different *interlocutors*, or even within a sentence. Intraspeaker variation is a necessary corollary of *inherent variability* in grammars.

Connections with theory

Regional dialectology has traditionally sought out older speakers, and especially those who have lived sedentary lives without much contact and experience outside of their immediate locality. The famous great surveys from the early twentieth century also mainly sampled male speakers. This target sample has been called the NORMS – non-mobile, older, rural, male speakers (Chambers and Trudgill 1998: 29). It was believed that such speakers used the most 'authentic' local variants. The dialectologist Harold Orton went so far as to say, 'in [England] men speak vernacular more frequently, more consistently, and more genuinely than women' (Orton *et al.* 1962: 15).

Counting variation: the use of index scores

Labov found that, even though the Vineyard was quite small, the variation in how speakers pronounced PRICE and MOUTH seem to divide the community along several distinct axes. He extracted every example of a PRICE or MOUTH word from all the recordings he had and coded them according to how raised and backed the onset of the diphthong was. Lower onsets received a lower score and more raised and centralised ones received a higher score. He was able to use these scores to obtain averages for each speaker. These individual speaker averages could be combined further to produce averages for groups of speakers. This process is illustrated in Figure 2.2.

For example, if a woman in her sixties produced 40 tokens of PRICE words in her interview, Labov would listen to each one. If a token had a very centralised onset he gave

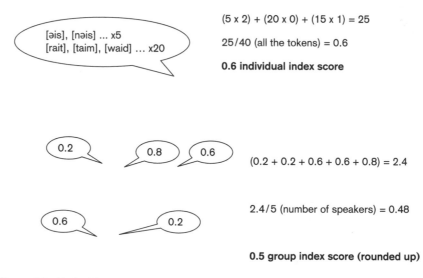

Figure 2.2   Method for calculating an index score for an individual speaker and a group of speakers. Raising and centralisation of the onset of PRICE words, or the (ay) variable, shown as an example.

that token a score of 2, for example. If it had a very low onset, he would give it a score of 0. Let's say this woman produced five very centralised tokens of PRICE (i.e., 2 points × 5 = 10 points) and 20 very low ones (i.e., 0 points × 10 = 0 points), and the remaining 15 were somewhere in between (i.e., 1 point × 15 = 15 points). She would end up with an index score of 25/40 or 0.6.

Once he had an index score for all the women in their sixties, he could group them and average that out. So if there were four others in that group and their index scores were 0.2, 0.2, 0.8, 0.6, then the average across the whole lot of them would give you an index for the group of 0.5 (rounded up); that is, it would show that this group of women raise the onset of PRICE words relatively infrequently compared to what is attested in the rest of the community.

exercise

Calculating index scores

Spanish from Mexico City allows two variants for /-r/ at the end of a word. One variant is a voiced alveolar flap [r] which is considered normal or standard; the other is a voiceless variant that is assibilated or fricated [ř] (Matus-Mendoza 2004). Imagine you have recorded a number of speakers from Mexico City and you have found the following distribution of the two variants in their speech.

Generation	Speaker	[r]	[ř]
I	Flora	24	80
I	Pablo	3	20
I	Luis	5	250
I	Carmen	12	30
II	Marta	30	250
II	Juan	12	171
II	Nico	2	200

Calculate a percentage average or an index score for each of the speakers. Who has the highest and lowest scores?

Now calculate averages or scores for the two generations: Generation I (the teenagers) and Generation II (their parents). Which group uses the standard flap variant more and which group uses the assibilated variant more?

Comparing index scores: towards the social meaning of variation

First of all, it is important to note that linguistic factors explained most of the variation Labov observed. When we considered the contrast between an aspirated and unaspirated /p/ in English earlier, we noted that which variant is used depends entirely on linguistic factors (where the /p/ occurs in the word). Likewise, Labov found that the kind of sound following the PRICE variable was the most important factor in determining which variant a speaker used. If it was followed by a voiceless fricative or stop (/t, s, p, f/) then speakers were more likely to use a centralised variant. We can say that when PRICE words are followed by these sounds they are in a phonetic environment that favours centralisation. If PRICE was followed by /l, r, n, m/ then speakers were more likely to use variants with a lower onset. In other words, a following nasal is an environment that does not favour centralisation.

But in addition to these linguistic constraints, Labov also found there were some very clear correlations with non-linguistic factors as well.

In general, Labov found that people 'Up-island' in the more rural areas and smaller towns were more likely to use the centralised variants than people from 'Down-island' in the bigger townships. But this regional divide wasn't the only, or most noticeable, distinction between the groups he recorded. He also found that if a person was associated with the fishing industry they were much more likely to use the centralised variants than if they were associated with any of the other occupations. He also found that if he looked at Vineyarders of different ages he found some regular differences. People between the ages of 31 and 45 used centralised variants of the PRICE and MOUTH diphthongs more often than speakers in any other age group.

Labov found that after he had talked to all these people he had a good sense of how they felt about Martha's Vineyard and what their attitudes were to living on a relatively isolated island which in winter becomes even more isolated. Most of them had fairly positive attitudes to living on the Vineyard. Some, for instance, had made the conscious decision to return to the island after having gone away to university. However, a smaller number of the people he talked to were more ambivalent about it, and some actively expressed negative attitudes towards being there. He decided to treat speakers' attitudes as a factor that might influence variation, along with the linguistic context and demographic features associated with different speakers. Labov discovered that the lowest rates of centralisation were found among the people who expressed active dislike or some ambivalence about living on the Vineyard.

A number of things about Labov's methods revolutionised the way in which dialectology could be approached. First of all, he tried to sit down with people in contexts that approximated ordinary everyday speech, and he recorded what they actually said, not just what they said they said, as had been true of most regional dialectology up until then. In addition, he investigated whether there were correlations between linguistic variants and a range of social factors. The factors he investigated were ones that seemed to be particularly relevant to life on Martha's Vineyard, and it turned out that they did correlate with the linguistic variation.

No, really?

The Martha's Vineyard survey was not the first piece of dialectology to observe social differences between speakers. Louis Gauchat (1905) observed five variables in the speech of the residents of the quite isolated village of Charmey (Switzerland). He noted younger speakers used innovative variants most, older speakers used them least, and middle-aged speakers alternated. He also noted that women in each group tended to use the innovative variants more than men. We return to the role of speaker's age in Chapter 7 and gender in Chapter 10.

With the benefit of this socially, as well as linguistically, detailed corpus of information, Labov was able to build up a larger picture than would otherwise have been possible. He had discovered that among the islanders, centralisation was highest among people who:

(i)   lived in the more rural, Up-island areas;

(ii)   engaged in the traditional island occupation of fishing;

(iii)   were in their thirties and forties; and

(iv)   liked living on the Vineyard and felt fondly towards life there.

Each of these correlations on its own is pretty arbitrary. That is, there is no reason why we might suppose people in their thirties and forties, or who are employed on fishing boats, *necessarily* would centralise more. Working amidst salt spray and fishing nets doesn't actually change the way you have to talk. But taken together, Labov perceived an overarching generalisation that unified all four characteristics.

The fourth correlation proved to be pivotal in the overall analysis. Contrasts between the year-round residents on Martha's Vineyard and the summer-only residents can be quite extreme. Labov proposed that centralisation was a means by which speakers could subtly but clearly stake a claim to being different from the mainlanders who come over for the summer only. All of the social factors that correlated with centralisation were consistent with this claim. The areas in which the invasion of summer residents was most localised was Down-island, and, as the finding in (i) shows, speakers who used the centralised variants of (ay) and (aw) most often were people who, by choice or tradition, lived Up-island. As (ii) indicates, centralisation also correlates with speakers who, by choice or tradition, were still trying to make a living in the traditional Vineyard way – from the sea. In addition, the most frequent users of centralised variants are also people of an age where they might well have children growing up on the Vineyard (as shown in (iii)), further reinforcing a qualitative difference between locals and summer residents. And finally, centralisation was much less frequent among locals who disliked living on the island and wished they lived somewhere else.

In short, by combining the linguistic facts with the social facts he had learnt about the island, Labov was able to argue that the variation was not free and unconstrained. He argued that the intraspeaker variability reflected and constructed an underlying social opposition: an opposition between locals and non-locals. Linguistic differentiation seems to serve the purpose of social differentiation.

Identifying relevant non-linguistic factors in a community

Labov found that the variation on Martha's Vineyard required him to pay attention to the social categories and issues that were most relevant to locals, e.g., changes in the economic base of the island, the increasing contrast between year-round and summer-only residents, the sense of isolation of living on an island.

What kinds of issues and social groups mattered the most in the town where you grew up? If you moved while you were growing up, or for university, did you have to change your ideas about what groups or issues were most important?

Do people seem to think they can 'hear' these social differences in the way people talk? What do they pay attention to? Vocabulary? Pronunciation? Grammar?

exercise

Connecting variation with change

In addition, Labov realised that his survey of Martha's Vineyard provided a snapshot of one point in ongoing change. By comparing older and younger speakers, a researcher could obtain a window into the long-term changes that linguists traditionally only studied at a much greater distance in time. In this case, a combination of the descriptive, linguistic facts about older and younger speakers, and an appreciation of the social changes taking place in the Vineyard, simulated a picture of how social and linguistic changes work their way through a community with the passage of time.

Prior to this study, linguists had believed that language change could only be studied once it had happened, but Labov's methods have established that there is a robust connection between the variation found in any community of speakers at a given point in time and the long-term processes of change studied by historical linguists. He showed that **synchronic variation** (variation right now) is very often the root of **diachronic change** (change over a period of time). Moreover, he showed that this relationship may emerge most clearly when researchers carefully consider the non-linguistic constraints on synchronic variation, such as speakers' age, their occupation and their attitudes or aspirations. (In Chapters 7 and 9 we return to the Martha's Vineyard study and see what happened in the 40 years after Labov conducted his research. We also consider the use of speakers' ages as a window on change, and the ways in which sociolinguistics and historical linguistics can be integrated.)

Synchronic variation

Variation occurring now.

Diachronic change

Change realised over chronological time.

Connections with theory

The connection between synchronic variation and diachronic change had been established by Hermann's (1929) restudy of Charmey. A generation after Gauchat's first visit, Hermann found that four of the five variables had indeed progressed in the direction Gauchat predicted on the basis of the age differentiation Gauchat had observed.

STEREOTYPES, MARKERS AND INDICATORS

Stereotype

A linguistic feature that is widely recognised and is very often the subject of (not always strictly accurate!) dialect performances and impersonations.

People sometimes have very clear perceptions about the features that differentiate linguistic varieties. These **stereotypes** are things people can comment on and discuss, and they often have very strong positive or negative opinions about them. They include, for instance, the Canadian use of *eh* at the end of sentences, or Australians' use of *dinkum*, and young people's (especially young women's) use of question intonation when they are making a statement or reporting an event (e.g., '*A bunch of us went down to see a movie at the Riverview on Friday?*'). Linguistic stereotypes are the kinds of features that make it into the Letters to the Editor section of local papers, and they are important features used when speakers are performing or putting on another accent or dialect. Upper-class speakers from England are known as *yahs* for their pronunciation of *yes* as /jaː/. The difference between the northern and southern English pronunciation of the vowel in the STRUT class of words, such as *cup* and *butter*, is one that most speakers in the UK are aware of, and, as Britain's study of the Fens showed, this level of awareness may be a factor contributing to the ongoing variability in how the community realises the vowel in this class of words.

However, the variables Labov was looking at on Martha's Vineyard, (ay) and (aw) centralisation, were aspects of the local dialect which speakers on the Vineyard were hardly aware of. Variables that speakers are less consciously aware of, and consequently which have not acquired strong stereotypes, provide some of the richest data for sociolinguists. They may be **markers** or **indicators** of important social factors in a community of speakers or the beginnings of language change, and because they are features which speakers are not consciously aware of (yet!), the variation a linguist finds is particularly revealing. **Markers** can be distinguished from indicators on the same continuum of speaker awareness that differentiates stereotypes and markers. Speakers show some subconscious awareness of markers, and this is made evident in the fact that they consistently use more of one variant in formal styles of speech and more of another variant in informal styles of speech.

Indicators, on the other hand, show no evidence that speakers are even subconsciously aware of them, and speakers consistently favour one variant over another regardless of who they are talking to or where. However, the relative frequency of one variant rather than another may differentiate groups of speakers as a whole.

In the next two chapters we will look at style-shifting more closely and you will see how markers work with some concrete examples. The importance of where speakers are and what interpersonal effect they want to create is also discussed in Chapters 5 and 6.

FACTORS MOTIVATING VARIATION

This chapter has already alluded to a number of factors that correlate with and seem to influence differences in how people use language. In the discussion of the studies conducted by Labov and Britain, we have seen how sociolinguists use both social and linguistic factors to explain or account for different patterns of usage. We have seen that even quite small differences in the ways speakers pronounce words are systematic and not free or unconstrained. The rest of this book is devoted to exploring such constraints even further.

We have also begun to touch on more difficult questions as well. Sociolinguists would like to know how people differ in the ways they use language and the linguistic variants available in their community at large; they also would like to ask why people differ in these ways: what motivates their differences in use? The conclusion that the (ay) variable marks the extent to which a speaker identifies as a 'real' Vineyarder, and the extent to which they might want to differentiate themselves from the swarm of summer visitors, moves towards addressing the questions of *why* as well as *how* people vary in their language use. Indeed, sociolinguistics would be a pretty dry business if all it did was document differences and similarities. But because sociolinguists are interested in the people and the use of language as much as they are interested in linguistic structure, the field is a bit more vibrant than that.

It is impossible to provide an exhaustive list of what motivates speakers to use language differently from each other or in different ways at different times. A lot of the context of language in use is very idiosyncratic. It pertains to the conditions associated with a single moment, an interaction between particular speakers, or the personal mood and intentions of a single speaker.

Notwithstanding this, though, it is possible to identify a smaller set of motives that recur frequently in sociolinguistic analyses. Variation in how people use language is often attributed to the following four motivations:

Marker

A *variable* that speakers are less aware of than a *stereotype*, but which shows consistent style effects. (See also *Indicator*.)

Indicator

A linguistic *variable* which shows limited or no *style-shifting*. Stratified principally between groups.

(i)   a desire to show how you fit in with some people and are different from others;
(ii)   a desire to do things that have value in the community (and associate yourself with that value);
(iii) a desire not to do things that are looked down on in the community (and have others look down on you);
(iv)   a desire to work out how others are orienting themselves to the concerns in (i)–(iii).

These are summarised in Table 2.1 where each of these important motivations is linked to an aphorism that may help you remember them.

The first motivation is developed especially in the examples discussed in Chapters 3–6. There we will see that sociolinguists frequently argue that variation in the speech of an individual is motivated by the speaker's desire to identify with some social groups, and/or differentiate themself from others. This requires balancing goals that may be in conflict with each other. This tension will be highlighted particularly when a speaker has to maximise their fit with others, while simultaneously maintaining individual distinctiveness.

We will also see that in many cases use of a specific linguistic variant can be interpreted as having a value within a community of speakers. Variation can be interpreted as speakers being motivated to use particular variants because they are responding to, or are orienting to, the value associated with a particular variant in their community. We saw this in the Martha's Vineyard study and will return to it in more detail, especially in Chapters 8 and 10 where we discuss social class and gender. We'll see that the community may value a variant consciously or unconsciously (as noted in the discussion of stereotypes, markers, and indicators above), and we will look at the methods we can use to work out directly or indirectly what groups of speakers consider 'better' or more valuable in their community.

Conversely, there is a similarly strong desire for speakers to avoid using forms that will bring them scorn or censure in their speech community. This may involve avoiding variants that sound 'old-fashioned', or that are strongly associated with another group that a speaker would rather not identify with. In other words, avoidance is sometimes just as important a factor as identification. Speakers may stay away from a variant if it has negative associations for them, and they may use another one if they feel that this will minimise the social risk they expose themselves to. Since this is the other side of the coin to *accentuate the positive*, these two factors are often relevant to the same examples. In a sense, a desire to accentuate the positive and to eliminate the negative is what gives rise to the tricky balancing act that we have already discussed.

The final motivation is a little different from the other three. Instead of being centred on the speaker's needs and desires, it stems from our intuition that others are motivated by the same things as we are. For the first three motivations speakers may be pretty clear about

Cultural identity

Table 2.1 Some common motivations for sociolinguistic variability, with everyday 'translations' into aphorisms, or adages. (Source, Meyerhoff 2001.)

General motivation	Associated aphorism
Fit in with some people; differentiate from others	'Life's a balancing act'
Do what has value	'Accentuate the positive'
Avoid what has costs	'Eliminate the negative'
Try to work out what others are up to	'It's a jungle out there'

what group or personal identities and attributes are available for them to identify with or differentiate themselves from at any one time. But often this is not so obvious. As we noted earlier, language not only *reflects* social and interpersonal dynamics, it also *constitutes* them. The constitutive role of language introduces a degree of indeterminacy in every interaction. It is not hard to find examples that seem to indicate that speakers are working quite hard to pin down what the relevant, or most salient, identities are for themselves and their interlocutors – or that they are trying to work out how the identities they have oriented to relate to the ones their interlocutors seem to have oriented to. Communication accommodation theory takes this indeterminacy to heart, and it argues that a lot of variation may result from speakers testing their hypotheses about these factors. Accommodation theory is introduced fully in Chapter 4, but the idea that language can be used to test hypotheses about social relationships recurs in several others.

We will return to these motives in the final chapter, by which time we will be able to assess them against specific linguistic examples. At that point, we will also be in a position to evaluate the extent to which they express distinct insights and the extent to which they articulate with each other.

CHAPTER SUMMARY

This chapter has covered a lot of theoretical and historical ground. It has tried to:

- acquaint you with the breadth of questions that fall within the domain of sociolinguistics, and
- begin to shape our focus on questions relating to how and why speakers alternate between different language varieties or different forms within a particular variety.

We have begun to see some of the important methodological and theoretical contributions that sociolinguistics has made to the study of language in general. These include:

- the shift to the use of naturally occurring speech as the basis for the description of variation, and
- the admission of social and attitudinal factors when analysing variation.

These complement and extend the purely linguistic factors which had been the stock-in-trade for linguists before, and they provide a basis for accounting for phenomena which formal linguistics had been unable to handle and had written off as unconstrained, free variation. The use of quantitative methods to demonstrate that non-linguistic factors pattern with language in non-random ways was an important step; later chapters will gradually flesh out some of the wide range of non-linguistic factors that pattern with speakers' different ways of using language.

It is important to bear in mind that even though the ground covered in this chapter leads most directly to the quantitative methods and studies associated with variationist sociolinguistics (discussed in more detail in Chapters 3–4 and 7–10), even approaches to more qualitative questions benefit if researchers recognise that their enterprise is to untangle and describe the sense and systematicity behind the apparent idiosyncrasy of surface patterns of language use and attitudes about language. These topics are discussed in more detail in Chapters 5 and 6 – but they will also prove to be relevant in Chapters 4, 9 and 10 (the overlap will, I hope, reinforce the complementarity of different approaches to all questions of sociolinguistic interest).

In the chapters that follow we will try to maintain a dual focus on how sociolinguistic research contributes to insights about both the structure of language and also social structure. There will be occasions where we focus mainly on individual speakers and occasions when the focus is more on the behaviour of groups of speakers, but again these complement each other.

In the next two chapters, for instance, we begin to look at how an individual's use of different forms or different language varieties tell us something about their relationship and attitudes to other individuals as well as to other social groups.

FURTHER READING

Article-length introductions to sociolinguistics and the study of language variation include:

Preston (1994), Wolfram (2006), a number of contributions in Newmeyer (1988), contributions in part II of Coulmas (1997).

Other general introductions to sociolinguistics include:

Chambers (2003) – a strong focus on variationist sociolinguistics and linguistic theory.
Holmes (2001), Mesthrie *et al.* (2000) – include more sociocultural discussions of language in use as well as a variationist backbone.
Milroy and Gordon (2003) – emphasis on methodology and principles for quantitative sociolinguistics.
Johnstone (2000) – emphasis on methods and issues for qualitative sociolinguistics.
Nevalainen and Raumolin-Brunberg (2003) – an emphasis on historical data, but provides a very solid introduction to principles and issues in the study of variation and change.
Wolfram and Schilling-Estes (2005) – focus on mainland US varieties of English.

There has been a recent burst of handbooks or encyclopaedias:

Chambers *et al.* (2001) – survey articles on quite specific topics of interest in the study of variation.
Ammon *et al.* (2005).
Mesthrie (2001) – very comprehensive coverage of terms, principles, trends and people in sociolinguistics generally (really gives you an idea of the breadth of the field).

Your library will have more.

On specific topics in this chapter:

Chambers and Trudgill (1998), Francis (1983) – good resources on methods and principles in dialectology and connections between regional and social dialectology.
Labov (1972a, 2001) – more on both the original Martha's Vineyard and NYC studies.
Blake and Josey (2003) – more on 'localness' on Martha's Vineyard.

CHAPTER 3

Variation and style

Key terms introduced in this chapter:

- accents
- dialects
- variety
- speech community
- style-shifting
- attention to speech
- audience design
- triangulation
- sociolinguistic interviews
- stratified

- monotonic
- trend
- rapid and anonymous
- speech community
- overt prestige
- covert prestige
- observer's paradox
- participant observation
- speaker design

INTRODUCTION

'And what do you do for a living?' her new acquaintance asked. Feeling somewhat pained by the man's inability to see she wasn't interested in talking to him, she replied tersely, 'I'm a sociolinguist.'

He doesn't get the message. 'Oh, yes?' (An ingratiating smile.) 'And what does a sociolinguist do?'

She pauses, then levels a steely look at him: 'It means I listen to the way people talk and I judge them on it.'

In general, the judgements sociolinguists make about other people's speech are pretty innocuous. Some sociolinguists know a lot about what features typify the **accents** or **dialects** of speakers from different regions, and these sociolinguists are pretty good at identifying speakers' origins from the way they speak. When linguists talk about **accents**, they are referring only to how speakers pronounce words, whereas they use **dialect** to refer to distinctive features at the level of pronunciation and vocabulary and sentence structure. So, for example, the English used by many Scots would be considered a dialect because it combines recognisable features of pronunciation, e.g., a backed short /a/ sound in words like *trap* or *man*, with constructions like *This data needs examined* . . . (i.e., 'needs to be examined') and the use of the preposition *outwith* (meaning 'beyond, outside'). Since all of

Accent

Where speakers differ (or vary) at the level of pronunciation only (phonetics and/or phonology), they have different accents. Their grammar may be wholly or largely the same. Accents can *index* a speaker's regional/geographic origin, or social factors such as level and type of education, or even their attitude.

Dialect

A term widely applied to what are considered sub-varieties of a single language. Generally, dialect and *accent* are distinguished by how much of the linguistic system differs. Dialects differ on more than just pronunciation, i.e., on the basis of morphosyntactic structure and/or how semantic relations are mapped into the syntax. (See also *Variety.*)

Variety

Relatively neutral term used to refer to languages and dialects. Avoids the problem of drawing a distinction between the two, and avoids negative attitudes often attached to the term *dialect*.

Style-shifting

Variation in an individual's speech correlating with differences in addressee, social context, personal goals or externally imposed tasks.

Attention to speech

Labov proposed that the different distribution of forms in different *styles* was motivated by the amount of attention the speaker was paying to the act of speaking. In activities, such as reading aloud, reading word lists or minimal pairs, Labov argued that speakers are paying more attention to their speech than they are in interviews and in interviews they pay more attention than when conversing with friends and family. Contrasts with *accommodation*-based accounts of style-shifting such as *audience design*. Also contrasts with more agentive theories of style-shifting such as *acts of identity*.

these features occur even in quite formal styles of speaking, they are quite reliable cues that the speaker comes from or has lived a long time in Scotland.

Outside linguistics, the term *dialect* may have quite negative connotations. These may be revealed implicitly rather than explicitly. For example, on Bequia (the Caribbean island mentioned in Chapter 2), people speak a variety of English which differs radically from the Standard English used in North America, the UK or Australasia. Bequians generally call the variety they speak *Dialect*. When researchers ask people to describe the local variety, locals will often contrast *Dialect* with what they call *proper* or *good English*. The opposition between *good* and *dialect* forms of English implies that dialect is bad and is linked to all sorts of attitudes about the local variety, such as where and when it is appropriate to talk Bequian.

Many linguists avoid the term 'dialect' because of these complicated, and sometimes negative, connotations in everyday speech. However, where they do use it, they intend it to be a neutral description or a cover-all term for a variety that differs systematically from others on the basis of pronunciation, grammar and vocabulary. (In Chapter 4 we will look at the ways in which people's perceptions and beliefs about different varieties can also be relevant factors in identifying different dialects.) I will often simply use the term **variety** because potentially it is less loaded.

Sometimes the kinds of judgements that sociolinguists make are about whether a person is speaking formally or informally, whether they sound like they grew up in a working-class or a middle-class neighbourhood – many of the judgements non-linguists make all the time about the people they are talking to.

Sociolinguists differ from the average listener, though, in trying to develop an awareness of language that goes below the level of social stereotypes. They are concerned with trying to determine how very subtle patterns of variation provide a systematic basis by which speakers can indicate or mark social cohesion and social difference. (We defined stereotypes, markers and indicators in Chapter 2.)

STUDYING VARIATION IN SPEAKERS' STYLE

In Chapter 2 we looked at the methods and findings used to identify this systematic variability on Martha's Vineyard. In this chapter we begin by looking at the next study Labov undertook, a social dialect survey in the Lower East Side of Manhattan. We will focus on Labov's finding that, for a number of variables, all speakers in the survey show the same general patterns in formal and informal styles. This apparent orientation to the same norms became critical for what he defined as a **speech community**. This consistency in the patterns between and within speakers across different styles provides further evidence against the notion of free variation (thereby developing the arguments introduced in Chapter 2).

We will look at three possible accounts for the consistency of **style-shifting** across individuals in a speech community. The first is the suggestion that people pay more or less **attention to their speech** when they are engaged in different kinds of verbal tasks. The second is the idea that speakers have an **audience** in mind, and they **design** their speech to suit that audience. The third is the idea that different linguistic styles present different personas that the speaker identifies with. We will consider the first two in most detail since they differ most radically and have been subject to the most careful empirical study.

After considering Labov's findings and the way he manipulated style in the Lower East Side study, we will examine two other studies that manipulated and examined speaker style somewhat differently. These focus on the speakers' relationships with their interlocutors.

This audience design account of style-shifting emphasises the dual role played by language variation in use: reflecting and constituting social meaning (see Chapter 2).

The Martha's Vineyard study established some basic methods for social dialect research and these remain well-used tools in sociolinguists' toolbox. However, Labov and other sociolinguists have subsequently added other creative methods for gathering the kinds of sociolinguistic information we seek. In this section, we look at some of the other methods he devised for reliably identifying the patterns underlying language variation and we focus on ways a researcher can manipulate data collection so as to elicit different styles of speech. We will consider what variation across different styles might tell us about the orderliness of language variation in a community of speakers.

THE NEW YORK CITY SOCIAL DIALECT SURVEY

After the success of the Martha's Vineyard study, Labov turned his attention to variability in the speech of New Yorkers. New York City (NYC) is an interesting site for fieldwork because historically it is a dialect pocket on the eastern coast of the United States; that is, it is surrounded by other varieties of US English from which it differs quite perceptibly. Generally speaking, the NYC accent is highly stereotyped in the United States; that is, residents and non-residents find the distinctive characteristics of the NYC accent highly salient and they are readily stereotyped (as defined in Chapter 2).

Historically, one of the more salient features that sets NYC speech apart from varieties spoken nearby (e.g., in New Jersey), and from the more general variety of Standard American, is that NYC has been r-less. This means that unless an orthographic 'r' occurs before a vowel, it is not pronounced as a constricted 'r' – in this respect NYC speech differs from most northern and western varieties of North America. Like British English, the post-colonial Englishes of the Pacific and southern Atlantic and some varieties of Caribbean English, words like *car, port, garden*, and *surprise* (i.e., words where the 'r' is in what phonologists call the coda of a syllable) do not get pronounced with a constricted, consonant [r.] This feature of the New York accent is widely stereotyped and is one that New Yorkers themselves may have quite negative feelings about – some of them say they dislike it even if they, their families and friends are all r-less speakers.

Labov's study of NYC was more ambitious than the study of Martha's Vineyard, and he looked at a wider range of variables. Some of these, like the (r) variable, were ones that speakers were consciously aware of; some of the others, though, were ones that speakers were much less aware of and seemed to be perceptible only to a trained linguist. (We will see results for some of the other variables in subsequent chapters.) However, even though speakers' level of awareness differed for the variables Labov identified, he found that there were some consistent patterns in the way the variables patterned across different groups of speakers and in different styles or activities.

Labov obtained his data on (r) using several different methods. The idea behind this is called **triangulation** and is basic to science. If, using different methods, you get results that are consistent with the same analysis or conclusion, then your conclusion is much stronger than it is if you arrive at it using only one means of measurement.

Audience design

Derived from *accommodation* theory. Proposal that *intraspeaker variation* arises because speakers are paying attention to who they are addressing or who might be listening to or overhearing them, and modify their speech accordingly.

Triangulation

A researcher's use of several independent tests to confirm their results and aid in the interpretation of their results. For example, use of data from *sociolinguistic interviews* and a *rapid and anonymous study*.

The sociolinguistic interview

Labov extended the basic interview paradigm he had used on Martha's Vineyard. He added several language tasks that he would ask people to do during the interview, and in the free conversation part of the interview he separated out speech directed at the interviewer and speech directed at friends and family members. A good interviewer can get several hours of speech from a single speaker and because the interviews are almost always conducted in the interviewee's home or somewhere they feel comfortable, a skilled (and somewhat lucky) interviewer may also have the chance to record the interviewee talking to other people who pass through while the interview is taking place.

Labov interviewed a random sample of people from the Lower East Side in New York in their own homes. The **sociolinguistic interviews** consisted of four structured parts. The interviewee was asked to:

Sociolinguistic interview

An interview, usually one on one, in which different tasks or activities are used to elicit different styles of speech. (You will sometimes hear it used simply to refer to a one-on-one interview lasting at least an hour covering a range of topics.)

(i)   read a list of minimal pairs (pairs of words that have different meanings but only differ from each other in one sound);

(ii)   read a list of words in isolation (some of which contain the variables under investigation and some of which do not);

(iii)   read aloud a short narrative (carefully constructed to contain the variables in as many linguistic environments as possible);

(iv)   talk with the interviewer about their life, some of their beliefs, and their life experiences.

Labov was aware that for a variable like (r) there were clear differences in which variant was considered appropriate for formal and informal speech. But there are problems with investigating the spontaneous production of different styles of speech. One problem is agreeing what constitute different 'styles' in the first place, another is agreeing which ones are more or less formal, and even if those problems can be overcome there can be problems with recording enough people using language in all those styles to allow the researcher to make valid generalisations.

Labov tackled these problems in defining and working with style by proposing that the formality or informality of styles was a function of speakers' attention to their own speech: in more formal styles they pay more attention; in more casual styles they pay less attention.

The activities in (i)–(iv) were intended to elicit different speech styles: (i) and (ii) require the speaker to pay much more attention to language, while in (iv) a good interviewer will foster quite animated and lively conversation between the interviewer and interviewee. This kind of speech can be called 'informal' speech, and Labov found that he had a lot of success in getting informal conversation by asking people questions about things like fights, dangerous situations the speaker had been in, the supernatural, their first girlfriend or boyfriend, and important events in their childhood. Side conversations that the interviewee might have with friends or family during this part of the sociolinguistic interview are presumed to involve the least attention to their speech, and these can be called 'casual' speech.

A minimal pair for the (r) variable would be *god* and *guard* – when *guard* is pronounced without a constricted /r/, it sounds just like *god*. *Dock* and *dark* are also minimal pairs in this variety of English because the vowel is the same, so only the presence or absence of an /r/ differentiates them. The layout of minimal pairs helps to focus the speaker on the form of the words. If you present someone with a card that looks like Figure 3.1 and ask them to read each line carefully and clearly, the speaker will be concentrating considerable attention on how they pronounce each word.

Connections with theory

Labov has never claimed that reading aloud, especially reading words in isolation or in minimal pairs, is related to conversational speech. He acknowledged that they are qualitatively different activities from having a conversation. The activities in (i)–(iii) are artificial strategies that enable the researcher to control how much attention the speaker pays to their speech. They therefore allow the researcher to test the hypothesis that attention to speech is an important constraint on variation.

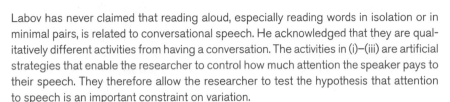

Please read across each line carefully and clearly:

guard	**god**
dock	**dark**
pin	**pen**
sauce	**source**
...	...

Figure 3.1 Example of a presentation of minimal pairs used to elicit most careful and attentive pronunciations.

The hypothesis is that if a speaker focuses all their attention on the pronunciation of a word in a task like this, then here, of all places, they will use a constricted /r/ – even if they don't usually do so in their casual speech. The reading list and the reading passage tasks were intended to require somewhat less attention to the form of individual words. Consequently, you would find progressively more of the local r-less variants in these activities.

Designing materials for a social dialect survey

It is not all that easy to create a plausible and moderately interesting narrative that includes a variable in a wide range of linguistic environments, e.g., sentence-finally, before a vowel, before different kinds of consonants, in common and in less common words, etc. (Sociolinguistic interview activity (iii), discussed on p. 30.)

Pick a sound that shows variability in your own speech or the dominant speech community you live in and try to construct a short (100–200 word) narrative that showcases this variable in as many environments as possible.

exercise

Interviewees can become surprisingly oblivious of a microphone even if they are attached to it, getting up to show you things, etc.

However, even someone you have got to know quite well may surprise you by showing they are paying attention to the recording, for instance by saying something like, 'That's enough for tonight' when a tape audibly comes to its end.

Finally the distinction between informal and casual speech in the interviews was also taken to reflect a (natural and spontaneous) difference in attention to speech. No matter how hard interviewers work or how skilled they are, unless they have invested a considerable amount of time in getting to know the interviewees, we assume that their conversations will always be subject to somewhat more attention than conversation with friends and family. Because of this, it was expected that they would also use the constricted variant of (r) less in casual conversation than in the informal part of the interview.

Labov's findings supported his hypothesis. On average, everyone used pronunciations with an [r] more when they were reading the narrative aloud than they did in casual conversation. They used even more [r] when they were reading the word lists, and they were most likely to use [r] variants when they were reading minimal pairs.

This sensitivity to style shows up in all the variables Labov examined. This is illustrated in Figure 3.2, where the frequency of constricted variants for (r) is shown in the four different styles averaged across everyone who was interviewed in the NYC study.

Figure 3.2 shows that the variants associated with these variables are **stratified** by style. This means that there is a consistent order for the styles across speakers. The rate of [r] presence drops steadily as you go left to right along the bottom axis of this figure. We can also say that the relationship between style and the variants is **monotonic**, or that the data show a **trend**, i.e., a consistent tendency to use less of the constricted variant as the researcher has manipulated the formality of the talk or the speaker's overt attention to speech.

The same monotonic relationship between style and linguistic variation can be seen in Figure 3.3, which plots the frequency of vernacular, raised variants in two vowel variables short (a) and (oh) (the TRAP and CLOTH vowels respectively – we'll return to these variables again in Chapter 8).

Stratified

See *Broad* and *Fine stratification*. The systematic and consistent patterning of a variant with respect to some independent factor

Monotonic

A steady increase or decrease in a feature along the x-axis of a graph.

Trend

Steady increase or decrease in the frequency of a form across a scale or set of measures.

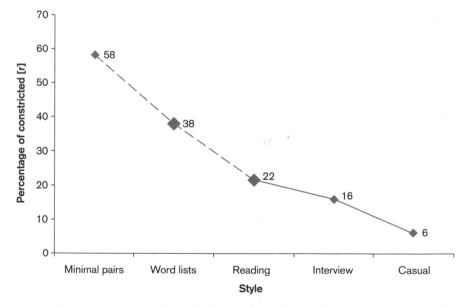

Figure 3.2   Occurrence of constricted [r] in New York City English in five speech styles. (Dashed line indicates the qualitatively different activities involving the use of unconnected speech.) (Source, Labov 1966: 221.)

Connections with theory

The results from the NYC study are frequently used to illustrate the systematic patterning of different groups of speakers from different social classes *across* different styles. As we will see in Chapter 8, the results for style and social class show patterns that are startlingly similar. The similarity of these trends was central to the analysis of the social meaning of the (r) variable in NYC.

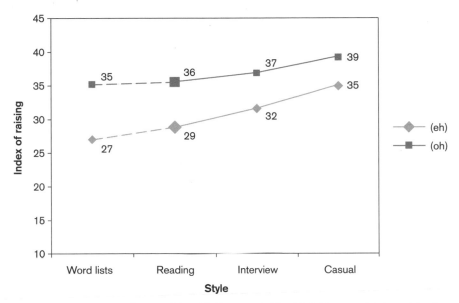

Figure 3.3   Raising index for short (a) and (oh) variants in New York City speech in four styles (TRAP and CLOTH vowels). Higher index means a more raised vowel. (Source, Labov 1966: 221.)

This monotonic relationship supports Labov's conjecture that the three artificial linguistic tasks that he included in the sociolinguistic interviews were, indeed, an effective means of modelling changes in stylistic formality. The trend that emerges between informal and casual speech in the free conversation part of the interview is continued in the manner predicted if style differences manifest a speaker's different level of attention to their speech.

A note on graph notation

Notice that the frequency with which the constricted tokens, [r], are used in each style in each activity is joined with a line. The line becomes a dashed line at the point where it is clear that there is a qualitative break between the kinds of activity represented. It is nevertheless continuous. This is very important because it makes a claim about the relationship *between* each of those points. The use of a continuous line asserts that style is a continuum. In other words, there might be an infinite number of degrees of attention to speech, of which these five activities or styles represent only a sample. If you were able to devise some other task that required a little bit more attention to speech than informal speech, but a little bit less attention than reading out loud, you would expect that the frequency with which speakers use constricted [r] would fall somewhere on or very close to where the line in Figure 3.2 runs between these two styles.

Rapid and anonymous surveys

A second method that Labov pioneered for studying variation was the use of rapid and anonymous surveys. The rapid and anonymous survey of the realisation of (r) in three department stores is one of the most famous studies in sociolinguistics. As well as trialling a novel and easily replicable methodology, the department store survey has made a significant theoretical contribution to variationist sociolinguistics. Together with the sociolinguistic interviews in the Lower East Side, it demonstrates that quite different methods for gathering data, including quite different ways of manipulating attention to speech, can produce similar and mutually informative results.

We noted that one advantage of the interview format for data collection is that it generates a large amount of information for subsequent analysis. Moreover, because the interviewer spends a fair amount of time getting to know the interviewee, they can make more sensitive evaluations when they come to assessing variation in and across social groups (we will return to the use of sociolinguistic interviews to gather this kind of data in Chapters 7–10). But one of the disadvantages of interviews is that they can take a long time to arrange and conduct. So it is often helpful to be able to complement them with methods that collect data more speedily.

Labov chose three department stores as the venue for some quick fieldwork. He tried to elicit as many tokens of the phrase *fourth floor* as possible from staff working in the three stores. This phrase was a good one from a linguistic point of view because it has one token of the (r) variable before a consonant and one token word and phrase finally. The decision to ask staff (and not, for instance, customers) was practical – staff were more likely to be able to give the desired answer. He would find some item on the store directory boards that was sold on the fourth floor, e.g., lamps or shoes, and he would ask staff where lamps, or shoes, were. They would say, 'Fourth floor', and then he'd pretend he hadn't heard and ask them to repeat it. With slightly more care, the staff member would repeat 'Fourth floor'. Labov would walk off and write down how often they had and had not used a constricted [r], and a few basic social facts about the speaker (their occupation in the store, their sex, a rough estimate of their age).

Connections with theory

Labov chose the three department stores according to the general socioeconomic level of their target customers. Because of this, he was able to employ his rapid and anonymous data to also check on the effects of social class found in the interviews. Social class is discussed further in Chapter 8.

This strategy was extremely productive. It provided:

- two casually uttered tokens of the (r) variable;
- two tokens of the variable uttered more carefully;
- tokens of the variable in different linguistic contexts (one preconsonantal environment, *fourth*, and one at the end of a word); and
- a speedy source of the information.

For these reasons the methodology is known as a **rapid and anonymous** survey.

In all three department stores, speakers were more likely to use the Standard American pronunciation with a constricted [r] when they repeated *fourth floor* carefully for a second time than they were the first time they uttered it. Because the pattern emerged across a considerable number of staff in all three stores, this supported the empirical findings in the interviews, and widely held attitudes about the (r) variable. The use of constricted variants with careful speech was robust and consistent across several measures. The parallels between the findings in the department store survey and the interview data can be seen in Figure 3.4.

Notice that in Figures 3.2–3.4 it is clear that even if style has a strong correlation with the use of [r], it doesn't *determine* which variant will be used. The results from these studies tell us about the probability with which a particular variant will occur. It is more likely that a person will use the constricted variant of (r) in a word list than in casual conversation. But in all styles, a speaker might use the other variant.

On the basis of the evidence accumulated in the New York studies, Labov argued that speakers could be considered co-members of a **speech community** if they share:

Rapid and anonymous study

A questionnaire used to gather data quickly in the public domain. (See also *Sociolinguistic interview; Triangulation.*)

Speech community

Variously defined on subjective or objective criteria. Objective criteria would group speakers together in a speech community if the distribution of a variable was consistent with respect to other factors (e.g., style). Subjective criteria would group speakers as a speech community if they shared a sense of and belief in co-membership.

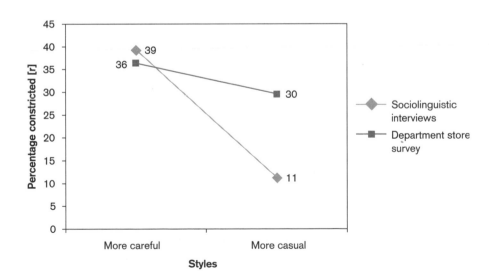

Figure 3.4 Frequency of constricted [r] in more careful styles of the sociolinguistic interview (reading passage, word lists and minimal pairs combined) and more casual styles (informal and casual combined) compared with careful and casual styles in the department store survey. (Source, Labov 1966: 74, 221.)

- the same variants in their repertoire, and
- the same, consciously or unconsciously held, attitudes to those variants.

In the case of (r), consciously held attitudes were reasonably accessible, but in the case of other variables, where speakers did not have much or any conscious awareness of the variation, consistent patterns of stratification in different speech styles provided crucial evidence that speakers share underlying attitudes about the variable.

Connections with theory

Labov assumed that when he got department store staff to repeat, 'Fourth floor', that he was getting them to pay more attention to their speech. This analysis focuses on style from the perspective of the researcher.

The analysis can be turned around so that it takes the perspective of the staff and focuses on the addressee, Labov himself. In this case, their variation might not be a function of an increase in the attention they paid to their own speech, but an increase in the attention they paid to their addressee. We will return to this alternative analysis shortly.

The effect of topic on style

There have been some efforts to break down the styles within the informal/casual speech parts of the sociolinguistic interviews. This has been done with some success on the basis of topic. It seems that when people are getting a bit preachy (about any topic) or when they are talking about 'language' itself, you elicit more careful styles than you do when the person is talking about, say, childhood memories.

Suppose you had been talking to someone for a few hours about their life history, their beliefs and their personal hopes. Make a list of some of the topics you might expect to come up. Would you expect some topics to elicit speech that is more careful and some to elicit speech that is more casual? Which ones? Why?

To sum up, each of the methods Labov used has its advantages. The rapid and anonymous survey quickly generates a lot of tokens of a restricted kind, and it is easily replicated. The interviews mean that the analysis can draw on more detailed facts about the interviewees and can be based on a wide range of tokens. They also enable the analyst to find out what kinds of social facts are important to the people being interviewed and what their attitudes are to different variables. Although both methods have advantages, it was the combination of the two that allowed Labov to forward a very strong claim that a person's attention to speech was an important constraint on the variable (r) in NYC.

Connections with theory

Attention to speech postulates a single grammar, of which the variation is an integral component: this is the notion of inherent variability. This highlights a fundamental difference between variationist sociolinguists and formal linguists. Sociolinguists consider intraspeaker variation to be evidence of inherent variability in a communal grammar. Formal linguists generally prefer to explain intraspeaker variation in terms of alternations between different grammars (akin to a bilingual speaker alternating between languages).

PRESTIGE OF A VARIABLE

It is tempting to think about the consistent orientation of speakers to a particular variant in more formal contexts, or careful tasks in terms of the relative **prestige** of the variants. But sociolinguists recognise *prestige* as a complex value that speakers orient to in different ways. In particular, we have to be careful that we do not define a *prestige* variant as 'a variant which has more status' if the only evidence we have for the variant being statusful is that it is used more by members of a speech community who themselves have more status (e.g., the upper class). If that is our only evidence, then our definition of *prestige* is circular and we might more accurately say that we have a variant that marks higher social class rather than a variant that is prestigious. Prestige is not necessarily something speakers are consciously aware of, nor something that is associated with the highest social classes or more powerful speakers in a community. These observations have led sociolinguists to make a distinction between **overt** and **covert prestige**.

Overt vs covert prestige

Overt prestige is understood to be the prestige associated with a variant that people are highly aware of and which is associated more with the speech of higher-status speakers. This would include a variant like the constricted [r] in NYC, which speakers will describe in evaluative terms as sounding 'better' or 'nicer' than the r-less variant.

But it is equally apparent that speakers orient themselves to other kinds of prestige. So, for example, most speakers of German have command over at least their local vernacular variety of German and Standard German (*Hochdeutsch*). They will have learnt their local vernacular variety with its characteristic pronunciations and lexical items at home, and continue to use it there, whereas Standard German is something they are taught at school and they use when they are speaking or writing in public (situations like this are discussed further in Chapter 6 in the section on diglossia).

The local variety carries strong connotations of naturalness and straightforwardness because it is acquired naturally and used in people's most informal and intimate styles. Standard German, on the other hand, may sound stilted and distant because it is so seldom used in intimate and friendly contexts. Politicians and other professional salespeople make strategic use of the positive connotations of different varieties, for example, by using the vernacular when they think it will be advantageous to sound like an everyday person and

Overt prestige

The prestige associated with a *variant* that speakers are aware of and can talk about in terms of standardness, or aesthetic and moral evaluations like being 'nicer' or 'better'. (See also *Covert prestige*.)

Covert prestige

A norm or target that is oriented to without the speaker even being aware that they are orienting to it. Evidence of covert prestige can be found in mismatches between speakers' self-report of using one *variant* and actual use of another variant. Often used (wrongly) to refer to the value associated with non-standard or *vernacular* varieties.

the Standard when they want to sound authoritative. (We return to perceptions about different linguistic varieties, and the connotations associated with them, in Chapters 4 and 6.)

This kind of local prestige is sometimes referred to as covert prestige, but in fact the use of the term for the value speakers associated with local or working class pronunciations is often far from covert. They can explain it to you quite clearly: 'I'd never talk like that with m' mates, they'd think I was a tosser.' Hence, there is often very little that is covert about the persistence of non-standard or highly regionalised veracular varieties.

The term **covert prestige** more accurately refers to cases where speakers' positive evaluation of a variant is genuinely covert or hidden. Peter Trudgill's (1972) early work on Norwich English found that some speakers recognise and overtly talk about one variant as being 'better' than another; furthermore, they claim to use the 'better' form, but in fact do not.

In this particular case, many of the men (not so many of the women) that Trudgill interviewed said that the Standard Southern British English pronunciations of *tune* and *dune*, i.e., [tjun] and [djun], were better than the local Norwich variant without the [j], i.e., [tun] and [dun], and reported to him that it was the form they used. That is, they were overtly oriented to the supra-local prestige of [tjun] and recognised the [tun] variants as being distinctively local and non-standard. Nevertheless, they used the local variant most often in their interviews with Trudgill. So their orientation to the local variant was covert: they believed they were doing something different from what they actually were doing.

Trudgill suggested that this *mismatch* between what the speakers say they do and what they actually do should be considered evidence of covert prestige. Chapter 4 discusses other examples of mismatches between how people think they are talking and how they are actually talking, and when we consider the notion of language vitality in Chapter 6, we will see another basis for distinguishing between institutionally based prestige and more locally based prestige.

Observer's paradox

The double-bind researchers find themselves in when what they are interested in knowing is how people behave when they are not being observed; but the only way to find out how they behave is to observe them.

IN SEARCH OF THE UNKNOWABLE: THE OBSERVER'S PARADOX

The paradox every sociolinguist faces in trying to account accurately for variation within a speech community is that they want to know what people say and do in their everyday lives, but as soon as they start to record them they change the dynamic even slightly. So what they want to know is, in one sense, unknowable. This has come to be known in sociolinguistics as the **observer's paradox**. Labov's rapid and anonymous surveys were an attempt to overcome this problem, as was his practice of trying to turn interview conversations to more lively and personal topics.

Connections with theory

The observer's paradox makes the same kind of generalisation about studying language that Heisenberg's uncertainty principle makes about studying particles. That is, we cannot observe something without changing it. One reason for the uncertainty principle in physics is that particles do not exist independently as *things*, they exist as sets of *relationships*. Sociolinguists, too, are actually studying sets of relationships when they look at variables. This will become more apparent as we progress.

Some sociolinguists take a leaf out of anthropologists' books in an attempt to overcome the observer's paradox. They spend long periods of time working and/or living with the people whose speech they are interested in, and they hope that by doing this they will eventually achieve insider status themselves. This is known as **participant observation**.

It is also possible to turn the observer's paradox to good use. It has also been pointed out that sometimes the way people talk when they are aware of being recorded can be sociolinguistically illuminating too. Natalie Schilling-Estes (1998a) noticed that some of the speakers she recorded from Ocracoke, an island off the North Carolina coast, seemed to enjoy giving quite flamboyant performances of stereotypes of the local accent. She found that these highly self-conscious performances of the local accent didn't produce anything that was inconsistent with what the same speaker produced in less self-conscious conversation. Moreover, the relatively extreme variants that one speaker produced in his performances provided telling evidence about the underlying system of phonological contrasts.

A widely recognised stereotype of Ocracoke speech is (ay), the diphthong in PRICE, which has a noticeably raised onset in the traditional Ocracoke brogue, e.g., [ʌ]. This is commented on by both islanders and outsiders. A comparison of one man's, Rex's, performances of (ay) and tokens of the variable in conversation showed that raising certainly was one dimension on which the (ay) variable contrasts with other Ocracoke vowels and with the non-raised variants, e.g., [ɑɪ], more typical of non-Southern varieties of American English. However, Rex also shortened the nucleus of (ay) in his performance speech (1998a: 67). Schilling-Estes argues that this means that Rex is maintaining a contrast between the Ocracoke diphthong and the Southern monophthong, e.g., [ɑː], which is typical of North Carolina and other Southern varieties of English.

Schilling-Estes points out that this is interesting because when Rex talks about the local variant he only ever contrasts his performance with non-raised variants, and gives no indication that the monophthongs associated with Southern accents are a relevant contrast for him in this variable. In other words, performance styles can provide otherwise unknowable information about the social and linguistic significance of a variant.

Surreptitious recording and other ethics issues

It is not possible for a sociolinguist to avoid the observer's paradox by gathering their data in secret. Surreptitious recording, i.e., using a hidden audio or video recorder without the speakers' knowledge, is not condoned by professional linguistic associations. It is also illegal in many parts of the world. Surreptitious recording is an abuse of the privacy of the people you are recording. You might think (as one linguist I know did) that it's OK to hang the headphones of your personal stereo around your neck, and give the impression that you have just paused in your listening, but in fact have the machine in record mode.

You might assume, as he did, that because you are just recording your family and friends, they would certainly give consent after the fact. But consent given after the fact is seldom free from some degree of coercion, and it may be especially hard for friends and family to assert their rights or preferences in this respect because they may fear doing (further) damage to the relationship.

Jennifer Coates, one of Britain's leading sociolinguists, has talked quite frankly about her attempt to get retrospective consent from a group of close friends that she had secretly recorded. She found that some of them were furious at her for the breach of trust.

Participant observation

The practice of spending longer periods of time with speakers observing how they use language, react to others' use of it, and how language interacts with and is embedded in other social practices and ideologies. A means of gathering qualitative data rather than quantitative data.

There are some forms of talk which it is generally agreed can be used as data without getting express permission from the speaker(s). This is talk that is already in the public domain, such as media broadcasts, or oral history archives. Standards vary as to whether or not recordings made for one purpose can be used freely for another, or whether permission has to be sought again from the speakers. Most universities have research ethics committees and specific staff in departments who can advise on all these questions.

CHALLENGING STYLE AS ATTENTION TO SPEECH

Many people were impressed by the consistency of the effects Labov had found across the four different activities that he included in his sociolinguistic interviews. However, not everyone was persuaded that the differences observed indicated that speakers were paying attention to their own speech. The British social psychologist Howard Giles had begun to look closely at the role language plays in shaping the dynamics of interaction between groups and between individuals.

Giles drew on principles that social psychologists had determined play a significant role in how people behave in intergroup and interpersonal interactions quite generally. Research had shown, for example, that people tend to favour other members of their group (ingroup members) at the expense of members of another group (outgroup members), especially in situations that involve some form of competition.

Giles therefore suggested that Labov was wrong in attributing speech differences across different styles to the effect of speakers' attention to their own speech. He argued that social behaviour is seldom so egocentric, and that interviewees would have interpreted their sociolinguistic interviews as intergroup or interpersonal interactions. The distinction Labov made between informal speech (to the interviewer) and casual speech (to family and friends) was a move in the right direction, but Giles argued that Labov's paradigm did not fully grasp or deal with the effects that our interlocutors may have on the way we talk.

Giles suggested that all the stylistic variation was actually caused by speakers attuning, or accommodating, to the norms associated with different addressees. Attunement and accommodation will be explained in detail in Chapter 4. For our purposes at the moment, we can adopt a common-sense understanding of the terms; that is, speakers fine-tune the way they talk according to the situation they find themselves in. And an important factor in determining how speakers make adjustments to their speech is *who* they are talking to. We are all aware that we are expected to speak differently when talking to friends than when talking to a teacher, a judge, a call centre, etc. Learning to make the expected attunements to others is part of the process of becoming socialised in a community of speakers, so it is very reasonable to assume that such processes might play a role in determining how respondents speak in sociolinguistic interviews.

Table 3.1 shows how a change in the addressee alone may be associated with quite marked changes in the way a speaker talks. This shows how often a speaker of Bislama (the English-based creole spoken in Vanuatu) omitted subject pronouns when telling a story, first to his extended family after dinner one evening, and then to me only.

In Bislama, as in many languages, you don't have to have a subject in every sentence. Instead of repeating a subject with a pronoun like you do in English (1), when the subject stays the same across sentences, you can have a gap as in (2):

Table 3.1 Number of sentences in which Sale omitted a pronoun subject as a percentage of all clauses in the conversation (two different audiences).

	Addressees			
	Extended family		MM only	
Speaker	Omitted pronoun	All clauses (%)	Omitted pronoun	All clauses (%)
Sale	N = 50	71	N = 40	62

(1) **The captain** told everyone to stay quiet. **He** waited until **he** thought it was safe. Then **he** signalled an advance.

(2) The captain told everyone to stay quiet. _Waited until _thought it was safe . . .

Table 3.1 shows that Sale generally omitted subjects in both tellings of the story, but you can see that he used more full subjects when he was telling me the story (even though it was, in fact, the second time he had told it to me). There are a number of reasons why he might use more subject pronouns with me than he does with his family. But one plausible factor is that by using more pronouns he is providing a non-native speaker with more overt information about who he is referring to in any given sentence. That is, he is trying to make the story clearer and easier to follow for the specific person he is addressing.

Style as 'attention to others'

Giles suggested that many of the effects observed in the New York studies might be caused by speakers attuning their speech to the more salient aspects of the context. These include the interviewer himself, a university-educated person (conducting a 'study', no less!). Giles noted that by inviting such a person into their home to conduct a study, the interviewee had already established a willingness to help out and accommodate the needs of the researcher. It would therefore be a small step indeed (in terms of interpersonal relations) for the interviewee to continue their accommodating manner and to attempt to produce the kind of speech they perceive to be most appropriate for the different tasks of the interview.

This means that the difference between informal and casual speech can be seen quite simply as a function of who the speaker is addressing, rather than pushing this dynamic to one remove (as Labov did) by proposing that a change in addressee changes how much attention the speaker pays to her/himself. Furthermore, when asked to perform non-conversational tasks like reading aloud, an accommodating person would be very likely to attune their behaviour to the norms they have been socialised to associate with reading aloud; that is, careful, school, or testing environments.

An important aspect of this alternative view of the way speakers shift between styles is that it foregrounds the importance of the speaker's and addressee's relationship and their attitudes towards one another. It presents a picture of speakers in which they come across more as thinking agents with interpersonal goals and desires than they do in the attention to speech model. In subsequent chapters, we'll see that an emphasis on agency and the dynamic quality of group and personal identities has become very influential in sociolinguistics. Many sociolinguists believe that people are really *doing* different things when they use different variants (see, in particular, discussions of communities based on shared practices in Chapter 9).

However, Giles's work – and most of the work following his lead – has been done within the experimental traditions of social psychology; that is, it has relied on data elicited under highly controlled circumstances rather than on the kind of naturally occurring speech favoured by sociolinguists. This is one reason why it has proved difficult to convince some sociolinguists that a speaker's attitude to and relationship with their addressee can and should be incorporated into models of variation and change.

One of the best-known proponents of the Gilesian view of variation has been Allan Bell, the sociolinguist who refined Giles's insight and tailored it more directly to the predictive and explanatory interests of sociolinguists. Bell believed that Giles's arguments captured a very powerful dynamic in sociolinguistic variation. Moreover, he saw its applicability beyond face-to-face interaction, and he argued that it could even account for phonological variation in radio broadcasts where announcers have no single or immediate addressee, and instead must be speaking with some kind of *Gestalt* idea about their audience as a group. He called this broader framework for analysing variation audience design.

Audience design

The term **audience design** both classifies the behaviour (the speaker is seen as proactively *designing* their speech to the needs of a particular audience) and encapsulates the presumed motive for the behaviour (who is the speaker's audience).

Bell had recorded several newscasters working for the national radio news network in New Zealand. These news readers would read on two of the government-owned stations, one of which was a middle-of-the-road, popular music station, and one of which was the classical station. The classical station generally attracted an audience from higher socioeconomic brackets, while the popular station attracted a broader range of listeners, including those from lower social classes.

Bell examined the occurrence of several variables, including the realisation of intervocalic /t/. Between vowels, (t) can be realised as either a stop or a flap in New Zealand English. This means words like *better* and *city* can either be pronounced [bɛtə] or [bɛɾə] (*better* or *bedder*) and [sɪti] or [sɪɾi] (*city* or *ciddy*). Although the news was essentially the same on both stations, and although the newscasters were exactly the same speakers, Bell found that there were more of the conservative, stop variants when the newscasters were reading on the classical station than when they were reading on the popular one. He argued that because the topics were held constant, and because the activity was the same, a plausible way to account for the differences was to assume that the newscasters were attuning their speech to what they believed the norms were for the different radio audiences.

This rather modest assertion actually has a very strong theoretical claim embedded within it. It claims that an individual's style-shifting (intraspeaker variation) derives from the differences probabilistically associated with different groups of speakers (interspeaker variation). If this is in fact true, then it means we can make a very specific prediction about the newscasters. If we compare the frequency of the innovative flapped variant of (t) in a single newsreader's speech on the popular and the classical shows, this intraspeaker variation will be *less than* the difference between the frequency of the innovative variant in the two target audiences. We will return to this prediction shortly and see what support has been found for it in empirical studies.

Different audience types

Bell's framework made another helpful contribution to the way sociolinguists might apply principles of accommodation and convergence to sociolinguistic variation. This was to distinguish between several kinds of audience that a speaker might be thinking about. He suggested that a person we are directly talking to has the greatest impact on how we talk. This person is our 'addressee'. But we also have to take other listeners into account when we are speaking, and he proposed that we distinguish between 'auditors', 'overhearers' and 'eavesdroppers'. Each of these other kinds of listeners would have progressively less and less influence on the way you speak, as is shown in Figure 3.5.

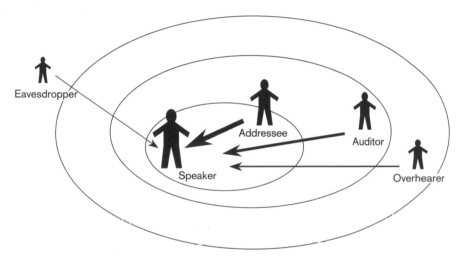

Figure 3.5   The strength of the effect of different interlocutors (known, ratified and addressed) on a speaker's choice of variants and different styles. (This representation is based on a figure in Hay *et al.* 1999, with kind permission of the authors.)

Bell proposed a system for distinguishing between these different kinds of addressee by using three criteria, whether someone is *known, ratified* or *addressed*. This is summarised in Table 3.2. An addressee is *known* to be part of the speech context, *ratified* (that is, the speaker acknowledges their presence in the speech context) and is *addressed* (that is, 'I'm talking to you'). If a teacher praises a student in front of the whole class she or he is communicating with both the student and the rest of the class (for whom the student is being held up as a model). Both the student and the class are the audience. The student is the addressee (known, ratified and addressed) and the rest of the class are auditors (known and ratified, but not addressed).

So audience design predicts that the speaker will attune their speech most to an addressee, next to an auditor, and then to any overhearers who the speaker thinks might be lurking around. The speaker will attune their speech less to auditors, overhearers and eaves-droppers because the speaker's relationship with them is more attenuated, and consequently the speaker has less clear relational goals. The speaker may also have much less detailed ideas about what kinds of people their auditors and overhearers might be, and this in turn means that the speaker will have less specific ideas about how they might attune their speech.

Table 3.2   Different types of audience according to their relationship with the speaker.
(Bell 1984: 160, table 3.)

	Known	Ratified	Addressed
Addressee	+	+	+
Auditor	+	+	−
Overhearer	+	−	−
Eavesdropper	−	−	−

By the time we move to the effect of eavesdroppers, we are talking about an audience that the speaker can probably only conceptualise in very rudimentary ways, so their effects will be very superficial in linguistic terms, e.g., we might be careful about the general topic or we might try to avoid swearing, but we won't alter our pronunciation or syntax much at all. Finally, Bell argued, any effect that the topic of conversation might have would also be extremely limited. Under this framework, topics would derive their effects from a speaker's stereotypes about *who* they are likely to be talking to when a topic comes up.

Connections with theory

A related approach to the idea of style-shifting as audience design is Coupland's (2001) suggestion that speakers use different styles to present themselves differently according to the context or who they are talking to. We might call this **speaker design**. The main differences between speaker and audience design models of style-shifting lie in what kinds of motives or goals are ascribed to the speaker and which are assumed to drive variation. For example, speaker design is readily compatible with the *accentuate the positive* and *eliminate the negative* motives (Chapter 2), but less so with the idea that one is testing hypotheses about others (*It's a jungle out there*). Speaker design is also compatible with style-shifting where there is no independent evidence of a change in the speaker's attention to their speech or their audience.

Speaker design

A further approach to analysing *style-shifting*. Stresses the speaker's desire to represent her/himself in certain ways. (See also *Acts of identity*.)

Relationship between social and linguistic constraints

Figure 3.6 summarises how Bell conceptualised the relationship between social variation (that is, variation between groups of speakers) and stylistic variation (that is, variation in a single speaker). This figure shows how, according to Bell, intraspeaker variability derives from the variability that differentiates social groups:

(variation between groups) > (variation in individuals)

Bell predicted that because it derives from social group differences, the variation any one individual shows in their speech will never be greater than the differences between the groups that their style-shifting is derived from. This may seem somewhat odd, since a group

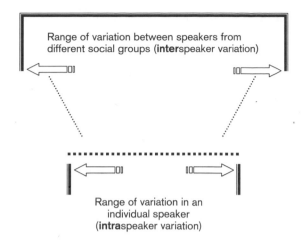

Figure 3.6   Bell's predicted relationship between linguistic differences across social groups and an individual's variability across styles.

is made up of many individuals, but one reason for it is that when a speaker attunes their speech to the norms of a group that they do not personally identify with, they will be approximating a target that they have only limited firsthand knowledge of. The variability triggered by topic alone should be even less than an individual's stylistic variation since topic effects are supposed to derive from the speaker's pre-existing variation space.

A few linguists have tried to test the details of Bell's audience design framework. Dennis Preston (1991) reviewed some of the data available to him using this framework and found that his data generally concurred with Bell's proposed ranking of constraints on variation. However, he also considered the relative strength of purely linguistic constraints on a variable. As is generally the case with a linguistic variable, the linguistic constraints have the most powerful effect of all on a variable (we noted this, in passing, for the Martha's Vineyard data in Chapter 2).

This means that, for instance, the nature of the following or preceding sound, or whether the variant is a subject or an object, accounts for far more of the variation we can observe than any social factors, such as who a speaker is talking to. The effect of any social constraints defines a smaller range of variation than the linguistic constraints do:

(linguistic factors) > (variation between groups) > (variation in individuals)

However, overall, empirical support for this ordering of factors is still rather shaky. Other researchers have found evidence that leads them to conclude the opposite to Bell and Preston – namely, that for some variables the range of a speaker's style-shifting exceeds the differences between social groups. John Baugh's work on African American Vernacular English in Los Angeles seemed to indicate that certain variables may rank social and individual factors differently. Some variables may show the relationship between interspeaker and intraspeaker variation that Bell suggested, but for some variables speakers' style-shifting may outweigh even the effects of linguistic constraints (Baugh 1979, cited in Rickford and McNair-Knox 1994). Thus, for the variable use of third-person singular -s and non-prevocalic (r), Baugh found that:

(variation in individuals) > (variation between groups)

Baugh suggested that whether a variable shows greater effects for linguistic or non-linguistic constraints depends on whether it carries much semantic information. He suggested that the two variables showing this pattern − (r) in non-prevocalic environments (the same variable as Labov studied in NYC) and third-person singular agreement on verbs (which may or may not be marked with -s, i.e., *she walks* or *she walk_*) − do not carry any crucial information.

For instance, there are relatively few minimal pairs created by variable presence or absence of [r] in English, so they will seldom cause confusion in conversation. Third-person singular agreement on verbs is actually redundant in English because there are very few contexts in which we do not have a full noun or pronoun as the subject of a sentence. So this, too, plays a very limited semantic role. Baugh suggested that when a variable carries limited informational or semantic load, it might show more variation within the speech of individuals than it does between groups.

Note that by invoking linguistic factors as a primary consideration in order to account for the reversal of the non-linguistic constraints on style-shifting, Baugh implies a fuller ordering of factors than even Preston did:

(linguistic factors: high information/semantic load) > (variation between groups)
> (variation in individuals)

(linguistic factors: low information/semantic load) > (variation in individuals)
> (variation between groups)

We still lack a lot of the detailed comparisons between individuals and groups to test Bell's framework thoroughly. A lot more research needs to be done in order to find out whether Bell is right in suggesting that there is a systematic or predictable relationship that derives intraspeaker variation from interspeaker variation. In the next two sections we examine empirical studies that have tried to test the predictions of Bell's framework.

---

exercise

Integrating topic shifts in audience design

Many people have found that in the informal part of a sociolinguistic interview, speakers use more of the standard or more conservative variants when they are talking about language than when they are talking about the supernatural. How could you account for this in terms of Bell's notion of audience design?

Do you think this is a more satisfactory account than one based on attention to speech?

---

exercise

'Attention to speech' vs 'audience design'?

Labov sees style-shifting as a linguistic reflex of changes in the amount of attention a speaker pays to their speech.

Do you think Bell's audience-design approach simply restates style-shifting in terms of how much attention speakers are paying to real or possible listeners? Or do you think the differences between the two approaches are more fundamental?

Reciprocal audience design?

Before leaving the topic of audience design, it is worth noting that the interviewer may also be attuning their speech to the audience. Peter Trudgill conducted a major social dialect study in his home town of Norwich and he found that, quite unconsciously, he had used more regional Norwich variants when he was talking to speakers who were themselves high users of those variants than he had when he was interviewing Norwich speakers who were low users of those variants (Trudgill 1986).

This raises the question of whether people consciously make these kinds of attunements or accommodations, and how much control they have over the success of their attunement. We will come back to these questions in the next chapter, where we examine some case studies showing that what people do and what they *think* they are doing may be somewhat at odds.

Attunement to different addressees: Foxy Boston's case study

The most serious test of Bell's audience design has been undertaken by John Rickford and Faye McNair-Knox in a case study involving repeated interviews over a period of years with a single speaker, a young woman they call Foxy Boston. Rickford and McNair-Knox's (1994) study represents an important milestone in the study of variation, and of stylistic variation in particular, because it draws both on detailed knowledge of an individual and quantitative information on the linguistic behaviour of the relevant social groups that the speaker's addressees represent.

Rickford and McNair-Knox decided the use the interviews that had been conducted with Foxy Boston as the basis for a rigorous test of Bell's proposals. They compared Foxy's use of a number of sociolinguistic variables when she was talking to Faye, an African-American, and when she was being interviewed (on very similar topics) by an Anglo-American interviewer, Beth. Rickford and McNair-Knox looked at several variables that are well known to favour one variant in African-American English and a complementary variant in White American English. Audience design predicts that with variables like these, Foxy would accommodate to the norms of the different groups when her addressee is a member of one or other of these groups. That is to say, she would use more of the variants that are typically used by African-American speakers (as a group) when she was talking to Faye, whereas she would use more of the variants typical of White American English when she was talking to Beth (and therefore fewer of the African-American variants). This follows from Bell's idea that style-shifting derives from social differences.

Two of the variables they looked at are shown in Table 3.3. They are the presence or absence of the verb BE and the presence or absence of third-person −s agreement on verbs. Examples of the variables and the variants that are statistically more likely to realise them in African American Vernacular English (AAVE) and White American Vernacular English (WAVE) are shown in Table 3.3.

There is a considerable body of work on AAVE showing that absence of third-person agreement and absence of BE are reliable markers of African American Vernacular English, differentiating speakers of varieties of AAVE from vernacular varieties of White Americans. Because the differences between AAVE and WAVE are so extreme for these variables, Rickford and McNair-Knox had to determine that Foxy wasn't just switching between different

Table 3.3 Two variables studied in Foxy Boston's speech, showing the variants statistically more likely to be used by speakers of African-American Vernacular English and speakers of White American Vernacular English.

	Variant more common in:	
Variable	African American Vernacular English	White American Vernacular English
Copula and auxiliary BE	*BE absent* He _ a teacher. She _ going downtown. You _ crazy.	*BE present* He is (He's) a teacher. She is (She's) going downtown. You are (You're) crazy.
Third-person −*s* agreement	*Subject agreement absent* She **think** you don't care.	*Subject agreement present* She **thinks** you don't care.

grammars (one AAVE syntax and one WAVE syntax) when she was talking to Faye and Beth (see Chapter 6 for more on code-switching). They took a lot of care to make sure that they really were comparing the same variables in the two interviews.

They did this by determining that when Foxy *did* use third-person singular agreement or BE that she did so in the same linguistic contexts in both interviews. Having determined that they were in fact comparing Foxy's use of the same variables in both interviews, they examined the frequency of the variants associated with AAVE norms; that is, absence of agreement and absence of BE. They found that Foxy did, indeed, have more absence of BE and −*s* agreement when she was talking to Faye than when she was talking to Beth. They interpreted these results as support for the notion of attunement through audience design.

But audience design made a stronger claim than simple attunement. Bell argued that the range of variation covered by a single speaker's accommodation to different addressees will be *less than* the range of variation between the groups that those addressees represent. Rickford and McNair-Knox found support for this crucial component of the audience design framework. The difference between how often Foxy omitted BE and −*s* agreement when she was talking to Faye compared to when she was talking to Beth was less than the differences between the frequency of these variants in African and White American Vernaculars taken from larger social dialect studies. This is shown in Table 3.4, where the final column shows

Table 3.4 Differences in frequency of copula and -*s* agreement absence for Foxy Boston talking to African-American and White American Vernacular English-speaking addressee. (Source, Rickford and McNair-Knox 1994, table 10.2 [modified].)

	Speakers of AAVE	Speakers of WAVE	Difference (in % points)
Foxy Boston's averages for absence with different addressee:			
copula	70% (N=283)	40% (N=176)	30 points
-s agreement	73% (83/114)	37% (46/124)	36 points

the difference (in percentage points) between when Foxy was addressing a speaker of AAVE and a speaker of WAVE.

Data from these variables in the vernacular speech of White Americans shows that rates for third-person singular -s absence are very low, and the rates of copula deletion are virtually zero. If we sample across a group of speakers, AAVE has a rate of about 65 per cent third-person singular -s absence and a rate of about 38 per cent copula deletion (these figures are taken from studies reported by Rickford and McNair-Knox, and in Labov 1972b). This means that the difference between the group averages for AAVE and WAVE speakers is greater than the range Foxy shows in her speech to an African-American and then a White American addressee.

There was less support for Bell's hypothesis about the effect of topic changes on an individual's style-shifting. We noted earlier that Bell proposed that the influence of topic would not exceed audience-based shifts. In fact, the frequency with which Foxy used the AAVE variants of BE and -s absence varied more within each interview (that is, depending on what topic she was talking about) than they did between the interviews overall (that is, depending on who she was talking to). So this result did not support Bell's hypothesis. The role that topic plays in style-shifting still needs a good deal of study.

Testing assumptions about topic-induced shift

Sumittra Suraratdecha tried to test audience design's predictions about the effect of topic in the speech of Thai university students living in the United States. She recorded them with different interlocutors and compared how often they switched back and forth between Thai and English during their group conversations.

She found that code-switching from English into Thai happened most often when the students were speaking about the supernatural, and switching from Thai into English happened more often when they were talking about travel and what they wanted to do after university.

Why do you think the code-switching might have gone in that direction for those topics?

exercise

So Rickford and McNair-Knox's study with Foxy provided a fine example of the ways in which quantitative studies of variation in groups and detailed analyses of one person's stylistic repertoire could complement each other. As far as testing audience design is concerned, it provided mixed support for the specific hypotheses of the framework. In addition, Rickford and McNair-Knox were cautious about claiming that their data from Foxy showed that she was attuning her speech for her addressee because they realised they had not controlled all social variables in their study.

The interviewers, Faye and Beth, certainly differed from each other in their ethnicity, but they also differed in how well they knew Foxy. Faye and Foxy had met before and knew each other pretty well by the time they had the conversation on which Rickford and McNair-Knox based their study. However, Beth and Foxy had never met before their interview. So, as Rickford and McNair-Knox point out, it is possible that differences in Foxy's speech in the two interviews were due to differences in how familiar her addressee was, rather than differences in their ethnicity. In the next section, we will see how sociolinguists might go about teasing these factors apart.

Attunement to groups or familiarity?

A lengthy and ongoing study of a speech community in a small town in Texas provided Patricia Cukor-Avila and Guy Bailey (2001) with exactly the opportunity to attempt to tackle the outstanding problem from the Foxy Boston study. Cukor-Avila and Bailey have been working in a small community, which they call Springville, since 1988. Over the years they have developed close friendship networks in the community and are now recognised by many locals as insiders themselves. They started out collecting data in recordings similar to the classic Labovian sociolinguistic interview, but over the years their recordings have become increasingly informal and are often controlled by the residents themselves. Cukor-Avila and Bailey realised that they were almost uniquely placed to try and resolve the ambiguities left from Rickford and McNair-Knox's study. Most of the residents of Springville are African-American, and this meant that they could examine the same AAVE variables in the Foxy Boston study. But their lengthy involvement with Springville meant they could also control for speech with familiar and unfamiliar WAVE-speaking addressees. This was important because the closer they could match the social and linguistic variables of Rickford and McNair-Knox's study, the more valid and the more informative the comparison between the two sets of data would be.

They decided to focus on the speech styles used by two African-American teenagers and one elderly African-American woman when talking to other African-Americans and with a White fieldworker. The teenagers, Samantha and Lashonda, had known both their interviewers for some time (and the interviews span a period a several years) so their familiarity with the two interviewers was high. Audrey, the older woman, was interviewed by her nephew and then also by two White fieldworkers that she had not met before. The differences in social factors characterising their interviews and Foxy's interviews are summarised in Table 3.5. For completeness, Cukor-Avila and Bailey also indicate whether the speakers share community membership, and whether other people were present during the interview, in case these non-linguistic factors might be relevant.

Cukor-Avila and Bailey found that there were minimal differences between Lashonda's and Samantha's styles in the interviews conducted by an African-American and a White interviewer, both of whom had known them for a long time. In other words, there was no evidence that, when talking to a White addressee, they attuned their speech so as to use more of the variants typical of White varieties of American English. The familiarity of the interviewer appears to have overridden any effect that her ethnic identity might have had. However, Audrey did exhibit style-shifting similar to Foxy's. Since they only found the same addressee effects that had been found with Foxy in Audrey's interviews, Cukor-Avila and Bailey suggested that this indicates that Foxy's lack of familiarity with Beth was more likely to have been the salient factor constraining Foxy's style-shifting than Beth's ethnicity.

As stated originally, Bell's audience design framework requires speakers to be aware of variation in the linguistic behaviour of different social groups in the larger speech community. An addressee is then perceived and categorised as a representative of one of those groups, and the speaker's understanding of the characteristic features of the group's speech is then used as the basis for designing a style appropriate to that addressee. This formulation of the framework gives primacy to social groups. However, the Springville data indicates that

Table 3.5 Comparison of social features characterising the interviews with African-American interviewees conducted by Rickford and McNair-Knox and Cukor-Avila and Bailey. (Source, Cukor-Avila and Bailey 2001: 256, 263, tables 1–3.)

| | Foxy's interviews | | Samantha and Lashonda's interviews | | Audrey's interviews | |
	Faye	Beth	Local teen	Fieldworker	Audrey's nephew	Fieldworkers
Race of interviewer	Afr.-Am.	White	Afr.-Am.	White	Afr.-Am.	White
Familiar?	Yes	No	Yes	Yes	Yes	No
Community member?	Yes	No	Yes	No (but 7 years' association)	Yes	No
Other people present?	Yes	No	Yes	Yes	Yes	Yes

speakers may principally perceive their audience in interpersonal terms (e.g., as a familiar friend or not), and that this kind of personal information trumps group information in constraining intraspeaker variation.

A lot more work is needed testing and replicating these kinds of studies in order to determine whether their findings are robust and whether the conclusions drawn from them are generalisable across speakers and communities. Many sociolinguists today believe that style-shifting is part of ongoing interpersonal negotiations, and it is these interpersonal negotiations that ultimately give reality and meaning to group identities and group memberships. The studies with Foxy and in Springville provide us with a basis for evaluating the relative importance of group factors and interpersonal factors for a sociolinguistic theory of style. The difficulty that they demonstrate in controlling for all the non-linguistic factors that might be relevant shows that this kind of careful comparative work often requires a long-term commitment to research in a community of speakers.

In turn, this is a good reminder to us of the importance of having sound information about the social backgrounds of our speakers, and an understanding of how they see themselves in relation to others in the larger social matrix. Because Cukor-Avila and Bailey have years of friendships and experiences in Springville based on extensive participant observation, they can draw on this information to add social and interpersonal meaning to their analysis of variation.

CHAPTER SUMMARY

This chapter has introduced stylistic variation – that is, variation within the speech of a single speaker – as a locus of sociolinguistic enquiry. It began by looking at the way in which style has been operationalised in social dialect surveys, including both the rapid and anonymous surveys and the different tasks built into a longer sociolinguistic survey. The fact of stylistic variation is undisputed in sociolinguistics, but there are some disagreements about its underlying causes and therefore the way in which this kind of variation should be characterised. Intraspeaker, or stylistic, variation can be characterised as the amount of attention the speaker is paying to their speech, or as the speaker's desire to attune their speech to their addressee's perceived norms. We have reviewed some of the more significant studies that reflect both frameworks. In doing so, we have highlighted differences in the methods required to test the two perspectives, but we have also drawn attention to the fundamental difference in the role of the speaker. The attention to speech framework presents a picture of the speaker that is fairly egocentric, while the attunement and audience design frameworks see speakers as co-participants in social and conversational interactions.

These different views of the speaker underpin a tension in sociolinguistics between generalisations made across large social groups such as social class or age (as is associated with the study of a speech community), and generalisations relevant only to much smaller, and sometimes quite idiosyncratic, communities that are constituted through members' shared practices (these 'communities of practice' are defined and discussed in more detail in Chapter 9). As Rickford and McNair-Knox showed, patterns that differentiate groups can be used to inform the details of an individual speaker's performance. The potential for such complementarity will recur again in later chapters.

This chapter has devoted considerable space to explaining the methods used to analyse style-shifting. These different methods are very important because they have implications beyond the study of style alone. The methods associated with the attention to speech accounts of style-shifting model variation as something that reflects non-linguistic information (e.g., how much attention the speaker is paying to their speech). The methods associated with audience (or speaker) design, on the other hand, treat variation as constitutive of non-linguistic factors (e.g., as selecting an intended audience, or attempting to stress similarity and identity with an audience). These differences are central to ongoing debates about how sociolinguistics should develop. This is why we have started this introductory text by examining research on style; several of the methodological and theoretical issues raised here have echoes in later chapters, where we will turn our attention to other social constraints on variation.

In the next chapter, we develop further the notion of accommodation that was introduced in the discussion of audience design. Although the focus in Chapter 4 is more solidly on attitudes that speakers have to other *groups* of language users and the varieties of language that they associate with those groups, discussions of multilingualism and code-switching in Chapter 6 again show how speakers balance considerations about the immediate needs of their conversation with their acquired knowledge about what is typical or expected across society as a whole.

FURTHER READING

In addition to the references provided in this chapter, you may find the following specific readings helpful:

Biber (1995) – a corpus linguistics approach to register and style; uses principal components analysis.
Bell (1991) – a more wide-ranging linguistic analysis of the forms and styles used in the news media.
Giles and Coupland (1991) – on linguistic accommodation and attunement.

Coupland (1984) – a study looking at one speaker's stylistic variation with different addressees.

Schiffrin *et al.* (2001) – a range of articles providing different perspectives on discourse analysis. Chapters in section III deal with styles of discourse in different domains or contexts.

CHAPTER 4

Language attitudes

Key terms introduced in this chapter:

- semantic shift
- semantic derogation
- linguistic relativism
- deterministic
- perceptual dialectology
- social identity theory
- salient
- accommodation theory
- convergence
- divergence
- subjective and objective measures

INTRODUCTION

Imagine you are sitting at home and the phone rings. You answer it and find yourself talking to a stranger on the other end of the line. What are you thinking as you listen to them?

When you talk to someone, you start to form opinions about them, sometimes solely on the basis of the way they talk (Chambers 2003: 2–11). The last time you rang a service centre to buy something over the phone, or to complain about something, you would have spoken to a complete stranger. And yet, within minutes or even seconds, you probably composed quite a detailed picture of who you were talking to. Were they male, or female? Were they a native speaker of English? Did they have a strong regional dialect, or could you perhaps only say very vaguely where they come from ('somewhere in Scotland' or 'probably the South')? You might decide that you think they are Asian or a Pacific Islander. You may also have strong ideas about whether they are 'nice', 'friendly' and 'competent', or whether they are 'rude', 'disinterested' and 'stupid'.

We draw very powerful inferences about people from the way they talk. Our attitudes to different varieties of a language colour the way we perceive the individuals that use those varieties. Sometimes this works to people's advantage; sometimes to their disadvantage. For instance, in the university where I work, a number of people speak with the southern British Oxbridge accents that are generally associated with privilege, respect and success. They seem to be found more often in the senior ranks of the university than people who don't. Of course, there are exceptions – the head of the university college who still speaks a clearly northern variety of English – and the exceptions are as interesting as the rule.

In this chapter we will consider how closely linked language and attitudes are. We will start by looking at examples that show how attitudes towards other people are expressed *through* language, by looking at the case of sexist language. We then examine people's positive and negative attitudes to different language varieties and we will see how these attitudes can shed light on the way people perceive to be organised.

Connections with theory

Language attitudes or language ideologies? The study of *language ideologies* is related to the study of language attitudes and perceptions about language discussed in this chapter. Woolard (1998) provides a discussion of the different ways in which the term *ideology* has been used in anthropology and anthropological linguistics; in general, its scope is necessarily broader than the study of language attitudes. The study of language ideologies considers how the beliefs and theories that speakers have about different forms of language help them to rationalise and relate highly complex social systems, such as access to power, and what social processes sustain those beliefs.

GENDER, LANGUAGE AND ATTITUDES

Language provides many windows on speakers' attitudes to themselves and others. Our everyday speech encodes a surprising amount of information on our attitudes. In this section, we start to investigate attitudes by looking at how attitudes to women and men are reflected in language. We will see that synchronic and historical data may provide telling attitudinal data.

Semantic shift and semantic derogation

> 'But the longer I live on this Crumpetty Tree,
> The plainer than ever it seems to me,
> That very few people come this way,
> And that life on the whole is far from gay!'
> Said the Quangle Wangle Quee.
>   Edward Lear 1877, *The Quangle Wangle's Hat*

When Edward Lear wrote *The Quangle Wangle's Hat* in 1877, the word *gay* already had several meanings. The Quangle Wangle Quee meant that his life was lacking in joy and mirth, which in fact is the oldest meaning that the word *gay* has – and some people still identify it with this meaning. But even by the late nineteenth century, *gay* had acquired a parallel set of meanings, most of which were decidedly negative and which focused on sexual promiscuity. At this time *gay* was used to refer to *women* who were sexually promiscuous; it was only in the early twentieth century that it seems to have started to be used to refer to homosexuals – probably the meaning we most strongly associate with the word now.

Over time, speakers may begin to use words in slightly different ways, and as these minor changes accumulate a word can end up meaning something very different from what it started out meaning. This process can be called **semantic shift** (or drift). For instance,

Semantic shift

Incremental changes to the meaning of a word or phrase. Sometimes included within the scope of grammaticalisation (or grammaticisation) theory, but unlike classic grammaticalisation, semantic shift need not entail structural reanalysis of the word/phrase. That is, a verb might stay a verb but its meaning might be severely weakened or altered over time.

the word *pretty* originally meant 'cunning' or 'skilful' and then went through a period when it meant 'gallant' or 'brave'. The meanings of 'pleasing' or 'attractive' that we associate with *pretty* appear in the fifteenth century, but it took a long time before these meanings edged the others out. Despite the wild trajectory *pretty* has had over semantic space, it has maintained an essentially positive set of meanings over time.

In this respect it contrasts with the history of *gay*, which has acquired negative connotations as it has moved from meaning 'joyful' to meaning 'immoral'. It is true that *gay* does not have a universally negative meaning now, but this process of reclaiming a positive meaning for *gay* only began comparatively recently. Even though in some circles it is a positive or neutral term of identification, this is not the case for all speakers of English, and some people still consider *gay* to be a derogatory epithet. (Recent shifts in the colloquial uses of *gay* have been decidedly negative.)

No, really?

'The question is,' said Alice, 'whether you can make words mean so many different things.'

'The question is,' said Humpty Dumpty, 'which is to be master – that's all.'

Martin Gardner's (1970) classic annotation of Lewis Carroll's *Alice* books notes that Humpty Dumpty's view on the meaning of words has a long history. He suggests it can be seen as a form of *nominalism*, which the philosopher William of Ockham defended in the Middle Ages. Ockham argued that the meanings of words derive from what we use them to signify.

Connections with theory

People sometimes end up in confused arguments about what words 'really' mean. Just because one meaning of a word is older than others, this doesn't make it the 'real' meaning of that word, and you would find yourself in all sorts of trouble if you tried to enforce this line. For instance, in Old English, *man* meant 'human being', irrespective of sex and age, but I doubt (m)any adult women would use this as grounds to use the 'Men's' room at a movie theatre. Similarly, *meat* originally meant '(solid) food in general', but this meaning is now wholly lost. You would be considered rather odd if you went around saying things like 'an egg is full of meat' (which was fine when Shakespeare wrote it in *Romeo and Juliet*).

Most linguists find the notion of 'real meaning' unhelpful. Instead, they find it more useful to talk about what is conventionally implied by a word when it is used, what other words it frequently occurs with (i.e., its collocations), and what it implies when it is used in different conversational contexts. In some contexts, such as religion, older meanings are still relevant even if they have fallen out of use in everyday speech. However, it is important to remember that in these cases the repetition of the rituals serves to (re)construct those meanings in just those particular contexts.

A semantics text, like Kearns (2000), will tell you more about these ways of thinking about meaning, and Eckert and McConnell-Ginet (2003) includes excellent discussion showing how the study of semantics can complement sociolinguistics.

In a study in the 1970s (now ripe for updating), Muriel Schultz noticed that when she looked at words used to describe women and men, there was a distinct tendency for words describing women to have acquired negative overtones (*bitch, tart, minx*), while this was not true for words about men. Moreover, the words for women also linked some kind of sexual activity with the negative attitudes, again in a way that was not paralleled by the words for men. So there is a big difference between the attitudes towards women and men having multiple partners, expressed in the contrast between *slut* and *stud*. And although younger speakers of English (especially, younger women) can use the word *slut* to refer negatively to a promiscuous man, generally speaking there is no way of expressing the kind of disapproval about a man that *slut* expresses about a woman. When a word's meaning shifts and acquires more negative connotations, it can be referred to as **semantic derogation**.

Semantic derogation

Semantic shift that results in a word acquiring more negative associations or meanings.

Semantic derogation

Do you think it is true that, in general, there is no way of expressing the kind of disapproval about a man that *slut* expresses about a woman? If it is true, why do you think this is?

In some varieties of English *rake* describes a promiscuous male. Do you think *slut* and *rake* differ only in the sex of the person they refer to?

exercise

Attitudes and context of use

Speakers of English sometimes differ in how negative they find a word like *minx* or *tart* (especially *tarty*). Are these words ever entirely positive or is their meaning always somewhat ambivalent? What determines how positively you might interpret them? The person who uses them or the actions they describe? Are there other factors?

exercise

This process of semantic derogation is seen particularly clearly in male/female pairs that have, as a result of semantic shift and derogation, acquired quite different meanings. So originally *courtier* and *courtesan* both simply referred to people attached to a princely court. However, *courtesan* quickly acquired derogatory connotations and became a euphemism for a mistress or prostitute. You see evidence of a similar process having applied in the different synchronic meanings for *master* and *mistress*.

Table 4.1 gives an even more detailed perspective on this process. It tracks the historical trajectory of a number of English words that currently refer, or once did refer, to women. But

exercise

Pretty nice?

When we discussed *pretty*, I said that it has essentially kept a set of positive meanings throughout its changes. But how positive do you think the word *pretty* actually is? Would an artist consider it positive if someone complimented their work by saying 'You paint the prettiest pictures'?

Table 4.1 Historical (diachronic) change affecting words that currently refer, or have at some time referred, to women.

	→ Semantic shift over time →				
gay (adj.)	(persons) full of joy and mirth (1310)	addicted to social pleasures and dissipations (1637)	(woman) leading an immoral life (1825)	homosexual (1935)	stupid, hopeless (1980s)
girl	a child of either sex e.g., *knave girl* (1290)	a female child, unmarried woman (1530)	a sweetheart, lady-love (1648)	a prostitute or mistress (1711)	a Black woman (1835)
harlot	a low fellow, knave (1330)	a male servant (1386)	an unchaste woman, a strumpet (1450)		
hussy	a mistress of a household, a thrifty woman (1530)	a (playfully) rude term of addressing a woman (17th C)	a female of the lower orders, of low or improper behaviour (18th C)		
tart	a delicious baked pastry (1430)	a young woman for whom some affection is felt (1864)	a female prostitute (1887)	a young favourite of an older man, a catamite, a male prostitute (1935)	
queen	a king's wife, woman of high rank (893, 900)	a term of endearment to a woman (1588)	an attractive woman, a girlfriend (1900)	a male homosexual (1924)	
whore	a female prostitute (1100)	a woman committing adultery (1440)	a general term of abuse (1633)	a male prostitute (1968)	
wench	a female child (1290)	a wanton woman (1362)	a servant (1380)	a working class girl (1575)	

it also shows some of the other directions in which their meanings have developed. The definitions and dates are taken from citations in the *Oxford English Dictionary*. What overarching generalisation do you think you could make based on this data?

All of these words have undergone a process of semantic derogation. Some start out simply describing femaleness in neutral or positive terms (*wench* or *hussy*) and some start out being ungendered (*gay*) or referring to males (*harlot*). In the last case, as the word began to denote women, it also acquired negative connotations, in the same manner that the neutral or positive words shift and acquire negative meanings over time.

Another thing you will notice from Table 4.1 is that the trajectory of these words tells us about more than just social attitudes towards femaleness. Attitudes to homosexual men, and specific groups of women – Black women and working-class women – are also embedded in the changes in meaning. Taken as a whole, even a small sample of words, like those shown in Table 4.2, suggests a picture of society in which the only group of people immune to this kind of derogation are heterosexual, White, middle-class men.

Connections with theory

White, middle-class, heterosexual males are often treated as the unmarked category in society and in research on language in society (Trechter 2003). This assumption of male unmarkedness also underpins the prescriptive norm of using the masculine pronoun *he* when referring to a non-specific person.

Saying that White, middle-class men are immune to this kind of semantic derogation is only true in a particular place at a particular time. There are, of course, derogatory words for them too (Henderson 2003), and some of these also show evidence of semantic drift. *Punk*, for example, is used to refer almost exclusively to White males on Union Island in the Grenadines, and children in Vanuatu use the word *turis* ('tourist') as a term of abuse to each other. Of course, *punk* started out negative, and *tourist* isn't necessarily male.

Increasingly, researchers on language and gender are emphasising how important it is to understand gender in relation to sexuality (see Cameron and Kulick 2003, and also Chapter 10). The importance of this is suggested very strongly by the data provided in Table 4.1. As Cameron and Kulick point out, class and race are also important in defining how we understand sexuality and gender. From even this small amount of data it is possible to see how attitudes to women, and the general eroticisation of women, are part of a complex set of links and attitudes to other groups that are candidates as the objects of White, middle-class heterosexual male desires.

In an interesting study, that foreshadows the more recent move linking attitudes to gender and sexuality, the sociolinguist Elizabeth Gordon (1997) found that listeners were highly likely to categorise a young woman with a broad, non-standard accent as (among other things) highly likely to be 'sleeping around'. By contrast, listeners did not categorise a young woman using a more refined, middle-class accent as so likely to be promiscuous. Gordon traces this association between lower-class varieties of English and sexual promiscuity back into the Victorian era (when something like modern class distinctions started to emerge due to the urbanisation and industrialisation of society). In later chapters we will see that there is a large body of data showing that different ways of speaking correlate with the social class and sex of the speaker. Gordon suggests that the different attitudes people have to women's use of broad or cultivated accents may play a role in determining the nature of some of these generalisations.

The linguistic derogation of women can be seen in many cultures. For example, Atiqa Hachimi (2001) shows there are aphorisms and sayings in Moroccan Arabic which cover all stages of a woman's life and which are revealing of social attitudes to women. Examples (1)–(3) are taken from her work:

(1) *I-bnat ma-ka-y-str-hum Rir trab.*
   'Only death can control girls.'
(2) *ʔumm-uk θumma ʔumm-uk θumma ʔumm-uk θumma ʔab-uːk.*
   'Your mother, then your mother, then your mother and then your father.'
(3) *I -ʕguz-a ktər mən ʃ-ʃitan.*
   'The old woman is worse than the devil.'

(Hachimi 2001: 42–44)

On the basis of a number of other linguistic examples, and an analysis of the sociocultural position of women, Hachimi argues that these kinds of aphorism encapsulate more widely held attitudes. She argues that they show that a Moroccan woman is positively valued only if she is actively producing children. Fulfilling the role of mother provides some insulation from the otherwise uniformly negative attitudes to women that are expressed in folk wisdom. A mother is to be treasured beyond all others, as indicated in (2), but before she starts having children (as in (1)) and after she stops (as in (3)), a woman is seen in very negative terms.

LINGUISTIC RELATIVISM

When people differentiate between groups, they almost inevitably make qualitative judgements about the basis of the differentiation. Comparisons between the members of a speaker's ingroup and members of outgroups tend to be made in such a way that they ensure a positive self-image. It stands to reason, therefore, that where one group holds more social power, the members of that group will be in a position to assert the validity of the way they perceive themselves and others, and they will try to assert the moral or aesthetic superiority of their ingroup.

Linguistic relativism

Weaker position than *determinism*. Holds that the value of one factor is not wholly independent of the value of another factor, but instead is somehow *constrained* by it. Associated with the Sapir–Whorf hypothesis which suggests that the way we perceive the world around us is in some way reflected in the way we talk. (See also *Reflexive*.)

This is one way of understanding what's going on with sexist or racist language. In turn, it provides a useful basis for understanding why people find racist or sexist language objectionable. Obviously it is not the words themselves that are objectionable. As virtually every introductory linguistics class tries to stress, words are simply arbitrary signs that communities of speakers use to denote something (that is, to pick out and identify a thing or event in the world). Hence, what people find objectionable about sexist or racist language is not the linguistic process of denotation, it is the underlying social and cultural assumptions about the way the world is and how it should be organised.

The term **linguistic relativism** can be used to refer to the hypothesis that the way we talk about others, and the words we use, does more than simply denote entities or events in the world. Linguistic relativism instead proposes that the way we perceive the world plays a part in how language is structured. Linguistic relativism is sometimes called the Sapir–Whorf hypothesis. Both Sapir and Whorf worked on Native American languages, and Whorf is famously associated with asserting that because the Native American language Hopi does not make the same tense and aspect distinctions that English does, Hopi speakers must perceive the world and the passage of time differently from the way English speakers do.

This argument has often been represented in extreme forms (usually by people who want to make fun of it).

For example, it has been suggested that Whorf was claiming that the grammar of Hopi imposed fundamental cognitive constraints on its speakers. That is, not only did the structure of the grammar mean that they do not perceive the passage of time as English speakers do, but they could never perceive the passage of time the way English speakers do. This would be a **deterministic** view of the relationship between language and thought because it contends that the shape of the language determines how its speakers perceive and experience the world.

Whorf did not actually make such deterministic claims himself. He argued a weaker, and less deterministic, position, which stressed the important links between how we talk (language), how we think about or perceive things (mind), and what it is that we perceive and have to talk about (the world). This is represented schematically in Figure 4.1.

Determinism/ deterministic

The idea that there is a strong causal relationship between two factors (i.e., one determines how the other will be). The idea that if you know the value for one factor, you can automatically and reliably predict the value for another. (See also *Linguistic relativism*.)

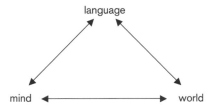

Figure 4.1 Mutually reinforcing influence of language, thought and the world that we perceive and talk about.

Connections with theory

The claim that words are completely arbitrary signs may need to be qualified a little. Some researchers have found that words that are closely related semantically have closer phonological forms than would be predicted by chance. It seems possible that speakers perceive patterns in the world and subconsciously map these into linguistic patterns.

There is some evidence to support this mutually constitutive model, some of which is particularly relevant to our discussion of sexist language. A number of experimental studies have been done with adults and children showing that the name of a professional occupation is explicitly marked as male or female – people find it hard to think of them being filled by someone of the opposite sex. So, it is much harder for people to think of a *fireman* as being a woman (small children will often simply reject this as impossible), whereas a *firefighter* can be imagined as a woman or a man. Similarly, research asking people to find images illustrating topics such as 'Urban man' versus 'Urban life' found that university students were much more likely to produce images that included only men in the first case, and images that either included women and men (or consisted of cityscapes) in the latter case.

Opposition to sexist, racist, or heterosexist language (by which we mean the unquestioning assumption that one sex, or one race, or one sexual orientation is better than another)

Generic reference terms

You can easily replicate Martyna's (1980) or Cassell's (1994) experiments on perceptions of gendered terms. For example, you could ask your subjects to go away and find you pictures to use in advertising chapters in a book. You could give half of them gendered titles like 'Man's relationship with the environment' and half of them ungendered titles like 'Relating to the environment'. Or you could provide people with a set of pictures you have chosen and ask some of them to tell you which ones are suitable illustrations of sentences that include gendered job titles, like *policeman, waitress*, and give some of them ungendered titles like *police officer, waiting staff*.

Once you start thinking about this, you will see that there are a number of interesting permutations you can do using different groups of informants or using different topics or titles as relatively neutral controls.

very often starts from the weak Whorfian position that language, thought and the world are interrelated. For example, people who actively promote language change by providing guidelines for how to avoid sexist language base their arguments on the assumption that if people choose their words more carefully this will in turn affect the way they think about the relationships between women and men. Advocates of non-sexist (non-racist, etc.) language policies hope that this process will destabilise the assumptions that people make about whether or not the group distinctions they are drawing are natural or just.

Similarly, arguments against providing guidelines for language use may dispute the details of this model. Instead of assuming that there is mutual influence between all three domains, counter-arguments contend that the direction of influence is asymmetric, and that language itself does not and cannot influence the way people think or the way they perceive the world. Notice that this seems to be based on a somewhat stronger and more deterministic position than the weaker, relativistic position outlined in the previous paragraph.

However, since a strong deterministic position clearly misrepresents the relationship between language and perception, this line of reasoning concludes that changing the language will make no difference. It is necessary to change the way people think first rather than trying to change the way people talk through language policies and publishing guidelines to avoid sexist or racist language. Under this model, once the way people think has changed, language change will follow.

Address and reference

Many linguists have drawn attention to the social importance of how people address and refer to one another (see Sally McConnell-Ginet 2003, for instance). You can explore this in several ways.

Either: What attitudes to you do you think are expressed in the ways other people address you? Keep a record of all the ways you are addressed over the period of a week (and note who addresses you like this and where). How do you feel about the different address terms? What would happen if someone at university tried to address you the way your family does? How would you feel?

Or: What kinds of attitudes to members of different social groups are expressed by the way they are addressed in public? Start to keep notes on all the terms you hear used to address customers in, e.g., stores, lunch stands. Is everyone addressed the same way? Do the customers and the servers use the same terms to address each other? It may help to pool your results with some friends for either of these exercises.

Whichever exercise you choose, consider how much your results support the idea that language, thought and the world are intertwined. If you think you have found any evidence for strong associations between attitudes and language, do you think it is possible to destabilise or even break those associations by changing the kinds of words used?

RECLAIMING DEROGATORY TERMS

Later in the chapter we will look in more detail at the pioneering work of Henri Tajfel in social identity theory. One of the principal motives for Tajfel's research was his desire to understand prejudice and racism – where does prejudice come from? How is it maintained as a social phenomenon? Tajfel observed that where there is an unequal relationship between groups, this inequality can be perceived as more or less legitimate, or as more or less permanent and stable. He proposed that when people believe they are being treated unequally, their responses to this situation will be constrained by the extent to which they think the current, unfair situation is legitimate and how readily they believe it could be changed.

So, to take a very simple example, people might think it is reasonable and legitimate for social power to be extended to people who possess physical power. If a woman believes this, then she might decide that it is legitimate for men in our society to have more social power than women because many men are bigger and physically more powerful than many women. Furthermore, if she generalises this observation and believes that it is a fundamental biological fact, she may also see the situation as permanent and unalterable. In this case, where the intergroup difference is understood as both legitimate and hard to change, Tajfel suggested that people are unlikely to contest or fight against the situation.

On the other hand, a woman might look around and see that not all men *are* in fact physically stronger than women. If that happens, she might perceive the larger inequalities between women and men that stem from this generalisation to be unstable. In addition, seeing that the situation is unstable, she might begin to question the fundamental legitimacy of the idea that physical power is a basis for accruing social power. In this case, Tajfel suggested she would be more likely to take active steps to combat the inequalities between the groups. (Tajfel actually works through all the possible combinations of perceived legitimacy and stability and makes even more fine-grained predictions about outcomes and actions than I have outlined here, but this rough summary will do for our purposes.)

Tajfel's observations about the social outcomes associated with different perceptions of the stability and justice of intergroup differences also have linguistic significance. If members of a social group do not perceive inequalities and biases against them to be legitimate or stable, then members of that group may seek to effect not only social change but language change as well. This occurs when linguistic practices become seen as part of a larger social

Connections with theory

The anthropologist David Aberle distinguished four types of social movement in terms that parallel Tajfel's continuum of personal–group identities. Aberle (1966) talks about *transformative* movements (which aim for a total change in supra-individual systems), *reformative* movements (which aim for partial change in supra-individual systems), *redemptive* movements (which aim at a total change in individuals) and *alterative* movements (which aim for partial change in individuals).

matrix. Once that matrix is contested and renegotiated, all practices sustaining the system of inequalities, including linguistic practices, become candidates for renegotiation and contestation. The words used to refer to or address a group are especially likely to be subject to scrutiny and reanalysis.

This is precisely what happened with both *nigger* and *girl* as general terms of reference for Blacks and women respectively. The proscription against Whites using *nigger* to refer to Blacks and against using *girl* to refer to adult women resulted from Blacks and women questioning the legitimacy and stability of intergroup differences that had been naturalised before then. These intergroup differences and the hierarchy associated with them had been naturalised partly through the repeated use of these words with negative or disdainful connotations (this provides another example of the manner in which language constructs social relations as well as reflecting them).

The hierarchies were, of course, constructed in other ways too, and through other social practices, but, crucially, the linguistic practices were seen as part of that broader context. It was because, of this that they became targets of contestation and eventual reanalysis. This reanalysis essentially proscribed their use as ways of referring to members of an outgroup in polite social situations. The use of both words as negative and trivialising terms of reference persists in some social contexts, of course. Perhaps of more interest is the fact that they are used with positive connotations among ingroup members. This process of reclaiming what was previously a negative term and redefining it in positive ways was a strategy for dealing with perceived inequalities that Tajfel also discussed.

A particularly successful example of reclaiming a negative word and redefining it positively is the word *queer*. For centuries, *queer* had more or less negative meanings in English, and these negative associations carried over into its use as an outgroup description of gays and lesbians. In the 1990s, the word began to be reclaimed and asserted with positive connotations within the lesbian and gay community, and is a relatively neutral term for a lot of speakers of English now. This positive redefinition of *queer* challenged the legitimacy of negative attitudes towards homosexuals, and it destabilised the privileged position of heterosexuality as an authority against which non-normative practices could be judged. The reclaiming and redefinition of *queer* was, initially, associated with quite radical attempts to destabilise the power of heterosexual norms (as discussed in Cameron and Kulick 2003: 27–29, 77). But this bold redefinition of the term has been less successful. Queer activists and queer theorists have not (yet) been able successfully to challenge the stability of the dominance of heterosexual norms in all the areas in which they might have hoped.

This discussion has covered some relatively familiar facts about the way speakers use language to express negative or derogatory attitudes to other groups in society. We have also

exercise

Reclaiming negative words

There are a number of examples where groups have reclaimed negative words and given those words a positive sense for ingroup use. Homosexuals reclaimed *queer*, some women use *bitch* as a term of strength.

Can you think of any others? (There may have been groups you knew at school who tried to redefine the terms others used to refer to them.) Were these attempts to reclaim a word successful? Did they succeed in questioning the legitimacy or stability of the intergroup differences they were based on? Alternatively, why did they fail?

What other factors were involved that are not covered in the discussion here?

seen that we can learn a lot about social attitudes through historical drift as well as the synchronic uses of a word. We have also seen that the meaning of derogatory terms may be contested and actively redefined by the groups they refer to, often with the express hope that changing how a word is used may change attitudes to the group of people it denotes.

In the remainder of this chapter we consider more subtle relationships between language and attitudes. We start by looking at research that shows people's perceptions of what different dialects there *are* are tightly bound up with their perceptions of what different dialects are *like*. We then return to the phenomenon of accommodation that was introduced in Chapter 3. We will see that accommodation theory is built on the supposition that speakers express their attitudes to themselves and others in the way they speak.

PERCEPTUAL DIALECTOLOGY

In Chapter 2 we looked at variationist sociolinguistics which emerged from the traditions of regional dialectology. Social dialect studies, such as the study of New York City, had very similar goals to the goals of regional dialectology; the chief differences between the two approaches were the kinds of data they collected. Dialectologists working in both of these traditions share the objective of describing language in all its richness and diversity, in order to thereby better understand what language is and how it works as a system.

There is yet another form of dialectology – **perceptual dialectology** – the methods and goals of which are more closely related to the methods and goals used in surveys of attitudes to language in social psychology. In social dialectology, boundaries between varieties are identified on the basis of trained linguists' observations of actual phonetic and grammatical features that constitute salient differences between varieties. In regional dialectology, boundaries are identified on the basis of what trained fieldworkers are able to elicit from speakers or speakers' reports of what they usually say. In perceptual dialectology, the beliefs and thoughts that non-linguists have about language are used to distinguish varieties. People's perceptions about language, whether descriptively accurate or not, are just as important to the researcher as the objective facts about how speakers talk.

In Chapter 1, we determined that sociolinguistics was concerned with the study of speech communities, and the manner in which an individual's linguistic performance relates to shared community norms. This dual concern means that we cannot focus exclusively on facts about production; that is, only on what people say. In addition, we would like to know

Perceptual dialectology

The study of people's subjectively held beliefs about different dialects or linguistic varieties. The focus on lay perceptions about language complements the regional dialectologists' more objective focus on the way people are recorded as speaking.

about perception; that is, how and what people hear. We will see that perception is a more complicated process than simply decoding the sounds and words that someone else has encoded and produced. Non-linguistic factors seem to act as quite strong filters or constraints.

Work in perceptual dialectology has been pioneered by the sociolinguist Dennis Preston, and it is closely linked to what has been called 'folk linguistics'. Folk linguistics looks more generally at non-linguists' beliefs and perceptions about language and language use – for example, asking what constitutes 'good' or 'bad' language. Here, I will only focus on perceptions about accents and dialect boundaries; more comprehensive resources are given in the 'Further reading' section at the end of the chapter.

Preston has developed a number of ways of eliciting people's perceptions of and attitudes to different varieties of a language. One method is to ask people simply to tell you where they think people speak differently. For example, Preston provided respondents with maps of the United States and asked them to draw lines showing where speakers have different accents. In addition, he invited them to label the areas they had marked off in any way they wanted to. Some people used geographic labels similar to the kind a regional dialectologist would use, e.g., 'Southern' or 'Midwestern'. An example can be seen in Figure 4.2.

Preston notes that even when you combine the responses from a large number of people (which minimises the effect of any one person's particular idiosyncrasies, such as being very aware of the Rhode Island accent because their boyfriend grew up there), this method produces a dialect map that looks rather different from the classic regional dialectology boundaries in the United States. The geographic labels are generally less detailed and discriminate fewer dialect boundaries than professional dialectologists do in, for instance, the historically complex area of the southern Atlantic states. This is unsurprising since the average person has neither the time to devote to making fine distinctions between varieties, and nor do they have the technical resources for categorising them at the level of detail that

Figure 4.2   Dialect map of the United States drawn by a Californian respondent showing perceived areas of difference and providing some labels for varieties. (Map courtesy of Dennis Preston.)

a dialectologist does. However, some of the perceptual boundaries between dialects do fall quite close to boundaries derived from linguists' dialect studies.

In a related study, Preston established that despite a lack of close professional study, the average listener was able to categorise speakers roughly according to where they come from. The method he used for showing this was as follows. He played nine recordings from speakers who came from towns running north–south through the Midwest and Southern US states. He played these in random order to untrained listeners, and asked the listeners to place the speakers in order (most southern to most northern variety). They were very good at differentiating southern varieties from northern varieties.

It is quite interesting that the discriminations respondents make in exercises like the map-drawing task and the accent-ordering task are often similar to the discriminations linguists make between varieties. If there was a mismatch, then this might indicate that perceptual dialectology tests simply measure something completely different to what linguists measure. But because some of the dialect boundaries recognised by linguists and non-linguists are very similar, this suggests that the two measures of dialects are mapping essentially the same thing. This suggests that if we do find differences between perceptual and regional dialect boundaries, we might want to pay closer attention to these differences. Preston's research suggests that lay listeners are filtering what they hear through some kind of social filter that then maps these phonetic differences on to social dialect boundaries that matter more to them than they do to dialectologists. In other words, these differences may provide us with information that is directly relevant to understanding all the cognitive processes that people use to perceive and classify language.

The filtering role that social information plays can also be seen in the labels for dialect regions that some respondents provide. These sometimes contain evaluative, as well as geographical, information. For instance, the label *Californiese Human Growthese* (in Figure 4.2) characterises a distinct regional variety, but it also suggests a somewhat dismissive or negative attitude to the variety it labels. One of Preston's respondents from Iowa labelled Hawai'i as being characterised by *Hawaii Intonation Pigeon*. This label provides geographic information (*Hawaii*), typological information (a kind of pidgin language), and structural information (the variety is distinctive for its *intonation*).

Linguists who have studied the sociolinguistic situation in Hawii would certainly agree with this respondent that there is at least one language variety spoken on Hawai'i that is unique to the islands. However, linguists would almost uniformly be thinking of the creole spoken there – a much more stable linguistic variety than a pidgin (a creole is a language that evolves from a pidgin as a consequence of contact between several mutually incomprehensible languages; see Chapter 11). And to a linguist, intonation is only one of many features that distinguish the creole in Hawai'i from mainland US varieties of English, and it is probably not the most salient of those differences. In addition, for linguists it is arguable that a creole based on English is actually a variety of English. So there are several dimensions on which linguists' and non-linguists' categorisations might differ. Perceptual dialectology is not so much interested in whether the Iowa respondent's perceptions about Hawai'i are 'right' or 'wrong'. Rather, it is interested in what those perceptions tell us about which features of language people most readily pay attention to, and how they integrate those features in a socially meaningful way into their further experiences of language.

It is also interesting that non-linguists sometimes perceive dialect boundaries where linguists do not. That is, they believe they hear differences differentiating areas that regional dialectologists do not consider to be distinctive. For example, *Eastern New Jersey* or (*Relaxed*) *Northwest*.

We can find examples of such discrepancies outside of the United States as well. In New Zealand, if you stopped people on the street and asked them whether they can tell where someone comes from in New Zealand just by the way they talk, the replies you would get would be different from the opinions you would get from linguists. People will often cite Southland (shown in Figure 4.3), and mention the use of 'rolled r's' there. There is some empirical basis for people's perceptions of Southland as a distinctive region. Southland had a very high proportion of Scottish settlers in the nineteenth century, and because of this many Pākehā(White) speakers of English in Southland had a Scots 'r'. This is very salient, or noticeable, in New Zealand because the rest of the country was non-rhotic (r-less). It is interesting to note here that even though the so-called 'Southland burr' is not widely used in Southland, a lot of New Zealanders still think of it as a distinctive regional feature of New Zealand English. They perceive it to be a distinct dialect area.

In addition to mentioning a variety that is now pretty much obsolete, people often say that the West Coast of the South Island has a distinct manner of speaking. As you can see in Figure 4.3, the West Coast is relatively isolated: the Southern Alps form a barrier to the

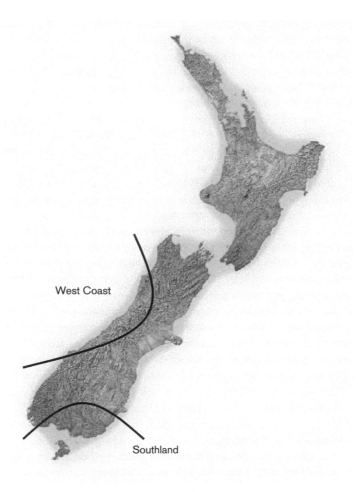

Figure 4.3   Map of New Zealand showing two perceived dialect areas.

east, and there are very few roads entering the region. For a long time, the West Coast made the most of this isolation, and, for instance, West Coast pubs opened on Sundays with apparent impunity while the law against this was policed throughout the rest of the country. Geographic and psychological isolation like this often foster regional linguistic differences, so it would not be surprising if we found that West Coasters in fact *do* speak differently from the rest of New Zealand, as many New Zealanders perceive them to. But linguists have been unable to find evidence of any clear, systematic basis for this perception of a regionally distinctive variety of English.

Connections with theory

Michael Montgomery (2000: 44–45) discusses several types of isolation that may have a linguistic impact. Isolation may be:

- physical, or geographic (how remote is a community?)
- sociological (what types of contact does it have with other communities?)
- economic (how much external exchange is there of goods, ideas, etc?)
- psychological (how open is a community to others? what attachments are there to its own culture?)
- cultural (does a community maintain distinctive practices and beliefs?)
- technological (are there mediated forms of external contact?)

Similarly, people may perceive social dialects that linguists do not. Many New Zealanders also believe that Māori speakers can be identified by the way they talk (Māori are the Polynesians who have lived in New Zealand for about a thousand years). Again, it has proved difficult for linguists to identify reliable, objective criteria that uniquely mark this subjective perception that a Māori English exists; some possible features are discussed in Holmes (1997), but it is not clear how exclusively these mark a particular ethnic variety.

So, in both of these examples, people have opinions about dialects or varieties for which there is limited objective (linguistic) evidence. What then are people responding to? Some sociolinguists would argue that these subjective perceptions are taking deeply held beliefs about social boundaries and projecting these beliefs into the linguistic system. The argument goes: because people perceive the boundary between Māori and Pākehā ethnic groups to be salient, then there must be a linguistic boundary between those groups; they must speak differently. Because they perceive the West Coast to stand apart from the rest of New Zealand, they believe that people there must speak differently from the rest of the country.

If this is, indeed, the way such perceptions of dialect differences emerge in the absence of objective support, then that is a very strong indicator of the crucial role language plays in reflecting and constituting different social identities. This is one reason why studies of perceptual dialectology can be important data for sociolinguists. They provide an independent measure – perception data, rather than production data – of how central language is to the formation and maintenance of social and personal identities. That is, how people perceive language provides evidence that is just as useful and relevant to the complicated *balancing act* between fitting in and being distinctive (introduced in Chapter 2) which may motivate differences in the way speakers use language.

Connections with theory

There is a lot of evidence showing a bleed-through between attitudes to a language and speakers of a language. This research was pioneered by the Canadian social psychologist Wallace Lambert who showed that the same speaker would be ranked very low on some social traits (e.g., power, wealth, trustworthiness) when speaking one language and high on the same traits when speaking another.

Recently, John Baugh and his colleagues (Purnell *et al.* 1999) have conducted a number of similar experiments and found clear evidence that landlords, for instance, respond negatively to the same speaker when they use features of Hispanic or Black English. Anita Henderson (2001) showed that personnel managers are acutely sensitive to and react very negatively to the presence of either features of AAVE pronunciation or AAVE syntax.

In subsequent chapters we will see that the social categories that are salient in a particular community may be reproduced in the production of linguistic variation. However, for now, the perceptual dialectology research provides a valuable reminder of the ways that social factors can be part of the process of perception as well as of the process of production.

ATTITUDES TO LANGUAGE: IDENTITIES AND ACCOMMODATION

Social identity theory

A social psychological theory holding that people identify with multiple identities, some of which are more personal and idiosyncratic and some of which are group identifications. Experimental work in this framework suggests that people readily see contrasts between groups in terms of competition, and seek to find means of favouring the co-members of the group they identify with over others.

In the last chapter we looked at ways in which speakers' attitudes to the individual they are talking to can affect the way they talk. Audience design proposed that speakers derive their style shifts to an addressee from the characteristics that they associate with the speech of the group as a whole. This presupposes that speakers perceive their interlocutors to be individual representatives of a group. This presupposition can be traced back through the social psychological theories that underlie audience design; namely, social identity theory (SIT) and communication accommodation theory (CAT), which was also introduced in Chapter 3. The next sections provide a brief outline of some of the features of both SIT and CAT that are salient for sociolinguists. We examine some of the linguistic effects of accommodation, focusing particularly on mismatches between what speakers perceive themselves to be doing, and what objective measures show that they actually are doing.

SOCIAL IDENTITY THEORY

Social identity theory (SIT) is a theory of intergroup relations in which language is one of many potent symbols that individuals can strategically use when testing or maintaining boundaries between groups. The theory was proposed by the social psychologist Henri Tajfel who had a deep interest in understanding the social and psychological processes under-pinning conflict between members of different ethnic and religious groups.

Tajfel's interest in identity and prejudice grew out of his own personal expe-riences. He was born in Poland in 1919, and moved to France in 1937 for university. During the Second World War he served in the French army and after being captured spent five years in German prisoner-of-war camps. He was able to survive the war by assuming a French identity, masking his Polishness and his Jewishness. He would later point out that regardless of the interpersonal relationships he had developed within the German camps, if his Slavic and Jewish group identities had been discovered they would have completely and unques-tionably determined his fate (Turner 1996).

To this end, Tajfel (1978) distinguishes between identities which are principally *personal* and identities which are principally associated with a *group*. SIT recognises that we all identify with many personas at different times and places and in different contexts; nevertheless, it assumes that we simplify away from a lot of this complexity in any given interaction and perceive it as being a more or less inter*group* or inter*personal* exchange. That is, we generally perceive a particular personal or group identity to be most **salient** at a particular stage in an interaction (where 'salient' here means the identity activated and oriented to by the immediate context of the interaction).

When a personal (rather than group) identity is salient, our behaviour is more likely to be constrained by idiosyncratic aspects of our personality, our mood, or the immediate context. This would predict that when personal identities are the basis for an interaction our behaviour – including the way we talk – will be subject to more variability. On the other hand, the theory predicts that if group identities are more salient, the way we behave and talk will tend to accentuate uniformity *within* groups. In other words, we would gravitate towards what we consider the normal or typical way of talking for a member of that group (and abstract away from the internal differences we know all groups have). In addition, SIT holds that when a contrast is made between the groups, our behaviour will accentuate the differences *between* the groups as well.

Recall that Bell proposed that intraspeaker stylistic differences derive from, and are therefore less than, differences between groups (Chapter 3). Bell's proposal follows from these last two points about intergroup communication. The accentuation of uniformity or similarities within a group would have allowed Foxy Boston to identify an appropriate level of, e.g., third person -*s* presence or absence, given the group identities she perceives to be salient. The accentuation of differences between groups might ensure that whatever the range of intraspeaker variation there is, it will not outstrip differences between the groups that are presently salient. (However, we must remember Baugh's suggestion that these prin-ciples of interaction and identity management may be subordinate to linguistic constraints.)

The salience of interactants' identities is not determined and fixed from the outset of an interaction, though it is certainly possible for speakers to go into an interaction with very fixed ideas of who they are talking to. Salience can also be negotiated during an interaction and emerge collaboratively, a point that is important in linking SIT with accommodation and, ultimately, sociolinguists' interests in style-shifting (as represented by audience design). Both

Salient/salience

A maddeningly under-defined term when used in sociolinguistics. Sometimes refers to how readily a particular variant is perceived/heard (this may be due to physiological factors affecting perception, or social and psychological factors that affect prime speakers and make them attend to a form). Sometimes refers to a non-linguistic factor that the context or participants appear to have foregrounded in discourse.

personal and group identities can be made more salient by others or selected on our own initiative.

Tajfel suggested that personal and group interactions fell at the opposite ends of a scale or continuum, though he was quick to note that this was something of an explanatory idealisation of the way interactions really take shape. A purely personal identity might not actually exist outside of the framework since even when we seem to be acting just as individuals, our behaviour may be interpreted as more or less consistent with the group identities we also possess. For instance, suppose you find yourself comforting a child who is crying hysterically after falling off some playground equipment. You would certainly be focused on meeting the immediate needs of the individual child before you, but your response as an individual may well be coloured by group identities, e.g., 'I hope *a parent* arrives soon, I'm hopeless with *kids*.'

SIT also supposes that we have different feelings about and attitudes to the social groups we differentiate. As a general rule, group identities are presumed to stabilise in contrast with other groups' identities, and this element of comparison or contrast translates into some groups being seen more positively than others. It is also a general rule that we try to find some basis for seeing groups we identify with in a better light than the ones we are contrasting them with. So the differentiation between groups has a useful social function. In order to feel good about Us, we need a Them to compare ourselves to.

In the previous chapter we examined two frameworks for analysing speaker style: attention to speech and audience design. We noted that one important dimension on which the approaches can be distinguished is the extent to which the speaker is portrayed as an active participant in the construction and negotiation of a speech event. However, it is also worth noting that both approaches share Tajfel's insight that individual and group identities are linked.

This was especially clear in Bell's audience design framework. As we saw in the previous chapter, he attributed some style-shifting to the effects of more personal relationships (i.e., design for an addressee) and some style-shifting to the effects of groups (i.e., design for what Bell called reference groups). In addition, as we have already noted, the mechanisms of audience design are presumed to operate with individuals standing in for a group.

It will be less clear at present how Labov's attention to speech framework also relates the group to the individual. However, this connection should become clearer in Chapter 8 when we consider parallels between the frequency of specific variants in different styles and the frequency of those variants in speakers from different social classes.

ACCOMMODATION THEORY

Accommodation theory has much in common with the tradition of social identity theory: accommodation theory is a bundle of principles that are intended to characterise the strategies speakers use to establish, contest or maintain relationships through talk. The original statement of the theory by Howard Giles (1973) focused on speech behaviours alone, but developments following in Giles's footsteps have expanded the scope of the research so as to include strategies in non-verbal communication behaviours as well. The field is, therefore, sometimes referred to as *speech* accommodation theory and sometimes as *communication* accommodation theory.

Regardless of its scope, accommodation theory rests on one pivotal process: *attunement.* The idea is that we all tailor, or attune, our behaviours according to the interaction, and this

Accommodation

The process by which speakers *attune* or adapt their linguistic behaviour in light of ➤ their interlocutors' behaviour and their attitudes towards their interlocutors (may be a conscious or unconcious process). Encompasses both *convergence* with or *divergence* from interlocutors' norms. (See also *Social identity theory.*)

process of attunement involves a range of communicative behaviours, like speech styles. Attunement renders the addressee(s) as equally important as the speaker and it also presents communicative behaviours as elements in a dynamic system. Drawing on the personal/group distinction of SIT, accommodation theory allows for attunement to attend primarily to very personal or very immediate factors, or else to occur in the context of intergroup contrast. Where an interaction is perceived in terms of group identities and group contrasts, accommodation theory also proposes that affective factors enter into the dynamic.

This, too, builds on the principles of SIT. An interaction that is perceived to be taking place between ingroup members (or between people who would like to negotiate a common group identity) will foster strategies that accentuate internal commonalities. This strategy, it is assumed, contributes to the social function of generating positive feelings about ourselves and the co-members of that group. This is often accompanied by a downgrading of the outgroups we might be contrasting ourselves with.

The two main strategies used in the process of attunement are **convergence** and **divergence**. Convergence involves a speaker altering the way they talk so that it approaches the norms of their interlocutor and accentuates commonality between the interlocutors (as discussed above). As we will see shortly, convergence can entail approaching the actual norms of the addressee, or it may involve approximating norms that the speaker believes (incorrectly) are characteristic of their addressee. On the other hand, divergence involves accentuating differences between the speaker and their addressee(s). Speakers may consciously undertake either strategy, but it is important to note that accommodation may occur well below the speaker's level of conscious awareness (this is sometimes misunderstood by linguists, who think that attunement and accommodation are consciously controlled moves in a conversation). In particular, it is important to note that the speaker may not be able to describe or identify the precise linguistic features that are altered through the attunement processes of accommodation. The next two sections provide examples of linguistic convergence and divergence.

Convergence

When the attunement involves increasing similarities between the speaker and their addressee, Giles called this *convergence*. This may happen at the level of very marked linguistic differences, such as the choice of language, or it may occur more subtly at the level of features such as pitch and speech rate. Speakers are generally reasonably aware of what motivates them to alternate between languages depending on the context and their addressee (and we return to switching between languages in Chapter 6). However, they may be quite unaware of changes that take place in their prosody, and their realisation of phonological or morphosyntactic variables.

Convergence with the addressee in choice of language is something that is learnt quite early, and there are obvious functional reasons for this. There's not much point talking to your Mandarin-speaking grandfather in English if he isn't going to understand a word you say, and vice versa with your Canadian cousins. However, children also seem to learn that alternating their dialect or accent may make for more effective communication, depending on their addressee. A little boy growing up in Scotland, with non-Scottish parents, was heard to do just this as early as 19 months. Sam was dropped off by a parent at kindergarten one morning and decided to go and look at the books. He walked across the room saying 'Book, book, book'. The vowel he used in 'book' when his parent first put him down was relatively centralised

Convergence

Accommodation towards the speech of one's interlocutors. Accentuates similarities between interlocutors' speech styles, and/or makes the speaker sound more like their interlocutor. It is assumed to be triggered by conscious or unconscious desires to emphasise similarity with interlocutors we like, and to increase attraction. (See also *Divergence; Social identity theory.*)

Divergence

Accommodation away from the speech of one's interlocutors. Accentuates differences between interlocutors' speech styles, and/or makes the speaker sound less like their interlocutor. It is assumed convergence is triggered by conscious or unconscious desires to emphasise difference and increase social distance. (See also *Convergence; Social identity theory.*)

[bʊək] – similar to what he would hear at home – but by the time he had crossed the floor of the nursery to the reading corner, he was using a backed and rounded vowel more like the one used by his Scottish caregivers, [buk]. Sam's kindergarten teachers would certainly understand [bʊək], just as his parents would understand [buk], so in this case his convergence on the Scottish norms in his daycare and his parents' norms at home is unlikely to be motivated by comprehension problems. Accommodation theory would suggest that his behaviour shows he associates other social and interactional benefits with speaking more like the different groups of people he moves in and out of.

Studies have also shown that people are quite quick to attune their speech rate to their addressee's. Generally, if we are talking to someone who talks more slowly than we do, we converge by slowing down our own rate of speech. Our interlocutor may also converge by speeding up slightly. This kind of mutual accommodation – some give and take by both parties – is an integral part of the theory.

Divergence

Attunement doesn't always entail convergence. Depending on the circumstances, speakers may decide that their interests are best served by maintaining, or even accentuating, distinctions between themselves and their interlocutors. This strategy is called **divergence**. Just as convergence in choice of language can facilitate comprehension, divergence in language choice can serve as a shield. For instance, in a report that tourists were being ripped off on visits to Prague, the journalist mentioned waiting staff who 'suddenly lose their ability to speak previously excellent English when questioned by foreigners about what they paid for' (Krosnar 2005).

Divergence at the level of accent can be equally functional. An American who has lived outside of the United States for many years says that she plays up her American accent, diverging from the locals, when she wants sympathy, or sometimes when she wants better service. So, for instance, if a police officer challenges her for stopping in a 'No Parking' zone, she replies in a broad accent suggesting she is perhaps a tourist and hopes it will make the police officer decide giving her a ticket isn't worth it. Similarly, she trades off the stereotype of Americans being vociferous complainers if service isn't good by accentuating her accent when she feels that the service she is getting isn't efficient or prompt.

And there are less Machiavellian functions to divergence. People may diverge linguistically from their interlocutors in order to accentuate differences if the comparison will foster positive feelings about their ingroup. Jokes are often made about how touchy Canadians and New Zealanders are if they are mistaken for Americans or Australians (respectively). A strong reaction accentuating their pride in being a Canadian or a New Zealander can be strengthened by the use of marked or unique features of their accent.

In the previous chapter we considered some examples of divergence, and these showed that the reasons why individuals might diverge are often related to their perceptions of and attitudes towards a group, as well as to individual members of that group. Our discussion of divergence illustrates the point made by social identity theory, namely that personal and group identities fall on a scale and are inherently blurred. We will return to this point in Chapter 6 when we look more specifically at accommodation in language choice.

Asymmetric convergence and divergence

As we have said, accommodation theory is a theory about interaction, and as such it is concerned with the negotiation of perceptions and identities between interlocutors in conversations. The examples given in the introduction to convergence and divergence are fairly straightforward ones, and they avoid dealing with disputes or contestation.

However, the theory allows for the possibility of an interaction in which one person converges and the other person diverges. These examples can be particularly enlightening, as they show how complicated and important people's attitudes towards others are and how these attitudes can be played out in language use. One such example is found in the debate about how to write Hawaiian.

Hawaiian is spoken in the US state of Hawai'i, where the dominant language is English. In Hawaiian, vowel length is phonemic; this means that a difference in vowel length alone can change the meaning of a word. So, for example, *kau* means (among other things) 'to place something' and *kāu* means 'your(s)'. The only difference is that the word meaning 'your(s)' has a long /a/ vowel and the verb meaning 'place' has a short one. Hawaiian also has a phonemic glottal stop /ʔ/ (the sound in the beginning and middle of the word marking surprise, 'uh-oh'), so the words *ulu* ('to grow') and *ʻulu* ('breadfruit') are only distinguished in meaning by the presence of the glottal stop in *ʻulu*.

Now, because these elements aren't phonemic in English, neither the glottal stop nor vowel length has any obvious way of being written in a spelling system that is based on the English alphabet. There are two options. You can omit them, or you can use orthographic conventions that are not used in English: you can write a line over a long vowel and you can write the glottal stop with an apostrophe or a single open quote (as in the word 'Hawai'i'). These are called the *ʻokina* and *kahakō*, respectively.

Generally, it is preferable to use these symbols – if you leave them out it would be a bit like skipping the final 'e' in English words like *bake* or *garbage*. That is to say, you could still read it, but it's just not standard spelling. So a lot of people in Hawai'i, even if they are not speakers of Hawaiian, try to learn where the *kahakō* and the *ʻokina* belong. This is seen as a gesture of respect for the language and its speakers. In other words, their attunement takes the shape of convergence, similar to the case of the little boy who uses Scots vowels when speaking to his Scottish daycare workers.

But the situation is complicated by the larger relationship between Hawaiian and English. Some people who speak Hawaiian are concerned about the influence that English is having on the language, and they would prefer to foster features that might create obstacles that would prevent further English-influenced incursions on it. So some Hawaiian language activists have argued that leaving the long vowel and glottal symbols out of Hawaiian is a good idea, because it makes the language more opaque to English speakers, and helps to maintain it as an ingroup code. In other words, by arguing in favour of making the spelling *less* transparent to people used to English norms, some speakers of Hawaiian advocate divergence. Interestingly, the *ʻokina* and *kahakō* are the linguistic focus for both attempted convergence and divergence.

Similar cases of asymmetric convergence and divergence can take place between individuals. The sociologist Ben Rampton provides some interesting examples (1998). In one recording, five teenage girls are talking and listening to music together. One of the Anglo girls starts talking about and expressing a passion for *bhangra* (a Punjabi music style). Her Indian friends give her very minimal feedback and encouragement to keep talking about it –

Rampton found in interviews that many of the Punjabi teenagers were quite unenthusiastic about their Anglo peers adopting 'their' music.

These examples show that convergence and divergence need not be symmetric. They can be asymmetric, with one group or person converging and the other group or person diverging.

Connections with theory

There have been a lot of experimental studies that show strong relationships between positive attitudes to an interlocutor and convergence in choice of language and some aspects of speech styles. People who are well disposed to each other have been found to converge on how often they interrupt each other, how long a pause they leave between turn, length of turns they take, and non-linguistic aspects of communication, like laughter. But we still lack a lot of work on more detailed aspects of the linguistic system, such as variables like (r).

Also, it is not clear how accommodative attunement relates to or complements priming. Priming is when a speaker follows the form or content of a preceding speaker's turn and it has been studied by a number of psychologists. They find that if I say, 'Why did you lend her your car?', you are more likely to use the same sentence structure in your reply. That is, you will probably say something like, 'But I didn't lend her my car', repeating my order of the verb, goal and object, rather than the equally used grammatical alternative, 'But I didn't lend my car to her'. It's not clear whether priming depends on speakers' attitudes to each other or to the task at hand. As far as I know, such questions have not been explored in the experiments on priming.

Subjective and objective measures

A speaker's perceptions of their own performance and their performance evaluated by some external measure.

Subjective and objective measures of convergence

The business of measuring convergence and divergence is complicated even further by the fact that interactants may *believe* they are converging or diverging, but they fail to achieve their goal. This may be because they misanalyse or misjudge their goal, or it may be because they do not have the necessary resources or skills to reach their goal accurately.

In Chapter 3 we mentioned the case of Peter Trudgill's convergence with the speakers he was interviewing in Norwich. In this case, he was not aware that he was converging even when he did. That is, there was a mismatch between his subjective perception of what was happening and the objective reality. He thought he was using the same interviewer style in every case, so from his subjective perspective there was no convergence to the norms of his interlocutors. But an objective measurement of what was going on after the fact showed that in fact he had converged.

If we distinguish between subjective and objective levels of convergence and divergence, there are four logical possibilities. These are shown in Table 4.2.

In cells A and D, there is a match between what the speaker subjectively believes is going on and what any objective observer would discover if they examined the interaction. In A, speakers believe they are converging and they succeed in doing so. In the other case, they

Table 4.2 Four possible kinds of interaction according to whether a speaker converges or diverges on subjective or objective measures. (Source, Thakerar *et al.* 1982: 238.)

		subjective	
		Convergence	Divergence
Objective	convergence	A	B
	divergence	C	D

believe they are diverging and again they succeed in this. When the subjective and objective measures of attunement coincide it is fairly easy for the researcher to invoke speakers' attitudes as an explanation for the behaviour observed, as I did in the examples in the previous sections. However, in the other two cells, B and C, there is a discrepancy between the strategy speakers believe they are employing and the actual details of their performance. We will look more closely at such situations in the next two sections.

Subjective convergence and objective divergence

Cell C represents the case where a speaker may be trying to converge with their interlocutor, but in the process of trying to converge they actually end up diverging. This seems to happen if the speaker:

■ incorrectly judges the situation, and
■ converges to the way they *perceive* their interlocutor to be talking (rather than to the way their interlocutor really does talk).

A study in Thailand found Thai children doing this when they were talking to ethnically Chinese speakers of Thai (Beebe 1981). There is a stereotypical Chinese accent associated with Chinese speakers of Thai, but the Chinese subjects in Beebe's study did not use this, they spoke standard Thai. Nevertheless, when the children in Beebe's experiment were talking to an ethnically Chinese experimenter, they began to use features stereotypically associated with Chinese pronunciations of Thai in their own speech, even though these features were absent in the speech of their interlocutor. In other words, the children seemed to be converging to what they (erroneously) perceived their interlocutor to be doing, and they were effectively unable to 'hear' what their interlocutor really was doing.

In this case, it appears that the children were converging not to their interlocutor's individual norms but rather to the norms widely associated with the group that they perceived their interlocutor to belong to (Chinese speakers of Thai). Notice that in this case, the motives for such behaviour are more complicated than they are in the more straightforward cases of cells A and D. Because the children's objectively divergent behaviour seems to be based on subjective notions of convergence, we have to analyse their unintentional divergence as an attempt to seem agreeable – that is, as if it were objective convergence.

Subjective divergence and objective convergence

An even more interesting example of a discrepancy between the strategy that the speaker perceives they are using and the strategy that an objective measure shows them to be using is found in cell B where there is subjective divergence but objective convergence. I am not aware of any studies that illustrate this process taking place in interactions between individuals, but work by Nancy Niedzielski on the perceptions and attitudes of groups of speakers seems to suggest that it is possible.

Niedzielski (1997) devised a simple but effective experiment. She had already determined that speakers of US English in Detroit (on the Canadian border) generally now pronounce words like MOUTH with a raised onset. However, Detroiters still perceive this raising of (aw) to be characteristic of Canadian English and not their own.

Previous perceptual dialectology studies in the Detroit area had shown that Detroiters are convinced that they speak 'Standard' American English, and it appears that they are completely unaware that a growing number of them use these raised, Canadian-like variants of (aw). Niedzielski drew on principles of SIT and accommodation theory and predicted that given Detroiters' social perception of themselves as speakers of 'Standard' American English they would be likely to perceive a recording of Detroit speech as sounding like General American, even if the speaker uses raised Canadian-like variants.

Niedzielski made up a tape with some sentences in which Detroiters used raised variants of (aw), e.g., *south, house* and *out.* These became the target words for the experiment. She then synthesised different versions of the target words and asked a number of listeners from Detroit to tell her which one of the options was closest to the variant they heard in the original sentence. One of the synthesised versions was identical to what the speaker actually said, and one was close to the historical norms for the Detroit accent. One was even more open, and in fact more typical of what is considered General American.

Niedzielski led half the people listening to the tapes to believe that the speaker was Canadian, and half of them to believe that the speaker was from Detroit, but in all other respects each respondent heard exactly the same thing. So half of the subjects thought they were trying to match synthesised versions of a local Michigander's vowels (i.e., a member of their ingroup) and half thought they were listening to a Canadian's vowels (i.e., that they were listening to someone from an outgroup).

Even though the objective facts of the case were that everyone heard a Detroiter using raised variants of the (aw) diphthong, Niedzielski found that respondents were much more likely to report hearing the diphthongs as raised if they thought the speaker was Canadian than they were if they thought the speaker was from Detroit. This is shown in Figure 4.4, which combines the results for several sentences.

When her subjects thought the speaker was from Detroit, they said that what they had heard was closer to the synthesised variants with lower onsets – either the ones people in Detroit traditionally used, or even an ultra-low variant that had never been used in Detroit. It seems that even when Detroiters heard a local who was objectively converging with their neighbouring Canadians' pronunciation of these words, their subjective perception was that the speaker uses the traditional open Detroit variant.

Since this study does not combine production and perception data from the same people, it does not technically fill out cell B in Table 4.2. However, Niedzielski's results suggest that it will be possible in fact, not just in theory, to find instances of subjective divergence with objective convergence.

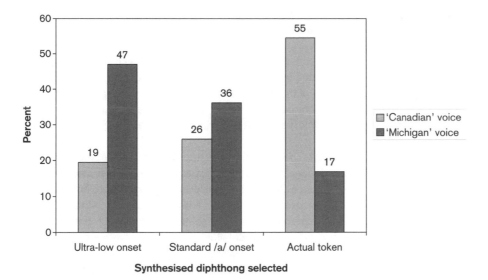

Figure 4.4   Influence of perceived nationality of speaker on choice of token in matching task. Pooled results for *south, about* and *out.* (Source, Niedzielski 1997: 71–72.)

The possibility of mismatches between speakers' perceptions of what they are doing and their objective performance raises some additional problems for the sociolinguist working from spontaneous speech. In recordings made from spontaneous conversation, the researcher doesn't have access to the privileged information about a speaker's attitudes to their interlocutor and the context is not controlled for such factors as it is in a social psychology experiment. This deficiency cannot be remedied by asking people afterwards either, because, as we have just seen, people may believe they are doing one thing and actually do something quite different.

However, we don't want to ignore these beliefs and perceptions even when they do not seem to be based on objective reality. They may tell us things about the structure of a speech community that even a trained linguist cannot detect. For example, Naomi Nagy has been part of a large team doing fieldwork in Montreal, Canada for some years now. This city is part of the French-speaking state Quebec, with an English-speaking minority. The Anglophone residents of Montreal all have to be (more or less) bilingual in French since that is the dominant language in the city. Many of the Anglophone Montrealers in the study claim that they have a distinctive way of speaking French which marks them as a group. However, to date, Nagy hasn't been able to find any linguistic features that distinctively mark the French of the Anglophone bilinguals as a group. This may also be a case of subjective divergence with objective convergence. But it is also possible that the speakers are attuned to differences that are very subtle and infrequent indeed, and which have so far escaped the attention even of researchers who know the community very well.

CHAPTER SUMMARY

This chapter has reviewed several rather different approaches to the study of language attitudes. It has tried to make the case for including attitudes about language and about different users of language as an important part of sociolinguistics, including the study of variation which generally relies almost exclusively on data from production and avoids issues related to perception.

It began by taking a look at how attitudes to others are revealed through language, specifically focusing on the paths through which word meanings change over time. This linked with subsequent sections of the chapter in which people's perceptions about different language varieties were brought back into focus, and strategies used to contest and renegotiate the meaning of words were related to principles of group and personal identity theory.

We saw that non-linguists' perceptions of dialect boundaries largely match the boundaries linguists draw, and suggested that this indicates that the variables being analysed by linguists and attended to (often quite subconsciously) by non-linguists are fundamentally similar. Where there are differences between the two, I have suggested that this may be an important indicator of social factors relevant to that speaker or their speech community.

The chapter has also looked in some detail at accommodation theory, which was introduced in the discussion of speakers' style-shifting in Chapter 3. The roots of audience design were traced back through accommodation theory to social identity theory in this chapter, and a wider range of strategies — symmetric and asymmetric convergence and divergence — were discussed. Accommodation theory stresses the importance of speakers' attitudes to their addressee, and the resulting dynamism in interactions. It also provides us with a context for comparing what speakers think they are doing with what they actually are doing.

In the next chapter, we continue to look at the way speakers balance between inter-personal and intergroup needs in conversation. The lens there is on the social significance of alternations between different languages, both at the national or institutional level and at the personal or individual level.

FURTHER READING

Pauwels (1998) — on non-sexist language.

Hellinger and Bussmann (2001–2003) — three-volume collection of articles on language and gender, many of which deal with attitudes to women expressed in a variety of languages.

Lucy (1992) — a more recent view on linguistic relativity.

There is an extensive literature on the analysis of racist language, especially among researchers coming out of the social psychology tradition, e.g., Wetherell and Potter (1992), Billig (1995), and see also Wodak and Reisigl (2001).

Niedzielski and Preston (2000), Preston and Long (1999) — folk perceptions of language and perceptual dialectology.

Gallois *et al.* (1995) — summary of theory and principles in communication accommodation and attunement.

Trudgill (1983) — case studies of accommodation in British pop and punk rock.

Warner (1999) — on the politics of Hawaiian language revitalisation; Schütz (1994) on the development of orthographic standards in Hawaiian.

Niedzielski (1999) — more accessible source of data on mismatches between perception and reality.

CHAPTER 5

Being polite as a variable in speech

Key terms in this chapter:

- ■ politeness
- ■ negative politeness strategies
- ■ positive politeness strategies
- ■ face wants
- ■ negative face
- ■ positive face
- ■ social distance
- ■ power
- ■ cost of imposition
- ■ bald, on record

- ■ inherently face-threatening acts
- ■ speech acts
- ■ envelope of variation
- ■ sociolinguistic competence
- ■ grammatical competence
- ■ pragmatic competence
- ■ contrastive analysis
- ■ individualistic
- ■ collectivist
- ■ *wakimae*

INTRODUCTION

'I'll have an iced mocha', my New York friend, Ellen, said. 'An iced mocha', repeated the server. 'Do you want whipped cream on that?' 'You have to ask?' said Ellen.

Politeness is a strange thing. Clearly the server at the Michigan restaurant where this exchange took place found Ellen's reply, 'You have to ask?' and her ironic tone of voice, somewhat hard to interpret. There was a long pause while she looked at Ellen waiting for her to say something more. When she said nothing and went back to studying the menu, the server finally looked at me. I raised my eyebrows and smiled slightly, and the server wrote the drink order on her notepad. Outside of New York, Ellen's answer didn't have the meaning of an enthusiastic 'yes' that it was intended to have. In Michigan, it seems waiting staff don't expect the kind of ironic jokes from strangers that you might find in talk between close friends.

Was it polite for her to say 'You have to ask?' like that? Your answer probably depends on where you grew up and what norms of politeness you acquired there. In many places, a reply like this would be considered terribly rude, and something like 'Yes, please' or 'Yes, thank you' would be expected. But by the standards of where Ellen grew up, she *was* being polite. By making a joke – moreover, a joke that suggests that the answer to her question is already shared knowledge between the speaker and the hearer – she was working to construct the business exchange in more friendly and intimate terms.

Intuitive notions of politeness

List five things that you consider *polite* and five things you consider *impolite*. (Decide beforehand if you will restrict yourself and focus only on talk or include other behaviours.)

Compare your lists with someone else's. Do you both agree entirely on what is polite/impolite?

What seems to be the main thing you were paying attention to when you drew up your lists?

As we will see in the discussion of speech levels in the next chapter, some languages even have different words for the same thing that have to be chosen depending on what the politeness and respect relationship is between the speakers. In Japanese, the form of some verbs, including the verb 'to eat' changes entirely, as you can see in the following example (the root form for 'eat' is shown in bold in each sentence):

(1)

Tanaka: Sensei,   keeki   **meshiagari**-mas-u-ka?
              Teacher   cake   eat(honorific)-polite-non.past-Q
              'Teacher, would you like some cake?'
Professor: Ee,   **tabe**-mas-u.   Tanaka-san wa?
              Yes, eat-polite-non.past.   Tanaka-san TOPIC
              'Yes, I'll have some. Will you, Tanaka?'
Tanaka: Hai,   **itadaki**-mas-u.   Doomo.
              Yes   eat(humble)-polite-non.past.   Thanks.
              'Yes, I'll have some. Thank you.'

(Adapted from Tsujimura 1996)

Here the student, Tanaka, uses the honorific form for 'eat' in his question. It is called an honorific form because it is used to show respect for the person who is (or will be) eating. The professor replies with the unmarked form (i.e., it makes no claims one way or another about the status of the person eating), and then Tanaka answers him using the form for 'eat' that indicates that Tanaka humbles himself with respect to his professor.

As you can see, regardless of which form of 'eat' they use, both Tanaka and his professor add a polite suffix, -*mas*-, on the verb, and the professor uses the respectful suffix -*san* when addressing Tanaka. Japanese requires speakers to make such decisions about what verb form to use, and what kind of suffixes to attach to verbs and nouns in everyday speech. Showing this kind of attention to each other and evaluating your relationship with your interlocutors in a particular place or at a particular time is, in a very general sense, what it means to be polite.

In this chapter we will look at the phenomenon of **politeness**, focusing on one framework for analysing different forms and levels of politeness. We will explore the usefulness of distinguishing between the politeness that we use among friends and with people we are less familiar with. This distinction will be useful because the kind of attention close friends pay to each other and the nature of our long-term relationships with each other are very different from the kind of attention we have been taught to pay to people with whom

Politeness

The actions taken by competent speakers in a community in order to attend to possible social or interpersonal disturbance. (See also *Wakimae*.)

Speech levels or respect in English vocabulary

English doesn't have speech levels or special respectful vocabulary to the same extent that Japanese and Sasak do (see discussion in Chapter 6). But we do have some areas of the vocabulary where we use euphemisms or avoidance strategies according to where we are or who we are talking to.

Make up a list of terms you know to say:

(i)   someone has died;
(ii)   someone has vomited;
(iii)   someone is wealthy;
(iv)   someone is attractive to you.

Now annotate each term according to where, when and who you would use it with.

we have more restricted relationships and with whom we are less well acquainted. This chapter will show how different forms of politeness attend to different social needs, and we will illustrate this by looking at examples of the different forms that requests and apologies can take. We will then consider the way in which frameworks of politeness have been applied to other fields, such as workplace interaction and intercultural communication. The chapter also considers some critiques of the most commonly used theory of politeness, and highlights some of the directions in which these critiques might help to advance work on politeness in the future.

THEORIES OF POLITENESS

There are a number of different ways in which linguists can analyse politeness. The various approaches differ primarily in the emphasis placed on the speaker, the addressee (or both), and the emphasis given to accounting for behaviour that would be considered polite or behaviour that would be considered impolite. Most of the frameworks proposed to account for politeness that are accessible to readers of English or other European languages have made the speaker central to the analysis rather than the addressee, and though they have tried to take into account the relationship between speaker and hearer, this has been limited by the focus on the speaker as a linguistic agent planning and evaluating their next move in a conversation. More recently, work by Japanese, Chinese, African and Middle Eastern scholars has begun to make more of an impact on the field of politeness studies. As a general rule, most of these researchers have emphasised the empirical and theoretical importance of seeing politeness and impoliteness as acts which involve consideration of the addressee's wants and desires as well as the speaker's own, and acts that involve consideration of the demands of the larger social group in which both the speaker and addressee have grown up and been socialised.

It is impossible in an introductory text to do justice to the range of perspectives that linguists and anthropologists have on politeness. Instead, I will introduce one major framework: Penelope Brown and Stephen Levinson's Politeness Theory, and discuss this in more detail.

Their framework is, without doubt, the most widely known and extensively used approach to the study of politeness. Its position in the field is so dominant that researchers who want to propose alternative treatments of politeness are obliged to state how and why they consider their framework to be preferable to Brown and Levinson's. So it is impossible to talk about politeness or to read most of the research that has been undertaken on politeness since the 1970s without understanding the basic tenets of Brown and Levinson's theory.

Brown and Levinson's Politeness Theory

Under Brown and Levinson's framework for analysing politeness, it is important to realise that both a deferential response and a joking response (as with Ellen's reply asking for whipped cream on her coffee) can be analysed as forms of politeness. Most people associate 'politeness' just with ways of speaking that avoid causing offence by showing deference to another person. But Brown and Levinson point out that in any speech community, in some contexts, deference would be inappropriate. Instead, comments that orient to ingroup membership may be what oil the wheels of an interaction and avoid causing offence. If Ellen had replied 'Well, if it's not too much trouble, I would be terribly grateful', such extreme deference would have also been peculiar, and perhaps even been interpreted as snobbish and uppity. In other words, under these circumstances, showing lots of deference would have seemed impolite and rude.

Brown and Levinson's goal was to provide a framework for analysing politeness that could accommodate considerations like this, and that might also provide a basis for discussing similarities and differences between cultures in how politeness works.

Positive and negative politeness; positive and negative face

Brown and Levinson suggested that it was useful to distinguish two types of politeness. They called the strategies that avoid offence by showing deference **negative politeness strategies** and the strategies that avoid offence by highlighting friendliness **positive politeness strategies**. They also suggest that whether we consider a strategy polite or impolite depends on how much attention or what kind of attention a speaker pays to their own and their addressee's **face wants**.

This technical use of the term 'face' is very similar to the way the word is used metaphorically in many varieties of English. If, for example, someone comes to a meeting unprepared and attention is drawn to their lack of preparation, you could say that person had 'lost face'. Similarly, if I do something embarassing in public, and you distract attention or say something to minimise the seriousness of what I did, you could say that you had 'saved my face'. (I'm told this use of the term may be less common in North American English than it is in other varieties.)

The notion of 'face' can be traced back to work by the sociologist Erving Goffman, who used the term to discuss some of the constraints on social interaction. In Goffman's work, 'face' was a personal attribute or quality that each of us works to protect or enhance. However, crucially, face is something that we only possess if it is recognised or granted to us by others in our community. Brown and Levinson narrowed this down somewhat, and their definition of 'face' emphasises less the interpersonal and communal nature of face wants. They propose that we want to guard our face against possible damage when we interact with others. The

---

Negative politeness strategies

An action, phrase or utterance that indicates attention is being paid to the *negative face wants* of an *interlocutor*. Often achieved through shows of deference. One type of action available to mitigate an *inherently face-threatening act*. (See also *Positive politeness strategies*.)

Positive politeness strategies

An action, phrase or utterance that indicates attention is being paid to the *positive face wants* of an *interlocutor*. Often achieved through shows of friendliness. One type of action available to mitigate an *inherently face-threatening act*. (See also *Negative politeness strategy*.)

Face and face wants

Erving Goffman's notion of face, our social persona, adopted into politeness theory. Face wants are the desire to protect our *positive face* and *negative face* from threat or damage.

reason that there are two types of politeness – positive and negative politeness – is because we are concerned with maintaining two distinct kinds of face:

(2)
- **Negative face** is the want of every competent adult member of a community that their actions be unimpeded by others.
- **Positive face** is the want of every member that their wants be desirable to at least some others.

(Brown and Levinson 1987: 62)

Notice the qualification that face wants are something 'competent adults' in a community have. In other words, we have to learn or acquire what we come to think of as our negative and positive face wants.

Negative face

The want of every competent adult member of a community that their actions be unimpeded by others. 'Don't tread on me.'

No, really?

What is and is not considered polite varies, of course, from place to place. Politeness conventions emerge gradually and consensually. A competent member of Arab society, for example, knows it is terribly rude to show the soles of your feet to someone. But in some cases, a ruling is required on whether a word or activity is impolite or not. Such a case occurred when one MP in the New Zealand Parliament referred to another MP as *wanker*. The epithet was licensed in the end, on the grounds that the dictionary defined *wanker* as 'a pretentious person' (Burchfield 1986).

In societies where interactions between strangers are conventionally oriented more to deferential (that is, paying more attention to negative face wants), it seems very rude to ignore the distance there might be between you and your addressee and to talk as if you know her or him better than you do (we will define this notion of **social distance** more fully in the section 'Choosing politeness strategies' on p. 87). A strong European stereotype of Asian politeness is that social conventions require Asian speakers to pay more attention to the hearer's negative face wants than, say, French society requires French speakers to. And in example (1) we saw some instances of the overt strategies required in Japanese to show that the speaker is deferential to (or respectful of) their addressee. These include the use of honorific address forms, humbling forms of the verb, and suffixes indicating politeness. These are all particularly noticeable to Western learners of the language and quite hard to master well. However, even within Europe, some speech communities are stereotyped as being more deference-oriented than others, e.g., the idea that Germans are more 'stand-offish' and Italians are more 'friendly'.

In Japan, students would usually address a university professor by his or her last name and then they will add the honorific suffix -*sensei* (meaning 'teacher'). By emphasising the social distance between the student and the professor, it attends to both parties' negative face wants. The situation in Germany is analogous. There, students and more junior faculty members almost invariably address university professors by their full professional titles. This

Positive face

The want of every competent adult member of a community that their wants be desirable to at least some others. 'Love me, love my dog.'

Social distance

See *Distance*.

means that if you are addressing a full professor who has a Ph.D., and who has also been awarded an honorary degree from another university, you are expected to use all those titles when you greet them: *Guten Tag, Frau Professor Doktor Doktor Nussbaum* ('Good afternoon Ms Professor, Doctor, Doctor Nussbaum').

Contrasting with this are societies where interactions between strangers are expected to be more personable and friendly (that is, where they often attend more directly to positive face wants), and it would be considered rude to talk in ways that emphasise or draw attention to the social distance between the interlocutors. The stereotype about Australians is that they are much more chummy and informal than other English speakers, i.e., more attentive to addressing positive face wants.

This greater orientation to positive face wants means that use of first names is the norm, even in professional contexts in much of the English-speaking world (though this seems to still be true more in North American and Australasian universities than in UK universities). This tendency interacts with other social factors, such as the addressee's age and sex. For example, younger university professors are more likely to be addressed by their first name than their older colleagues are. Moreover, many women report an asymmetry between the way that they are addressed (e.g., 'First Name' or 'Mrs + Surname') and their male peers (e.g., 'Title + Surname'). The fact that the politeness strategies speakers choose depends on their evaluation of a number of social factors is an important point that we will return to shortly, and later in the chapter we will also return to the broad social stereotypes that have provided us with our examples here and find that they too are not so straightforward.

The specific linguistic and non-linguistic strategies that display attention to either the speaker's or the addressee's face wants can therefore be referred to as 'positive' and 'negative politeness strategies'. Even a very brief exchange such as a greeting can illustrate some of the different linguistic strategies used to express the two kinds of politeness. For example, suppose you were passing by the outdoor tables of a coffee shop and you recognise an old friend who you haven't seen for some time. You might call out to them using a nickname:

(3)   'Mouse! I haven't seen you in years. You look terrific! What are you up to?'

Brown and Levinson provide an extensive list of linguistic strategies that express positive politeness, several of which are illustrated in this example. The use of ingroup code (here, a nickname *Mouse*), showing attention to the addressee's interests (*what are you up to?*) and exaggerating the speaker's interest or approval (*you look terrific!*) are all strategies that attend to the addressee's positive face wants.

Other greetings attend more to the hearer's negative face wants, for example:

(4)   'Excuse me, Dr Michaels, I'm sorry but could I just interrupt you for one moment?'

The politeness strategies in (4) include a deferential form of address (*Dr Michaels*), an apology (*Excuse me; I'm sorry*) and an attempt to minimise the request (*just; one moment*). These are negative politeness strategies because they attend to the addressee's negative face wants, that is, to their desire to be left alone to pursue their own actions or interests unimpeded.

exercise

Orienting to different kinds of politeness

Would you say that the community you grew up in was oriented more to negative or positive politeness? What are some examples of behaviour supporting this?

How does it compare with other places where you have lived or that you are familiar with? Have you ever found yourself living somewhere where the general orientation to positive or negative politeness was different to the norms you grew up with?

Did this cause you problems? How did you resolve them (if at all)?

Choosing politeness strategies: power, distance and cost of the imposition

Our decisions about exactly what kinds of strategies would be polite or impolite in a given situation involve an evaluation of a number of different factors. Brown and Levinson identify three specific factors. We consider how great a **power** difference there is between the speaker and the addressee; we consider how great the social **distance** is between the speaker and the addressee; and we evaluate the **cost of the imposition** (I have modified their terminology very slightly here).

We generally put more effort into being polite to people who are in positions of greater social power than we are. For instance, I am more polite to the government official processing my passport application than I am to the telemarketer who rings me during dinner. That is because I want the official in the passport office to do me a favour and speed up my application, but when the telemarketer rings me I am the one with the power and they need something from me. That is the effect of power on politeness.

Similarly, the social distance between speakers has a tremendous impact on how they speak to each other. We are generally more polite to people who we don't know very well, and we generally feel we can be more abrupt with people who are close friends. If you are cooking a meal with a close friend or family member, you might simply say 'You've got the butter' instead of 'I think the butter is closer to you than it is to me, so could you pass it to me'. However, if you are working on a task with someone you are not so close to, you might ask in a less direct way, showing more attention to their negative face wants – 'Excuse me, are those the telephone accounts? Could I have them for a second?'

Power

A vertical relationship between speaker and hearer in Brown and Levinson's theory of *politeness*. Along with *distance* and *cost of imposition*, power determines how much and what kind of redressive action the speaker might take with a face-threatening act.

Cost of imposition

Modified term from Brown and Levinson's *politeness* theory. A scalar measure of how serious a *face-threatening act* is in a particular society, and given the *power* and *distance* difference between speaker and hearer.

No, really?

Being family members doesn't necessarily mean you can assume closeness. In a lot of places, some kinship relationships are conventionally considered respectful ones, and you must use respect forms when addressing that member of your family.

In Tamambo (spoken in Vanuatu), a mother's brother is addressed with *kamim* **and the subject agreement marker** *no-* **('you, plural') as a show of respect (like** *vous* **in French) (Jauncey 1997: 107.)**

The third factor that Brown and Levinson believed was important in order to understand the different politeness strategies people use was how big the social infraction is. This was what they meant by the cost of the imposition. So, to continue the example of requests that we have been looking at, different requests have different social weight. Asking someone for the time is generally considered a minor imposition. As a consequence, you can ask complete strangers for the time and the politeness strategies we use pay relatively little attention to face wants, e.g., 'Sorry, do you have the time?' or even just 'What's the time?' However, asking for money is generally considered a greater imposition, and usually you would only do this with someone you are fairly close to. And the more money you want to request, the better you will probably want to know them. For example, in the last few months I have found myself needing 5 pence so I can get the bus home and I borrowed this from an acquaintance, but the day when I left my credit cards at home I had to ask a very close friend to lend me enough money to buy my groceries.

No, really?

In many languages in Vanuatu, polite registers or respectful ways of speaking are spoken of in terms of 'heaviness'. So, in Mwotlap, spoken in the north, the phrase is *hohole map* ('talk respectfully, lit. heavy'), which shows that the speaker 'thinks heavy' (*dēm map*), or respects the addressee or the person being talked about. The metaphor of heaviness carries over into the English-lexified creole, Bislama, where *ting hevi* alternates with the more English *rispektem*.

Costs of an imposition

How would you rank the cost of the imposition involved in asking someone to:

(i)   check on your flat or house while you are on holiday,
(ii) feed your pets and water the plants, and
(iii) answer and deal with any mail?

What are the ways in which you can try to address the differences in cost to them?

So under this framework there are three social variables that shape how people choose which politeness strategies they will use. Their attention to others' positive and negative face wants will be determined by the relative power and social distance of the interactants, and by the social cost of the imposition. As a number of people working within this framework have noted, the three factors are by no means independent. You are often not very close to someone who is in a position of power or authority over you, so power and distance are overlapping measures. And how we evaluate cost is also partly a function of interlocutors' social distance or the power one interlocutor has over the other. This was shown clearly in the examples I gave in the last paragraph, where the scenarios I drew on to illustrate the notion of cost made direct reference to how well I knew the person I was borrowing money from. Similarly, we do not feel that asking someone to tell you the time carries much cost for a number of reasons. One is that the time is not considered to be privileged property of anyone (if you give me the time, I haven't taken it away from you), nor is the activity particularly onerous (it takes moments to either tell me the time or say that you don't know). But it is also relatively low in cost because it doesn't change anything about the social order in doing so. The social distance and relative power of everyone involved remain unchanged.

Despite this lack in independence, I believe they are still useful factors for us to bear in mind when we consider the variable ways in which people are polite or impolite to each other.

Inherently face-threatening acts

Brown and Levinson suggest that some conversational events are **inherently face-threatening acts**. That is, once you undertake one of these acts, it is impossible not to have somebody's positive or negative face wants threatened (sometimes it will be the speaker's, sometimes it will be the hearer's). This means that whenever one of these acts happens in a conversational exchange, the participants have to make a decision about how polite they will be.

> ## Connections with theory
>
> The term 'face-threatening *act*' builds on the notion of **speech acts** from the field of semantics and pragmatics. Naming something, wagering something, requesting something, are considered speech *acts* because when said they perform some activity. Saying 'I bet you . . .' lays a wager; saying 'We'll call the bear Erasmus' names the bear, and so forth. Some of the face-threatening acts discussed in the politeness literature are classic examples of speech acts. But some vary a lot in their syntactic form, e.g., an apology can take a number of forms – some direct and some indirect – and still be considered an apology.

Table 5.1 shows that we can divide speech acts up according to whether they constitute a threat to the addressee's or the speaker's face wants. Giving an order or making a request are threats to the addressee's face wants, and so are expressions of disagreement. But giving an order threatens the addressee's negative face wants because it is at odds with their desire to have their actions unimpeded, while expressing disagreement threatens their positive face wants because it is at odds with their desire to have their wants seen as desirable by others (if I don't agree with you then at least some of what you want is not desirable to me).

The table also reminds us that some politeness strategies are speaker-centred and attend to the speaker's face wants. This is shown in the bottom row of the table, where expressing thanks and making an apology are identified as examples of threats to the speaker's face wants. Saying 'thank you' establishes indebtedness to the other person,

Inherently face-threatening acts

Speech acts which necessarily threaten the speaker's and/or hearer's *positive face* and/or *negative face*. In Brown and Levinson's framework, they require the speaker to decide whether or not to mitigate the threat and which *politeness strategies* to use.

Speech acts

Utterances which, in saying, do something.

A compliment can have a serious impact on the addressee's desire to have their actions proceed unimpeded. In some societies, there is an obligation or strong expectation to offer the speaker something they have complimented.

Table 5.1 Examples of inherently face-threatening acts illustrating threats to positive and negative face of speaker or hearer. (Source, Brown and Levinson 1987: 65–68.)

| | Type of face threatened | |
Whose face is threatened	Negative face	Positive face
Addressee	Orders or requests Threats or warnings Compliments, or expressions of envy	Disapproval or criticisms Disagreements Bringing bad news about H, or good news about S Non-cooperation, like interrupting
Speaker	Accepting an apology Saying *thank you*	Making an apology Showing lack of (physical or emotional) control

hence a speaker may be setting themself up to have their actions impeded at some time in the future.

Making an apology is a threat to the speaker's positive face because it involves going on record with the fact that we have done something that is socially frowned on. In other words, you have to state publicly that you did something stupid or unkind or tasteless. For example, you apologise if you forget your partner's birthday, or put a dent in your friend's car. If you are on record as having acted stupidly, unkindly or tastelessly, then other people are unlikely to identify with you. Hence they will be unwilling to suggest that they share your wants and desires since it is now a matter of public record that your actions include things like this.

Untangling face threats

Whose face is threatened if someone starts to speak and instead burps loudly? Why?

Can you think of cases where an interruption is *not* a threat to the addressee's positive face?

Why do you think a compliment or expression of envy constitutes a threat to the addressee's negative face?

Bald, on record

A technical term in Brown and Levinson's theory of *politeness*. Refers to an *inherently face-threatening act* made without any softening through *positive* or *negative politeness strategies*. Notice they do not call this 'impolite'.

Depending on how serious an FTA is, it will require more or less action to mitigate (or reduce) the potential damage to the addressee's or the speaker's face. At one extreme, an extremely trivial FTA can simply be done without requiring very much mitigating action. Brown and Levinson call this 'going on record' or doing the FTA 'baldly'. Going on record means that the speaker simply does the face-threatening act and doesn't wrap it up with any positive or negative politeness strategies.

At the other extreme, an FTA might be judged to be so serious that the speaker simply cannot bear to undertake it – in this case, silence, or self-censorship, is the ultimate mitigation. In between, various kinds of actions can be taken to redress or mitigate potential damage to either participant's face. This includes hinting at or indirectly committing the FTA, or doing things that directly attend to either positive or negative face wants. We will shortly see some specific examples of all these strategies and this will help to ground the theory in everyday language use.

In Figure 5.1, FTAs are shown on a scale from least to most threatening to someone's face wants, and degree of threat is defined in terms of the relative power (P) and distance (D) of the interlocutors and/or the cost (C) of the imposition. The kinds of actions associated are arranged on the left of the figure, showing how they correspond roughly to being increasingly polite. We will be principally concerned with discussing the first four, since they have overt linguistic consequences. We will have less comment on the fifth option since it involves not saying anything; but just as we have seen that linguistic variables may involve an alternation between presence and absence of a sound, absence of an FTA is sociolinguistically meaningful.

It is worth noting that there is a problem with trying to analyse absent FTAs, and the problem highlights the difference between what we are doing when we analyse variation in how people are polite and variations in how people pronounce words. The difference is quite simple and depends on whether there is a predictable context in which the variable occurs. For example, it is possible to describe each and every context in which (r) could occur and then we can investigate whether for each context it is present or absent. This is known as the **envelope of variation** for (r). But there is no clear envelope of variation for FTAs. We can't predict when FTAs will occur, so when an FTA is not present in conversation we don't usually know whether a speaker thought of undertaking the FTA, and then chose silence as the option for mitigating it, or whether the speaker simply didn't think of undertaking the FTA in the first place.

Some examples of going baldly on record with an FTA will illustrate how this is typically associated with impositions that have very low cost or might be uttered in a context where the interlocutors are working on a task together (so social distance would be low). In the examples in (5), the FTA is identified as in Table 5.1:

Envelope of variation

All, and only, the contexts in which a *variable* occurs.

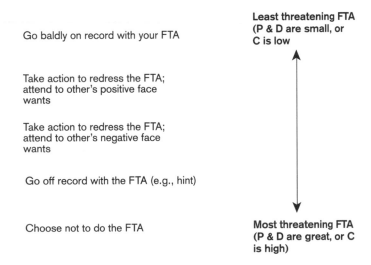

Go baldly on record with your FTA

Least threatening FTA (P & D are small, or C is low

Take action to redress the FTA; attend to other's positive face wants

Take action to redress the FTA; attend to other's negative face wants

Go off record with the FTA (e.g., hint)

Choose not to do the FTA

Most threatening FTA (P & D are great, or C is high)

Figure 5.1   Actions that can be taken to mitigate or redress a face-threatening act (FTA), ordered in terms of the difference in power and distance between interlocutors and the cost of the imposition.

(5)   What's the time? (*request*)
Pass the salt. (*order*)
You've got toothpaste on your shirt. (*criticism* or *bad news about H*)
It's not ready yet. (*warning*)
Sorry. (*make apology*)

Going bald or on record means saying what you want to say without couching the statement or utterance in any politeness strategies. However, a lot of FTAs are couched in some form of redressive or mitigating action. Redressive actions that attend to a threat to negative face wants are the kinds of linguistic strategies we think of first when we talk about someone being polite or impolite. Since negative face wants refer to a person's desire not to have their actions impeded, if you want to redress the threat to someone's negative face you might qualify the FTA in some way. For example, you might suggest that the addressee has options in how they respond to it, or that minimise the FTA, show deference or depersonalise it. In (6), both the type of FTA and the redressive action (underlined in the examples) are identified:

(6)   <u>Could you</u> tell me the time? (*request: does not assume compliance*)
<u>There's something</u> on your shirt. (*bad news about H: minimise; depersonalise*)
<u>Gentlemen</u>, you can't park there. (*warning: show deference*)
<u>I'm sorry</u> to interrupt . . . (*interrupting: apologise*)

On the other hand, because positive face wants refer to people's desire to have their wants and desires shared by others, redressive action that attends to a threat to positive face wants might suggest that the speaker and the addressee do share similar wants and desires, or they may imply this by suggesting that the interlocutors are members of an ingroup (see Chapter 4).

(7)   Pass the salt, <u>honey</u>? (*request: ingroup identity marker*)
A: Sorry about that. B: <u>Oh it could happen to anyone</u>. That's OK. (*accept apology: suggest common ground*)
<u>For your safety and the safety of others</u>, do not inflate the life vest until you leave the aircraft. (*warning* or *order: give reason; be inclusive*)
<u>You've done a great job with the model</u>, but <u>we</u> ought to also try Liz's idea. (*disagreement: show attention to positive face wants; be inclusive*)

If you compare the examples in (6) and (7) with Table 5.1, you will notice that attention to positive and negative face wants can redress potential threats to *either* negative *or* positive face. For instance, a request, which in Table 5.1 is classified as a threat to the addressee's negative face, can be redressed either by showing attention to their negative face wants in (6), or by showing attention to their positive face wants in (7). So the relationship between a threat to a participant's face wants and the type of redressive action taken to mitigate that threat is complex, and becomes even more complicated when speakers combine attention to negative and positive face wants in one utterance; for example, *Could you tell me the time, love?* where the negative politeness of *could you* is paired with the positive politeness of *love*.

When the cost of the imposition becomes very high or when the distance and power differential between the speaker and addressee is very great, then even more linguistically

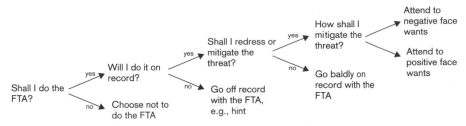

Figure 5.2   Flow-chart showing conscious or subconscious decisions leading to choice of a particular politeness strategy. (Adapted from Brown and Levinson 1987: 69.)

complicated redressive action is required. This may involve going 'off record' and trying to convey the message by means of hints or suggestions; for example, 'Is that the salt?' for *pass the salt.*

Brown and Levinson presented these different actions as being the rational outcomes selected by speakers as they evaluate the social dynamics of a situation. Figure 5.2 shows how different outcomes might arise from the speaker asking her or himself different questions.

Some case studies of the theory at work

Let's look at how this system operates by examining some specific examples of what would be considered face-threatening acts. The first one we will consider is making a request or giving an order. As we have seen, these present a potential threat to the addressee's negative face wants, because they necessarily involve infringing on the addressee's actions by getting them to do something they had not planned to do. The second example is an apology which presents a threat to the speaker's positive face since it involves admitting to having done something socially frowned upon.

Here is the scenario for the request or order. It's a bitterly cold day and the room you are in has a window open. You feel like you are freezing. The open window is much closer to your friend Sam than it is to you. You can:

Say nothing and keep on freezing	**Don't do the FTA**
	Do the FTA but redress the threat to face:
'Isn't it cold in here?'	**Off record (hint)**
'I'm sorry. Could you do me a favour and shut the window?'	**Negative politeness**
'You look cold, Sam. Should we shut the window?'	**Positive politeness**
	Do the FTA without redress to face:
'Shut the window, Sam.'	**Bald request/order**

Now consider the scenario for the apology. A friend asked you to look after her tropical fish while she was on holiday. You overfed them and they died. You can:

exercise

Linguistic features expressing attention to face wants

Find the specific linguistic features that attend to negative and positive face wants in 'I'm sorry. Could you do me a favour and shut the window?' and 'You look cold, Sam. Should we shut the window?' Now explain whose negative and positive face wants they attend to and how.

exercise

Manipulating cost of an imposition

Try increasing the cost of the imposition and see what different kinds of politeness work you have to imagine doing. Instead of asking for a fairly trivial service (like shutting the window), imagine asking someone for:

- money: £1 vs £100/$1 vs $100
- a ride in their car: they drop you off on the way home vs a special trip
- access to space they are in: crossing someone's path in the street vs use of a terminal in a busy computer lab.

Say nothing *or*
Tell her that it was the fishes' fault,
    they ate too much.   **Don't do the FTA**

                                    Do the FTA but redress the threat to face:
'These fish are awfully hard to look   **Off record (be vague)**
    after, aren't they, no matter
    how hard you try?'
'I'm sorry your fish died. I'd like to   **Negative politeness**
    replace them, if I can.'
'I hate having to tell you this, but your   **Positive politeness**
    beautiful fish died while you were gone.
    Can we replace them?'

                                    Do the FTA without redress to face:
'Sorry. I killed your fish.'   **Bald apology**

Now try increasing the power differential between you and the fish owner. Imagine that instead of being a close friend's fish, they belonged to one of your university professors. You will probably find yourself tying yourself in complicated knots as you try and attend to both their negative and positive face wants and your own.

As we noted earlier, people sometimes pay attention to both positive and negative face wants in the same sentence. In addition, they can pay attention to both the speaker *and* the addressee's face wants in one utterance. For example, the request that started 'I'm sorry, could you do me a favour . . .' was categorised as negative politeness. Certainly, it is true that this whole formula shows acute sensitivity to the addressee's right and desire to have their actions unimpeded: the formulaic apology (*'I'm sorry'*) makes clear that the speaker understands they are disturbing the addressee's right to have their actions unimpeded. And yet, as we have also seen, an apology constitutes a threat to the speaker's positive face. In this case it signals that the speaker is about to do something to disturb the social peace.

One advantage of representing the system, as in Figure 5.2, is that it indicates a bit more clearly that politeness does not work via a set of checks and balances. In other words, whether a speaker uses strategies that pay attention to positive or negative face wants is not dependent on what kind of face is threatened by the FTA. A potential threat to the addressee's negative face can be redressed with positive politeness strategies (and you would certainly have noticed this if you did the exercise analysing request forms in more detail), just as we saw that the face threat of an apology can be attended to and reduced with negative politeness strategies, e.g., 'I'd like to replace them'. That is because the offer to replace the fish puts the speaker under further, future obligations – i.e., it impedes their own future actions.

APPLICATIONS OF POLITENESS THEORY: INTERCULTURAL COMMUNICATION

We have noted on several occasions that there are significant differences in how the basic elements of the system – power, social distance, and cost of the imposition – are calculated in different groups. The differences can account for a good deal of variation in how politeness is realised. This raises the interesting question of whether Brown and Levinson's framework can be used to better understand what happens when speakers from different social or cultural backgrounds interact. Some researchers have found this framework useful for deconstructing problems and misunderstandings in how politeness is expressed in cross-cultural situations. In this section, we will look at one such example.

At the start of the chapter, we contrasted the politeness norms for speakers from different sociolinguistic backgrounds. For example, we briefly considered the differences in how students address university professors in English-speaking universities and in German universities. What happens when people who have acquired the politeness norms of one community find themselves in a completely different community? At a superficial level, such intercultural contact often reinforces stereotypes about groups, e.g., New Zealanders' and Australians' perceptions that the English are distant and unfriendly can perhaps be reduced to a difference in what the conventional assumptions are about the social distance between new acquaintances. These differences can lead to misunderstandings between individuals: an Australian working in England may interpret English social distance as indicating that co-workers don't like them as a person.

Intercultural contact can create some quite interesting day-to-day dilemmas for individuals. What happens, for instance, when Japanese students who are used to attending overtly to the negative face wants of their professors move to the US or New Zealand, where the norms are more geared towards attention to positive face wants – e.g., through reciprocal use of first names? This can present them with a clash between their own sociolinguistic norms and the norms of the community they are now sudying in. They can respond to this dilemma in a number of ways. One would be to remain true to the politeness norms they grew up with, and to continue to use the most respectful address forms available to them in English

Sociolinguistic competence

The skills and resources speakers need to deploy in order to be competent members of a speech community using language, not only grammatically but appropriately in different contexts, *domains* or with different *interlocutors*. (See also *Grammatical competence; Pragmatic competence*.)

Grammatical competence

See *Competence and performance*.

(e.g., *Professor Thompson* or *Dr Heycock*), or they can adopt the foreign norms and address their professors as *Roumi* or *Dave*.

Along the way to resolving this issue there can be a stage in which there is some uncertainty, and these points are particularly interesting for the sociolinguist because they highlight both the enormous creativity of language users and the ways in which their creativity can be constrained by the systems that they are most familiar with (this issue will be explored again in Chapter 11). One example was the way that Japanese students in linguistics at the University of Hawai'i converged on a short-term solution that satisfied both US and Japanese sociolinguistic norms.

The Japanese norms for interacting with professors are to use deferential forms of address, such as (*Last Name*) + *Title*, as Tanaka does in the example at the start of the chapter when he calls his professor *Sensei* ('teacher'). At the University of Hawai'i, however, most graduate students would call professors by their first name, especially a younger professor. For a period, the Japanese students in linguistics took to calling the youngest professor by her first name, but they would add the respectful address term *sensei* to it at the end. For example, instead of the canonical Japanese form, *Yoshimi-sensei* ('Professor Yoshimi'), they used *Patricia-sensei* (roughly, 'Professor Patricia'). In this way, they ended up with something that satisfied the US norms of positive politeness (based on reciprocal first naming) and their own Japanese negative politeness norms based on respect and social distance (achieved through the use of titles). This was a very clever strategy, because the end product fulfilled the expectations both of the speakers and the addressee.

Connections with theory

We could say that these students found themselves in a situation that tests their **sociolinguistic competence**.

Dell Hymes proposed that formal linguistic systems (our **grammatical competence**) are part of different sociolinguistic systems. Our sociolinguistic competence allows us to select the appropriate utterance from all the possible grammatical utterances made available to us by our grammatical competence (1974: 75). That is, competence goes beyond simply knowing the rules for combining words into phrases and then phrases into clauses. In order to be a truly competent speaker of a language, you also have to know when to use certain styles or registers, what variants are generally (though subconsciously) recognised as being appropriate for different groups of speakers, appropriate politeness routines, and even when to speak or stay silent. Some of this kind of knowledge may also be described as **pragmatic competence** in the literature, but the important point here is that some linguists recognise forms of competence that go beyond syntax and semantics.

Pragmatic competence

The ability of a well-socialised speaker to know when certain speech acts are

The Brown and Levinson framework has provided a fairly useful foundation for researchers who are interested in describing in detail the mechanics of intercultural communication and miscommunication (e.g., Kasper and Blum-Kulka 1993; Blum-Kulka 1997). There are several reasons for this. For example, the framework provides a simple classification or typological system under which the norms of any group of speakers in any particular context can be defined as more or less oriented to positive or negative face wants. Once the differences between the norms of different groups of speakers have been identified, points of possible intervention and specific training can be proposed in order to avoid cross-cultural miscommunication.

Researchers such as Gabrielle Kasper have looked at a number of the kinds of FTAs that are central to Brown and Levinson's theory, and they have tried to determine how the sociolinguistic strategies most frequently associated with a particular FTA in the learner's first language compare with the sociolinguistic strategies used by native speakers of the learner's target language. If specific differences can be identified (e.g., one language tends to conventionally use negative politeness strategies while the other uses positive or negative politeness strategies), teaching can be focused on areas in which the different social and linguistic skills are most marked and are therefore most likely to be problematic.

required, appropriate or inappropriate. A competence required over and above *grammatical competence* in order to successfully participate as a member of a speech community. (See also *Sociolinguistic competence*.)

Connections with theory

The method of comparing the linguistic strategies associated with FTAs in different languages is a form of **contrastive analysis**. The use of contrastive analysis has been widely used as the basis for devising second-language teaching materials that target areas of greatest difference – and it is assumed, greatest difficulty – between learners' first language and their target language.

For instance, if you want to request a drink in a bar in English you usually use some strategies that attend to the addressee's (bartender's) negative face wants, e.g., *Could I have a glass of red wine, please?* However, in German there is less attention to the server's negative face wants, and it is perfectly appropriate to say something like, *Ich kriege ein Rotwein* ('I'll get red wine'), with no 'please' or 'could'. It is possible to add *bitte* ('please') and to say *könnte* ('could'), but if you used both the request would sound absurd and slightly snooty. In some cases, you can imagine that these sorts of differences can cause real social difficulties when learners try to transfer their native-language strategies into the language they are learning, so it is useful for researchers like Kasper to have a framework in which they can describe these differences and prescribe solutions for language teachers.

Contrastive analysis

An approach to second-language acquisition that focuses on points of similarity and differ-ence in two varieties. The assumption is that where they differ, learners will have most difficulty.

Translating politeness

Make a list of three possible contexts in which you might have to *refuse* an offer made to you. Try to vary the contexts as much as possible in terms of P, D and C. Present them as short scenarios like this:

A friend suggests you should skip your 4 o'clock lecture to come to the movies. You don't want to. You say: _____

(Be sure to allow them to say 'nothing', i.e., to avoid the FTA too.)

exercise

Ask a native speaker of English to complete the scenarios.

Now ask native speakers of other languages to imagine being in this situation. Ask them to complete the sentences first in their own language, and then to translate the response (try and make the translation as literal as possible).

What differences can you see, and how would you describe them in terms of the notions of attention to positive and negative face wants?

CRITIQUES OF POLITENESS THEORY

As we have seen, Brown and Levinson's politeness theory can be quite a powerful and effective way of describing the ways in which people are perceived to 'be polite/impolite' to each other. We have also seen that it has been readily adopted by some researchers into intercultural communication, and we have seen how the insights from politeness theory have sometimes been used to shed light on more practical and applied questions of language teaching.

There are also a number of criticisms of this framework (these are discussed in detail in Watts (2003), and see also the suggestions for further reading). I will present three critiques which have been alluded to in our discussion already: the interdependence of the three variables that form the foundation of Brown and Levinson's approach, the (Western) emphasis on individualism and free choice, and the tendency to mix positive and negative politeness.

The interdependence of power, distance and cost of the imposition

As we have seen, power in this framework is essentially a vertical measure – a relation of superiority and subordination – and distance is essentially horizontal – how well people know each other. We have already noted that this provides a tidy theoretical distinction but that representing power and distance as independent factors is misleading. In practice, power and distance are very often heavily dependent on each other. This can make it difficult, if not artificial, to try and keep them separate. Generally the people we know best – that is, the people where there is least social distance – are also roughly our equals, neither our superiors nor our subordinates. When there is a relatively big power differential between individuals, it is also likely that they will be less close to each other socially. So in many cases, if you know the relative distance between interactants, you can fairly reliably predict the relative power between them as well (and vice versa).

Moreover, social distance can be simultaneously measured in different ways. When there are multiple dimensions on which distance can be calculated it can be difficult to predict whether interactants will orient themselves to one dimension or another. For example, some students from Hawai'i were trying to organise and systematically describe the decisions they make about whether to use Standard American English or Pidgin (discussed fully in the next chapter). They felt that they were aware of two very important dimensions for evaluating social distance.

As we will see in Chapter 6, part of a speaker's sociolinguistic competence in Hawai'i is knowing when to use Pidgin and with whom. The students all agreed that power and social distance are relevant factors in determining whether they will use Standard American English or Pidgin with an interlocutor, but they also agreed that the first and most salient question was whether or not their addressee was *Local*, too (in Hawai'i, people talk about those born there as *Locals*).

Many of the students felt that *Localness* overrides any other constraints there might be on using a language. If their interlocutor was clearly Local, they reported that they would always start out using Pidgin, no matter how formal the context or how little they knew the other person. They reported that even if they were discussing formal matters to do with their enrolment at university or getting a driver's licence, their first concern would be with whether or not their addressee was Local or not. If the addressee was, they said they would start out using Pidgin, and then adjust as necessary, depending on other cues their addressee might give about the social distance or power differential in that setting.

In short, choosing to use Pidgin in Hawai'i is an important (essentially, positive) politeness strategy for upwardly mobile or middle-class people like these students. However, the decision to use one language rather than another turns out to involve a lot of complicated and sometimes quite rapid calculations about the social nature of an unfolding interaction. These calculations are based on a rich history of other interactions that together shape an individual's sociolinguistic competence in Hawai'i. Even an apparently straightforward question about language choice requires speakers simultaneously to track power and distance in their relationships with other people along dimensions that are specific to Hawai'i (Localness) and that are shared with other Americans (previous acquaintance, institutional roles, etc.).

The emphasis on a speaker's choices

A number of researchers on politeness have criticised the Brown and Levinson model for focusing too heavily on the speaker. Sachiko Ide, a Japanese sociolinguist, has suggested that this reflects Western values of individualism and does not fit well with societies like Japan where a person's identity is perceived to be bound up in their group membership, with all the collective rights and responsibilities associated with the group, rather than with the exercise of rational self-interest that is at the heart of Western theories of identity (Ide 1989).

Some work on intercultural communication has tried to group societies according to how **individualistic** or how **collectivist** they are. It might be appropriate to describe politeness primarily in terms of the concerns of the speaker and addressee as individuals in prototypically individualistic societies, such as Australia or the US. Setting a high value on autonomy and having choices are attributes that cluster together and help define individualistic societies. But in societies with collectivist values, such as Japan, Thailand and China, this misses key features organising the social order, including requirements for polite behaviour. In these societies, Ide argues that Japanese society (and other collectivist communities) values attention to people's interdependence and to reciprocal relationships (see also Ting-Toomey 1988). In this context, the importance of discerning social behaviour appropriate to the social situation is emphasised. The Japanese word for this discernment is **wakimae**. Ide argues that *wakimae* is a much better basis for formulating models of politeness in Japan than the kind of individualistic decisions shown in Figure 5.2.

It should be noted that the clusters of social attributes and the contrast between individualistic and collectivist cultures are derived from a study of one multinational corporation

Individualistic

A society that emphasises and celebrates the individual over relationships (cf. *Collectivist*).

Collectivist

A collectivist society emphasises the relationships and interdependence of the individuals it is comprised of (cf. *individualistic*). (See also *Wakamae*.)

Wakimae

A Japanese term introduced to the study of *politeness* by Sachiko Ide. Refers to the attention paid to people's interdependence and to the reciprocity of relationships, and, specifically, the discernment of appropriate behaviour based on this.

(Hofstede 1980). Hofstede presented his findings in terms of the national origin of the employees surveyed, but his research was neither intended nor designed to thoroughly probe the values and behavioural norms of the nations themselves. This means sociolinguists should be a little cautious (or self-critical) about incorporating the distinction between collectivist and individualistic cultures into their research. Moreover, work by Morales and his associates suggests that when these constructs are brought down to the level of individuals, the associations between politeness and collectivist/individualistic attitudes become very shaky. They found that classifying an individual as individualistic or collectivist did not allow them to make reliable predictions about what politeness strategies they would choose under different circumstances (Morales *et al.* 1998).

Mixed messages: showing attention to both positive and negative face

Relatedly, in some of the earlier examples we saw that attention to positive and negative face wants can be bundled into a single utterance, and we noted that it is not clear how such examples should be analysed. They certainly don't cancel each other out, but would we want to categorise the utterance as an example of positive politeness, or negative politeness? The problem can be extended beyond the individual to the group: there are no groups of speakers who solely use positive or negative politeness strategies or that are wholly collectivist or individualistic. I have relied on national stereotypes in a number of illustrations of how politeness works, but by definition a stereotype simplifies and abstracts away from complexity and diversity. An American reader might justly object that the valorisation of individualism in the US should be offset against the strong sense of a community that is manifested in the large number of hyphenated group identities: Italian-Americans, African-Americans, Polish-Americans, etc. Likewise, a Japanese reader might object that Japanese society is just as well known for the celebration of highly idiosyncratic expressions of individual difference in personal fashion as it is for its emphasis on discernment.

One of the criticisms of Brown and Levinson's framework is that it very easily leads analysts towards overly simplistic categorisations, such as Thai society attends to deference and negative face, while Australian society attends to familiarity and positive face. Such generalisations are especially unwarranted if they depend on studies of only one or two FTAs (e.g., requests or orders).

CHAPTER SUMMARY

Politeness strategies can in some ways also be construed as sociolinguistic variables. To the extent that they are used to negotiate a position for a speaker in relation to others in the complicated social space we live in, they perform similar functions to the alternations between languages or styles within a language that we have looked at, and even the alternation between sounds that can mark identity or differentiation from others. However, politeness strategies do differ from the kinds of sociolinguistic variables that we have looked at already in previous chapters. Those variables are realised by variants which stand in mutual opposition to each other, and are semantically equivalent (that is, they do not change the linguistic meaning of the utterance even if, as we have seen, their social meaning differs). Politeness strategies are not like this. In the exercises, you have seen many cases where different strategies nest and pile up on each other, reinforcing each other or adding nuances to the entire message. Politeness strategies generally do add some meaning to the utterance. In some cases it may not be great, but in other cases − say when the speaker establishes an obligation to perform some action at some time in the future − the politeness strategy also clearly conveys some kind of proposition or idea.

Brown and Levinson's politeness theory is an attempt to formalise how our choice of phrases, or even single words, fits into the complexities of the social order. Like other work in sociolinguistics, it attempts to show how apparently diverse and heterogeneous linguistic routines are nonetheless constrained and systematic. One reason why it remains attractive, despite the very valid critiques that have been levelled at it, is that it provides a clear framework for studying the systematicity of linguistic variation above the level of sounds and inflections. Moreover, some of the criticisms are quite constructive; they might focus our attention on ways in which work on politeness needs to develop next if it is to fully capture all the cross-linguistic and cross-cultural richness we are interested in.

In the next chapters we move away from the discussion of how interpersonal factors constrain speakers' choice of language. We will begin to look at how speakers use language as a means for organising and giving meaning to larger social groupings. We have seen that politeness is about satisfying the needs of individual speakers and addressees, but also that it is about satisfying social or cultural norms. Similarly, in the next chapters it is worth bearing in mind that generalisations about the orderliness of talk between subgroups in a speech community are only possible because of the orderliness of individuals in those groups.

FURTHER READING

Watts (2003) − for a comprehensive summary of research on politeness.

Eelen (2001) − an overview and criticism of various approaches to politeness.

Leech (1980) − another widely used framework for analysing politeness with greater emphasis on the hearer.

Holmes (1995) − on gender and politeness.

Mills (2003) − also on gender and politeness, but requires more engagement with theory.

Holmes and Stubbe (2003) − on workplace culture and 'relational practice'.

Jaworski (1993) − more on silence.

Ting-Toomey (1994) − articles providing further perspectives on *face* and *facework*.

If you are interested in this topic, the relatively new *Journal of Politeness Research* will be useful.

CHAPTER 6

Multilingualism and language choice

Key terms in this chapter:

- **vitality**
- **diglossia**
- **High variety**
- **Low variety**
- **code switching**
- **domain**

- **situational**
- **passive knowledge**
- **active knowledge**
- **code mixing**
- **speech levels**

INTRODUCTION

It's late evening on the hills above the town of Tórshavn, in the Faroe Islands. Because the islands are so far north, even in August the sky is light until quite late and the children can play outside until 10 p.m. or later. Tonight some boys – about ten years old – are playing in an outdoor playground that belongs to the local nursery. The language of everyday life in the Faroes is Føroyske (Faroese), a Germanic language closely related to Icelandic, and the boys are talking in Faroese as they play. One of them climbs to the front of a mock ship and straddles the foredeck and the cabin with one foot on each. As he does this, another boy reaches up trying to slap his backside. With each swipe, the second boy calls out in English, 'Nice ass, nice ass'.

The use of English at this point obviously means something more than the words themselves do. All of these boys would have been completely fluent in Faroese, and by the age of ten they would have been very fluent in Danish. Both Faroese and Danish certainly have the lexical resources to say 'nice ass'. So why did he choose English instead?

In Chapters 3 and 4, we have already seen a number of cases where the choice of a word or even the pronunciation of a word may signal social and attitudinal information over and above the purely referential information carried by the word itself. We've also looked at analyses that explain intraspeaker variation in terms of who the speaker is talking to and whether they want to stress likeness and commonality with their addressee. In the different approaches to style-shifting, we have seen that different ways of talking carry different social meaning, perhaps signalling casualness and intimacy, or authority, formality and prestige.

In this chapter, we are going to look at how choosing between languages can be invested with the same kinds of social and affective meaning as choosing *styles* in one language. The

If you ever do need to say 'nice ass' to someone in Faroese, it's *deilig reyv*. And in Danish, *skøn røv*.

fact that languages can be invested with this kind of additional interactional meaning means the process of drawing up official policies of language planning and language in education can be a charged one. Decisions made about the official use and recognition of languages can have a powerful impact on the long-term strength of a language. We will use the term **vitality** to describe the likelihood that a language will continue being used for a range of social functions by a community of speakers, and we will see that vitality is influenced by institutional, social and demographic factors.

We will then examine some more specific cases where the vitality of different language varieties manifests itself in a division of social labour. That is, we will see that in multilingual communities, different languages have more or less vitality in different (institutional, social or personal) domains. In multilingual settings, the choice between languages carries interactional force or implies something about the situation or the interlocutors. One language may be used for some social functions or in a specific social context, while another language is reserved for other functions and contexts. This can be called **diglossia**, and we will look at some communities that have been described as diglossic, including speech communities with elaborated registers that are used in different situations and with different addressees.

LANGUAGE POLICY AND LANGUAGE PLANNING IN MULTILINGUAL SOCIETIES

No nation in the world is completely monolingual. In some cases, this is due to the way modern nation-states have been composed on the basis of rough geographic boundaries and because of historical political allegiances and conquest. Nowadays, it is also because of the ease and speed of movements of people between different nations. However, some nations officially consider themselves to be monolingual (e.g., Greece), and the historical reasons why they decide to foreground a single language in education and politics gives us interesting insights into how ideas about culture, race, self-determination and identity have developed in parallel to one another.

However, even in communities or nations that embrace their multilingualism, issues of self-determination, identity and culture are central. As we have seen in earlier chapters, speakers can use quite fine phonetic detail as the means for establishing group boundaries or personal identities. In other words, quite subtle and even unconsciously controlled forms of linguistic variation can have strong social effects. It is, therefore, hardly surprising that intense negotiation of collective values takes place when a community is making decisions about which language(s) will be officially or nationally recognised. In the next sections I outline how two new nations dealt with intense multilingualism and a colonial history when it came to shaping language policies that would contribute to defining a new national identity.

National languages and language policies

Two examples of highly multilingual societies can be compared in this respect: the Republic of South Africa and the Republic of Vanuatu, one located in the southern-most part of the African continent, and one in the south-west Pacific. Both, relatively recently, have had the task of formulating a national constitution, and as multilingual nations both wanted to codify language policies in their constitutions.

Vitality

Demographic, social and institutional strength of a language and its speakers.

Diglossia

Classically defined as a situation where two closely related languages are used in a speech community. One for *High (H)* functions (e.g., church, newspapers) and one for *Low* (L) functions (e.g., in the home, or market). The situation is supposed to be relatively stable and the languages/ varieties remain distinct (cf. *creole* outcomes of language contact). Now often extended to refer to any two languages (even typologically unrelated ones) that have this kind of social and functional distribution.

LANGUAGE RIGHTS IN SOUTH AFRICA'S CONSTITUTION

The South African Constitution was drawn up with the shift to full suffrage and equal rights for all citizens following the dismantling of the apartheid regime in 1994. *Apartheid* means 'separation' in Afrikaans, the language of the White Afrikaner population who were socially – though by no means numerically – dominant in South Africa until the 1990s. Under apartheid, legislation concentrated power and control of land and other economic resources in the hands of the 15 per cent of the population who were ethnically White, while the very large Black majority and the Indian and mixed-race sectors of the population were actively discriminated against. They were not, for instance, allowed to vote or have a say in changes to land law and local educational policy. The White population subdivided into two further groups: the English (descendants of the English settlers of South Africa) and the Afrikaners (who traced their descent to the first Dutch colonists). The two groups maintained their heritage languages, though of course they were subject to the kinds of changes that would affect any language over that time. Afrikaans looks and sounds quite different from Dutch today, and South African English has undergone a number of independent changes to the vowel system and its vocabulary, all of which make it sound quite distinct from modern British English (Lass 2002).

With the dominance of these two groups came the authority to legislate and control matters relating to language. Under apartheid, the ruling class of Afrikaners was able to stipulate that official business in the nation-state should be conducted in their language, Afrikaans. The law that dictated that Afrikaans would be the medium of instruction in Black schools became one of the most hated aspects of the apartheid regime and served as a lightning rod for acts of resistance. During the apartheid years this language law was often the focus of protests in the Black community against the injustice of the whole apartheid regime. The most widely known instance was the student uprising in Soweto that started in 1976, when Black students began protesting about the required use of Afrikaans as the medium of education. Protests continued into the 1980s and hundreds of protesters (including more than a hundred schoolchildren) were killed in clashes with the government's armed forces.

Connections with theory

Review the discussion of Tajfel in Chapter 4 (p. 63). How does the student protest in Soweto fit into his theory of intergroup relations? What does this form of creativity say about students' perceptions of the *justice* and *stability* of the situation? Why do you think they felt they had to boycott the classes rather than, for instance, try using their preferred language(s) in school instead of Afrikaans? What more does that suggest to you about the perceived stability of the situation?

Language choice in education

Why do you think the Black population of South Africa hated the law requiring them to be taught in Afrikaans in school so much?

Do you think that there is any similarity between the resistance to use of Afrikaans as a medium of education in South Africa and calls for 'Ebonics', or African American English, to be recognised and used in US schools?

You can also find coverage of the Soweto uprising from 16 June 1976 on the Internet or by searching back-files of major newspapers in a library. To what extent is the role of language discussed in the media reports? Do you think linguistic issues are well-covered? Why (not)?

A new start and new language policies

The apartheid regime in South Africa finally collapsed in the 1990s, partly as a consequence of political, sporting and economic boycotts. Equal rights and full suffrage were extended to all ethnic groups, and power transferred from the White minority to the Black majority (though to say it like this papers over a good deal of political and social diversity among different groups of Black Africans in the new South Africa). A new constitution was drawn up for the new state, and all of section 6 – which includes many paragraphs – is given over to language rights in the new nation.

The Constitutional Court of South Africa reproduces the Constitution on its website. The first thing the Constitution says about language is:

> 6.(1) The official languages of the Republic are Sepedi, Sesotho, Setswana, siSwati, Tshivenda, Xitsonga, Afrikaans, English, isiNdebele, isiXhosa and isiZulu.

In other words, the new state was to define itself in terms of linguistic pluralities, giving equal status to 11 languages. There are, of course, smaller language groups whose languages have not been given official recognition and support, and this does create a hierarchy within the larger sociolinguistic picture of the new South Africa. Another thing to note about the principal statement on national languages is that in the Constitution the official languages are not seen as being purely functional, but also as of affective importance. A few clauses later, the Constitution says 'all official languages must enjoy parity of esteem and must be treated equitably'.

Enjoyment of language

Why do you think the writers used the verb 'enjoy' in the last quote? What is 'enjoy' trying to capture? In your opinion, to what extent can or should 'enjoyment' of a language be considered a basic human or constitutional right?

The South African Constitution then goes on to say a number of other things, some of which clearly reflect the new nation's desire to distance itself from values and unjust practices of the past:

> 6.(2) Recognising the historically diminished use and status of the indigenous languages of our people, the state must take practical and positive measures to elevate the status and advance the use of these languages.

As we have already noted, there are many other languages used in daily interaction and for specific purposes in South Africa. While these are not afforded the institutional support of the official languages, the Constitution again recognises the linguistic pluralism of the new nation. So, the rights of speakers of other languages should be addressed in future language planning and policy. To this end, the Constitution specifies that a Language Board, functioning independently of the government, must be established, whose brief is to promote official and non-official languages in South Africa.

This examination of the South African Constitution indicates how vitally important the new nation perceives language rights to be. They help define core values which the nation wants in order to shape the development of a new South African identity now and into the future. The multilingual, multicultural nature of South Africa is a synchronic fact that contributes to these needs, but the needs also arise from the historical role that language has played in a history of oppression. For that reason, the Constitution writers have felt it important to address aspects specific to the *history* of South Africa, aspects of its *current* state of affairs, and their *aspirations* for the future in the document. What is interesting, sociolinguistically, is that they have recognised all of these dimensions as being directly related to policy and planning about language use, and spelled this out overtly in a way that is rather unusual.

LANGUAGE RIGHTS IN VANUATU'S CONSTITUTION

The challenges of linguistic self-determination also arise in other post-colonial contexts around the world. Many Pacific nations gained full independence only in the latter half of the twentieth century. The Republic of Vanuatu is one such example. Vanuatu was jointly administered as a colonial outpost by both the British and French (in a unique arrangement known officially as the 'Joint Condominium' government, but generally referred to locally as the 'Joint Pandemonium') until 1980 when it became an independent nation.

The new nation was highly diverse linguistically, and as in South Africa this raised a number of issues, some practical and some ideological. In addition to the many indigenous Eastern Oceanic languages spoken on the islands, there is an English-based creole called Bislama which is widely used, especially in the main centres (the capital Port Vila and the northern town Luganville/Santo). Finally, there are the two colonial languages, French and English, which were the official languages of the Condominium government.

National and official languages in Vanuatu

Upon gaining independence, Vanuatu inscribed slightly different decisions into their Constitution than South Africa did. The relevant section on 'National and official languages'

No, really?

Vanuatu is a nation made up of an archipelago of 83 islands. Its population is growing rapidly, and currently stands at around 200,000 people. As many as 114 distinct languages may be spoken there – linguists are still arguing and counting. They all agree that it is the country with the highest density of languages per head of population anywhere in the world.

in the English version of the Constitution is much shorter than the comparable section in the South African Constitution (and, interestingly, is somewhat less expansive than the Bislama version of the Constitution).

NATIONAL AND OFFICIAL LANGUAGES

3.(1) The national language of the Republic of Vanuatu is Bislama. The official languages are Bislama, English and French. The principal languages of education are English and French.

3.(2) The Republic of Vanuatu shall protect the different local languages which are part of the national heritage, and may declare one of them as a national language.

What clause 3.(1) does is make a three-way distinction between a *national* language, *official* languages and languages of *education*. It divides up these functions between French, English and Bislama, while in the next paragraph it addresses the importance and value placed on the indigenous languages which do not have any institutional status. This is articulated more explicitly in the Bislama version of the Constitution, which says: 'The indigenous languages of Vanuatu are part of the many good, traditional aspects of the country, and the government of the Republic will ensure that they are maintained' (my translation).

Clause 3.(2) allows one of the 'different local languages' to have national language status instead of or as well as Bislama. This aligns Bislama with the indigenous Eastern Oceanic languages, and suggests that Bislama's status as a national language is partly because it is *not* a colonial language but is considered more like an indigenous language of Vanuatu. As Ni-Vanuatu will readily tell you (*Ni-Vanuatu* is the adjective formed from *Vanuatu*), Bislama 'belongs to everyone'. Unlike the indigenous Eastern Oceanic or colonial languages it is not linked to any particular group or any particular set of vested interests. It is widely seen by Ni-Vanuatu as part of the common property of the nation, and an important way of establishing a bond between Ni-Vanuatu when they meet overseas.

ETHNOLINGUISTIC VITALITY

The negotiation of official status for languages in multilingual communities or nations involves a number of social, political and attitudinal factors. These factors all contribute to what we can call the 'ethnolinguistic vitality' of the different linguistic varieties. The concept of ethno-linguistic vitality comes from work on the social psychology of language. Researchers were interested initially in the relationship between groups of speakers and the languages in use in their community. They asked questions such as 'why do some languages remain strong in the face of social change, while others are abandoned within a few generations?' and 'what role does language play in defining a group or ethnic identity?' The term 'ethnolinguistic vitality' takes its name from two issues that were fundamental to the early research. A linguistic variety has relatively high 'vitality' if it is spoken and used widely. This kind of vitality is a good indicator of whether or not that particular language will continue to be spoken in successive generations, or whether speakers are likely to shift to another language. The word 'ethnolinguistic' reflects the researchers' belief that the use of a particular language variety is an extremely significant factor in defining a cultural or ethnic identity. The demographics of the (ethnic) group speaking a language, the status afforded to a language, and the institutional support provided for a language are all important considerations for evaluating the relative strength or vitality of languages.

The model of ethnolinguistic vitality that we are going to look at was not only intended to provide a reasonably reliable means for describing and comparing the relative vitality or strength of languages but has also been used as a frame for discussing what kinds of action or intervention might promote long-term maintenance of less vital varieties. We will see shortly that some work in this framework has been conducted in active collaboration with speakers of languages that are threatened by, for instance, the increasing use of English. The three pillars of ethnolinguistic vitality are represented in Figure 6.1. This figure represents vitality as being a function of three clusters of factors: the status (of a variety or of the speakers of that variety in different contexts), the demographics of the group identified and identifying with that variety, and institutional measures supporting or recognising a variety.

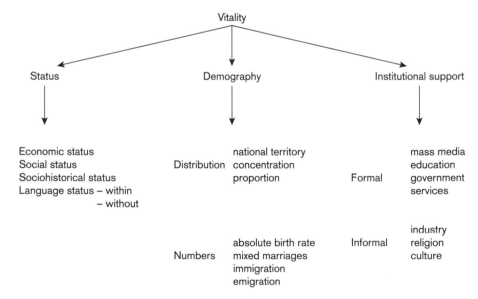

Figure 6.1 Factors contributing to ethnolinguistic vitality. (Source, Giles *et al.* 1977.)

Status factors influencing language vitality

If the speakers of a language have relatively high social status within the larger community – perhaps because they have higher social or economic status – the ethnolinguistic vitality of that variety will be higher too. This is the situation with what we would call the 'standard' language. The status of the language within the community *and* outside the community also matters. So too does the historical status that variety has had in the community in question. For example, Latin maintained relatively high vitality in Europe many centuries after it died out as a language of day-to-day communication. This was partly because it scored highly on all the status measures. The people who did acquire proficiency in Latin had greater economic and social status, and even people who did not have command of the language respected others' acquisition of it (that is, it had high status outside of the community of Latin users).

Institutional factors influencing language vitality

Institutional support also contributes to increased vitality of a language and therefore promotes its maintenance and use. Widespread use of a language in the popular mass media, as the medium of education, and in official government business all increase its relative vitality. This is the kind of vitality that both the South African and Vanuatu Constitutions try to foster by naming official and/or national languages.

More local and home-based activities, such as maintenance of a language for religious purposes and for regular cultural events, mean that even if the language is not widely used for daily conversation, it can retain a degree of vitality; this will also favour its long-term maintenance. A case of this can be found in the complex sociolinguistic situation found in Mauritius.

Mauritius is an ethnically and linguistically diverse nation in the Indian Ocean. The population mainly speaks Mauritian Creole at home and in daily business interactions, but English and French also have official uses. In addition, the very large population of Indo-Mauritians maintain (to a greater or lesser extent) use of their heritage Indian languages (e.g., Gujarati, Punjabi, Hindi and Urdu). These are the languages, still sometimes used in the home, of the descendants of the migrant indentured labourers who came to Mauritius from what is now India and Pakistan. So French and English have high vitality on formal institutional measures, and Mauritian Creole has high vitality on other (mainly demographic) measures.

At the same time, *informal* institutional support can also play a significant part in determining the vitality of a language. In the last two Mauritian censuses, a number of people identified 'Arabic' as their heritage language (Rajah-Carrim 2003). Closer analysis of trends across the last few censuses suggests that some Muslim respondents are reporting Arabic as their heritage language. Virtually all the Muslims on Mauritius are Indo-Mauritian and not Middle Eastern, so we would expect that they would indicate something like Urdu or Gujarati as their heritage language (indeed, this is what earlier censuses seemed to show). One interpretation of this increase in how many people report using Arabic is that because Arabic is the language of the Koran and Hadith this gives it considerable informal institutional vitality within the Muslim community. Furthermore, the language of the Koran and Hadith have high sociohistorical status in the Muslim community (the books are an important factor in providing a sense of cultural continuity for the community). It is possible that under the influence of these measures of high vitality, some Indo-Mauritians are now identifying Arabic as their 'heritage' language, even though, unlike the other heritage languages of the community, Arabic is seldom – if ever – spoken in anyone's home.

Demographic factors influencing vitality

Finally, the model notes the importance of demographic factors in determining the ethno-linguistic vitality of a language. A language might have relatively little social and economic status and relatively little institutional support, but if the group of people speaking the language appreciably outnumber the speakers of other languages, and particularly if they are relatively concentrated in a specific area, then the long-term prognosis for the maintenance of that language is improved. We can see the importance of having concentrated popula-tions of speakers of a language by considering the impact of New Zealand's policies of relocating Māori in the mid-twentieth century. The movement of Māori into urban areas was accompanied by a deliberate policy that was known as 'pepper-potting'; that is, Māori were housed so as to avoid significant concentrations of Māori in one area. This rupture of Māori social networks had a profound effect on the transmission of key cultural information – including the language – to the next generation, a disruption that is only gradually, and with tremendous effort, being reversed.

USING THE MODEL OF LANGUAGE VITALITY

Although Figure 6.1 is a useful overview of the many factors that are involved in maintaining a lively and vital linguistic community, there are a few reasons why we should use it carefully. First of all, although each factor itemised in Figure 6.1 is presented as if it were discrete and independent of the other factors, this is something of an idealisation. In particular, you can probably see how measures of institutional support overlap with measures of status. Similarly, some measures of (informal) institutional support might be more likely to follow from demographic facts, such as high concentrations of speakers in one area and whether there are high rates of immigration. Immigration is important because it provides a ready 'top-up' of proficient users of a language variety and the associated social and cultural traditions. Some varieties of Central American Spanish spoken in the US have benefited from the vitality of steady immigration over several generations.

It might be possible to correct for some of these problems by weighting the different factors shown in Figure 6.1. Deciding on which factors to weight more than others would have to be based on in-depth research in a particular community. In fact, this is how the framework has been deployed by some researchers, and we will look at the results of some of the work on language revitalisation and language maintenance that have drawn on this framework.

Canada's First Nations languages

Canada is well known as a multicultural and multilingual nation. Both French and English are recognised as national languages and, in the province of Quebec, French is keenly protected and promoted as a language of all official and public discourse. In addition, there are numerous languages spoken by more recent immigrants to Canada, such as Mandarin, Cantonese, Punjabi and Spanish. Some of these languages, while lacking the formal institutional support that gives French and English their relative vitality, nonetheless retain a degree of vitality by virtue of informal and demographic factors.

Canada is also home to the languages of the First Nations. 'First Nations' is the term used in Canada to refer to the native North American peoples who lived in what is now Canada before it became a European colony. They currently make up about 2 per cent of Canada's overall population. Many of the First Nations people have left their traditional or reservation lands in Canada and more than 25 per cent now live in Canada's 11 largest cities. In general, the language rights of the First Nations have little formal institutional support. Quebec, the Northwest Territories, and the recently formed Nunavut are the only states with language policies affording protection to First Nation languages.

Itesh Sachdev is a sociolinguist who has worked for many years with speakers of various minority language communities in Canada, including speakers of First Nations languages. Some of his more recent work has been in the Fisher River Cree community (in Manitoba) (Sachdev 1998) and the Haida Gwaii community (on Queen Charlotte Island in British Columbia). In both these communities English is the dominant language and has high status and a lot of institutional support. Cree and Haida have comparatively low status and little institutional support. They are taught as subjects in the schools, but do not serve as the medium for education in any subject. They are only spoken fluently by a small number of elders in each community – indeed, the number of native speakers is so small that Sachdev has been able to meet *all* the fluent speakers in both communities.

Despite the low vitality of Cree and Haida, the communities are keen to find ways of promoting their use and maintaining them in the younger generations. Sachdev has worked with both communities to try and determine what kinds of intervention strategies are most likely to work in each place. In doing this, he is trying to make practical use of the model of ethnolinguistic vitality discussed above, combining it with the strength of local researchers' knowledge and interview skills. Some striking findings emerged from his combination of interviews, surveys and language attitudes questionnaires.

He found that in both communities there was an almost universal perception that the Haida and Cree languages are a very important index of Haida or Cree identity. However, he also found that people who were taught Cree or Haida in school expressed more negative attitudes towards the language than towards English, while people who had learnt Haida or Cree at home, or people who had never learnt the languages, evaluated English and their heritage language roughly equally.

Obviously, this poses problems for possible intervention. It suggests that maintenance of the languages in these communities may actually be harmed if the principal efforts towards their revitalisation are made in the schools. And yet promoting use of the languages in families requires quite subtle forms of intervention and support.

Sachdev and his colleagues in the Cree and Haida communities turned their attention to other kinds of markers that might play an important role in influencing the long-term vitality and maintenance of these languages. Among other things, they have looked at how individuals label themselves within those communities, and how these labels correlate with other factors.

Group labels can be tremendously rich in the kinds of attitudes and values they evoke. Research in Canada has found that when White Canadians were asked about their attitudes to the First Nations, they gave very different responses depending on the label or name the researchers used to describe the First Nations. Similarly, Sachdev found that there were big differences in how members of the Haida and Cree communities described themselves and their language profile. For example, people who self-categorised as 'Indian' showed greater identification with colonial ideologies, and these people tended to favour use of English over use of Haida or Cree. On the other hand, members of the community who self-categorised as 'Cree' or 'Haida' showed the opposite tendency, and they favoured the First Nations languages.

Sachdev and the local researchers in both communities concluded that language revitalisation is likely to be more successful if underlying ideologies about colonialism and self-determination are addressed. In terms of ethnolinguistic vitality, they have found that status issues need to be addressed as urgently as institutional ones if the Cree and Haida languages are going to thrive in coming generations.

Wales: identity and language post-devolution

The challenges facing a language like Welsh are rather different from those of the First Nations. Aggressive revitalisation and language maintenance efforts have been a feature of the social and political landscape in Wales for somewhat longer than they have been among the Canadian First Nations. The (partial) devolution of political and economic decision-making from the British Parliament to the Welsh Assembly has enabled even more direct funding of language maintenance initiatives.

However, the activities that are emphasised in Wales are beginning to shift from promoting Welsh as a core cultural value to dealing with the difficulties that are associated with funding and staffing the revitalisation programmes that have already been established. What this means is that the groups responsible for promoting the status of Welsh within the country are critically evaluating where they get the best return on funding and resources, and they are trying to identify key, and successful, groups and strategies. There has been a shift from simply bolstering the vitality of the language in terms of social status, or institutional support. This involves a careful evaluation of how demographic factors interact with the newly achieved institutional support.

Colin Williams, of the Welsh Language Board (WLB), notes that in most cases statistics on minority language use are woefully inadequate. Census data may give a rough idea about how many speakers there are of a language, but these figures can be very misleading. The 1991 census records 600,000 speakers of Welsh, which seems like a very healthy base figure and suggests that current policies and practices encouraging language maintenance have been very successful. However, this figure may include people who do not use Welsh daily, and it may exclude people who hesitate to call themselves 'Welsh speakers' because they are comparing their abilities with those of native speakers.

To date, most of the efforts towards revitalising Welsh have been focused in the formal institutional domain of school and regional government. Twenty-seven per cent of Welsh children are now in Welsh immersion programmes, and all children under 16 have to take Welsh along with English and Maths as a core subject in school. The promotion of Welsh has led to some changes in its status. In the past, research on language attitudes has shown appreciable distrust of bilingualism in the wider community, but this is much less true now. Promotion of the language in school, along with work on perceptions of bilingualism, has had as much impact on increasing the use of Welsh as statutory reform has.

Because of the relatively high institutional support for Welsh in Wales, the focus of the WLB is now shifting to status and demographic issues affecting the long-term vitality of the language. Among the demographic facts that give cause for concern at this stage is the finding that 50 per cent of families have only one parent who is competent in Welsh and in these families that the children tend not to speak the language at all. In addition, the WLB has found that bilingual teenagers use less and less Welsh as they get older, and it has identified the ages of 9, 14–15 and 18–20 as being particularly important points at which people tend to shift away from using Welsh. Intervening to promote and maintain the language at these points requires close work with the individuals, and the WLB has found that this is not easily done by a national body. As a response to the need for very local responses to language shift, they have established Mentrau Iaith Cymru.

Mentrau Iaith Cymru are small and very local groups that identify local domains and practices that can be targeted for introducing Welsh into. They are likened to linguistic *animateurs*, little cells of political activists, and the kinds of activities they have undertaken include (in West Wales) providing special gift packs for new parents. These are distributed by midwives, and the information provided in them seems to have led to a doubling of the intake in Welsh medium nurseries over recent years. The Mentrau Iaith Cymru have also targeted specific workplaces, working closely with fire stations or police stations, in order to promote the use of Welsh there.

Some promoters of Welsh now argue that the community needs to move beyond the old rhetoric of protection of Welsh to a discourse that focuses on promoting bilingualism. That is, the community needs to move beyond seeing Welsh as a marker of nationalism to a point where it becomes an index of inclusive pluralism. This might entail the community changing its tactics from producing reactive policies to pursuing purposive growth. These activists argue that just as languages and the communities that use them are constantly changing, so too must the strategies and discourses change for effective maintenance of the vitality of a minority language.

No, really?

Colin Williams also stresses that real language revitalisation means that a language functions in *all* social networks and all social domains. He tells a story about a Harvard professor visiting Caernarvon, in north-west Wales, for a conference on minority languages. Walking back to his hotel, he was approached by a man speaking to him in Welsh. Though he understood nothing of what the man said, it was clear from his tone and gestures that he was not friendly. After unsuccessful attempts to communicate, the professor was soundly thumped, abused and his wallet was stolen. As he picked himself up from his mugging, he took some small consolation: 'My, my. Welsh *is* a living language.'

DIGLOSSIA IN A COMMUNITY

In some multilingual communities, the different measures that determine the vitality of language varieties are more rigidly demarcated than in others. Charles Ferguson noted this when writing about the relationship between Classical Arabic and the vernacular spoken varieties of Arabic used throughout the Middle East, and the relationship between European French and Haitian Creole in Haiti. In both the Middle East and Haiti, Ferguson observed that although the languages in each locale were more or less historically related, there was strict differentiation of the domains and functions for which the different languages were used.

Diglossia

Ferguson's 1959 article brought the term into widespread use in Anglophone linguistics, but the term appeared at least as early as 1930 in a French language article by William Marcais.

High (H) variety

See *Diglossia*.

Low (L) variety

See *Diglossia*.

Vernacular varieties of Arabic and Haitian were acquired naturally by children and were the everyday medium of communication in the home and with family and friends. On the other hand, Classical Arabic and European French were used for written media (e.g., newspapers and government documents) and when reading aloud from a script or set texts (e.g., radio news broadcasts or teachings in a church or a mosque). In addition, no one natively acquired Classical Arabic or European French in these speech communities. The languages had to be formally taught, and had thoroughly standardised grammars which were the subject of conscious study. Ferguson called this situation of societal bilingualism and institutionalised code-switching, **diglossia** (from Greek, meaning 'two languages').

Ferguson called the language with higher overt prestige, and which is used in more formal contexts and for writing, the **High variety** (or H, for short), and the vernacular variety the **Low variety** (or L). In his original case studies of diglossia, the two varieties in use in the community had some historical link to each other, and one could be argued to have its roots in the other.

Since then, the notion of diglossia has been applied more widely. Joshua Fishman suggested that it should be extended to apply to a functional or domain-based distinction in when you use different languages, registers or styles. He argued that on functional grounds, there was no reason to limit diglossia only to situations where the varieties were diachronically related. This shifts the emphasis from language structure to shared norms for acquisition and use in the community, thus making diglossia very clearly a sociolinguistic phenomenon.

Since then, researchers have noted numerous situations in which more than two languages seem to enter into the same kind of sociohistorical relationships that characterise the classic cases of (either Ferguson's or Fishman's) diglossia. So, among other things, you can find references to 'nested' or 'overlapping' diglossia. An overlap might occur if you had three or more languages. Some people have argued that the sociolinguistic situation in Tanzania is a case of this. In some domains the local vernaculars function as the L to Swahili's H. But in other domains, Swahili is the L to English's H.

For the rest of this chapter, the notion of diglossia will not play a large part. In general, the chapter will try to keep focused on the notions of vitality, and also on how domain of use determines which variety of language a speaker chooses. However, there are obvious connections with the key characteristics of diglossia, and moreover the term is still often used in linguistics. So it is worth having a sense of how it complements or sometimes intersects with the sociolinguistic perspectives that will be developed more fully.

IS 'VITALITY' THE SAME AS 'PRESTIGE'?

An obvious point of possible intersection is between *vitality* and *prestige*. The two terms capture similar intuitions about the importance of institutional support and attitudes to the use of a variety. But the terms do not mean the same thing. Probably if a language ranks highly in terms of institutional measures of vitality, it will always have a degree of overt prestige associated with it (see Chapter 3). For example, government jobs usually pay reasonably well and are usually pretty steady, so as soon as knowing a language becomes a requirement for holding a government position, it is going to become reasonably desirable to a number of people. And if the official business of state and governance takes place in that language it will have external recognition, which also affords it a measure of overt prestige.

The notion of ethnolinguistic vitality therefore has some advantages over prestige. It gets away from any confusion or indeterminacy surrounding terms like prestige, because it avoids

No, really?

In 1998 the Mauritian government issued new bank notes. As with the old notes, there were inscriptions in English, Tamil and Hindi. But on the new notes, Tamil followed Hindi. Bitter arguments followed. Tamils argued that, as one of the first communities in Mauritius, Tamil should precede Hindi. Hindus argued that because they make up a larger section of the population, Hindi should precede Tamil. Finally, at huge cost, the government recalled the notes and replaced them with new ones on which the old order of languages was reinstated. The dispute highlighted differences in the sociohistorical and demographic vitality of the two languages and their associated ethnic groups.

the need to make a distinction between norms that people are consciously orienting to (overt prestige) and those that they seem to be less consciously orienting to (covert prestige). For this reason, it may sometimes be a more useful framework for discussing the social dynamic between languages or language varieties. On the other hand, if you are actually interested in the question of *how* speakers orient to different linguistic norms, then it may be more appropriate to focus on the conscious awareness that is inherent in the notions of (c)overt prestige.

Connections with theory

In studies of language contact, emphasis is placed on determining when different groups of speakers came into contact with one another. Many researchers have noted that the first speakers to arrive when dialects or languages come into contact may have a greater effect on the ultimate structure of the newly emergent variety than later arrivals do. This has been variously called things like the principle of first-past-the-post (Sankoff 1980) or the founder principle (Mufwene (1996), who borrows the term from population genetics). These principles draw on demographic factors and sociohistorical status for describing diachronic processes in a manner very similar to the way ethnolinguistic vitality does to describe synchronic states of affairs.

CODE SWITCHING AND CODE MIXING

People who speak more than one language, or who have command over more than one variety of any language, are generally very sensitive to the differences in the vitality of the languages they use and they are equally aware that in some contexts one variety will serve their needs better than another. This may lead them to change the variety they use depending on where they are. So a speaker of African American Vernacular English (AAVE) may know that when they are applying for a building permit to add an extension on their house, things may simply go a lot faster if they switch into Standard American English (or the regional White vernacular) when they are talking to the White clerk at City Hall. However, when they go home and are telling their neighbours about what kind of extension they are putting in, it may be more appropriate to use AAVE.

Code switching

In its most specific sense, the alternation between varieties, or codes, across sentences or clause boundaries. Often used as a cover term including *code mixing* as well.

This phenomenon of moving between distinct varieties is known as **code switching**. When code switching is constrained by where speakers happen to be, it can be called **domain**-based or **situational** code switching. When it is constrained by who a speaker happens to be talking to it can be called addressee-based. In addition, there are other more metaphorical motivations for code switching, and we will look at examples that illustrate these points.

It might be fair to say that a diglossic community is one that is characterised by highly predictable domain-based code switching. I would prefer to treat code switching as distinct from diglossia because code switching is not necessarily insitutionalised in the way diglossia is. There is more individual creativity and flexibility involved.

Domain

The social and physical setting in which speakers find themselves.

It is sometimes difficut to say just whether it is the domain of the interaction that determines what linguistic variety a speaker will choose, or whether the person they are talking to is what determines their choice. As we have seen in earlier chapters, speakers choose different styles of a language depending on where they are, who they are talking to and what kind of impression or persona they want to communicate to their interlocutors. The same thing holds for shifts between different language varieties when people code-switch.

---

exercise

Switching styles and languages

Guy is a lawyer in Honolulu. In court, and when meeting with clients, he wears a suit and tie and he speaks the supra-localised variety of American English he acquired growing up in a family that moved often. Outside work hours he wears T-shirts and jeans, and when he stops an employee at the drugstore to ask for help, he switches into Pidgin, 'Cuz, get dakine pukka beads here?' ('Hey mate, do you have any of those, like, surfer beads here?').

Why do you think Guy uses Pidgin instead of Standard American English in the local store? Can you imagine situations where he might want to use Pidgin in his legal work?

Situation(al)

A more idiosyncratic and personalised view of the context or situation of language use (cf. *domain*). In this text, used to describe one of the motivations for *code switching*.

A nice example that shows how domain and addressee influences can blur into each other are the factors determining which language you might speak in the market in Kondoa, a township in inland Tanzania. Swahili is the national language of Tanzania and is the language generally used for education, politics and business. However, the vernacular language spoken in the region around Kondoa is Rangi, so there are at least two languages to choose from when you go to market to do business.

Suppose you want to buy the favourite vegetable of the area (it looks something like spinach but, when cooked, has a consistency like okra or bhindi). You would go to the Kondoa town market, the only permanent one in the area, and you could say to a market vendor '*Naomba mlenda*' ('I want spinach/okra' in Swahili). If you point to a large bundle sufficient to feed ten people, the seller will tell you it costs around 300 Tanzanian shillings (the equivalent of about 50 US cents in 2004). You might haggle a bit, saying something like,

'*Naomba unipunguzie bei*' ('I want you to decrease the price' in Swahili), and they might give it to you for 250 shillings. Good job.

Well, no. Because if you had asked the vendor the same thing in Rangi, '*Nooloomba kɪruumbu*' ('I want spinach/okra'), they still would have initially asked 300 shillings for the bundle of spinach. But if, during the process of haggling, you use the traditional Rangi formula '*Heeriheeri*' ('What's your bottom-line price?'), chances are they will sell it to you for 200 shillings. In other words, speaking Rangi is worth a 20 per cent discount. The local community uses people's language skills as a means of identifying ingroup members over outgroup members, and once they have been identified they favour them.

On the other hand, if you have business to conduct at the Kondoa branch of the national bank, you better be able to speak Swahili. Banks draw on a national pool of employees, so many are non-Rangi and simply won't understand you unless you speak Swahili. Secondly, coming in speaking Rangi may leave you open to a charge of political tribalism. As a consequence you may be seen as a bad risk for a loan or in a business contract.

These examples show that domain (where you are) is important in determining which language variety you would choose to use in Kondoa, but they also very clearly show that deciding which variety to use requires a good deal of cultural knowledge. The use of Swahili in the bank is not just dictated by the domain, it is also determined by who your interlocutor is likely to be, their linguistic skills, and the inferences about your political stance that might be drawn from your use of either Rangi or Swahili. The convention of using Swahili in a bank arises not just from associations between Swahili and a certain level of education, though this is certainly part of it, but also from people's conventional understanding of what different languages represent about a speaker's political and interpersonal disposition. In other words, there are several ideologies about language that converge in making Swahili the unmarked choice in finance.

Similarly, the use of Rangi in the marketplace requires more than just knowing that both Swahili and Rangi are acceptable means of communication in the Kondoa market. It requires knowing more than just that the vegetable seller is a speaker of Rangi. In order to get the Rangi discount, you also need to know a conventional formula, *heeriheeri*, and you have to know when it is the right time to use it. In other words, you have to understand the conversational give-and-take for buying and selling, and how these are the same and different from turn-taking in conversation. So, this requires a lot of knowledge about Rangi culture and interactional norms.

Deciding when to use which code

Speakers may conceptualise the relationship between location, addressee and ingroup identity in different ways. Figures 6.2 and 6.3 are decision trees, representing what two groups of students at the University of Hawai'i said they bear in mind when they try to decide whether to use Pidgin or Standard American English. Each box in a decision tree marks a point where the students felt they would ask themselves a crucial question. If they answered 'yes' to that question, they would follow one path out from that box; if they answered 'no' they would follow another path from the box. Sometimes the domain and addressee factors pile up on each other and they felt that one decision follows another before they would come to a decision about which variety to use. At other times, the decision is simple, and a 'yes' answer would take them directly to the choice of one variety rather than another.

In Figure 6.2, the students have used the classic notation of a decision tree and there is almost always a 'yes' and a 'no' route out from each question they ask themselves. (The only exception to this is the box 'At work?', where there is only a 'yes' route out. Presumably, if the answer is 'no' there are other domains that might be checked.) The second group of students (Figure 6.3) felt that their domain or location was the most meaningful place to start. But notice how important it is for them whether or not their addressee can speak Pidgin. Whereas the first group in Figure 6.2 indicate that they would always use Pidgin with their friends, the second group say they would generally only do so if they were speaking to a friend who also speaks Pidgin. You might think it is a little odd to address someone in a language that they cannot speak, but there are several reasons why speakers might choose to use Pidgin with friends and peers regardless. One is that friends may have **passive knowledge** of Pidgin even if they are not fluent speakers themselves (passive knowledge of a language

Passive knowledge

The ability to understand, but not speak, a language. (See also *Active knowledge.*)

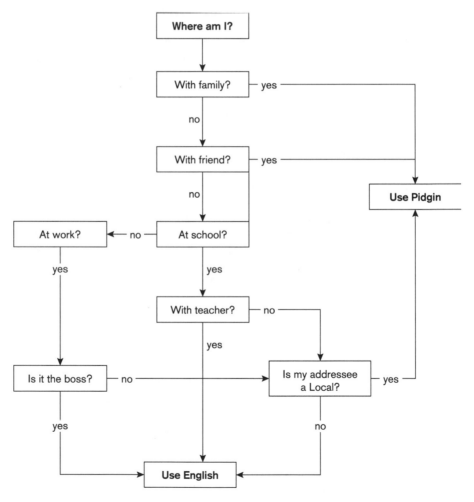

Figure 6.2   Decision tree for when to use Pidgin or Standard US English for six university students in Honolulu, Hawai'i. (Note the ranking of addressee above domain or location and above social role of the interlocutor.)

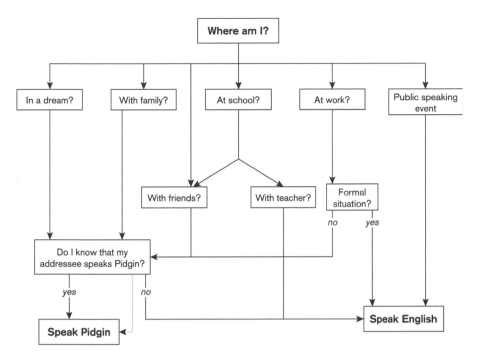

Figure 6.3   Decision tree for when to use Pidgin or Standard US English for four university students in Honolulu, Hawai'i. (Note the ranking of domain above speaker and hearer social roles, and consideration of the interlocutor's own competence in Pidgin. The dotted line indicates a less frequent, but possible, choice.)

means you can understand it, while **active knowledge** means you can understand and produce it). Another reason is that using Pidgin in every peer interaction may be a way in which these students can assert the importance of Pidgin as a marker of ingroup and Local (native to Hawai'i) identity.

Another thing that is interesting about the second group of students' decision tree is that they explicitly note that sometimes they violate their own norms or expectations. The dotted line shows that under some circumstances they would deliberately choose to use Pidgin with an addressee even if they know that person doesn't speak the language and may have trouble understanding. Many of the junctures in the decision trees are completely below the level of conscious control or awareness. People will tell you that they simply know that it feels right to speak one variety or another in certain places or with certain people. However, on occasions speakers will play with and flout those norms or expectations.

Active knowledge

Knowledge of a linguistic *variety* that includes the ability to produce and use that variety, and not only understand it. (See also *Passive knowledge*.)

Mapping your language choices

A lot of people use a different language variety at home than they do in school or at work. If you are someone who falls into this category, try drawing a decision tree for yourself, mapping the process by which you consciously or subsconsciously choose one variety

exercise

over another. Give it to someone else and ask them to interpret it. (You may be surprised how much socolinguistic work you have bundled into any one point.)

If you do not have appreciably different language varieties to choose from, try finding someone else to interview and draw a decision tree for them. Drawing one for yourself and one for someone else requires very different skills.

Switching within and between turns

The kinds of code switching we have looked at up to this point present the choice between languages or varieties as being something like an 'either–or' question. Either the interaction takes place in Rangi, or it takes place in Swahili. Either it is in Pidgin or it is in English. In practice, there can be a lot of mixing of codes during a single exchange or even within a single speaker's turn. If we want to, we can talk about switches within turns as **code mixing**, but not all researchers think the processes underlying switches within turns and between different conversational episodes are sufficiently different to warrant completely separate terminology.

It seems that the kinds of interpersonal or affective functions associated with use of Pidgin in Hawai'i or use of Rangi in Kondoa also play a role in switching within turns. So there are mixed codes which signal ingroup humour and affection. Conversely, they can show hostility to outsiders who may not understand all the mixed constituents or may not understand the conventions governing how the codes are mixed.

Miki Makihara's work on Rapa Nui (Easter Island) discusses the way in which a mixed code has been emerging there since the 1970s or 1980s. This indigenous interactional code is now used by children and adults alike. It involves extensive mixing of Rapa Nui (a Polynesian language) and Spanish (Rapa Nui is administered as part of Chile, so both Chilean Spanish and a Rapa Nui variety of Spanish are spoken in Rapa Nui). Makihara believes that this mixed variety functions as an important marker of an emerging sense of Rapa Nui solidarity and identity, and probably first emerged in informal conversations; Makihara also discusses the social functions it seems to index within informal conversations. For instance, in Example 1 we can see it being used for teasing and joking between a married couple and their friends. (I follow Makihara's layout of the text: the original forms are on the left, the English translation is on the right. Text in *italics* is Rapa Nui; text that is <u>underlined</u> is Spanish.)

There are switches between Rapa Nui and Spanish after turn 1 and turn 5, and within turns 2 and 5. Notice that the husband and wife also playfully use the resources of Spanish in turns 2–4, with the husband using the formal 'you' to his wife, which she returns with the informal 'you'. So the ingroup nature of the exchange is realised at a number of different levels – the teasing about who can or should be called *korohu'a* ('old man') and the husband's mock formal way of addressing of his wife. In addition, the switching between Rapa Nui and Spanish forms between and within turns is characteristic of local and intimate conversation on Rapa Nui.

The extent of the mixing between Rapa Nui and Spanish can involve some (syntactically) quite complex alternations, going well beyond the use of a noun or adverb as in turns 2, 5 and 6 in Example 1. Makihara also gives examples where speakers mix nouns and determiners or verbs and tense markers from different languages.

Code mixing

Generally refers to alternations between varieties, or codes, within a clause or phrase. Often elicits more strongly negative evaluations than alternations or *code switching* across clauses.

Wife:	*'I hē ia te korohu'a nei?*	1 W:	*Where's the old man?*
Husband:	Me está diciendo *korohu'a* otra vez.	2 H:	You (formal) are calling me *old man again.*
	¿A quién está diciendo *korohu'a* mi amor?		Who are you (formal) calling *old man* my dear?
All:	[laughter]	3 All:	[laughter]
Wife:	No, a tí no, a mi papa.	4 W:	No, not to you (informal), to my dad.
Husband:	Acuérdese que yo soy joven *'ā*	5 H:	Remember (formal) that I am *still young.*
Friend:	Cómo será *ia, ahani e 'apa pa'ari ro 'ā, ko ture mai 'ā.*	6 F:	What will *it* be, *(he) is barely half-adult but is already talking back.*
All:	[laughter]	7 All:	[laughter]

Example 1   Mixed Rapa Nui interactional code being used for joking among intimates. *Italics* = Rapa Nui, underline = Spanish. (Source, Makihara 2004: 532; slightly modified.)

Connections with theory

There is a lot of debate among linguists about whether switching within turns can happen at any point or whether there are formal linguistic constraints that make it possible or impossible to switch between different constituents. Some linguists argue that switching within turns happens at the level of surface strings (so constraints may be determined by processing or linear word order of the languages involved). Other linguists argue that more subtle factors are involved and that these are consistent with theories of syntax that posit underlying structure to a clause. Mahootian (2006) gives a good summary of different formal perspectives on code switching.

In longer stretches of interaction it also becomes quite clear that the mixing is very much a dynamic process, involving call and response from different participants. This, too, adds to the sense that the mixed code serves as a solidarity marker. You can see this echoing effect across turns in Example 2 where Mario (a 6-year-old) is talking to his grandfather, his aunt Elena and his 6-year-old cousin Mariana. Elena's joking comment recycles Mariana's previous turn and incorporates Mariana's Spanish into Elena's Rapa Nui sentence. Speakers can use a discourse strategy like this to create coherence within a text.

Mario:	*Koro!* Vamo al *uta* mañana?	1 Mario:	*Grandpa!* Let's go *inland* tomorrow?
Mariana:	¡A pie!	2 Mariana:	By foot!
Aunts:	[laughter]	3 Aunts:	[laughter]
Elena:	*He kī ki ta'a korohu'a he iri* a pie!	4 E:	*Tell the old man [grandpa] to go up* by foot!

Example 2   Mixed Rapa Nui interactional code showing switches within turns that echo previous discourse. *Italics* = Rapa Nui, underline = Spanish. (Source, Makihara 2005 [modified].)

Attitudes to switching between varieties

In some multilingual communities mixing constituents from one language with another language can be seriously frowned upon. The terms used to describe the mixed utterances are often pejorative or jocular, like *Spanglish* or *Franglais*. Such labels provide another basis for identifying the close association between attitudes to language use and language users which we discussed in more detail in Chapter 4.

In the Tariana community, in north-west Amazonia (Brazil), many languages are in use because of cultural traditions that favour marrying someone from outside your own immediate clan or tribe. So new speakers of neighbouring languages are regularly brought into the Tariana community, and many people grow up with passive or active command of a number of local languages as well as Brazilian Portuguese and some English. But there is surprisingly little mixing of other languages into Tariana. Alexandra Aikhenvald talks about the negative reactions such internal code switching generates on the rare occasions that it happens. For example, a very old man once greeted her with the following (Tariana is in *italics* and Tucano is <u>underlined</u>):

> Example 3   *Pi-nu-nikha*   <u>mahkõ</u>
>   'Have you come   <u>daughter</u>?' (Aikhenvald 2003: 10)

After the old man had left, people explained his slip, saying he was 'not all there any more' (Aikhenvald 2003: 10). Aikhenvald explains that Tariana people have very negative feelings about the insertion of Tucano into Tariana, but that attitudes about sentence internal switches (like in 3) involving other languages are seen in somewhat different ways.

For example, people seem to feel that using Baniwa (also spoken nearby) in a Tariana sentence is kind of funny rather than being just 'wrong' (as use of Tucano is). She explains this in terms of the relative vitality of the languages concerned. Tucano is spreading rapidly in the region as a *lingua franca* (these are discussed further in Chapter 11); that is, more and more people are using it to communicate when they don't share a native language, and it is the only language in the region with any significant growth in overall numbers of speakers. Baniwa, on the other hand, is still only spoken within the traditional Baniwa villages. So Tucano is policed because it is a threat to Tariana. Baniwa is not a threat and so the occasional use of it in Tariana discourse is seen as amusing more than anything else.

exercise

Borrowing or co-opting?

What do you think when someone borrows extensively from languages or styles that they don't (as it were) 'natively' command? For example, if an English speaker uses words like *hombre* or *mucho* in a predominantly English sentence? Do you feel the same way about borrowing from non-native languages when it occurs in, for example, the media personalities adopted by someone like Sasha Baron-Cohen (for instance, his personas Ali G and Borat Sagdiyev)?

SPEECH LEVELS AS DIFFERENT CODES

As we saw in Chapter 3 and have seen again here, the person you are talking to may have a considerable effect on your speaking style. In some languages these effects are codified, and there are different **speech levels** that must be used when you are talking to someone of higher or lower status than you. These speech levels are characterised by vocabularies that sometimes differentiate thousands of words. Some of the best-known examples of these kinds of speech levels come from Indonesian languages such as Javanese, which is typical of the languages in Indonesia in distinguishing *low, mid* and *high* speech levels. The structure of a sentence does not change radically according to speech level, but the vocabulary can be entirely replaced.

In Sasak, spoken by about 3 million people on Lombok, an island about 65 km long and 65 km wide in eastern Indonesia, all dialects have three speech levels. Sasak has a traditional (and still strong) caste system: the highest caste are the *mènak* (about 6 per cent of the population), there is a very small second caste called the *prewangse*, a third caste known as *jajarkarang* (about 80–85 per cent of the population), and the lowest caste is the *sepangan* (traditionally the servants of the *mènak*). What caste someone belongs to determines what speech style you should use when you are talking to them. So a *mènak* speaker will use the high style and should also have high forms addressed to him or her (this mark of honour is nowadays also extended to Muslims who have completed the *hajj* – the pilgrimage to Mecca).

Sasak speakers have high conscious awareness of this system, and the styles have specific names. The ordinary or low speech level is called *biase* or *jamaq*. The middle level is called *madie*, and the high level is called *alus* ('smooth, refined'); there is also another style known as *kasar* ('coarse, vulgar'), which will not concern us here.

The differences between *biase/jamaq, madie* and *alus* are illustrated in Table 6.1. This shows how the sentence 'I have already eaten but you have not yet eaten' would be rendered in three speech levels for Sasak.

Speech levels

Replacement of vocabulary with sometimes radically different forms in the different styles associated with different social groups or *castes*.

Table 6.1 Speech levels in Sasak illustrated in the sentence 'I have already eaten but you have not yet eaten'. (N.B. In *alus* the order of 'I' and 'already' are reversed.) (Source, Nothofer 2000: 60.)

Jamaq	*aku*	*uah*	*mangan*	*kamu*	*ndèq man*	*mangan*
Madie	*aku*	*uah*	*mangan*	*side*	*ndèq man*	*bekelór*
Alus	*sampun*	*tiang*	*mangan*	*pelinggih*	*nènten man*	*madaran*
gloss	I	already	eat	you	not yet	eat

No, really?

People on Lombok recognise five different varieties of Sasak. These are identified by a shibboleth. The different pronunciations of 'like this' are generalised as the name for the variety. So people who pronounce 'like this' *menó* are *Menó-Mené*. People who pronounce it *Menu* are *Menu-meni*. And likewise there are the *Ngenó-Ngené*, the *Meriaq-Meriku* and *Kuto-Kuté*. The independent linguistic status of the last one is somewhat disputed, and indeed all five may have more to do with five historical Sasak kingdoms than they do with different linguistic systems.

A *jajarkarang* speaker would use *jamaq* (low level) to another *jajarkarang*, and *madie* (middle) when speaking to or about their father (same caste but where you want to show some respect). *Alus* would typically be used from one *mènak* to another. *Mènak* will insist on use of *alus*, but many *jajarkarang* do not know very many *alus* forms. They therefore adopt various avoidance strategies, such as getting someone else to speak to a *mènak* for them.

Variations in the use of speech levels

It is important to note that the situation with speech levels in Sasak (and other Indonesian languages) is not cast in stone. There are a number of social considerations that temper whether or not the speech styles are used in the idealised manner. A speaker's competence may override what is prescribed as the ideal – not all speakers know all the *alus* vocabulary. Similarly, a speaker's interactional goals can override the ideal.

The speech levels of Javanese, spoken by 75 million people on the most populous island in Indonesia, were described by the anthropologist Clifford Geertz in the 1960s, and Geertz's data and analysis have been widely cited in linguistics texts ever since. But E. Uhlenbeck, a scholar of Javanese, provides a critical evaluation of Geertz's description of the system. Uhlenbeck – taking his lead from Indonesian scholars themselves – shows that in actual practice the way people use these speech levels is tempered by sometimes highly local or immediate needs and goals.

The Javanese low, middle and high levels are (respectively) *ngoko, madya* and *krama*. Uhlenbeck shows that in a popular novel, dialogues between the hero and his sister illustrate nicely the social and psychological complexity governing use of these forms. Early in the book, the sister is pleading with her brother to tell her a secret he is hiding. She uses *krama* (the high forms) as she tries to coax an answer from him. However, shortly afterwards she interrupts him when he says something that she disagrees with. To do this she uses *ngoko* (with a *madya* pronoun). Towards the end of the book, she is trying to persuade her brother to go to his bride, and for this she uses *madya* with some *krama* forms (Uhlenbeck 1970: 454).

---

exercise

Cross-over between speech levels in Sasak

Look at the third column of Table 6.1, the first token of 'eat' in Sasak. Compare this to the last column, and the second token of 'eat'. The first token remains in the 'low' or *jamaq* form. Why do you think a *mènak* would use a low form here instead of the *alus* form *madaran*? (How do the two halves of the sentence differ?)

Uhlenbeck is not trying to dispute the fact that there are different speech levels in Javanese; what he is trying to do is to bring to our attention some of the tricky questions about *how many* speech levels there are, questions which have troubled Indonesian linguists for some time. Perhaps a useful consequence of his work is that the Javanese situation looks a little less exotic to readers unfamilar with languages like these. It makes the fundamental way in which people use the system seem a bit more familiar to those of us who are used to other kinds of register and style-shifting.

CHAPTER SUMMARY

So why do 10-year-olds in Tórshavn switch into English to tease each other? In this chapter we have looked at a number of different ways in which we might understand the relationship between languages or varieties in multilingual communities, and we have seen that the choice of one language rather than another can serve a number of different purposes.

We have seen that language can play a key part in the collective definition of a national identity. Some nations write principles and beliefs about language rights and language use into their Constitution. The fact that some nations do not mention language in their founding documents at all doesn't necessarily mean language is not important to them. On the contrary, it may simply tell us something about what is marked and unmarked or taken for granted.

We also saw that institutional measures like legal protection for a language or for a language's users are only one means of ensuring the vitality of a language. Other social and attitudinal factors, some historical, some economic and some demographic, are all also important in determining the relative and long-term vitality of a variety. Since these factors vary depending on the particular community under investigation, we can't talk about a language (e.g., Brazilian Portuguese) having 'high vitality' or 'low vitality'. It depends where you are when you ask about its vitality. Brazilian Portuguese has very high vitality in Brazil, but in the sometimes quite large immigrant communities of Brazilians in New Jersey it may have relatively low vitality compared to American English – especially among younger speakers. And as we saw, languages can be relatively high in vitality on some measures but not on others. How we might want to weight these disparate factors – or even whether weighting of them is the most appropriate step forward – remains an open question. Nevertheless, some speakers of minority languages that are threatened by languages with higher vitality have found this framework useful for diagnosing where intervention might be best directed.

Prestige, vitality and even the technical term 'diglossia' all capture interesting facts about the way languages in multilingual communities are specialised. But they differ in the extent to which they focus on speakers' creativity, societal rigidity, and the role of the addressee. In the section on code switching we saw that even groups of students who are much the same age and who have much the same fluency in two community languages can see their linguistic choices very differently, some focusing more on whether they are talking to ingroup or outgroup addressees and others focusing more on where they are. Our example from Rangi showed us how the two factors are entwined with each other.

Even other formalised systems of alternating codes, such as the different speech levels or registers used in Sasak and Javanese, involved balancing different, and sometimes competing, norms for how speakers talk about themselves and about others. These addressee effects were more constrained than the ones we looked at in Chapters 3 and 4, but ultimately we are struck by similarities between the kinds of factors that play a role in determining what forms speakers will choose or whether code switching and mixing is considered a mark of a speaker's competence or a sign of their lack of competence.

I can't say for sure what the boys in Tórshavn were doing when they switched into English to say 'nice ass', because I can't get inside their heads, and it was just a chance comment that I overheard. The fact that they made the switch suggests to me something about the relative vitality of Faroese and English – clearly English is felt to be an effective medium for teasing, perhaps drawing attention to the tease, perhaps making the speaker appear more cool and in command of (yet another) language.

I suspect that this example tells us something about the functions of code switching in that community. The evolution of ingroup norms that involve teasing or even coercion

– strengthening ingroup ties by explicitly or implicitly contrasting 'us' and 'them' – will play a part in the next chapters we are moving into. We'll see that just as it is difficult to talk about a single motivation or function for a switch between codes, it is sometimes difficult to say how or why a particular form 'fits' or not.

As we continue to examine the complexity of addressee effects and speakers' attitudes to language, this complexity will become a backdrop for our discussion in later chapters of how differences in the way people talk simultaneously constitute and reflect membership in or identification with social categories like gender, age, and social class or social network.

FURTHER READING

In addition to the references provided in the text of this chapter, you may find the following works helpful:

Haeri (2003) and Joseph (2004) – on language ideology and politics of standard languages.
Mesthrie (2002) and Early (1999) – on the linguistic situation in South Africa and Vanuatu.
Landry and Bourhis (1997) – ethnolinguistic vitality of French in Canada.
Barker *et al.* (2001) – on the English Only movement in the US.
Edwards (1998) – on languages in Canada generally.
Williams (2000) – on Welsh revitalisation.
Makihara (2001) – structural factors in Rapa Nui mixed languages.
Aikhenvald (2002: chapters 8, 9, 11) – on Tariana code-switching norms.
Laver (1981) and Holmes (2001) – more examples of decision trees with sociolinguistic
    variables.

There is a vast literature on code switching and code mixing. Some useful starting points, providing very different perspectives, are: Auer (1998), Myers-Scotton (1993a, 1993b), Poplack (1980), McCormick (2002, with a focus on a South African community), Mahootian and Santorini (1996), Rampton (1995).

CHAPTER 7

Real time and apparent time

> **Key terms in this chapter:**
>
> - **real time**
> - **apparent time**
> - **trend studies**
> - **panel studies**
> - **critical period**
> - **acquiring language**
> - **learning language**
>
> - **generational change**
> - **lifespan change**
> - **age-grading**
> - **stable variable**
> - **linguistic marketplace**
> - **community-wide change**
> - **ageing deficits**

INTRODUCTION

So far we have looked at variation as a phenomenon constrained by:

- space or geographic features (regional variation);
- who the speaker is talking to (addressee effects and accommodation);
- a speaker's expression of style;
- where the speaker is (social domains and diglossia);
- the relationship between speaker and hearer and the social cost of the interaction (politeness).

At this point, we begin to examine some of the factors that are strongly associated with what is called variationist sociolinguistics. In this chapter, we will look at how variation plays an important role in language change. The evidence for this can be seen in what are known as **real time** studies (because they involve comparing the way people talk at one point in time with the way they talk a decade, or a generation, or a hundred years later). We will also see how sociolinguists have found ways of getting around the problem of having limited access to historical records, by looking at changes in **apparent time**. This notion of time is a more abstract one; as we will see it involves abstracting from the way speakers of different ages talk at a single point in time.

In the following chapters we will look at other variables that influence variation (and which often interact with ongoing change in important ways). These include social class (Chapter 8), and social networks (Chapter 9) and gender (Chapter 10). All these factors (age, social class, gender) have played an important role in formulating general principles of variation,

Real time

Augustinian time. The passing of years, hours, minutes and seconds that we measure with calendars and clocks and that we think we understand until we really think about it.

Apparent time

The apparent passage of time is measured by comparing speakers of different ages in a single-speech community at a single time. If younger speakers behave differently from older speakers, it is assumed that change has taken place within the community. The apparent time construct relies on the assumption that speakers only minimally change the way they speak after the *critical period* or in adulthood. A useful method where *real time* data is absent.

and these principles are of interest to us because they sometimes make predictions about the direction and path of language change. By building on what we have learnt about individual style and interpersonal politeness in the preceding chapters, the chapters we are moving into now will deepen our appreciation of what a sociolinguistic perspective on language entails.

STUDYING CHANGE OVER TIME

In *Blade Runner*, director Ridley Scott imagines Los Angeles street scenes in the twenty-first century, where locals talk in a mixture of English, Japanese, Korean, German and Hungarian. Rick Deckard, the movie's central character, responds just as quickly and easily (when he chooses!) to Japanese, English and in a mixed language, Cityspeak, that is characterised by rapid code switching or borrowing (see Chapter 6). Ridley Scott uses this mixed language, with its predominantly Asian base, to tell us how he expects the California social matrix to change in the next hundred years.

No, really?

Blade Runner has a number of publications and websites given over to detailed analysis of themes and events in the story. Cityspeak gets its fair share of attention, with various attempts to transcribe and translate (literally and freely) what is said. You can see it broken down into its constituent parts here: <http://www.brmovie.com/FAQs/BR_FAQ_Language.htm> You'll notice that Scott's fantasy language of the future is still made up of unchanged pieces of twentieth-century languages.

A more radical vision of the way in which language might change in the future is given in Russell Hoban's book *Riddley Walker*. The language used by the eponymous main character is a more radical transformation of the English we speak today than the Cityspeak of *Blade Runner* is. Part of the reason why Hoban's text is comprehensible to us is that he cleverly creates a coherent linguistic system that generalises and regularises non-standard variants we are familiar with from many present-day varieties of English. Hoban's vision also includes differences in the discourse style of our descendants in the future. This means in some places the rhythms of Riddley Walker's speech seem as odd as Shakespeare's rhythms and discourse structures are to us now. Here are some examples from early in the book:

> *I tried to plot the parbeltys of it and program what to do ncx. I knowit we bes put a farness behynt us qwicks we cud . . . Theywd fynd the dead hevvy and for all they knowit him and the kid boath ben jumpt by dogs when he unbart the doar.*
>
> ['I tried to work out the likelihood of it and plan what to do next. I knew we had best put some distance behind us as quick as we could . . . They'd find the dead guard but for all they knew, he and the kid had both been jumped by some dogs when he unbarred the door.']

(Hoban 1980: 75)

Like a gull I seen 1 time with a broakin wing and Dad kilt it. Them yeller eyes staret scareless to the las. They jus happent to be in the gull but they dint care nothing for it.

['Like a gull I saw once with a broken wing and Dad killed it. Those yellow eyes stared fearlessly to the last. They just happened to be in the gull but they didn't care.']

(Hoban 1980: 79)

Projecting variation into the future

In the extracts from *Riddley Walker* given here, you will see that Hoban is sensitive to the variable deletion of final /t/ in consonant clusters – this is a feature of all varieties of present-day English. Our 'next', 'best' and 'last' become *nex, bes* and *las*. You'll also see that he regularises past-tense forms: our 'knew', 'killed' and 'stared' become *knowit, kilt* and *staret*.

Either work from these short extracts, or find some more examples from the original text. Compare words like 'next' and 'last', where the final consonant is simply part of the word (i.e., monomorphemic words), and examples of verbs where the final consonant sound is what marks past tense. Can you identify any rules or principles that seem to underlie Hoban's new form of English?

No, really?

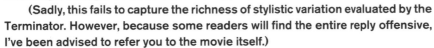

Other movies set in the future or involving travel between time usually ignore the question of language change. In James Cameron's *The Terminator*, the only indication we have that a time-travelling cyborg might have trouble communicating with twentieth-century interlocutors occurs when a cleaner suggests the Terminator should keep the noise down in his room. The cyborg runs through responses in several registers ('No', 'Go away', 'Please come back later'), before selecting a stronger one deemed most appropriate to the situation: 'F*** you!'

(Sadly, this fails to capture the richness of stylistic variation evaluated by the Terminator. However, because some readers will find the entire reply offensive, I've been advised to refer you to the movie itself.)

How language will change in the future and how it will differ from what it is now is a huge question. Understanding language change has been at the heart of variationist sociolinguistics from the start of the field. But one of the reasons why we don't have very clear ideas about how linguistic variation might progress and develop in the future is that we don't have an awful lot of information about how changes have taken place in the past. Our earliest sound recordings only go back as far as people born in the middle of the nineteenth century. The rest of the time we have to make educated guesses about what people used to talk like based on how they wrote and what written records have lasted over the centuries. But if we were to find out enough about the regularity of language changes in progress, and if we could work out some generalisations about how changes work their way through communities of speakers, we could use that information and make informed guesses about the general directions a language might take in the future. (This is essentially what Hoban has done in his book.)

In this chapter, we are going to look at two ways of thinking about linguistic variation over time. Perhaps the obvious way would be to look at variation within communities over a period of many years (even centuries). We'll see in this chapter that we can call this 'real time'. The other way we can look at time will be by means of what is called 'apparent time'. This involves comparing the speech of individuals of different ages at one point in time in a speech community. Both methods have advantages and disadvantages, and we will discuss these in turn.

REAL TIME STUDIES OF CHANGE

In an ideal world, sociolinguists would have access to corpora of recorded conversational data from a wide range of different speech communities, tracking speakers in each one over a long period of real time. Some of the studies we have already looked at draw on real time data – for instance, Rickford and McNair-Knox's (1994) full study of Foxy Boston compared interviews done with Foxy while she was at high school with ones done after she had moved on to university.

But in the real world such real time corpora are rare. In the chapter on social class that follows, we will see that some sociolinguists working with historical data have managed to get around this, and make very good use of what limited information about the speech community is available to them. But occasionally researchers have access to a corpus that is sufficiently detailed that they can use the older data to complement modern data. When this happens, they can turn a synchronic picture of variation (variation at one point in time) into a diachronic picture (change over time).

Researchers at Canterbury University in New Zealand were fortunate enough to find (and purchase) an archive of national radio service interviews done in the 1930s and 1940s with early settlers of New Zealand. Because the speakers were being interviewed about the settlement of the country in the nineteenth century, they told the interviewers a reasonable amount about who they were and where their parents had come from – all information that's important for deciding how it might be appropriate to compare these historical recordings with twenty-first century speakers of New Zealand English (Gordon *et al.* 2004). But many old recorded archives were not collected for social, historical or linguistic purposes, and so this kind of detailed information on the speakers' background is limited or completely missing. Under these circumstances, it is hard, if not impossible, to find an appropriate group of present-day speakers to compare them with.

On the other hand, some corpora are controlled for their genre, or style, so we can be less concerned that we don't know much about the individual speakers. For example, radio and television announcers are usually expected to conform to their station's 'house style', so they will approximate either some regional or social dialect standard for the station (this was especially true in the early years of broadcasting, when people believed that one function of the media was to model appropriate social and linguistic behaviour). Bell's (1991) research on linguistic variation across several stations concluded that individual stations have their own sense of what is standard or appropriate, tailored to the kind of listeners they attract (see Chapter 3). So even though we may not have a lot of information about who individual newsreaders are, where they grew up, or even how old they are, archives of news from a single radio or TV station can give us some idea of how standards have changed over the years.

(Recent changes in attitude to regional accents at the BBC and some major North American broadcasters, such as CNN, will mean that broadcast corpora may provide more challenges for future sociolinguists to interpret.)

When we have data from the same community at two or more periods in time, socio-linguists would say that they have real time data on which to base their comparisons. In the next sections, we look at some examples of real time studies and we will see that variation is crucial to understanding language change. We will then build on this by looking at ways in which language variation can be interpreted as a forecast of changes that may be starting to take place, but which have not yet reached the level of social awareness. (And in the following chapters we will begin to see how variation that marks ongoing change is influenced by a complex mixture of non-linguistic factors.)

Trend studies

The first kind of real time studies we will examine are **trend studies**. A trend study uses data from corpora that include comparable speakers who have been recorded at different points in time. They provide one kind of diachronic perspective on how language varies and changes. They are called 'trend studies' because the real time lag between the first set of data and later sets of data allows you to observe how trends progress through a community.

Figure 7.1 shows the results of a real time study looking at the devoicing of fricatives Northern Standard Dutch (NSD) and Southern Standard Dutch (SSD) in radio broadcasts

Trend studies

A trend study involves comparing speech from members of the same community at different points in time. (See also *Panel studies; Real time.*)

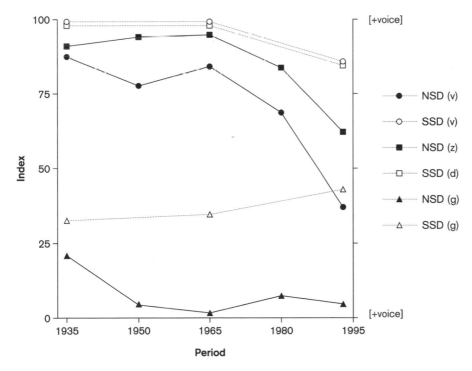

Figure 7.1   Increase in devoicing of final (z) and (v) over real time in corpora from Dutch radio broadcasts. (Source, Van der Velde *et al.* 1996: 165.)

recorded in 1935 through to 1995. As you can see, there is a steady, monotonic increase in devoicing of (v) and (z) during this period. By 1995, the norm for NSD radio announcers clearly favours the innovative devoiced variant.

With concerted effort, a good deal of planning and the support of funding agencies, it is possible to compile a real time corpus of more conversational speech as well. This is valuable, because as we saw in Chapter 3, different styles or genres of speech provide different perspectives on community norms. So if our real time data is restricted solely to relatively formal-speaking styles (like newsreading) we may miss something.

Connections with theory

Some sociolinguists think that researchers have overemphasised the importance of speakers' everyday, most casual speech. They argue that, among other things, this creates a cult of 'authenticity' where speakers using the most non-standard forms are seen as the 'real' speakers of a vernacular variety. (These issues are discussed in Schilling-Estes (1998a) and a special issue of the *Journal of Sociolinguistics* in 2003.) Nonetheless, they still agree on the fundamental integrity of spoken, spontaneous discourse as a source of data. Sociolinguists and functional linguists share a respect for discourse-based data (though they differ radically in how they understand variation in such a discourse-based system). Most formal linguists and psycholinguists, on the other hand, consider discourse-based data to be less than informative, as it is uncontrolled and subject to gaps.

Connections with theory

We can also use historical sources to track some kinds of sociolinguistic variation. Written historical sources are usually best suited to studying syntactic change, but Trousdale (2005) looks at how we can use data in very old texts to explore variability in pronunciation.

Panel studies

Studies of variation across *real time* when the participants are held constant (cf. *Trend studies*.)

In addition to trend studies, there are two other ways of looking at variation and change over time. You can constrain a real time study so that it compares data from exactly the same speakers over a period of years. Corpora like these are even more uncommon than real time trend studies because they require painstaking work tracking down the same people over a period of time. They are called **panel studies** because they involve sampling and resampling a single panel or group of speakers. The other way of exploring how variation is related to change over time is by comparing the speech of speakers of different ages within a community at a single point in time. Sociolinguists call these studies in **apparent time**.

In the next section we find out how the apparent time construct works. But we should not forget about panel studies, because we will return to them later and we'll see how well they support the inferences sociolinguists make using the apparent time methodology.

APPARENT TIME STUDIES OF CHANGE

Apparent time studies of variation and change involve sampling speakers of different ages and comparing the frequency of a variant in the speech of successive generations. Apparent time is a way of simulating and modelling real time change using synchronic data, when the diachronic corpora we discussed in the previous section are not available to researchers or when researchers do not have the time or money to construct their own real time corpus.

However, by drawing on insights from other fields of linguistics, sociolinguists can use synchronic patterns of variation as a window on what has been happening in a community over the last few generations. One such insight that is very important is the notion of a **critical period** for language acquisition.

Why is the critical period important? If you were lucky enough to learn a second or third language when you were a small child, you probably found it relatively easy. In fact, it may have been so easy and natural that you can't even remember the process of acquiring it. If you have tried learning a language since you were in your teens, you will have found the whole experience a lot more like hard work. Lenneberg (1967) noted how widespread this phenomenon is, and suggested that humans have a critical period during which they are primed and ready to acquire language(s). After this critical period, though, acquisition seems to get harder and it may be impossible for an adult to learn a language to a native-like standard after the critical period, even if they are immersed in a community speaking a new language. Even an accomplished learner will be given away by subtle differences in their pronunciation or how they use the grammar (White and Genesee 1996).

These basic generalisations have been well known for a long time (and not just to linguists). Recent advances in the study of language acquisition and cognitive neuroscience indicate that there may be a solid physiological component to them (one which some individuals can, nonetheless, override).

Critical period

The period during which language learning seems to be easiest; that is, in childhood and for some people going into early adolescence. Exposure to language outside the critical period usually results in less than native-like acquisition. Some researchers believe the critical period is an artefact of (i) developmental changes in the brain, or (ii) changes in the receptiveness or attitudes of language learners, or (iii) a mixture of physiological and social factors.

Connections with theory

People who study multilingualism in individuals distinguish between **acquiring** a language – that is, the relatively effortless and subconscious process typical of young children – and **learning** a language – the more conscious process associated with adults. Lenneberg's hypothesis, and subsequent psycholinguistic work, suggests that there may be a biological basis to the critical period.

Obviously there are also differences between how the average adult thinks about her or himself in relation to language and how small children do, and these non-biological, attitudinal factors may also play a part in making it more difficult to learn a language to native-like levels after the critical period.

The assumption, therefore, is that the linguistic system we acquire on the basis of linguistic input in childhood is qualitatively different from any other system that a person might be exposed to later in their life. Their 'native' system, for want of a better word, will be more stable and less readily altered by subsequent input than a system learnt later in life is.

Acquiring (language)

It is sometimes useful to distinguish between the natural acquisition of a language variety (e.g., a mother tongue) and learning of a language variety (e.g., in the classroom).

Learning (language)

See *Acquiring (language)*.

Sociolinguists have found that they can use this principle to their advantage. When they believe there are changes taking place in a group of speakers, but they don't have real time, longitudinal studies of that speech community, sociolinguists have adopted the practice of examining variation in speakers of different ages. Then they can compare the relative frequency of different variants in the speech of people who were born at different times.

The idea is that, because the basics of a speaker's phonological system have been laid down in their youth, when we listen to speakers who are 75 years old today we get an idea about what the community norms were when they were children (70 years ago). Similarly, when we listen to speakers who are 45 years old today, we get an idea about what the community norms were when they were children (40 years ago). And so on. In this way, sociolinguists model the passage of time. (Of course, because this is only a model of time, it is especially helpful to test it against real time data when possible. We will return to this shortly when we look more closely at some panel studies.)

By simulating the apparent passage of time like this, sociolinguists are able to make informed comments about the rate and directions of change in a speech community. This is very helpful to them no matter what their larger goals are as sociolinguists. Those who see social dialectology as a branch of historical linguistics naturally value the detail that apparent time studies can offer them by showing intra-individual as well as inter-individual variation. Some sociolinguists, of course, are more interested in the dynamics of face-to-face interaction and they want to understand how speakers use language (among other social resources) to align or differentiate themselves from others. But even if a linguist is principally interested in language as a tool in personal identity formation, it is still very informative to know either where the linguistic resources that speakers are using come from, or how the linguistic resources speakers use to signal personal identities can feed patterns of change across the whole community over time. So apparent time is a tremendously important concept for sociolinguistics.

We will get a better idea of how the apparent time construct works in practice if we consider studies of a variable in English and in Spanish. The first one involves non-standard verb forms in Yorkshire English and the second involves non-canonical verbs for reporting speech and thought in Puerto Rican Spanish.

During the 1990s, Sali Tagliamonte gathered a very large corpus of conversational speech in Yorkshire (north England). Although there are some almost universal changes taking place in British English (such as the spread of the glottal stop in place of oral stops, which will be discussed further in Chapter 10), non-standard regional varieties are still alive and well. What seems to be happening is that speakers are making room for some of the supra-regional changes that are taking place and accommodating them within their own vernacular. For sociolinguists, it is very interesting to see how people accommodate new variants into their vernacular. In Britain, this can be especially interesting because there is competition and tension between:

(i)   supra-local, non-standard variants (like the glottal and *th*-fronting),
(ii) local vernacular variants, and
(iii) the supra-local prestige forms of Standard English.

There are a several methods for understanding how these tensions get worked out within a particular variety. One method that can be used is to examine closely the speech of a small group of speakers and interpret intraspeaker, as well as interspeaker, variation in light of the individuals' life histories and their current goals and activities (see the discussion of communities of practice in Chapter 9).

While such particular studies are useful, at some point we need to get a picture of how such local, ingroup tensions get transformed into larger-scale patterns of community-wide change. Larger social dialect studies provide us with a different lens through which we can look at such changes, and Tagliamonte's corpus provides us with this sort of perspective.

One of the traditional vernacular variables that she looked at in Yorkshire English was the non-standard use of *was* (in existential sentences, as in 1a–b) and *were* (in negative tag questions, affirmative declarative sentences and negative sentences, as shown in 2a–c) (from Tagliamonte 1998):

(1) a. There *was* these concerts.
     b. There *was* no roads.   [expect *were* in Standard English]

(2) a. Bit before our time, *weren't* it?
     b. Everything *were* going great.
     c. It *weren't* very satisfactory.   [expect *was* in Standard English]

Tagliamonte used apparent time to infer whether or not these variables were remaining involved in ongoing change in Yorkshire English. So she grouped her sample of informants according to their age. In Figure 7.2 you can see how she grouped her speakers into four age groups to see what the overall trends are. This figure shows that younger female speakers are using non-standard *was* almost 90 per cent of the time, and that among younger men the variant is also on the increase.

In Figure 7.3, Tagliamonte shows the data for non-standard *were* among female speakers only. Although there is little use of the non-standard variant in the affirmative declarative sentences (2b), in negatives and negative tags there appears to be a jump between the 30–50 year age group and the 50–70 year age group. The non-standard variant has increased in the speech of women under 50.

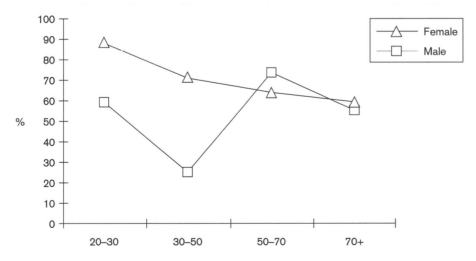

Figure 7.2   Distribution of non-standard was in existential sentences by sex and generation. (Source, Tagliamonte 1998: 182.)

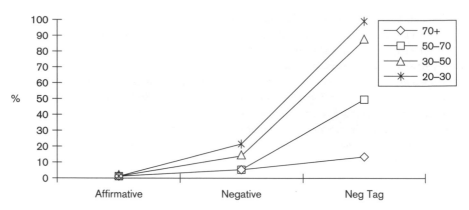

Figure 7.3 Distribution of *were* in standard was contexts: affirmative declarative sentences, negative sentences, negative tag questions. Female speakers only. (Source, Tagliamonte 1998: 179.)

exercise

Two variables or one?

Look at the data for female speakers only in Figure 7.2 and compare them to the data for women in Figure 7.3. They seem to show two changes in progress – non-standard *was* (shown in Figure 7.2) and non-standard *were* (shown in Figure 7.3).

Do you think these are related changes in progress or do you think they are moving through the community independently of each other? Why (not)?

Richard Cameron (1998) also used apparent time data to explore variable use of verbs of quotation in Puerto Rican Spanish. These are verbs used to introduce reported speech (or thought), like *say* in English. As in English, where there are several common options for introducing reported speech (*so she says . . ., so she goes . . .* and *so she's like/all . . .*), speakers of Puerto Rican Spanish have several strategies for introducing direct reports of speech or thought. Cameron found the following variants:

(i)   canonical verbs of direct report (e.g., *decir* 'say', *pensar* 'think');
(ii) a speaker-centred form, i.e., the speaker is introduced with no verb of report, *y Maria ". . ."* 'and Maria ["says" understood] ". . ."'; and
(iii) a freestanding quote with no speaker or verb to introduce it (this option is also very frequent in English, as we will see in Chapter 11).

Because Cameron was looking at a variable where there were more than two variants, the way he measures the distribution of each variant is slightly different from the ways we have looked at up until now. The previous studies we have looked at have had two variants – e.g., presence vs absence of (r). For these, we can talk about the frequency or the likelihood with which we will find one or other variant in a particular style pretty intuitively. Contexts where we are more likely to find the innovative variant are shown as being over 50 per cent of the tokens. Or where we want to be more precise, we have talked about the probability of finding a form in that context as being over 0.5 (you can think of probabilities as weighted percentages, if you like). On the other hand, contexts where the innovative variant is not favoured have a probability of less than 0.5.

However, Cameron's study is examining the distribution of three variants, so the cut between favouring and disfavouring falls at 0.33 (rather than 0.5). A probability below 0.33 indicates that the variant is not favoured among those speakers; probabilities over 0.33 indicate it is favoured; and a probability of 0.33 essentially says that this group of speakers neither particularly favour nor particularly disfavour the variant.

In Figure 7.4 we see the results for the three variables – canonical verbs, the speaker-centred variant and freestanding quotes – plotted for four different age groups of speakers: pre-teens, teens, 20–39-year-olds and over 40-year-olds. This apparent time data clearly suggests that the variation in Puerto Rican Spanish reflects an ongoing change. The canonical verbs of reported speech are favoured by speakers who are more than 20 years old, while both the other variants are favoured by pre-teen and teenage speakers. In particular, the speaker-centred variant *y Maria ". . ."* is favoured by younger speakers. In fact, the line for freestanding quotes hovers pretty close to 0.3 for all age groups (i.e., neutral weighting for a three-way competition between variants), and that seems to suggest that whatever constrains the use of this variant, it is not really dependent on the speaker's age. So the apparent shift away from the canonical verbs must really be towards the *y NP* variant.

Finally, consider the way apparent time informs us about final vowel epenthesis in Faetar, a Franco-Provençal dialect spoken in an isolated village in southern Italy. Work by Naomi Nagy found that Faetar speakers might say *kutteje* or *kuttej* for 'knife'. The form without the final vowel, *kuttej*, maintains the older Franco-Provençal pattern, while the form with the final vowel, *kutteje*, seems to reflect the increasing influence of Italian (which prefers CVCV syllable structure). She found that the frequency of these forms in different age groups was quite informative (see Figure 7.6). This figure shows the increasing use of the vowel-final forms in apparent time – young speakers use more of the Italian-like forms with a final vowel, and older speakers use more of the consonant-final forms. This was typical of the pattern found across a number of lexical items.

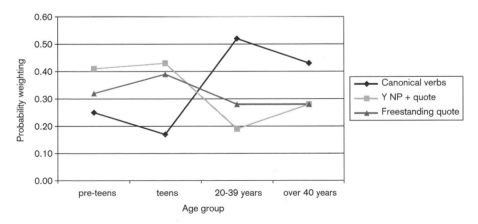

Figure 7.4   Reported discourse strategies in Puerto Rican Spanish, broken down into four age groups. (Source, Cameron 1998: 70.)

exercise

Puerto Rican reported discourse

Cameron also breaks down the variation in use of these strategies for reporting discourse according to speakers' sex. The results for female speakers are shown in Figure 7.5.

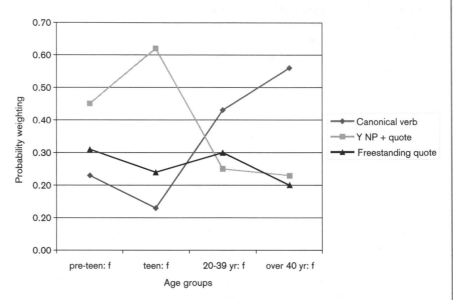

Figure 7.5 Apparent time data on strategies used to report discourse in Puerto Rican Spanish, females only. (Source, Cameron 1998: 73.)

What extra information does the apparent time data for women and girls give you? Does it support the idea that there is a change taking place away from canonical verbs to *y NP* variants?

REAL TIME TESTS OF THE APPARENT TIME CONSTRUCT

Traditionally, the apparent time method has been used as a way for linguists to obtain a quick check on the kind of longitudinal data that they don't always have access to. In Labov's study of Martha's Vineyard (Chapter 2), he combined apparent time data with the patterns that had been noted in earlier dialect atlas surveys. This earlier data gave him a real time perspective on the variable he was studying, but since the earlier dialect surveys had not considered the relative frequency of different forms in individuals' speech, there were limits on the extent to which his apparent time data could be compared with the dialect survey's real time information. Nevertheless, he was able to use the apparent time information to infer that the general trends were for younger Vineyarders to centralise the onsets of (ay) and (aw) more, especially if they did not have negative feelings about the island.

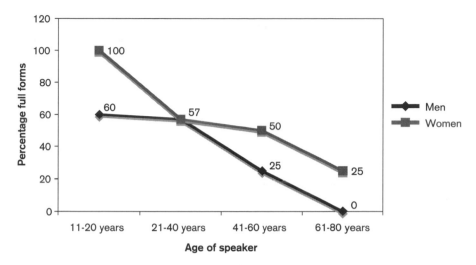

Figure 7.6   Frequency of vowel final variants (*kutteje*) for 'knife' in Faetar. Note increasing use of Italian-
like forms in younger speakers. (Data kindly provided by Naomi Nagy.)

Panel studies of change over time

As the field of sociolinguistics has developed, though, we are starting to see more studies
include a real time component in their methods. A particularly interesting branch of research
has been the studies that have tried to follow the same individuals over a period of real time.
These are called 'panel studies'. They are especially important for empirical and theoretical
reasons because they provide a check on the validity of the apparent time construct. How
stable really is an individual speaker's linguistic system once they are past the critical period?

   One such panel study has involved repeatedly interviewing the same speakers in the
city of Montreal. Researchers now have data from 1971, 1984 and 1995 interviews and can
compare the speakers' behaviour with respect to several phonological, morphological and
lexical variables. We also have similar panel study data from a Swedish town, Eskilstuna, that
retested speakers after thirty years (1967 and 1996), and a recent study looking at a whole
suite of variables in Finnish comparing data gathered in 1986 and 1996.

No, really?

**One of the best-known panel studies is still underway in Britain. Director Michael
Apted has reinterviewed the same people every seven years since they were
7 years old as part of a remarkable set of documentaries known as the *Seven Up*
series (World in Action, Granada Television). The focus is on social development,
but naturally there is a treasure trove of sociolinguistic data in them after so many
years (Sankoff 2004).**

One of the clearest findings emerging from panel studies is that not all linguistic variables behave the same across a speaker's lifespan. As a general rule, a speaker's phonology is more stable than their vocabulary. You will certainly have acquired or learnt new words for concepts and things after the critical period, and we keep acquiring vocabulary throughout our entire lives. In between phonology and lexicon, though, variables behave a bit differently. Some syntactic and morphological variables seem to be treated by speakers as if they were essentially lexical, and so we see the ability for individuals to restructure their systems radically over real time. Some morphological variables seem relatively stable though, and this suggests that speakers understand them as being more like phonological variables.

The Montreal study provides a rare opportunity to get to grips with how the stratification of variables in a community relates to individuals' adoption and maintenance of idiosyncratic patterns of variation (recall from Chapter 3 that stratification refers to the systematic and consistent pattern of a variant with respect to some independent factor – in this case, speaker age).

For many years there has been a gradual shift in Montreal French in how speakers pronounce the trilled or rolled (r). The older Montreal norm was an alveolar variant [r], but this is gradually being replaced with a uvular variant [R] (like the one used in European French). The general trend across the community is clear when you compare the average frequency of the uvular variant at three points in real time – 1971, 1984 and 1995 (see Figure 7.7). This figure shows that the community as a whole is using more of the uvular variant in place of the alveolar one. Like the Dutch radio broadcast corpus, sampling a comparable group of speakers at several points in chronological time shows compellingly how pronunciations have changed.

However, Hélène Blondeau and her colleagues (2003) also examined specific individuals' behaviour over time. They compared the results for the individuals in their study with the inferences a sociolinguist would draw based on the apparent time distribution of

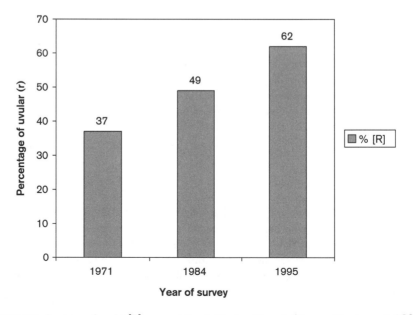

Figure 7.7   Increase of uvular [R] over real time in Montreal French. (Source, Blondeau *et al.* 2003.)

Table 7.1   Mean [R]/([R]+[r]) for Montreal speakers, 1971–1995.

Speaker groups	Number of speakers in 1984*	Mean age in 1971	Mean [R] 1971(%)	Mean [R] 1984(%)	Mean [R] 1995(%)
I	8	23	95	98	100
II	9	34	45	68	70
III	8	27	9	7	3

Note *The base line sample in 1971 was 23 speakers. In 1984, two younger speakers were added and in 1995 only 14 speakers were re-recorded. (Source, Sankoff 2005.)

variants across different age groups. They found that the panel study results largely vindicated the assumptions made using the apparent time method. In general, people remained relatively stable in their use of one variant or another. Not completely stable, but relatively stable, and where there were changes in individuals' speech, they were consistent with the overall direction of the change in the speech community, thus affirming the usefulness of the apparent time method.

Nahkola and Saanilahti (2004) found similar stability in individuals' use of variants over time in a study of Finnish. So far, their panel study has not run as long as Blondeau et al.'s, but it is notable for including data on a very large number of phonological variables.

Let us examine exactly how stable speakers are in their use of the (r) variable in Montreal French. Table 7.1 shows that the Montreal speakers fell into three groups. Two groups, comprising 16 speakers in the panel study, are remarkably stable. Half of these speakers (Group I) were those who started out in 1971 as users of the newer variant [R] – and they have remained users of [R]. The other half (Group III) were those who started out as users of the older alveolar variant [r] – and they have remained users of [r].

But nine speakers fell in between these groups. These were speakers who started out using the innovative uvular [R] a little less than half the time and in the following quarter century increased their use of the uvular variant to a little less than three-quarters of the time. For seven of these nine speakers, the increases were statistically significant (for two they were not, so their behaviour is actually as stable as the speakers in Groups I and III). As Gillian Sankoff notes, it is hard to link the behaviour of these seven individuals up with developmental factors: 'one was a teenager, three were in their twenties, two were in their forties and one was in his early fifties!' (2005).

Nahkola and Saanilahti (2004) also suggest that if there is likely to be any adjustment in a speaker's behaviour, age of the speaker is less important than the nature of the variable. They suggest that if your input when acquiring a variable is characterised by a lot of variability (e.g., roughly half of the tokens you hear are one variant and roughly half are a second variant), then it is more likely you will change the frequency with which you use the competing variants during your life. If, on the other hand, there is relatively little variation in your input as a child, they suggest you will be more likely to remain stable across the lifespan.

Do the seven speakers in Group II who have significantly changed their use of [R] challenge or contradict the assumptions underlying the apparent time method? Not in the slightest. The majority of the speakers in the Montreal study (18 out of 25) have remained extremely stable in their use of [R]. Only seven have changed at all. And, crucially, their shift has been in the same direction as the community is shifting overall (as shown in Figure 7.7). In other words, the Montreal panel study shows that the apparent time method is by and large

Connections with theory

Nahkola and Saanilahti (2004) suggest that variables which were acquired with little variation will remain stable across the lifespan, but that individuals may alter the frequency with which they use variants that are acquired with a high degree of variability. They go on to suggest that variables acquired with a lot of variation might be responsible for the typical S-shaped curve associated with linguistic change. That is, individuals pass through a 'phase of maximal variation' quickly, and the cumulative effect of this is the S-shaped curve well known to historical linguists.

a very good method for inferring directions and speed of language change in a community. The seven unusual speakers show that inferences drawn from apparent time may *under-estimate the speed* of a change, but not the direction.

In other work (Blondeau *et al.* 2003), Sankoff and her collaborators have explored in more detail how an individual's personal life history might be having an impact on their participation in and orientation to ongoing community-wide change. This, of course, opens the door for researchers to turn common sociolinguistic modes of enquiry on their head. Instead of asking, 'How can we explain why these individuals are behaving differently from the group?', we can start to ask, 'How can we explain why group behaviours have the meaning they do, if we must necessarily understand them through individuals' behaviours?' This invites a broader critique of what 'innovative' and 'conservative' mean, perhaps leading us to think about them in a wider social sense rather than in a strictly chronological sense.

Martha's Vineyard revisited

In 2002, a couple of attempts were made to replicate Labov's now classic study of Martha's Vineyard and to see what has happened there in the 40 years since it was first studied. One researcher, Jenny Pope, set out to replicate Labov's study as closely as possible. She hoped that by using the same or similar sociolinguistic tasks (recording a reading passage, word lists and conversational speech) her results would provide real time data that was maximally comparable with Labov's. To further improve the comparability of her results with Labov's, she also grouped speakers according to the year they were born.

As in the Montreal study, Pope's results provide broad support for the practice of drawing inferences about change in progress from the distribution of variants in speakers of different age groups. Where her results diverged from the apparent time predictions, this was consistent with the findings from the Montreal study of (r). That is, where Pope's results differed from Labov's, they suggest that inferences about change in progress that are drawn on the basis of apparent time data underestimates the rate of a change but in no way challenge the basic inference about the nature of the change in progress. (Note that Pope's study is a real time trend study, and not a real time panel study like the Montreal data.)

Figure 7.8 shows the results for centralisation of (ay) and (aw) on Martha's Vineyard in Labov's and Pope's studies. In order to see both samples on one graph, speakers are represented according to their year of birth along the x-axis (bottom axis). This models the passage of time for the whole community.

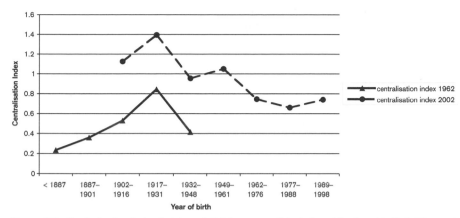

Figure 7.8 Centralisation index (raising of diphthong onset) in (ay) and (aw) on Martha's Vineyard comparing community recordings in 1962 and 2002. (Sources, Labov 1972a; Pope 2003.)

Following Labov's original work, the higher the centralisation index, the more raised the onset of the diphthongs (ay) and (aw). The peak and fall of overall centralisation in 2002 is absolutely consistent with the peak and fall documented in 1962. (Remember from Chapter 2 that Labov found evidence from regional dialect surveys indicating that centralisation of (ay) and (aw) has gone in waves on Martha's Vineyard for more than a hundred years. Pope's results confirm this.)

However, it is equally clear that Pope's results differ from Labov's in the overall rate of centralisation. The index in her study is consistently higher than it was in Labov's, even when we consider the cohorts of speakers who were recorded in both studies (those born between 1902 and 1948). Figure 7.9 shows that this is very largely due to a dramatic increase in centralisation of the (aw) variable (the MOUTH set of words), and much less so due to an increase in the centralisation of the (ay) variable (the PRICE set of words).

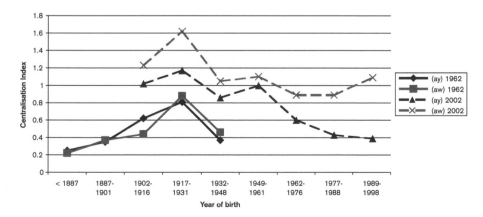

Figure 7.9 Different degree of (ay) and (aw) centralisation on Martha's Vineyard over time (1962 and 2002 compared). Note increased centralisation of (aw) and decrease in (ay) centralisation in post-1962 speakers. (Sources, Labov 1972a; Pope 2003.)

We'll return to Pope's finding that (aw) and (ay) are developing differently on Martha's Vineyard towards the end of the chapter because they will illuminate one of the problems associated with conducting and interpreting the results of real time studies.

PROFILES OF CHANGE

Let us use the data we have looked at so far to take stock of the possible ways in which variation and time intersect. Table 7.2 shows the five possibilities for change in an individual speaker's behaviour over time, and change in a community of speakers over time. It also indicates how we would interpret each possible combination and gives the kind of pattern associated with such a relationship in a graph: whether it would be trending consistently up, down, or not changing at all. The three central rows are the ones we are most concerned with in this chapter, and their crucial points of similarity and difference are shown in bold.

Rows 2–4 are variables where there is a steady increase or decrease in a particular variant over time. When time is measured on an individual scale, this means we are talking about an individual changing the way they speak during their lifetime. Where time is measured over more than the average lifespan, we are talking about change in the norms of a community.

The discussion of the shift from [r] to [R] in Montreal French illustrated the **generational change** (row 4) that occurs when each new generation of speakers gradually uses more and more of the innovative variant. This accounts for the overall increase in use of [R] from 1971 to 1994 that we saw in Figure 7.7.

Closer examination of the Montreal data also revealed a related phenomenon which only some members of the speech community exemplify. This is **lifespan change** (row 3), when an individual changes their own speech after the critical period, but in a manner that is consistent with the gradual change taking place in the community as a whole.

The real time study of Martha's Vineyard also linked generational change with lifespan change, showing a gradual increase in the community's use of centralised onsets for PRICE and MOUTH words up to the 1930s, and then a decrease in centralisation (especially of (ay)) after that. The comparison between Labov's and Pope's data showed a boost in frequency

Generational change

Each generation in a community shows progressively more and more frequent use of a *variant*. A change that can be inferred to be taking place on the basis of *apparent time* evidence is a generational change.

Lifespan change

A term introduced to the study of language variation and change by Gillian Sankoff. A change to a speaker's pronunciation or grammar that take place after the *critical period* can be described as a lifespan change. Lifespan changes in pronunciation appear to be severely restricted in their form: they generally only move in the direction of the community overall (see also *generational change*) and they may also be *constrained* to certain input or starting points for a speaker. On the other hand, lifespan change is well-attested for vocabulary.

Table 7.2   Relationship between variation and change in the individual and the community. (Sources, Labov 1994: 83; Sankoff, 2005.)

	Type of change	Individual	Community	Synchronic pattern
1	Stability – no change	Invariant	Invariant	Flat, no slope with age
2	Age-grading	**Changes abruptly**	Invariant	Steady increase/decrease with age
3	Lifespan change	**Changes abruptly**	**Changes gradually**	Steady increase/decrease with age
4	Generational change (change over 'apparent time')	Invariant	**Changes gradually**	Steady increase/decrease with age
5	Community-wide change	Changes abruptly	Changes abruptly	Flat, no slope with age

rates consistent with some (or all) speakers born between 1902 and 1948 increasing their use of the innovative variants over their lifetime in a direction that is consistent with the communal change.

The second row of Table 7.2 shows one other possible relationship between variation and change, which we have not yet considered. This also involves changes over an individual's lifetime, but in this case it is not associated with communal change. It is therefore called **age-grading**, a term which emphasises that the variation is associated with individuals of different age groups.

Age-graded variation

The individual change and communal stability that is associated with age-grading defines a **stable variable**, that is, where there is no ongoing shift towards or away from one variant or another. Until now, this chapter has only looked at cases where variants show change over real or apparent time. However, not all variation involves change in progress (we already looked at some macro-level variation that is very stable – e.g., diglossia in Chapter 6 – and in the next chapter we will see some more examples of stable variation).

If you look back to the discussion of apparent time studies you will notice that Tagliamonte and Cameron both present their findings in four age bands. Variationists like to see multiple points plotted on an age axis for several reasons. One reason is that it provides more convincing evidence for the claim that there is a steady, monotonic increase or decrease in a variant over time.

It is important to establish this because with stable variables, speakers increase and then subsequently retreat from a variant during their lifetime. With stable variables, the different variants realising the variable maintain their social significance within the speech community, and the variable's role as a signifier of social meaning is recreated by each new generation. The (ing) variable, which we look at in more detail in the next chapter, is a very good example of this in English. The variation between [ɪn] and [ɪŋ] has existed in English for centuries now, and even though [ɪŋ] is considered the 'better' or more standard variant, [ɪn] has proved to be a remarkably resilient alternative. The same is also true for the use of a stop [t] or [d] instead of a fricative [θ] or [ð] in words like *tooth* or *this* in some varieties of English. Both sets of variants are very robust and the stops show no signs of edging out the fricatives completely (or vice versa).

The linguistic marketplace

An early and highly influential paper by the sociolinguists David Sankoff and Suzanne Laberge took the notion of the **linguistic marketplace** from the work of the French sociologist Pierre Bourdieu and introduced it to sociolinguistics as a means for understanding these kinds of variables. Sankoff and Laberge noticed that there is often a peak in use of the standard variant in people as they reach their early twenties, and then a subsequent decline in the frequency of that same variant among speakers in later middle age. So if you came back to that community and restudied the sample variable over three successive generations – i.e., conducted a real time trend study – you would end up with a pattern like that in Figure 7.10. Figure 7.10 doesn't represent an actual real world variable, it just schematises the general pattern of age-graded variation.

Age-grading

If, as a rule, all speakers of a community use more tokens of one variant at a certain age and more tokens of another variant at another age, the variable is said to be age-graded.

Stable variable

If there is no evidence (e.g., from *generational change*) that one variant is pushing out another variant, the variable can be considered stable. A classic example is the alternation between the alveolar and velar nasals in the word-final *-ing* which has existed for centuries and shows no signs of disappearing at present. Stable variables may exhibit *age-grading* (i.e., avoidance of a stigmatised variant in adulthood).

Linguistic marketplace

A way of talking about the extent to which an occupation or activity is associated with use of the standard language.

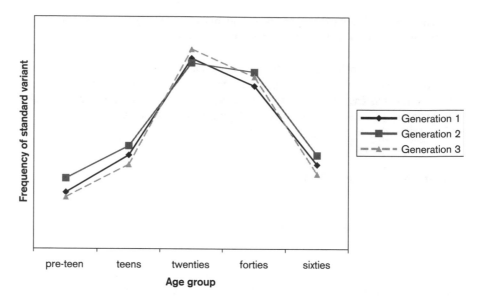

Figure 7.10   A hypothetical age-graded variable, showing pattern across four age groups and three generations in a speech community. Note increased use of the standard at about the same time in each generation and the subsequent retreat.

But now look at what happens if you were to group exactly the same information into only two age groups, either of which might make sense – say, teens and pre-teens vs adults; or people 20 years old and younger vs people 40 and over. In one case, the aggregation results in something that resembles a change in progress; in the other case, the aggregation results in a pattern that suggests there is no change (in individuals or the community). This is shown in Figures 7.11 and 7.12 using the same hypothetical data set as in Figure 7.10.

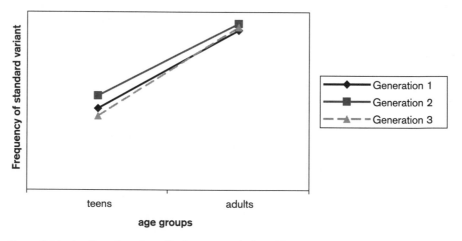

Figure 7.11   An alternative schematic of an age-graded variable where only two age groups are shown. Note the apparently monotonic relationship between frequency of the standard and age of speaker; this would suggest communal change in progress.

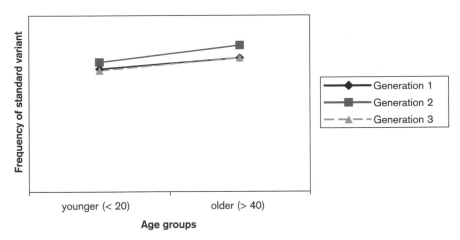

Figure 7.12   Another alternative schematic of an age-graded variable where only two age groups are shown. Note the apparently monotonic relationship between frequency of the standard and age of speaker here would suggest neither change in community nor individuals.

Even though Figures 7.11 and 7.12 are both based on the same information as Figure 7.10, they mislead us because of their oversimplification. Cutting up the data into more than two age groups demonstrates that there is change in individuals but no change in the community.

Theoretically, it is possible for an age-graded variable to show a steady increase in the use of one variant across all points in the lifespan over successive generations. But it is more typical to find some form of peak and retreat as in Figure 7.10, and it is typical for this to occur with speakers in their teens or early twenties. Of course, with a real stable variable the overall peak and retreat may be less marked than in this stylised representation.

Sankoff and Laberge wondered what might account for an increase in standard variants at this time and they drew their answer from Bourdieu's analysis of the dynamics of social power. Bourdieu had talked about the centralisation of power in the (upper) middle class, and had linked the middle class's control over a number of different kinds of 'capital' to explain this. He observed that control of material wealth was one means of exercising social control, but he also argued that control of more evanescent resources, such as language, is also important.

Bourdieu argued that the middle class not only decide what are appropriate and inappropriate modes of discourse, but that they also guard the status of their particular social dialect, ensuring it retains overt prestige in the speech community. In this way, the language itself acquires symbolic power. Moreover, because it appears to have this power by virtue of some immanent social force, it allows the middle class to gate keep access to other resources of power. So you can't get a job as a banker unless you can talk the way a banker is supposed to talk, and you won't talk like a banker is supposed to talk unless you've grown up in a part of the speech community that is made up of bankers and people like them. Catch-22. If language can function as a form of capital, we can talk about there being a linguistic marketplace where certain ways of talking are more valuable 'coin' or have greater social capital than others.

Sankoff and Laberge pointed out that in their late teens and early twenties people start to become more involved in the broader linguistic marketplace through their participation in the workforce. For many jobs, it is expected that the holder will be able to use standard language norms and/or show a command of relatively formal styles when appropriate. The influence of the standard language market will be seen even among people whose jobs do not place a high value on use of the standard. This is because, during our working years, we are all much more likely to come into contact with people who are thoroughly integrated in the standard language market, even if we aren't ourselves. So an increase in use of standard forms among speakers in their late teens or early twenties might result from speakers' increased involvement in the domains where standard language is (a) expected and (b) rewarded most directly. This explanation can then be extended to any subsequent retreat from the standard when speakers become older. As people's intimate involvement with the standard language market becomes attenuated, they can revert to the non-standard forms.

Connections with theory

A similar see-sawing pattern is also found in the frequency with which migrants use their home language and the language of their host country. So you might start out speaking Cantonese all the time with your family at home. But when you get to school, you might start to use English more frequently. Then when you start working, your daily interactions might be overwhelmingly in English. But as you get older, you may find yourself seeing more of the people you grew up with, and when you talk to them you might well revert to Cantonese, the first language and ingroup code which you all share.

The connections with Bourdieu's analysis of symbolic power are also helpful in understanding how stable variables can persist as they do, and what we meant when we said that their meaning is recreated anew by successive generations. Once certain groups of speakers have control over the variants that are most valuable in the linguistic marketplace, they will expend a certain amount of effort in making sure that this resource remains valuable (think of the way a cartel, like the diamond cartel, restricts access to diamonds to keep their value high). So it follows that stable variables:

- have often been in existence for a long time, and
- are often above the level of conscious awareness.

As mentioned above, a classic example in English is the alternation between [ɪn] and [ɪŋ]. Houston (1985) provides an extremely comprehensive survey of the history of this variable, and even though some speech communities are characterised by higher rates of the alveolar variant overall than others are, there is at present no indication that either the alveolar or the velar variant is going to push out the other completely. For a typical pattern for the (ing) variable, see Figure 7.13. It shows the retreat away from the alveolar variants in the middle age group (speakers in their forties), in particular in the speech of middle-class women (I have not broken down the data for the working-class speakers by speaker sex because the percentages for working-class women and men are not transparent in the source document). The middle-class women also show increased use of the less formal

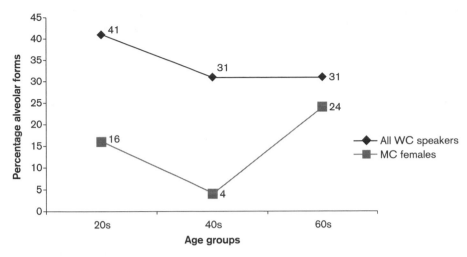

Figure 7.13   Frequency of alveolar [ɪn] in the interview speech of working-class (WC) and middle-class (MC) women in Porirua, New Zealand. (Source, Holmes *et al.* 1991: 59–60.)

variant in the 60-year age group, at the time when their involvement in the standard language marketplace would, in most cases, be waning.

It is also possible to have an age-graded pattern that shows a peak in use of a non-standard variable in the teens and pre-teens with a retreat away from the non-standard in adulthood. You might say that use of slang or non-standard vocabulary shows this kind of age-grading (though the vocabulary items differ from one generation of slang users to the next).

Connections with theory

Some generational changes also feature a small peak among teenage speakers. Like the peak associated with stable variables, it is assumed that the peak found with changes in progress reflects the sensitivity of that group of speakers to the symbolic meaning of the incoming variant and (in this case) the social cache attached to being a leader of a change. A discussion of the complex manner in which generational change and age-grading may combine in a change in progress is not possible here, but there are good discussions of this in Chambers (2003) and Labov (1994).

Community-wide change

Finally, we consider the possible relationship between variation and change that is shown in the bottom row of Table 7.2. Where everyone in a community changes the way they speak at pretty much the same time, we can speak of **community-wide change**.

One example of community-wide change would be a case of a linguistic taboo. For example, when a respected leader dies, some communities will avoid terms of reference that

Community-wide change

An entire group or community switch to use of a new *variant* at about the same time.

made up part of his or her name. Another term, perhaps co-opted from elsewhere in the lexicon or even borrowed from a neighbouring language, will be used to refer to things originally denoted by that person's name. So, if the deceased's name was *Rose*, the community as a whole, as a token of their respect, would no longer use the word *rose* to refer to the flower. They might extend the word *daisy* to do the work *rose* used to do, or they might borrow a word from somewhere else.

These kinds of community shifts are not just restricted to vocabulary. Sankoff (2005) reviews several cases where structural variables seem to have been subject to community-wide shifts, with all individuals adopting a new variant at roughly the same time.

No, really?

Apolonia Tamata (2004) discusses an interesting case of taboo-related language change in Fiji. In the village she looked at, there is an expectation that the community will avoid using a high-ranking person's language completely when they die. But because this is very onerous and communicatively disruptive, the community decides who will undertake the change on behalf of everyone else. Tamata discusses how the village decided which speakers – all women, as it happens – would bear the symbolic duty of language shift on behalf of the entire community.

Connections with theory

Community-wide shifts can present special problems for historical linguists trying to determine the historical relationships between languages and establish language families. The process of building up sets of cognates and determining shared patterns of change can be disrupted by community-wide changes. If language taboos and such community-wide shifts are factors in the language families they are reconstructing, historical linguists also necessarily become experts in social and historical facts (Simons 1982).

Summary of variation across time

The important features of Table 7.2 that have shaped our discussion of variation over time are:

- the characterisation of change as occurring in an individual or the community;
- the characterisation of change as gradual or abrupt.

This has allowed us to discriminate four types of change: age-grading, lifespan change, generational change, and community change. The nature of lifespan change, and its relationship to generational change, is something that sociolinguists have only recently begun to deal with. It has emerged as an additional possibility only recently, as better corpora have been carefully constructed that resample both the same individuals and the same community over a period of time. Sankoff (2005) suggests that we 'reserve the term "age grading" for those situations in which groups of speakers . . . find it appropriate to employ a particular pattern (say, . . . higher values of [an often stable] prestige variant) among young adults as they enter the labor market . . . [Where] individual speakers change over their lifespan in the direction of a change in progress in the rest of the community, I propose we dub these cases of "lifespan change"'.

The relationship between these forms of lifespan change and the kind of developmental change we all pass through in acquiring the constraints on variation in our first language is still an open question, and we can be sure that some of the more interesting sociolinguistic research in the next decade or so will be focused on better understanding issues like this.

In the next section I want to take a slightly more critical look at the practicalities of real and apparent time studies. Both present some challenges for the researcher. Finally, the chapter concludes with a brief consideration of a slightly different perspective on lifespan change, and discusses some of the recent work on language and ageing. Future developments in our understanding of the relationship between variation and change over time might well find that this research complements or converges with sociolinguistics.

CHALLENGES ASSOCIATED WITH REAL AND APPARENT TIME SAMPLING

When we first introduced the notion of real time studies, we mentioned some of the challenges that face the researcher wanting to do either a trend or a panel study. Obviously the main one is time itself. Researchers are increasingly under pressure to produce results from their research quickly. It is impossible to imagine a situation where someone would be allowed to take the 20 or 30 years of their entire academic career to collect data on a real time study and only publish the results on their retirement. Also, a lot of researchers can't bear to wait that long for a result (even if we know it will be worth it). For that reason, the apparent time construct is not only a practical means for analysing change in progess, it has also provided several generations of sociolinguists with the quick turn-around of results that they need.

We also noted that panel studies have to deal with drop-outs from their sample. Drop-out rates in any large social science study can be high (especially when participants aren't being paid), and it takes a lot of careful forward planning to combat this. A panel study needs to finish with enough people still there to make any generalisations sensible and reliable.

Another challenge for real time trend studies is harder to deal with. If there have been major social or demographic changes in a community between the time it was first studied and when researchers come back to look at it again, you may find that you are not actually comparing exactly 'the same' speech community. For example, we looked at Pope's replication of Labov's Martha's Vineyard study earlier in this chapter, and we noted that overall there was more centralisation of (ay) and (aw) in 2002 than there had been in 1962. But when she broke the data down and compared (ay) with (aw), she found that the two variables were going in different directions. Centralisation of (aw) seemed to be increasing; centralisation of (ay) seemed to be decreasing. However, in Labov's study (ay) centralisation seemed to be more important than (aw) centralisation for marking a local Vineyarder identity. Using the same procedure as Labov, Pope shows that Vineyarders with a positive attitude to the island were using (aw) centralisation in 2002. In other words, the real time data seemed to indicate that there had been a reversal in the marking of these variables on Martha's Vineyard.

Pope considers several reasons why she might have found this apparently quite recent increase in (aw) centralisation, and she argues that any interpretation of the 2002 Martha's Vineyard data needs to take into account social changes in the Vineyard since Labov conducted his study. Migration of workers from the mainland (largely Massachusetts) in the intervening 40 years, the increased economic polarisation of rich summer visitors and struggling year-round residents, and the transformation of the fishing industry into sports fishing have all changed the profile of the Vineyard. Nevertheless, in some respects the island has stayed the same. Pope found the same desire among locals to differentiate themselves from the summer folk, and the same urge to mark themselves as local through values or behaviours. But it is perhaps not surprising that as so many new residents have moved to the island, including a now substantial population from the mainland, the linguistic resources for marking local-ness have been reassigned from (ay) in the 1960s to (aw) in the 2000s.

The apparent time method has its own challenges. Although it has proved the basis for a very robust methodology, we have seen that it is limited in the extent to which it can usefully be deployed in the study of lexical (or quasi-lexical) variables because people can easily add to their vocabulary throughout their lives. In addition, questions are starting to emerge about how we should interpret the small sector of a population who seem to be riding the wave, and who show some variability across their lifespan.

There are also open questions about whether all speech communities are equally likely to show generational grading. It is possible, for example, that speech communities characterised by very rapid internal change might be less inclined to show this kind of stratification of variables. So, for instance, research into variables associated with some of the newer pidgins and creoles spoken in the Pacific have not found clean generational grading, even if the bulk of the evidence seems to indicate that ongoing, community-wide change is taking place. (We will return to variation in pidgins and creoles in Chapter 11.) It is possible that in such socially and linguistically dynamic situations, the speech community is sufficiently diffuse that generational change will only show up at very local levels. Indeed, even when there is a general absence of stratification by generation of speaker, some Pacific creole variables seem to be generationally stratified within families (Labov 1995; Meyerhoff 2000).

LANGUAGE AND AGEING

My great-uncle Richard served in the New Zealand delegation to the United Nations in the 1960s, and as he got older it seemed to the rest of the family that we heard the story of Khrushchev banging his shoe on the lectern during the 1960 General Assembly at every family gathering, with stupifying regularity. Most people have stereotypes about how ageing affects a person's way of talking, and they include things like forgetting whether you have told someone something already, rambling on self-indulgently, and so forth.

Most of these stereotypes are tangential to the discussion of age that I have been pursuing in this chapter, but before leaving the topic of age entirely I want to draw attention to some of the major themes emerging from research into language and ageing being done in discourse analysis and social psychology. There are an increasing number of researchers working in this area, and as the demographics of Western nations sees more and more people move into the 65-plus age bracket we are likely to see research in this area grow even more. One very likely demographic-led development will be a trend not to lump the 'elderly' together in one age cohort, but to look at narrow age bands (paralleling the current sociolinguistic interest in narrow age bands among the pre-teens and teens). It is already common practice in other fields of research.

Most of the research on language and ageing has, until recently, focused on what would be considered **ageing deficits**. These include hearing loss, processing problems and memory loss, or clearly degenerative conditions like Alzheimer's disease. Of course research on the impact that Alzheimer's has on a speaker's linguistic capabilities can make very positive contributions both to linguistics and gerontology. But there are also a number of good reasons to look beyond a focus on ageing deficits.

First, what younger members of the speech community consider a deficit may be viewed positively, as an *improvement*, by older speakers themselves. Collaborative research led by Nik and Justine Coupland looked at the phenomenon of 'painful self-disclosure' in elderly conversation (Coupland *et al.* 1988). They point out that these stories about illness or bereavement, which younger interlocutors may find unpleasant or overly intimate, can have a positive function for older speakers. They may be deployed as a way of managing what an older speaker perceives as an age-related face threat (see Chapter 5 on politeness); that is, they may be an example of variable discourse strategies being used to avoid costs ('eliminate the negative' in Chapter 2).

Second, a focus on deficit issues means that the areas in which older speakers may continue to become more proficient are simply ignored. Harwood (2006) points to several areas in which it seems that we continue to get better and better as we get older. An obvious area of increment (already discussed in this chapter) is in vocabulary and conceptual development. In addition, it seems likely that we continue to develop and hone our narrative skills as we get older. Harwood notes: 'We have little systematic knowledge of older adults' abilities in group decision making, public speaking, or emotional expression, yet each of these seems open to improvement into late old age.'

Finally, although problems like dementia have a serious impact on the language production and comprehension of those who are afflicted by the conditions, such people make up only a small proportion of the elderly. It's been pointed out that the features of ageing that researchers have traditionally focused on reflect very deeply embedded attitudes we have towards the elderly. These attitudes are by no means shared across cultures. It has been suggested, for example, that in communities where the elderly aren't expected to become more forgetful, they don't seem to have as many problems with memory recall. So it seems that at least some of what we stereotype as being part of the 'normal' ageing process is socially or discursively constructed.

Ageing deficits

Changes in individuals' performance in later stages of their lifespan. 'Deficits' refers to impaired performance on tasks or activities compared with younger speakers (e.g., recall, hearing). Focused on more than improvements that are associated with increased age (e.g., narrative skill, vocabulary).

CHAPTER SUMMARY

This chapter has tried to show how much is encompassed by the study of variation stratified by apparent or real time. The use of apparent time and real time as measures in the study of variation provides clear connections between the synchronic study of sociolinguistic variability and the diachronic perspective of historical linguistics. We have seen that the apparent time construct and the methods associated with it for studying variation and change have been largely vindicated in the very few studies where we have real time data from individuals that we can compare the apparent time construct against. The majority of speakers do maintain the same rough distribution of variants over their lifespan. Among the minority who change, the change is always in the direction of the change that the apparent time method reveals. This means that the inferences about change in progress made using apparent time data are quite robust, but our inferences about the speed with which a change is taking place may be on the conservative side.

In earlier chapters we have talked about the interdependence of group factors and the individual, but once we start looking at apparent and real time the connection between individual and group becomes more concrete. These methods for studying variation focus our attention on both the developmental (i.e., individual) and social (i.e., group) phenomenon that language variation is.

This chapter has barely scratched the surface of the research currently being done on the relationship between variation in individuals over time, in communities over time and within communities at any one point in time. Connections are being strengthened with other sub-fields of linguistics, so, for example, there are increasingly areas of overlapping interest between research on intraspeaker variability while a child is acquiring a language and what, in this chapter, we have called lifespan changes and generational changes. As we learn more about the nature of change over an individual's lifespan or across a community, the process by which children (and even second-language-speaking adults) acquire variable phenomena becomes more open to investigation. Finally, studies of language variation in small groups of speakers are becoming more sensitive to the age of the speakers and their life histories or experiences.

The methods by which change over time is studied in individuals and groups are, necessarily, somewhat different from each other. But, taken together, there is a tremendous vitality to the research in this area. It currently overshadows research being undertaken on language and social class (Chapter 8), and is at least as active a sub-field in sociolinguistics as the study of language and gender is (Chapter 10).

FURTHER READING

There are some excellent survey articles which would serve well as starting points for further work in this area: Sankoff (2005), Bailey (2002).

In addition, you may find the following helpful:

Nevalainen and Raumolin-Brunberg (2003) – introduction to historical sociolinguistics.
Kroch (2001) – surveys diachronic studies of variation.
Gordon *et al.* (2004) and Trudgill (2004) – development of colonial Englishes.
Bourdieu (1990) and Cameron (2000) – commodification of language varieties and linguistic styles and the linguistic marketplace.
Bailey (2002) – problems with real time resampling of a community.
Shenk *et al.* (2002) – narrative structures of elderly speakers, one of whom has Alzheimer's.

CHAPTER 8

Social class

Key terms in this chapter:

- social class
- status
- cross-over effect
- fine stratification
- broad stratification

- change from above
- change from below
- hypercorrection
- linguistic insecurity
- negative concord

INTRODUCTION

In Chapters 2–6 we examined the systematicity of variation in the speech of individuals, and saw that there are a number of different ways in which speaker style, or the choice of a particular linguistic code, or the use of different kinds of politeness routines, can be understood as part of an orderly relationship between language and society. In Chapter 7 we saw that the variation in how speakers of different ages in a single community use language is also revealing. We saw that age provides a useful synchronic measure through which we can draw inferences about the directions (if not the speed) of diachronic change.

In this chapter we will look at social class: a measure of social organisation at the level of the larger speech community. Although it is obviously true that interactions take place between individuals, we will see that individuals' linguistic behaviour nevertheless patterns with groups. Among other things, in this chapter we will start to discover the way in which the range of non-linguistic variables discussed in the next three chapters interact with stylistic variation (Chapter 3). Crucially, we will see that these interactions are not random; there are robust parallels between the way variables pattern with respect to all these factors. These common patterns in the distribution of variants can be drawn on to strengthen our interpretation of the social meaning of a variable. In this chapter, and the ones immediately following it, we return to some of the factors that were proposed in Chapter 2 as general motivations for variation: the desire to maximise fit with others in a group, and sometimes to maximise benefits or minimise costs associated with identifying with a particular group.

SOCIAL CLASS

Social class

A measure of *status* which is often based on occupation, income and wealth, but also can be measured in terms of aspirations and mobility. These factors can then be used to group individuals scoring similarly on these factors into socioeconomic classes.

Social class is a notion that has its intellectual basis in theories of social and political economies dating from the nineteenth century, and theories of social class are associated with figures like Karl Marx and Max Weber.

There are a number of ways of theorising and, therefore, defining *social class*. Though we generally think of it now as being a function of a person's occupation (and/or their personal wealth), this is only one way of theorising it. Marx drew a fundamental distinction between those who produce capital or resources and those who control the production of capital which others produce. The former are the working class (Marx's *proletariat*, derived from a word meaning 'worker') and the latter, the middle class (Marx's *capitalists*).

However, many sociologists reacted against this very simple definition of class. In Weber's work, class is theorised in terms of social actions, and a great many more social divisions/classes are recognised than Marx's pair. Individuals' economic situation might be an important factor in defining what class they belong to, but the influence of economic factors is tempered by people's life style and life chances. Weber argued that all three of these factors define a person's status. The shift in definition from Marx to Weber is of particular interest to sociolinguists because Weber's conceptualisation of class tries to capture the significance of an individual's participation in a complex set of associated behaviours (including speech, his *life style*), and also the importance of aspirations and attitudes (*life chances*). Another well-known sociologist, Talcott Parsons (who played a large role in introducing Weber's work to US sociology), also emphasised the importance of social action in how we make social divisions within a society.

No, really?

Weber (1864–1920) is considered one of the founders of sociology. His work deals equally with religion as it does with class, and he is especially well known for one essay which links his thoughts on religion, economics and social order: *The Protestant Ethic and the Spirit of Capitalism*. He also wrote about Eastern religions and was interested in their relationship to emergent social orders in China and India.

Like the notion of the speech community, class can be seen as being inherently about division or it can be seen as a construct that emphasises consensuality. The divisions inherent in Marx's theory of social class were fundamental to his ideas about class conflict. Weber's theory, on the other hand, allowed for class identity to be shaped by perceived similarity as well as difference.

As we will see, the notion of contrast (and sometimes conflict) has been influential in shaping how some sociolinguists interpret linguistic variation that is stratified by social class, and it colours the explanation for some patterns of variability within a larger speech community. In this work, the term 'class' is used more in the sense of Weber's notion of class as being based on a series of social actions. When we come to discuss the concept of *communities of practice* later in this chapter, we will see that this takes Weber's notion of participation in shared social actions to an even more refined level of analysis.

Mobility and determinism: class vs caste

Another important feature of social class that we inherit from the Weber tradition is that however we define class it allows for the possibility of individual mobility. This potential for mobility makes social class different from a caste system. In a caste system, the caste you are born into determines your position within the larger social order for your whole life. Social class may turn out to be similarly fixed; however, it need not be. Before the nineteenth century when English writers talked about 'class' they actually meant something more like a deterministic, caste system. Mobility really only arises during the nineteenth century. Lynda Mugglestone (2003) has documented how the possibility of class mobility had an impact on people's attitudes to regional accents.

Nowadays, potential mobility between classes is taken as given. Just because you are born into a working-class family this does not blindly determine that you will be working class forever, and a major change in an individual's life may profoundly affect the kind of social class they find themselves a part of. When Victoria Beckham, the former Spice Girl, announces that she is 'the second Queen of England' (Nicholl 2003), she asserts and claims her rights to move her way up the class hierarchy, purchasing access to upper-class social circles by throwing lavish parties and jetting around the world with private stylists in tow.

People who are upwardly mobile may feel that living in their old neighbourhood is incongruent with their new social aspirations and so they will move to a larger house or to a street with a 'better' address. In a similar way, they may acquire ways of talking that are slightly different to the ones they acquired when growing up. However, there seem to be limits on how much we can change the way we talk as adults (which we discussed much more in Chapter 7), and you can probably think of someone you know whose accent and/or ways of speaking send a different message from the rest of the social picture they present. Changing your accent or native discourse patterns is much harder than moving house. An upwardly mobile Yorkshireman might pick up Received Pronunciation as he makes his way through the British higher education system, but more than twenty years later, his continued use of a short *a* vowel in the BATH lexical set and the occasional use of [ʊ] where RP has [ʌ] (e.g., in 'cup') may give his roots away.

The reason why it is harder to change your vowels than your address if you are upwardly mobile may be due to developmental factors (the critical period hypothesis discussed in the previous chapter). But it is partly also to do with social and psychological factors. Because language is such an integral part of our self-identity, we may also not be prepared to abandon our original accent as readily as we might abandon our home. A New Zealander might spend 15 years living in the United States, but hardly shift her vowels at all. And increasingly, it wouldn't even occur to young speakers of regional varieties of British English to try and pick up RP just because they have secured a place in an Oxford or Cambridge college.

People may also move down the class and status ladder because of changes to their life chances. For example, a doctor, forced to flee her home because of war or persecution, may find that as an immigrant to a new country she has to work as a hospital orderly or nursing aide because her qualifications as a consultant are not recognised in her new home. Her lifestyle and status – that is, her social class – will necessarily drop. She'll no longer be able to acquire the usual trappings of middle-class life or to participate in middle-class activities such as buying art or going on regular holidays. We would like to know what the linguistic consequences of this kind of social mobility are too.

The consequences of a downward change in social class are varied and interact with a number of linguistic and social factors. If the drop is involuntary (e.g., because of forced migration) a person might maintain the linguistic markers associated with the higher social class they grew up in. This would be an indirect way of reminding listeners that the speaker's current social standing is not one they identify with. On the other hand, she might not want to sound 'uppity', in which case she may make an effort to accommodate to the working-class norms her lifestyle now identifies with more.

Connections with theory

Data from the way films are dubbed into foreign languages often provide interesting perspectives on social variation. An ethnically marked variety such as AAVE has no obvious ethnically marked analogue in much of Europe. Instead, dialect varieties that used to primarily mark regional differences are acquiring the function of social-class markers. For example, when US films featuring AAVE speakers are dubbed into German, working-class varieties from the Ruhr region or from Berlin are used (Queen 2004).

Of course, a number of facts suggest that class is to a certain extent something you are born into. An astounding number of people in graduate school are the children of academics, the US political system is full of family dynasties, and the notion of 'trust fund kids' all speak to the stability of class. Nevertheless, we collectively nurture the ideal that anyone can make what they want of themselves and move out of one class, up into another one, and we tend to gloss over the potential for downward movement in the scale.

Measuring social class

Social class is a function of the intersection of a whole lot of different social (and sometimes even personal) attributes. So there are a number of different ways in which class can be measured, and sociolinguists have tried to use a number of different metrics in their studies of speech communities. Some of the more careful work on class has taken such factors as people's accommodation into account, giving higher scores to people that own their own homes rather than rent, and even more points to people depending on how much their home is worth and whether they have made structural improvements on the property and carefully maintain its appearance. But perhaps the most frequently used measure is a person's occupation and/or the occupation of the primary breadwinner in their family when they were growing up. On the basis of factors like this, a speech community can be subdivided into different socioeconomic classes (SECs).

It is important to note that professions differ in their status in different communities. Most countries have research boards that rank professions according to their local status. This ranking is based partly on the earning power of a typical member of that profession, but it also factors in things like the results from attitude surveys that are regularly conducted by

Census Boards or Economic Research Councils. These attitude surveys ask people to indicate how much they 'respect' different professions (you have probably come across the results of these in the media for instance, they regularly show that politicians rank near the bottom with used car sellers).

But how reliable is it to use occupation as the principal basis for assigning them to a particular socioeconomic class? If we adopt the more Weberian view that social status or class is derived from a range of social actions, then we would seriously question the validity of this. Perhaps a more sensitive and accurate measure of social class or social status would combine a number of objective factors (like personal wealth and value of home) with subjective factors (like people's aspirations to social mobility, or their friendship networks).

In Labov's (2001) work on variation in Philadelphia, he systematically tried to work out whether social class is best represented by a bundle of features – occupation, level of education and house value – or if it can be reduced to occupation alone. He found that for some variables, occupation was just as good an indicator of the variability as all three factors combined, but for most the combined measure did a better job of accounting for the variation observed.

It would be useful to have Labov's test replicated in superficially similar urban, industrialised centres. Recent studies have drawn attention to the increasing complexity of measures of social class in cities. For instance, work based on the 2001 UK Census concludes that neighbourhood is a better predictor of attitudes and behaviours than occupation alone, because the effects of occupation interact with a number of other factors, such as more complex family structures, whether or not a household has two incomes, the marital status of the heads of household, and whether there are any children in the household at all. Neighbourhoods seem to focus similarities on a lot of these measures, so you have concentrations of dinky (double-income-no-kids) households in certain areas, or upwardly mobile families of second-generation immigrants, etc.

These neighbourhood categorisations are used by marketers (they determine what leaflets arrive in your mail) and by teachers, police and other public sector planning groups. They have not yet been widely used in sociolinguistic research, but as social scientists employ greater finesse in identifying social classes we can expect to see benefits flowing on from this to the study of linguistic variation.

No, really?

On 25 January 2004, the *Observer* newspaper in Britain reported a new classification system that ranks British households into one of 61 different profiles. Obviously, these get quite detailed and cover only small segments of the population, which then get combined to form larger classes. What is known in Britain as 'the chattering class(es)' – that is, people with metropolitan values, attitudes and spending patterns – break down into more specific categories. (Do you feel like you are, or aspire to be, one of these? What do you think of the labels for the groups the marketers have chosen?)

The New Urban Columnist: Well-qualified young professionals working in occupations such as financial services, PR and the media. Open to new fashions

in taste and thinking. Drawn to inner-city life as they find it more stimulating than suburbia.

The Counter-Cultural: Young and mobile people in their twenties and thirties. Live on their own or in transient relationships. Many associated with the gay scene. Thoughtful, well educated. Tend to live in areas with a diverse mix of people.

The University Challenge: Typically a student. Lives in rented accommodation in areas that come to life in the evening. Displays a strong belief in informality and authenticity.

CLASS AS A FACTOR IN LINGUISTIC VARIATION

We have already seen a lot of evidence that variables are subject to quite systematic stratification in the speech of individuals and groups. For instance, we saw stratification according to speaker style (Chapter 3), and stratification according to age (Chapter 7). And any sociolinguistic variables are stratified according to social class or social groupings. This means that one variant is more frequent in the speech of members of a higher social class and another variant is found more often in the speech of members of a lower class. It is very important to note that these differences are not deterministic – generally, all speakers will use both variants some of the time regardless of their social class. What distinguishes the groups is the relative frequency with which they use each variant, so it is helpful to draw on quantitative methods for analysing this kind of variation.

Many of the linguistic variables that have different distributions in the speech of different social classes are also involved in ongoing change. This means that their distribution is sensitive to more than one non-linguistic factor: the distribution is stratified by, for example, social class of the speaker as well the age of the speaker. As we saw in the previous chapter, when a variant incrementally increases in frequency in the speech of younger and younger speakers in a speech community, this is a good diagnostic of a change in progress. In this chapter we will also see that variations resulting from changes in progress are also stratified by social groupings such as class or social networks. In other words, a monotonic trend across apparent time may be paralleled by a monotonic trend across classes. In the next chapter we will add gender to the picture. The combination of all these factors adds depth and colour to our picture of how different variants in language are used in socially significant ways.

Status

Max Weber's theory of *social class* held that it was based on a person's status, measured in terms of their lifestyle and life choices in addition to measures of wealth and occupation (as per Marx).

Class stratification of stable variables

Here it may be helpful to reminder ourselves of Weber's definition of class or **status** as a composite of economic wealth, linguistic (and other social) behaviour, and attitudes and aspirations. These factors can be used to a varying degree in order to better understand the social meaning of the patterns of variation we find.

However, as we saw in the previous chapter, it is important to remember that not all variation involves language change. Some variables are stable, meaning the variants can co-exist for many, many years (even centuries) without one ousting the other. These variables may also show stratification according to social class. In some ways, they provide a more straightforward starting point for exploring the way in which social groups like class may intersect with language variation, so we will begin with an example of one of them in the next section.

If a variable is relatively stable, that is to say, it has been around in the speech community for some time and shows no signs of going away, speakers may be much more aware of the variation. In this case, speakers very often have positive or negative evaluations associated with different variants, and the different variants will come to be associated with different non-linguistic attributes. Where one variant is widely perceived to be 'better', this very often correlates with more frequent use of this variant by speakers from higher SECs (in the chapters on style and attitudes to language we have discussed different ways in which a sociolinguist might determine what is perceived as 'better'). These variants are usually the ones prescribed in standard speech.

We have a bit of a chicken-and-the-egg situation here: does a variant get perceived as 'better' or as part of the standard because it is more frequently used by speakers from a higher social class? Or do speakers from higher social classes use that variant more often in order to stake out, or reify, their position as more powerful and prestigious speakers? This question can't be resolved solely from looking at distributions of forms. We have to combine data on which age groups use the more statusful variant (as we did in Chapter 7), and also where the more statusful variants are used and with whom (as discussed in Chapter 3, and see also Chapter 10 on gender). For the time being, let us accept the generalisation that higher-status variants are used more frequently by higher-status speakers, but acknowledge that this oversimplifies the picture a good deal.

Notice that I am using the term 'status' here, rather than 'prestige'. Different kinds of prestige were discussed in Chapter 3. Here, we are talking about variants that have overt prestige, which speakers either orient to directly through their stereotypes and judgements about language use, or indirectly through their consistent shifting towards one variant in more carefully or more outgroup-directed speech. (One of the general goals of this book is to arrive at a better understanding of how different social factors relate to one another and to concepts like 'status' and 'prestige' and 'power' in a dynamic way. We don't want to conflate prestige and standard uniformly, but we are interested in how they overlap or can become confused with each other!)

One of the best-known and best-described stable variables in English is the (ing) variable. This is the alternation between [ɪn] and [ɪŋ] in word-final position (e.g., *ceiling, pudding, drawing, expecting*). Variation between these two variants has been found in every variety of English in which it has been studied so far, though (as we will see shortly) different varieties of English differ quite a lot in how often they use the different forms. Moreover, the variation can be traced back to structural differences in English that are hundreds of years old. In all varieties of English the velar nasal variant, [ɪŋ], is considered to be 'better' than the alveolar variant, [ɪn]. This is partly due to the influence of the orthographic convention of writing these words with <-ing> at the end, and we can see evidence of this evaluation in the consistent pattern of shift towards the velar variant that occurs in outgroup or careful speech.

Figure 8.1 shows how the variable patterns in four Australasian varieties of English: Cessnock and Sydney in New South Wales, Brisbane in Queensland (all in Australia) and the city of Porirua (in New Zealand). This figure, clearly shows that all four communities differ in the overall frequency with which the less prestigious form [ɪn] is used. Brisbane has the highest rates of [ɪn] overall (40 per cent when you average across both SECs), and Sydney

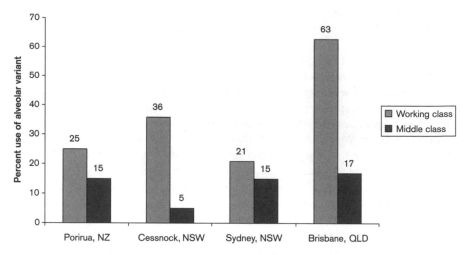

Figure 8.1 Frequency of the alveolar (non-standard) variant [ɪn] according to socioeconomic class of the speaker in four localities in Australia and New Zealand. (Source, Holmes *et al.* 1991: 59.)

the lowest (18 per cent averaged across working- and middle-class speech). However, all four communities show the same effect for socioeconomic class. Working-class speakers use more of the non-standard variant [ɪn] and middle-class speakers use more of the standard variant [ɪŋ]. And if you plot the distribution of [ɪn] and [ɪŋ] in the speech of different social classes according to style, you find that in all speech styles there is the same separation between speakers of different social classes. This makes it even clearer why we talk about this as stratification. (We consider the parallelisms between stylistic and class stratification of variables in more detail in a separate section later in this chapter.)

Literary records show that the alternation between [ɪn] and [ɪŋ] has been a very salient marker of social class for several centuries. A number of eighteenth- and nineteenth-century writers make good use of such variation to indicate the social status of their characters. So, for example, in Dickens we find an ex-prisoner and charwoman talking about 'the buryin' ground' (Mugglestone 2003: 130).

Connections with theory

Mugglestone also reproduces a cartoon from *Punch* magazine in 1873 (2003: 133). In the cartoon, a little boy asks 'Ain't yer goin' to have some Puddin', Miss Richards?' where the [ɪn] variant occurs in the verb *goin'* and the noun *puddin'*. Sociolinguists' work has found that [ɪn] is more frequent in verbal forms (*going, assuming*) and less frequent in nouns and adjectives (*morning, pudding, interesting*).

In their study of Foxy Boston (Chapter 3), Rickford and McNair-Knox suggested that not all tokens of a variant are equally salient or are as likely to be 'heard'. By providing an example of [ɪn] in a noun – a context in which it is less frequently heard – *Punch* provides readers with a particularly telling social marker.

Class stratification with changes in progress

By looking at a stable variable we have established that speakers' use of different variants may be a rough marker of social class within a speech community at large. I now turn to some examples where the variable involves a change in progress. As I have already indicated, the overlap and intersection between class stratification and other non-linguistic factors such as style (and gender, in the next chapter) is in my opinion infinitely more interesting when it is enriched by the dynamism of a change in progress.

In Montreal French there is variable deletion of /l/ in words like *il* 'he' and *elle(s)* 'she (they, fem.)', as well as in words like *la*, the feminine object pronoun. The forms with /l/ are the standard variants, while the variants without the /l/ are considered non-standard (though the (l) variable in French is a bit like the (ing) variable in English, it appears to occur in all varieties). The constraints on /l/-deletion have been studied by a number of sociolinguists in several varieties of French. Figure 8.2 shows how often /l/ is absent in the speech of three different socioeconomic groups in Montreal in a study conducted by Shana Poplack. Poplack based her socioeconomic categorisations on speakers' occupation. The bar chart indicates that speakers of Montreal French from higher occupational groups use more of the conservative form than speakers from the lower SECs do. There is a consistent, monotonic relationship between social class and deletion of /l/.

Sociolinguistics can point to numerous cases where the higher social classes retain the conservative form, and the lower classes lead in the shift to a new norm. The pattern is very well attested and can be seen in descriptions of many ongoing language changes. There is also evidence that the same generalisation held historically. Mugglestone (2003) reviews evidence about the spread of long [ɑː] before the fricatives /f, s, θ/, as in *staff, pass* and *bath*. The long *a* variant started among lower-class speakers and spread to the upper class. As Mugglestone notes, there has been a complete flip-flop in evaluations of this variant in the space of a couple of hundred years. What is now the standard in the UK and southern hemisphere varieties of English, [ɑː], was for a long time considered a Cockney vulgarism.

We can see similar stratification by speakers' social class in two ongoing changes affecting /t/ in New Zealand English. Although both changes involve /t/, they seem to

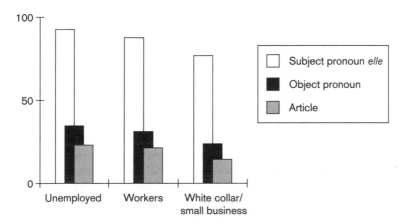

Figure 8.2   Absence of syllable-final /l/ in Montreal French according to socioeconomic class of speakers. (Source, Poplack and Walker 1986: 189.)

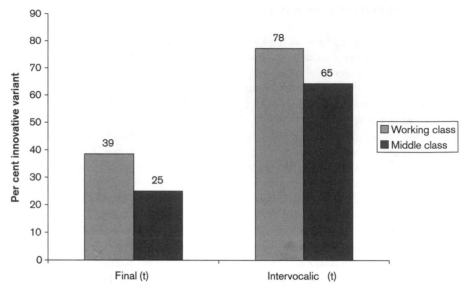

Figure 8.3   Frequency of word final (t) realised as glottal stop and intervocalic (t) realised as a voiced flap by socioeconomic class of the speaker. Conversational speech of young New Zealanders. (Source, Holmes 1995: 59, 63.)

be independent of each other. One change affects syllable final /-t/, which is variably realised as a glottal stop [ʔ] in New Zealand English. The second change affects intervocalic /-t-/, which is variably realised as a flap [ɾ]. Both the non-standard variants, the flap and the glottal, are more common in the speech of young working-class New Zealanders than they are in the speech of young middle-class New Zealanders. This can be seen in Figure 8.3.

These are very simple examples, which contrast only two social classes, but as we saw in the section 'Measuring social class', a number of factors can be used to group speakers in different classes, and it can sometimes be useful to discriminate among more classes than just a higher and lower one.

Figure 8.4 shows how as many as ten different socioeconomic groups can be plotted for a single variable if your corpus is large enough and if you have gathered sufficient detail about your speakers' backgrounds. This shows the relative raising and centring of the vowel in words like *lost, talk* and *wash* in New York City. Labov called this the (oh) variable (the class of words it covers is very broad) and its realisation ranges from low variants [ɑ] and [ɔ] through to a very raised and centralised realisation, [ʊːə], which results in (near) homophones of *shore* and *sure*. The degree of raising is shown as an index and plotted iconically so that the index scores higher up the y-axis representing more raised variants (higher vowels). Figure 8.4 also shows how the different socioeconomic class groups realise this variable in three styles: casual speech, formal speech and in a reading passage. The different social classes have been grouped for increased clarity. You can see that speakers in the highest SEC use lower variants of (oh) and speakers in the lowest SEC use raised ones more often. All the SEC groups use more of the lower variants in the more formal speech to an interviewer and in a reading passage, and most tokens of the innovative, raised variants in casual speech to friends and family.

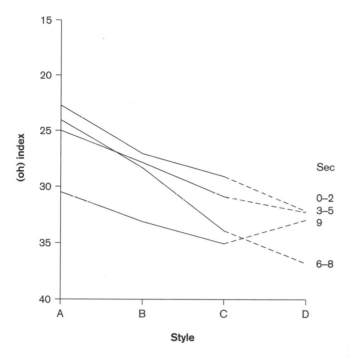

Figure 8.4 Raising of (oh) by social class of speaker. (Source, Labov 1972a: 129.)

Notice that Figure 8.4 shows very clearly that speakers in the highest social class are not necessarily the models for change. Here, as with the majority of documented sound changes, change is led by what Labov has called the 'interior' groups − neither the topmost, nor the bottommost SECs. Typically, changes like this are led by the lower middle class or the upper working class. (The special role played by the lower middle class will be reaffirmed in the discussion of the **cross-over effect** later in this chapter.)

FINE AND BROAD STRATIFICATION

A sociolinguistic variable can show **fine stratification** with respect to a non-linguistic variable such as social class, or it can show **broad stratification**. Fine stratification means that small changes in overall frequency differentiate the averages for different groups; broad stratification means the frequency with which a given variant occurs in different social classes is relatively more marked. In terms of a line graph, fine stratification results in lines that are bunched closer together, and broad stratification results in lines that have more space between them. The important thing about fine and broad stratification is that each emphasises the orderliness of the data. The order in these patterns reaffirms the point we noted earlier with respect to style-shifting: there is no free variation. Superficial differences are underpinned by regular processes.

Figures 8.6 and 8.7 show schematically what fine and broad stratification between social classes looks like across four different styles of speech. Most of the examples we consider in this chapter follow an attention to speech model for style-shifting and compare the different speaking styles identified and pioneered by Labov. However, in order to remind

Cross-over effect

The cross-over effect emerges at the intersection of style and class. Typically it refers to the breakdown in the most careful speech styles of clear *stratification* between speakers of different *social classes*. For example, when reading word lists, speakers from the **second** highest social class will suddenly produce more tokens of an incoming or prestige form than speakers in the **highest** social class do, instead of producing slightly fewer tokens as they do in their conversation or interview styles (cf. *Hypercorrection*).

New York vowels

Consider the data in Figure 8.5, which is adapted from the New York City survey. It shows the degree of raising of (oh) and in short (a), the TRAP vowel in words like *bad*. Both casual and formal speech styles have been combined and are contrasted with readings style.

Who leads with raising of short (a)? To what extent does it pattern with (oh)?

Do you think it makes sense for higher SECs to follow patterns established in lower-status groups? How is this consistent or at odds with the progress of other trends you can think of?

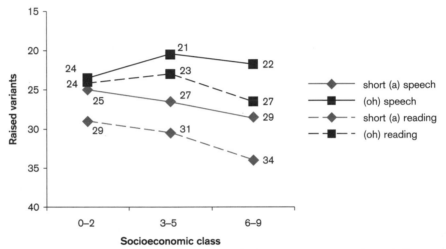

Figure 8.5 Raising of short (a) and (oh) in New York City in reading and connected speech. (Source, Labov 1966: 221.)

us that audience design or accommodation to the interlocutor is an alternative and equally sensible way of viewing style-shifting, I have plotted the hypothetical examples of fine and broad stratification in Figures 8.6 and 8.7 across styles that are more compatible with an audience design view of stylistic variation.

What this means in practice is that the orderly distribution of variants across social classes holds with respect to other factors such as style. For instance, if a variable is socially stratified according to class, like (ing), and middle-class speakers favour use of the standard [ɪŋ], this generalisation will hold in each of the styles identified with Labov's attention to speech model of style (Chapter 3). That is, in casual speech to friends or family, middle-class speakers will use more [ɪn] than the working-class speakers; in an interview with a researcher both groups will use more [ɪn] than they do with their ingroup, but the frequency for middle-class speakers will still be higher than for working-class speakers.

However, because social class or status is a complex category involving both subjective and objective factors, we want to be careful that any apparent effects we observe for class

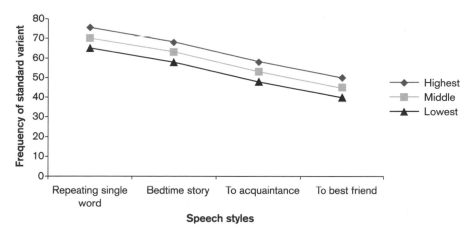

Figure 8.6 A (hypothetical) variable showing fine social class stratification. Distribution of a standard variant with overt prestige in speech to different kinds of addressee or in different tasks (distribution of standard variant in highest, middle and lowest classes bunches together in all styles, but groups form discrete strata).

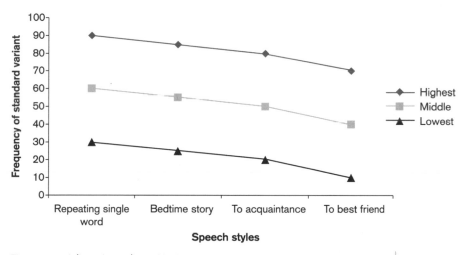

Figure 8.7 A (hypothetical) variable showing broad social class stratification. Distribution of a standard variant with overt prestige in speech to different kinds of addressee or in different tasks (highest, middle and lowest classes clearly discrete; distribution of standard variant markedly different for each class in all styles).

can't be attributed to other factors. For example, we might find that more middle-class speakers use [ɪŋ] than working-class speakers do. But what if the middle-class speakers happened to use more low frequency, 'formal' words (e.g., *exasperating, utilising*) than the working-class speakers did? What if we happened to catch working-class speakers talking to their family more often? Suppose presence of [ɪŋ] is favoured by everyone before a following /k/, and our sample of middle-class speakers just happened to include lots of tokens of [ɪŋ] before /k/?

There are several ways sociolinguists test whether class really is important. One way is to use statistical tests that adjust for the relative frequency of a variant in different contexts and among different speakers. Although programs that can do these kinds of tests are quite straightforward to use (and are widely available), if you are just starting out in sociolinguistics they may seem a bit fearsome. These programs allow us to make adjusted calculations of the frequency of a variant – the weightings Cameron used to express the distribution of different introductions of quotes in the previous chapter were an example of just this kind of adjustment.

However, if you're not into this level of quantitative analysis you can still do a very easy check of whether the variation you see really is a function of social class. You can plot results for class against some other factor, such as style or gender, for instance. If you find that in all styles (however you choose to understand style), you get a consistent effect for speaker status, then you would feel much more confident in saying that a variable is sensitive to social class. This consistent effect might show up as fine or broad stratification (Figures 8.6, 8.7) – the *size* of the difference between speakers with different status, occupational or educational backgrounds is not what is important. What is important is the *fact* of difference.

Social significance of fine and broad class stratification

Some researchers have suggested that patterns of broad and fine class stratification reflect the relative rigidity of class structures in a speech community. It's been observed, for example, that the differences between social classes for a stable variable like (ing) seem to be more broadly stratified in British varieties of English than they are in North American varieties. Data for Norwich, in England, is compared with data from the major cities of New York and Detroit in the United States in Figure 8.8.

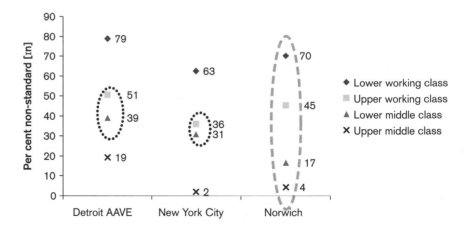

Figure 8.8   Use of [ɪn] variant rather than [ɪŋ] in two US social dialect surveys and one British one. Relatively broad stratification in Norwich circled with dashed line; relatively fine stratification between upper working and lower middle classes in Detroit and NYC circled with dotted lines. (Note: Norwich data combines original lower working and middle working class. Sources, Trudgill 1974; Labov 1966; Wolfram 1981.)

Here you can see that the differences between the social classes in Norwich are more widely spread out; that is, they appear to be more broadly stratified than the differences between classes in Detroit and New York City, where the class stratification, especially between the internal groups of upper working class and lower middle class, is very fine. Some researchers have generalised from data like these and suggested that the reason there is broader class stratification in the UK and finer stratification in the US is that there is greater potential for individual mobility across social classes in North America than there is in Britain. I think we need to be a little cautious about assuming that broad or fine stratification is necessarily related to how fixed the class structure is in any given speech community. First, the data in support of it is rather limited. Second, it seems to focus on only part of the overall distribution of variants. In Figure 8.8, the overall range from highest to lowest class for each city is roughly the same: 60 percentage points for Detroit, 61 percentage points for New York, and 64 percentage points for Norwich. So it is only with respect to part of the distribution that the British data shows broader stratification than the US data does.

Another possible problem with drawing parallels between the relative class rigidity or mobility of a society and broad or fine class stratification of linguistic variables can be seen in Figure 8.9. Relative freedom from the strictures of British social class is widely taken as a characteristic of New Zealand and Australian social life, yet as we saw earlier, some communities there are characterised by relatively fine stratification between social classes and some by relatively broad linguistic stratification. Moreover, the differences do not straightforwardly correlate with the size and metropolitan nature of the city. Figure 8.9 combines data from Australasia, Norwich, Detroit and New York. To make it easier to compare across studies, it collapses the variation in New York, Detroit and Norwich to a contrast between middle and working class, because we only have data on two social classes for the Australasian cities. We can see that Porirua (a fairly small peri-urban city near the capital, Wellington) and Sydney (a major metropolitan area) pattern together with little class differentiation for (ing). On the other hand, Brisbane (another major metropolitan area in Australia) and Norwich (a comparatively small city in England) pattern together in showing quite broad class differences for (ing). The stratification in the US is broader than in Sydney, but finer than it is in Brisbane.

Fine stratification

A distribution of variants, e.g., across groups of speakers in different styles, which shows each group of speakers patterning minimally differently from each other in each style. Shows up as small gaps between *trend* lines on a line graph.

Broad stratification

A distribution of variants – for example, across groups of speakers in different styles – which shows each group of speakers patterning markedly differently from each other in each style. Shows up as a big gap between *trend* lines on a line graph.

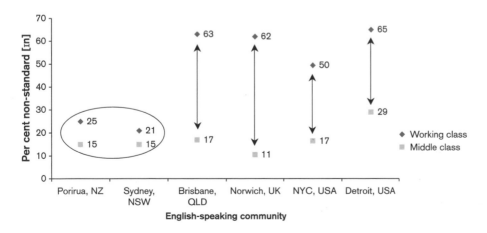

Figure 8.9 Comparison of class stratification in six English-speaking cities, showing very fine stratification in Sydney and Porirua, but broad stratification in Brisbane, Norwich and the US.

It may prove to be true that there is a relationship between how fine the class stratification for a variable is and the rigidity of the social matrix in the community. However, this survey of studies shows that we can't support sweeping statements about correspondences between linguistic variation and the ease or lack of mobility in 'the United States' or 'the United Kingdom'. A degree of caution is required when making such generalisations, and probably a good deal more primary research specifically designed to shed light on this.

CROSS-OVER EFFECTS AND CHANGE FROM ABOVE/BELOW

So far we have emphasised the orderliness of the stratification of speakers in different social classes. However, there is a famous exception to this orderliness. This is the case where speakers from one social class use even more tokens of a variant that has overt prestige than speakers in the next higher social class do. This phenomenon has been called the **cross-over effect**. It usually occurs in the most monitored styles such as reading word lists or minimal pairs, and this is taken to reflect the high social value associated with a particular variant. This means the phenomenon is associated with one particular view of style (something that will become even more clear shortly when we consider how cross-over effects have been interpreted).

The effect is attested most often with the lower middle class and/or upper working class. Speakers in these groups 'jump over' the next higher classes up. For this reason, it is sometimes identified even more specifically as the 'lower middle class cross-over effect'. However, as we will see, it is perhaps useful to divorce it from specific classes, because it can even show up in the second highest social group in speech communities where urban, Western notions of class are less relevant.

Because the cross-over effect is associated with changes in progress – e.g., Montreal (l), rather than English (ing) – it is consistent with the important role that the lower middle class and the upper working class play in leading changes in progress. In conjunction with data on speakers' attitudes to different variants, a cross-over effect can provide important clues about how sound changes disperse through a community.

A cross-over effect was famously first observed in the study of New Yorkers' use of (r) – the presence or absence of a constricted [r] before consonants and word finally. This is shown in Figure 8.10. Here, the locally innovative variant [r] is plotted in two speech styles for four SECs groups in New York City in word-final contexts (such as *car*, so [kaː] or [kar]) or pre-consonantally (such as *dart*). (Labov (1966, 1972a) discusses the factors underlying the ten SECs 0–9 he used and his subsequent regrouping of them.) It is clear from this figure that in casual speech use of the [r] variant is restricted to the middle middle-class speakers (SEC 9), and does not occur in any of the other classes with very high frequency (0 per cent in SEC 0–1, 3 per cent in SEC 2–5 and 2 per cent in SEC 6–8). However, when they are reading word lists, all speakers use a lot more of the incoming, prestigious variant, and the speakers in SEC 6–8, the lower middle class, use it most of all (at 90 per cent).

Similar effects show up with other variables. Figure 8.10 shows the frequency of one of the non-standard vowel variants in the same sample of New York City speakers. This plots the frequency of raised variants for the short *a* vowel in words like *bad* and *bag*; that is, [bɛːᵊd] or even raised as much as [bɪːᵊg]. The short (a) variable and the (r) variable are both changes in progress in New York. But attitudes to the two variables differ markedly.

Speakers are more aware of the alternation between the innovative constricted [r] and

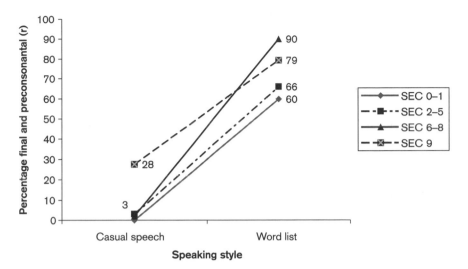

Figure 8.10   Frequency of use of [r] in final and pre-consonantal position in New York City in four socioeconomic class (SEC) groupings: 0 = lowest SEC; 9 = highest SEC. (Adapted from Labov 1972a, tables 9.5 and 9.6.)

the local r-less vernacular, and the incoming form is generally considered 'better'. When New Yorkers are asked to evaluate a sentence with constricted [r] and without, they give strong, positive evaluations to the r-ful version. Changes like this, which people are consciously aware of, have been dubbed **change from above**. 'Above' means 'above the level of conscious awareness', not necessarily that they originate in higher status social groups (the two may go together, but it is important not to confuse these two senses of 'above').

New Yorkers do not have the same attitudes to the raised variants of short (a). When they are asked to evaluate pairs of sentences that differ only in the use of raised or low (a) variants, they give strong, *negative* evaluations to the sentences with raised (a). Moreover, even speakers who use raised variants of short (a) claim that they don't. Their negative evaluations seem to act as a filter, and they 'hear' themselves sounding not as they really are but as how they would like to be (cf. discussion of covert prestige in Chapter 3). Nevertheless, like (r), the short (a) variable shows a cross-over effect in the most formal reading styles and this is shown in Figure 8.11. Because of this lack of conscious awareness a variable like short (a) raising can be called a **change from below** (as in 'below conscious awareness').

In Figure 8.11 the cross-over seems to go downwards (as opposed to up, as with (r) in Figure 8.10). This is a bit confusing, unfortunately, but it comes about because Labov has converted speakers' short (a) tokens into an index of raising, and then represented this raising index iconically on the y-axis. So the higher up the y-axis score you go, the more raised the realisations of short (a) are.

Labov suggested that the cross-over effect in Figures 8.10 and 8.11 could be called **hypercorrection**. This was an extension of a term usually used to describe overgeneralisations based on imperfect learning of a rule in a new language or dialect. Such overgeneralisations have been recognised for a long time, not only by linguists. For example, suppose you are a speaker of some variety of English that almost always uses [ɪn] and seldom uses [ɪŋ] variants of the (ing) variable. You may be aware that the velar forms are somehow 'better' than the alveolar ones, but because the velar variants are so rare in your own variety you really

Change from above

Changes taking place in a *speech community* above the level of individuals' conscious awareness. Able to be commented on. One *variant* is clearly standard or has clear *overt prestige*. It does **not** refer to changes led by higher social classes (though this may often be the case). (See also *Change from below*.)

Change from below

Changes taking place in a *speech community* below the level of conscious awareness. Not the subject of overt comment. It does **not** refer to changes led by lower social classes. (See also *Change from above*.)

Hypercorrection

The production of a form which never occurs in a native variety on the basis of the speaker's misanalysis of the input (cf. *Cross-over effect*).

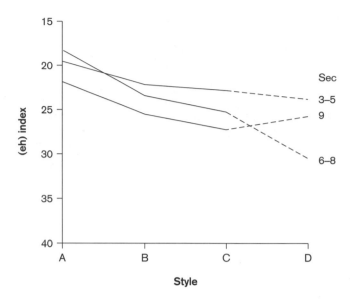

Figure 8.11   Raised variants of short (a) in New York City, showing cross-over effect for lower middle class (so-called 'interior' class). (Source, Labov 1972a: 127.)

Linguistic insecurity

Speakers' feeling that the variety they use is somehow inferior, ugly or bad. Negative attitudes to one's own variety expressed in aesthetic or moral terms.

are at a loss as to where to put them. You become uncertain about what the 'correct' pronunciation of any word with a final [ɪn] is. For a word like *captain*, is this really an [ɪn] final word, or should it be pronounced with a velar nasal in formal or nice company? Thackeray's novel *Vanity Fair* indicates that precisely this kind of **linguistic insecurity** has surrounded (ing) for a long time. Jos Sedley's valet refers to one of Sedley's friends as *the Capting* [kæptɪŋ]. A form like *capting* can be called hypercorrection because the perceived 'correction' actually produces something that is not attested in any native variety of English.

It is easy to understand why it was attractive to borrow the notion of hypercorrection from the behaviour of learners overshooting their second language or second dialect target. Remember that under Labov's attention to the speech model of style-shifting, the hypothesis

No, really?

Hypercorrection occurs with borrowings from foreign languages as well. Sometimes when speakers borrow a word from another language they produce a 'foreign' pronunciation that is not attested in the original language. An English example is the use of a palatalised [nj] (corresponding to the written *ñ*) in Spanish borrowings where there is no [nj] in the Spanish original. The words *empanada* (a folded-over pastry) and *habanero* (a type of chile from Havana) are frequently pronounced *empañada* and *habañero*. It seems that people find the sound [nj] so iconic of Spanish that they insert it in words borrowed from Spanish, simply to mark them as borrowings (or to suggest they are sophisticated bilinguals!), even when the original had the plain [n].

was that speakers were monitoring their speech more and more as the tasks got more and more focused on linguistic forms rather than content. The consistency of style-shifting across classes and individuals suggested that speakers shared a perception of what was considered better or more appropriate in the speech community as a whole. Consistent stratification of variants across styles and classes has been interpreted as indicating that the social meaning of a variant results from an association between careful and considered styles of speech and higher social class.

However, there are two reasons why it may not be entirely helpful to call the lower middle class cross-over 'hypercorrection'. The first is empirical. When a working-class speaker says *Capting*, they are producing something which, quite simply, does not exist in any variety of English. This is not actually what the lower middle-class speakers in Labov's study were doing. It is very likely that the r-ful forms they produced are actually attested in the speech of middle-class New Yorkers. That is, they are producing forms like [kɑrd] for *card* which certainly occur in middle-class speech, but they are simply producing them more often than middle-class speakers do in that style. Hypercorrection in the classic sense of the term would be if they were producing forms like [gɑrd] for *god* where no speaker of an r-ful variety would ever produce an [r].

The second reason is more conceptual. In order to describe the behaviour of the lower middle class in Figures 8.10 and 8.11 as hypercorrect, we have to treat

(i)   social class membership; and
(ii)   the social meaning of linguistic variation

as more fixed than they are. We have been at pains to stress the fact that class is not rigidly deterministic, and, as the discussion in other chapters has shown, many social categories and identities are defined through negotiated interaction. Moreover, when we are talking about a change in progress, we are necessarily talking about a linguistic system with a moving target (or targets); the significance of a variant that occurs at a particular frequency is subject to negotiation and contestation within the speech community.

Connections with theory

The use of hypercorrection in sociolinguistics may date from Labov's 1966 study of NYC. But the idea was around before that. Bloomfield (1933: 302) talked about *over-elegant* and *hyperurban* forms. Hockett (1958: 436) discusses *overcorrections* and *hyperurbanisms*. Bynon (1977) uses the term to translate the French *régression*.

The term 'cross-over effect' directs our attention to what speakers are doing, rather than reifying class divisions in an empirically and theoretically questionable way. It also provides a more meaningful basis for comparison between speakers' performance (as shown in Figures 8.10 and 8.11), and their sensitivity and reactions to the variables when others use them. It therefore seems on balance a less loaded and more appropriate term than 'hypercorrection'.

Meaning of the cross-over

Labov conducted a number of tests to investigate attitudes to the presence or absence of /r/ and the raising of short (a). He found that in the case of (r), lower middle-class (SEC 6–8) respondents gave strongly positive evaluations to speakers using the supra-local variant with overt prestige, and in the case of short *a* they gave strongly negative evaluations of the more stigmatised, regional variant. This is shown in Table 8.1.

Table 8.1   New Yorkers' evaluations of speakers using /r/ and raised short *a*. (Source, Labov 1972a: 130, 131.)

Class	SEC	Percentage positive response to r-ful speech	Percentage negative response to raised short a
Lower class	0–2	50	63
Working class	3–5	53	81
Lower middle class	6–8	86	86
Upper middle class	9	75	67

The results of these attitude tests suggest that the lower middle class are more sensitive to, and hence view more positively, the use of the incoming variant [r], and evaluate more negatively the use of the non-standard, raised New York variant for short *a*, than even upper middle-class speakers (who actually use more of the Standard US English forms themselves in casual speech).

exercise

The lower middle-class leaders in change

If it is true that lower middle-class speakers are particularly sensitive to the incoming variant, why do you think that might be?

How might this relate to Weber's definitions of class, and the position of the lower middle class within a larger class structure?

Both the subjective responses to the attitude tests and the performance of speakers in different tasks converge, indicating the important role played by the second highest social class in linguistic variation. Both their production and their perception of variables suggest that in order to understand the trajectory of sound changes in progress or the social significance of innovative variants we need to consider the relationship between innovativeness/ conservatism and being in the second highest class.

Use of (r) in North Carolina

Figure 8.12 shows the distribution of pre-consonantal and final (r) in North Carolina. This is the same linguistic variable as Labov studied in New York City. North Carolina, like NYC, is traditionally an r-less area.

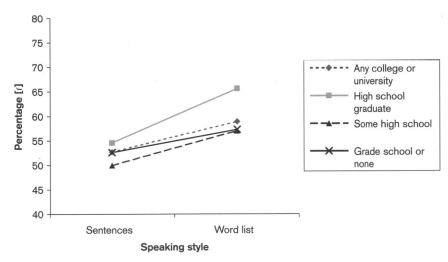

Figure 8.12   Frequency of constricted [r] before consonants and pauses in North Carolina in two reading styles (sentences and isolated words). Respondents categorised according to level of formal education received.

The speakers are broken up into four groups who differ in the amount of formal education they have had (least = grade school or none; most = any college/university). The frequency of [r] presence is shown for two activities: reading sentences (less careful) and reading word lists (more careful).

What kind of cross-over effect can you see here? How does it differ from the cross-over effect documented by Labov?

Do you think the North Carolina cross-over effect can be explained in the same way that the NYC cross-over effect was? How do you have to modify or extend Labov's argument?

CLASS AND HISTORICAL SOCIOLINGUISTICS

Historical sociolinguistics analyses the variation that is found in written historical texts. Often we are lucky if we know very much about the writers in these corpora at all, or the circumstances under which the texts were written. Nevertheless, even very basic information on writers' social backgrounds can yield systematic patterns – very like those found in recent studies of spoken variation. That is, we find stratification of variants according to the writers' social class or sex. Here we will look at two variables that show effects for class in the historical record: the first gives evidence for how and when a particular strategy for expressing negatives was lost from Standard English, and the second involves the introduction of a new form of verb agreement.

The decline of negative concord in English

Negative concord

A language where a negative element/constituent in a sentence requires all other indefinites to also be negative has a rule of negative concord.

Negative concord refers to a pattern of agreement between a negative constituent early on in a sentence and any indefinites that follow it. It is strongly stigmatised in Standard English, but widely used in non-standard varieties spoken around the world. You may know it as using 'double negatives', but this term underestimates how many negative elements you can end up with in a single sentence. A rule of negative concord can produce sentences like:

(1) I didn't have nothing to do with none of it.

Here, *nothing* and *none* occur following the negative element *not* (*-n't*), where Standard English would have *anything* and *any*. Modern Standard English has lost the agreement between negatives and indefinites that it once had.

Historically, English did have negative concord, and the equivalent of (1) was perfectly standard. Romance languages still have this rule. In most cases, the negative element that triggers this switch is *not* or *-n't* attached to the verb in a sentence, but it can be other negative constituents as well. So Standard English says (2) and not (3), but (3) is perfectly grammatical in Spanish (in the following sentences the negative trigger is in **bold** and the indefinite showing concord is in *italics*):

(2) **Nobody** said *anything* about that.

(3) a. **Nobody** said *nothing* about it.
        (English: non-standard with negative concord)
     b. **Nadie** me dijo *nada* de eso.
        (Spanish: standard with negative concord)

Connections with theory

Try pushing this norm of non-standard and vernacular English. How far can you force negative indefinites with a negative element in the main clause? Can you have more than the three negative indefinites in (1)? Now try and see if you have one in a subordinate clause – for example, 'translate' these Standard English sentences into ones with negative concord:

(a) *I didn't tell anybody who was waiting for anyone.*
(b) *She better not do anything to hurt anybody.*

Do *anyone* or *anybody* change into *no one* and *nobody*?

Languages differ in how far the agreement effects of an earlier negative reach down into the rest of the sentence. In some languages, the clause boundary between a main and subordinate clause (marked by *who* in (a) and *to* in (b)) is permeable and the negative can trigger agreement even in the subordinate clause. In other languages, this boundary is stronger and it blocks a lot of syntactic phenomena. Negative concord can be one of them.

Since this boundary differs cross-linguistically in its strength, we should not be too surprised if different varieties of English treat it differently. We might not be surprised, for example, if we found that the boundary is strong for lower middle-class speakers and weaker for working-class speakers. So, a working-class speaker might produce *She better not do nothing to hurt nobody*, while in theory a lower middle-class speaker might produce *She better not do nothing to hurt anybody*.

An important rider on this generalisation is that we are talking about modern *Standard English*. Most, if not all, varieties of non-standard English spoken today continue to use the older patterns of negative concord, but because the variable carries very strong negative sanctions it shows quite pronounced stratification across social classes, with upper middle-class speakers using it seldom, if ever, even in casual speech and lower working-class speakers using it quite often.

However, up until the sixteenth century, it was perfectly acceptable to use negative concord in English, so we find examples like (4) written by Mary, Queen of Scots, and examples like (5) written by the English chancellor, Thomas Cromwell.

(4) I'l **never** be so lasie **no more** but rise by five a cloke rather then mise wrighting any more.

['I won't be so lazy anymore, and will rise by five o'clock rather than miss writing anymore.']

(Mary Stuart, 1577(?))

(5) And wher as I accordinglye haue not in lyke wise remembrid and rescribid it hath bene for that I haue **not** hade **anything** to wryt of to your aduancement.

['And whereas I accordingly have not in the same manner remembered and written in reply, it has been because I have not had anything to write about to your advancement.']

(Thomas Cromwell, 1523)

One of the interesting things about this variable is how early the association with different social classes emerges. Terttu Nevalainen's work shows that by the end of the sixteenth century the patterns we find in today's sociolinguistic studies of this variable are already apparent. In Figure 8.13 we can see the decline of negative concord in the letters written by men from three social classes (data from women is very limited, except in the highest social class). The ranks in this hierarchy are what Nevalainen (1999) calls Gentry, the Middle Ranks and Other Non-gentry. She establishes through careful sociohistorical research that these social ranks were highly salient in sixteenth- and seventeenth-century society; Gentry and

No, really?

The 1510 parliamentary *Act Against the Wearing of Costly Apparel* legislated detailed restrictions on the colour and substance of clothing according to social station: 'No serving man under the Degree of a Gentleman [shall] use or wear any Gown or Coat or such like apparel of more Clothe than two broad yards and a half in a short Gown and three broad yards in a long Gowne.' Infringements of such laws were subject to punishment – for example, 'imprisonment in the Stocks by three days' (Nevalainen 1999).

the Middle Ranks would not make their living through manual labour, while other Non-gentry would.

Figure 8.13 shows that the men in the Middle Ranks lose negative concord fastest. It is worth noting that this group includes men who were classified as socially mobile, that is, men who might have started out life in lower ranks but had risen to very powerful positions and/or been ennobled during their lives. The highest social rank follows behind these speakers, and by the start of the seventeenth century they have closed the gap with the Middle Ranks. The Other Non-gentry lag in the loss of negative concord. While the decrease in negative concord from 1520 to 1680 is statistically significant for the Gentry and Middle Ranks, the apparent reduction for Other Non-gentry is not significant – there are just very few negative sentences in this group's letters (so when you adjust for this the difference turns out to be no greater than you'd expect by chance alone).

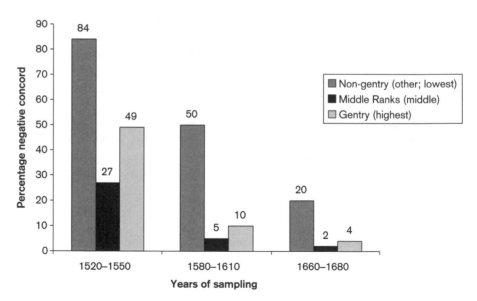

Figure 8.13   Frequency of negative concord in English letters written by men of three social ranks in the sixteenth and seventeenth centuries. (Classes here are: Gentry = nobility, upper and lower gentry, upper clergy; Middle Ranks = socially mobile men, lower clergy, other professional, merchants; Non-gentry (other) = manual workers.) (Source, Nevalainen 1999.)

By the end of the seventeenth century there is a clear class split with respect to this variable. Speakers who fall into what is roughly analogous to the modern upper and middle classes seldom if ever use negative concord; speakers from the working class use it regularly. The class stratification that is associated with this variable in English today started to emerge from the very earliest stages of the variable's existence.

The emergence of 3s -s agreement on verbs

Nevalainen's work also shows that the change from -*th* to -*s* marking third person singular agreement on verbs was stratified by social class. English lacks the richness of verbal morphology that characterises most of the other Germanic languages, and the only really productive inflections are the -*ed* marker of past tense on regular verbs and the use of -*s* in the present tense indicating that the subject of the verb is third person singular (*he, she, it*). All the other persons (first and second – *I, we, you*) and third-person plural have no agreement marking on them.

The third person -*s* marker that we use today was not always the standard form. Originally, it was only found in northern varieties of English, and the agreement marker used in southern and midland varieties of English was -*th*. However, as (6) shows, the northern -*s* had gained a foothold in the south by the fifteenth century, and as (7) shows, for several hundred years individuals alternated between the northern and southern variants:

(6) *The Kyng **purposeth** as to morow to be at Wendesor, and from thens to Notyngham. My Lord Chamberlyn **rides** to morue hame to Leycestre.*

['The King intends to be at Windsor tomorrow and from thence [goes] to Nottingham. My Lord Chamberlain rides home to Leicester tomorrow.']
(Richard Page, 1478(?))]

(7) *thy father **remembers** his loue to the and take thy wrightinge to him very kindly . . . I had thought to haue written to mr Roberts this time. but this sudene lornye of the mesinger **affordethe** me not so much time.*

['Your father sends his love to you and is touched by your writing him . . . I had intended to have written to Mr Roberts this time [too], but the sudden departure of the messenger does not afford [=give] me enough time.']
(Katherine Paston, 1626)

The northern variant made its way south because of massive internal migrations in England at this time. Starting in the fifteenth and sixteenth centuries, large numbers of northerners (mostly young men) moved to London looking for work as apprentices, and this changed the social make-up of the city enormously. The population in London in 1550 was around 100,000; by 1750 it was around 500,000. Sixteenth- and seventeenth-century court records suggest that more than 80 per cent of all Londoners were migrants and had not been born there (Nevalainen and Raumolin-Brunberg 2003: 38–39).

Ultimately, the -*th* ending became associated with formal and written style such as is found in the King James Translation of the Bible and the Book of Common Prayer (ritual language is very often archaic or more conservative than speech).

Connections with theory

You may have noticed a third variant for marking third person singular verbs in the extract from Katherine Paston. She writes *and [thy father]* **take** *thy wrightinge very kindly,* where the verb appears in its bare form, and has neither *-th* nor *-s* agreement marking on it.

This variant is particularly robust in East Anglia, where it is still an option. Peter Trudgill (2002) has analysed this variation as the consequence of massive immigration of Flemish and French speakers to Norwich in the sixteenth and seventeenth centuries – in 1579, 37 per cent of the population of Norwich were French- or Dutch-speaking immigrants.

Just as the huge numbers of northerners moving to London and the south were probably the vectors by which the northern *-s* variant gradually became the southern standard, Trudgill suggests that the large number of second-language speakers in Norwich at this time may have allowed the unmarked third-person variant to stabilise. Marking *only* third person singular is typologically unusual. Generally, if a language has *any* unmarked forms of the verb, third person singular lacks overt inflection; English is very unusual in having inflection only on 3s. So second-language learners of English might drop 3s agreement in order to level out an irregularity in the English verb paradigm, and native speakers of English might pick up this second-language strategy because it makes English less typologically marked.

In addition, the influx of Europeans to Norwich occurred at the same time that the southern agreement system was more widely destabilised by the introduction of the northern *-s.* Norwich was clearly affected by this as well (as shown by Katherine Paston's letter). This additional variability might have favoured the emergence of an unmarked third person singular form and encouraged it to stabilise in the region.

THE INTERSECTION OF CLASS AND STYLE

When we looked at stratification and cross-over effects, we started to see the important interplay between the way the speech community can be divided into social classes and the way speakers can differentiate within their stylistic repertoire. This interplay is more than a descriptive curiosity. When similar patterns in different domains occur sufficiently often, we have to ask what their co-occurrence tells us. What does it *mean* for two different (and largely independent) factors to pattern alike? In this section, we examine some of the parallels between class and style stratification.

The principal generalisation about class and style is that a variant which is favoured in the speech of higher social classes also tends to be the variant that is favoured in more careful styles of speaking overall. We can see this in Figure 8.14 which shows how often the non-standard variant of (ing), [ɪn], is used in Norwich English in five social classes and in four styles – casual conversation, formal conversation, reading passage and word list (following Labov (1972), I have used a solid line between the points marking conversational styles and reading, but used a broken line to connect with performance in word lists on the grounds that this is a very different kind of activity).

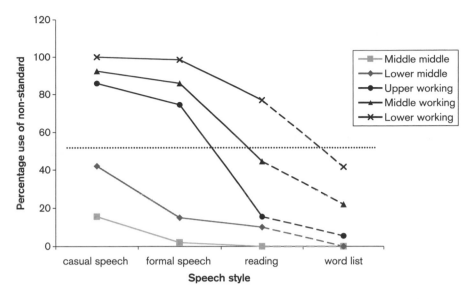

Figure 8.14 Frequency of non-standard (ing) in Norwich English in four styles for five SECs. (Data from Trudgill 1974, table 7.2.)

All social classes use [ɪn] most in conversation and least in reading and word lists. Moreover, in any one speech style there is positive correlation between class and use of [ɪn]. That is, the higher the socioeconomic class of the speaker, the more likely the speaker is to use the standard form [ɪŋ]. It is also clear that the range of variants used by speakers in the different groups overlap considerably. This is shown in the lower half of the graph, below the horizontal line. Here, you can see that the frequency with which the standard [ɪŋ] is used by lower working-, middle working- and upper working-class speakers in the reading and word list styles actually overlaps the frequency with which lower middle- and middle middle-class speakers use the standard variant in their casual and formal speech styles. Even though the overall frequency of the non-standard variant is lower in higher-class speakers, each socioeconomic group shows the same general tendencies with respect to style.

An idealised schema of the parallel between style and socioeconomic class is given in Figure 8.15. The arrows between the different social classes draw our attention to the overlap between more careful speech among one group of speakers and more casual speech among another.

In Chapter 3 we discussed different ways of analysing style-shifting, and we contrasted the idea that attention to speech motivates style-shifting with the idea that style-shifting is motivated by accommodation to the addressee (or imagined addressee). One way of reading Figure 8.15 is as a means of explicitly drawing both those explanations of style-shifting together. The leftmost arrow maps the frequency of a non-standard variant in the conversational style of the highest social class and shows how this overlaps with the frequency of that variant in the reading passage style of the speakers in the next socioeconomic class. In turn we can see that the frequency of the non-standard variant in reading-passage style for this mid-class overlaps with the frequency of the same variant in the word list style for the speakers in the lowest social class.

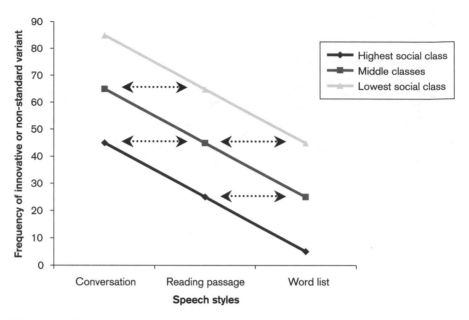

Figure 8.15   Idealisation of the parallelism between speaking style and speaker class, showing overlapping frequencies in speakers of different classes in different styles.

This suggests that when speakers pay more attention to their speech, they are in a
sense using their mental map of what the speech community as a whole sounds like to
guide them. That is, speakers seem to be treating the task of talking more carefully as if it
requires them to talk like someone of a higher social class (or, as we saw in the discussion
of accommodation-based analyses of style, the task makes them imagine talking to someone
representing the standard). All in all, it suggests speakers have a very sensitive appreciation
of what the linguistic norms are for different social groups in their community and that they
can and do draw on those norms for social purposes.

CHAPTER SUMMARY

Social class has fallen somewhat out of favour in sociolinguistics these days as a non-
linguistic variable for study. This is true in other social sciences too. One of the problems has
been that a lot of researchers feel categorisations into social class have been used uncritically
and as if they determine individuals' lives. Rather than providing the starting point for analysis,
researchers have been concerned that something like social class substitutes for analysis.
As a result, research on more local or personal identities has largely eclipsed the study of
social class.

However, even if we believe that a move to analysing variation in terms of personal
identities is the right thing to do for empirical and explanatory reasons, it is important not to
leave anything valuable behind. Where we have found systematic relationships between
larger social categories like class and very personal phenomena like style-shifting, we
have been given extremely important clues about what a specific variant means to the
speakers using it. In addition, the relationship between highly individual behaviours and group

behaviours gives us extremely valuable information about how intra-individual variability might be transformed into collective change. In other words, the information about larger group behaviour and individuals' behaviour complements and enriches both.

In this chapter we have seen examples that illustrate some of the reasons why broad categorisations like social class should remain part of the sociolinguistic tool kit. And the reasons are both practical and theoretical.

At a practical level, as we saw in the discussion of historical sociolinguistics, superficial information about people's occupations or their upward mobility within the larger class structure may be the only information available to us. The results from Nevalainen and her associates' work on the history of English show that even a modest amount of information about individuals or groups can be transformed into patterns of variation and change that bear a very strong resemblance to patterns found in recent, oral corpora. There are increasing numbers of oral and written corpora that are available in the public domain, many of which are very rich in data on variation but which were not deliberately gathered with this in mind. As Nevalainen's work shows, we would be short-changing ourselves as a profession if we were to turn our backs on these entirely just because they only offer basic demographic information on, for example, age, sex and occupation.

From a more theoretical perspective, social-class analyses have highlighted some interesting patterns across independent factors. In this chapter we have noted on numerous occasions the parallels between stratification of a variable according to social class and according to style. We have seen that these kinds of parallelisms are highly suggestive about what different linguistic variants signify or mean when speakers use them. In addition, these parallels can be used as a basis for drawing somewhat richer inferences about what the wider meaning of a category such as class is.

Social class is a categorisation system that is based on attributes like occupation or aspirations or life choices, and these attributes provide a useful basis for grouping individuals together. They are also sometimes eminently sensible groupings, since the indicators that define class membership also define who we associate with. In the next chapter, we examine social networks and communities of practice as the basis for analysing language variation and change. These analytical frameworks focus more explicitly on the importance of patterns of association and how we mark our identifications with (and distinctiveness from) others.

FURTHER READING

In addition to the works referred to in the text, you may also find the following interesting:

Guy (1988) and Ash (2002) – overviews of social class and variation and change.
Milroy and Milroy (1991) – the rise of standard varieties and their interplay with class (and other social factors).
Lippi-Green (1997) – the social impact of ideologies of Standard English and non-standard varieties on different social groups.
Chambers (2003) – different measures of social class by occupation, neighbourhood, etc.

CHAPTER 9

Social networks and communities of practice

Key terms in this chapter:

- core, peripheral, secondary network members
- dense and loose networks
- uniplex and multiplex ties
- community of practice
- brokers

INTRODUCTION

In the previous chapter we looked at the way in which linguistic variation can be analysed in terms of social classes. Social class can be used to group large swathes of people without the researcher needing to know them very well, whereas social networks are groupings based on frequency and quality of members' interaction. Communities of practice are defined by shared practices and goals, whose salience and meaning can only be determined through detailed or ingroup knowledge. Because these three levels of social categorisation ask different questions about the social meaning of a linguistic variable, they can be used effectively with different kinds of data to analyse – and, more importantly, – to understand the meaning of linguistic variation.

In this chapter, we turn to social groupings that may have more local meaning or more salience in the day-to-day workings of speakers' lives. They will gradually form a bridge between the way variation patterns in larger social groupings of class to the more inter-personal view of variation that informed Chapters 3–6 when we considered the impact of addressee and domain on the way speakers talk.

SOCIAL NETWORKS

Social networks can be defined as 'the relationships [individuals] contract with others . . . [reaching] out through social and geographical space linking many individuals' (Milroy and Gordon 2003: 117). Whereas grouping people into social classes involves compartmental-ising them on the basis of factors that may matter to society as a whole (e.g., how prestigious their jobs are), social networks group people on the basis of factors that are more idiosyncratic. Social networks are defined by who your friends are, who you live near, who you have dinner or have drinks with, and who you work with. Network analyses also ask how often the members of all these groups are the same, and how often they are completely different?

It is very important for sociolinguists to have a sense of what the patterns of associations are between people who are friends or roughly social equals within a community. This is because the diffusion of linguistic change happens relatively fast and very efficiently along what we might call horizontal channels (e.g., within one age group and a social cohort). What we might call vertical channels (e.g., channels between generations or across big social divides) are a comparatively slow and inefficient means of transmitting innovation. So it is common knowledge that kids talk like their friends, not their parents (hence the nice age differences underpinning the apparent time construct discussed in Chapter 7).

The significance of social networks emerges implicitly in sociolinguistics as early as Labov's study of Martha's Vineyard. There, as we saw, the networks of the Chilmark fishermen and the Menemsha Native Americans were characterised (respectively) by higher levels of (ay) and (aw) centralisation than were found in other groups. The Native American community was a relatively self-contained network of individuals because of the regional and cultural isolation of the reservation. The fishing community also formed a reasonably self-contained network. Partly this was because they were located at the end of the island furthest from the growing tourism industry, but their network was also characterised by a more general orientation to traditional Island ways of life.

However, the systematic use of social networks as the basis for analysing linguistic variation is most closely associated with James and Lesley Milroy's research in Belfast, Northern Ireland. The Milroys found that the patterns of language change that they observed correlated in very informative ways with the web of relationships making up social networks. They argued, therefore, that social networks are at least as important as macro-social categories like class for understanding how changes take hold and spread across a community (or communities). In the next two sections, some basic terminology associated with network analysis is introduced, as well as ways in which an analyst can identify social networks. I then introduce the concept of the community of practice. We will see that communities of practice are a specific form of social network. They are defined even more strictly by members' negotiated shared behaviour(s). Then we look at some case studies where social networks have been usefully deployed for analysing linguistic variation. (We will examine more case studies of communities of practice in Chapter 10.)

Finally, the chapter will conclude with a discussion of some more theoretical issues arising from the discussion of social class or social status and social networks, especially the relationship between class and style.

Defining networks

If membership in a particular social class can be determined on the basis of all sorts of external factors, but especially an individual's occupation, what determines membership in a social network?

Social network theory was introduced to sociolinguistics from sociology. In other fields of the social sciences, social networks have been found to have a big impact on how innovations are spread through society. You can look, for instance, at how fashions for sneakers/trainers spread, or how new forms of technology spread using social networks (so, as you can imagine, marketers love studying social networks). Naturally, if we can show that networks influence the social dispersion of innovations in fields like knowledge and technology, it would be nice to know whether they also affect the spread of linguistic innovation.

How can you identify a social network? One way of going about it is for the researcher to observe who interacts with who in a community and to note how or why they are interacting with each other. Slowly, patterns of interaction will emerge and these can be said to constitute individuals' social networks. This method has the advantage of being objective and, like a census, can provide a comprehensive slice-of-life picture of the way the community was structured at the time the research took place.

Another way of identifying networks is for the researcher to let the people s/he is observing define their own social networks. That is, you can simply ask the subjects in your study something like 'who are your best friends?' or 'name all the people that you had a conversation with yesterday'. The researcher can then build up a network on the basis of all the answers. Some problems inevitably arise: Tim might name Nick as a best friend, but Nick doesn't return the favour. This might be because Nick doesn't think as much of Tim as Tim thinks of Nick, or it might simply be because Nick forgot to name Tim (it happens, even with good friends).

The researcher has to decide how to deal with a situation like this if and when it comes up. If you are using subjects' own reports as the basis for building up a picture of their social networks you can either try and factor in all the information that you are given, or you can be stricter and only count those naming relationships that are reciprocal (i.e., ones where Ann names Joe and Joe names Ann). Jenny Cheshire (1982) and Penny Eckert (2000) both used naming when constructing the social networks of the adolescents in their studies. Taking into account reciprocal naming patterns and other social characteristics such as use of swearing and clothing style, Cheshire distinguished between people who were central to the network (**core members**) and those who were less integrated into it (**peripheral** and **secondary members**). Eckert composed the social networks in the high school where she was working based on responses to the question of who are 'the main people you hang out with', regardless of whether the naming was reciprocal. We will look at both these studies in more detail later in the chapter.

Core network member

Term used by Jenny Cheshire to describe the members centrally involved and actively participating in a friendship *network*. Distinguished from peripheral and secondary members who were progressively less involved.

Peripheral network members

See *Core network members*.

Secondary network members

See *Core network members*.

---

exercise

Identifying social networks

Child's name	Answer to 'Who are your best friends?'
Sam	Max, Leah, Leon, Corbin
Max	Sam, Corbin, Leon, Leah
Corbin	Leah, Sam, Max
Leah	Sam, Katie, Corbin
Katie	Leah, Max, Corbin
Leon	Corbin, Max

The table above gives the names of six children and their replies to the question 'Who are your best friends?' All the children know each other, but not all of them name each other as 'best friends'.

Write the children's names on a piece of paper in a rough circle. Now link them up in a network by drawing an arrow between everyone whenever they name another child as a 'best friend'. For example, you'd draw an arrow pointing from Sam to Max and another back from Max to Sam.

Now do the network again, but this time only connect the children where there is reciprocal naming; that is, where both children give each other's name in response to the question.

How different do the two networks look? What information seems to be missing or added in either one?

Dense and loose networks

Networks can be differentiated on the basis of whether they are **dense** or **loose**. A dense network is one where the members all know each other. So, for example, if you asked the question 'who did you have a conversation with yesterday?' of five people, and the only people each individual named were the other four people, then you would have a very dense network. However, if you asked that question and you got only minimal overlap in people's replies you would be dealing with very loose networks.

Dense and loose networks

Dense networks are characterised by everyone within the network knowing each other. In loose *social networks* not all members know each other.

Dense or loose networks?

Go back to the network you constructed for the kids in the previous exercise. Would you say that network is dense or loose? (You might want to characterise part of the network as more dense than another.)

Again, is this information retained where you construct the network on the basis of all naming relationships, as well as when you construct it based on reciprocal naming only?

exercise

The distinction between dense and loose networks may be important for understanding how changes progress through communities. Milroy (1987: 202–203, 213) suggested that, in general – regardless of whether you are studying an innovation in speech or an innovation in technology – dense networks slow down or inhibit change. Researchers hypothesise that in dense networks members police each other's behaviour (consciously or unconsciously) because of the intensity of their contact. Moreover, because in a dense network members' contacts outside their network are comparatively superficial, there is less chance of being systematically exposed to innovations from outside.

Loose networks make individuals more open to change. The ties that the individual members have to other networks provide an opportunity for them to be exposed to and pick up innovations from outside their network. In addition, the normative pressure of any single network will be attenuated, because we assume speakers have to attend to the norms of the numerous different networks that their loose social ties give them membership to.

Megan Melancon (2000) studied the patterns of language use among Louisiana African-Americans who identify as Creoles and found that network density was a useful non-linguistic variable for accounting for patterns of language maintenance and language loss. Melancon assigned a network score to all the people in her study. The score was based on five factors:

(handwritten margin note: applicable to BC?)

- ■ How long has the individual lived in the area?
- ■ Is the individual's spouse a member of a long-time local family in town?
- ■ Does the individual work in town?
- ■ How many of the individual's recreational activities take place in town?
- ■ How many of the individual's friends live in town?

For each of these factors, if an individual answered 'always' or 'all', they were given a score of 1. For 'usually/most' they were assigned a score of 2; for 'sometimes/some' a score of 3; and for 'never/none' a score of 4. Her results ranged from someone with the densest network (who scored 5) to people with the most open networks who had scores of 18.

Melancon compared these network scores with how often an individual used Creole French. She found that there was a very strong correlation between a person's social network and their use of Creole French. The speakers who used Creole most often had network scores of 5–7.

Multiplex and uniplex ties within networks

Uniplex tie

A network tie between individuals that expresses one role or basis for contact and interaction. (See also *Multiplex tie*.)

Multiplex ties

Individuals in a social network can be linked through a single social relationship (a *uniplex tie*; e.g. mother~daughter) or through several social relationships (multiplex ties; e.g. cousins~co-workers~neighbours).

Networks can also be distinguished in terms of the quality of the ties between individuals. That is, if the network tie between two individuals is based only on one relationship, e.g., the two people work together, or are family members, or have children in the same swim club, then this tie is called a **uniplex tie**. However, if two people know each other in several different roles, then the tie is called **multiplex**. So if two individuals are best friends, and they take the same courses at university, and they work in the same pub on the weekend, their tie would be a three-way one – a multiplex tie.

Again, the assumption is that a loose network based largely on many uniplex ties is going to be more open to the introduction and transmission of innovations than a dense one where members share multiplex ties. In practice though, these kinds of qualitative distinctions between types of network tie have not been exploited as a basis for much sociolinguistic analysis. Most sociolinguists would share the intuition that some network ties are likely to be more important to speakers than others. However, in practice we find this intuition is integrated much more fully in research that looks at speakers as members of communities of practice.

---

exercise

Multiplex ties within networks

It has been suggested that working-class networks in the British Isles are almost always more multiplex and denser than middle-class networks (Milroy 1987: 52).

Why do you think that might be? What characteristics define a network as multiplex? How well does a stereotyped working-class or middle-class lifestyle correspond to that definition?

COMMUNITIES OF PRACTICE: HIGHLY LOCAL NETWORKS

Like social networks, the **community of practice** has been borrowed into sociolinguistics from another field of the social sciences. Communities of practice were initially developed as part of a social theory of learning. So, for example, Jean Lave looked at how tailors in Liberia learnt the skills of tailoring as part of a larger social process that involved getting to know how to be a constructive member of the community of all tailors. The tailoring practices were only one of many social practices that apprentices had to learn. Similarly, Etienne Wenger studied a US insurance company, identifying the range of social practices that characterised experienced members of the workplace community as opposed to novices who had only recently joined. Wenger, too, examined the process of learning that was involved in transforming new employees into core members of the workplace group (Lave and Wenger 1991; Wenger 1998).

A community of practice is a specific kind of social network. Communities of practice are characterised by:

- mutual engagement;
- a jointly negotiated enterprise;
- a shared repertoire.

'Mutual engagement' means coming together in direct personal contact. The requirement for mutual engagement is a stricter measure for membership than is required for either social networks or social classes. It is possible to build up a social network that extends to and includes individual members who have no direct contact with each other but who inherit ties from others (you might say members can be linked transitively). Likewise, not everyone in the middle class meets everyone else in the middle class. The spheres of social engagement that define a community of practice are much narrower than anything an entire social class could participate in.

A 'shared repertoire' may be speech styles, but it also includes other social practices. In the domain of language, it includes shared ways of pronouncing words, shared jargon or slang, and in-jokes. A shared repertoire also enables some conversations to be continued over a period of days or weeks without any fuss, or without a sense that participants need much reorienting to the topic. Note that a shared repertoire need not suppose contact between members or face-to-face engagement. So a shared repertoire is a necessary, but not sufficient, condition for defining a community of practice. Work in sociolinguistics over the last 40 years has clearly demonstrated that innovations or norms can be distributed around a speech community or a large social network without there being direct contact between all members of the community or network.

A 'jointly negotiated enterprise' is perhaps the most crucial criterion for defining a community of practice. Without this, it is easy to subsume the community of practice under the notion of social networks. The criterion of a jointly negotiated enterprise tells us that the members of a community of practice are not just in contact with each other, but they are working towards some shared goal, or are defining and satisfying some specific enterprise. In workplace studies (like those of Lave and Wenger, (1991)), a jointly negotiated enterprise may be local or specific, such as training new recruits to maintain an online ordering system, solving the problem of how to staff the office over the summer when everyone wants to take holidays, or increasing efficiency and output among a factory team.

Community of practice

Unit of analysis introduced to sociolinguistics by Penelope Eckert and Sally McConnell-Ginet in their research on language and gender. A smaller unit than a *social network*. Co-membership is defined on three criteria: mutual engagement, a jointly negotiated enterprise, and a shared repertoire. Associated with analyses of variation that emphasise speakers' agency. (See also *Acts of identity; Speaker design*.)

The community of practice works very well as an analytic framework in studies of workplace interaction. There, it is fairly easy to identify the relevance of all three criteria: mutual engagement, a jointly negotiated enterprise and a shared repertoire. As well as providing an alternative framework for answering linguistic questions about how new linguistic forms take hold and spread in a community, the community of practice provides a framework that is well suited to more applied goals in linguistics. It is a bit of a cliché that workplaces can't function without 'good communication'. The community of practice framework provides a good basis for linguistics to talk about what constitutes 'good communication' and bring some of our research out of the academy and into practical applications for training; for example, sharing ideas about what works well or what doesn't work in achieving some jointly negotiated enterprise.

---

exercise

The importance of individual variation

In Chapter 6 we saw that grouping speakers into multiple age bands is considered advantageous because it sometimes means overall trends emerge more clearly – the preferences of individual speakers won't distract from the overall picture.

But given the community of practice as an alternative level for analysis, what disadvantages might there be in grouping speakers in social classes? If large groups erase individual variation, why might this matter?

This chapter will not examine studies based on communities of practice in detail. We will return to them in Chapter 10, where we look at how gender has been treated as a sociolinguistic variable. Some of the most systematic studies of communities of practice to date happen to have been undertaken by researchers interested in how society perceives and reifies gender roles. Nevertheless, it is important at this stage to be aware of the history running from the study of speech communities to social networks and, most recently, to communities of practice.

The rest of this chapter will focus more squarely on social network studies. It reviews the methods and the empirical insights into the nature of language variation and change that sociolinguistics has gained from them. After the review of network case studies, we'll reconsider the significance of social class to the study of variation and change.

CASE STUDIES OF SOCIAL NETWORKS AND LANGUAGE VARIATION

We now examine results from three studies that have highlighted the significance of social networks. The first two come from research in Britain (Reading and Belfast), and the third comes from research in Los Angeles. The networks in Reading and Los Angeles are teenage networks, while the networks in Belfast are neighbourhood-based.

Reading, England

One of the first studies of language variation to use social networks in its analysis was conducted by Jenny Cheshire in Reading. Cheshire spent time hanging out with and recording the speech of a group of Reading teenagers, and she found that reciprocal naming and objective observations of the teenagers' patterns of association allowed her to distinguish between members of the group who were core and members who were peripheral. This distinction correlated with the extent to which different kids engaged in socially sanctioned and unsanctioned activities, such as going to school or cutting classes. This distinction mapped very neatly on to linguistic variation as well. (Note that by combining naming data, and also observations of what activities the teenagers were engaged in, Cheshire's work foreshadows the later turn to communities of practice.)

For example, with three linguistic variables, a teenager's place in the social network had a robust correlation with which variant they used more often. The three variables were use of non-standard pronouns to introduce a relative clause (1), the use of non-standard subject–verb agreement, i.e., -s present-tense agreement with non-3s subjects (2), and the use of *never* as a general negator, corresponding to the use of *not* or -*n't* in the standard (3).

(1) Are you the little bastards **what** hit my son over the head?
     (Standard: **who** or **that**)

(2) a. I just **lets** her beat me.
         (Standard: **let**)
     b. We **buses** it down the town.
         (Standard: **bus**, i.e., 'take the bus')

(3) I **never** went to school today.
     (Standard: **didn't go**)

The distribution of these forms according to how integrated the speaker was in the network of teenagers showed that core members always used more non-standard forms, followed by what Cheshire called secondary members; the peripheral members were always the ones who used standard variants most. This is shown in Figure 9.1. It indicates that non-standard *what* is the variable that is the most sensitive indicator of a speaker's position within the social network. Core members almost always use the non-standard variant, while peripheral members categorically use the Standard English *who*.

On the other hand, the stratification of non-standard *never* according to a speaker's position within the network is not so extreme. In particular, it is a poor marker differentiating secondary from peripheral members. The most salient difference for this variable is between core and non-core members.

We can represent the variation Cheshire documented in a line graph, because the distinctions between core, secondary and peripheral members in the network are related to each other on a scale. Membership in each category is defined by how much or how little an individual participates in a range of activities. So even though Cheshire distinguished three groups, we can imagine even more fine-grained groupings of the teenagers she worked with, also based on how much they see of each other and what activities they engage in together. And if we were to do this, we would expect more fine-grained categorisations to fall roughly along the lines plotted in Figure 9.1.

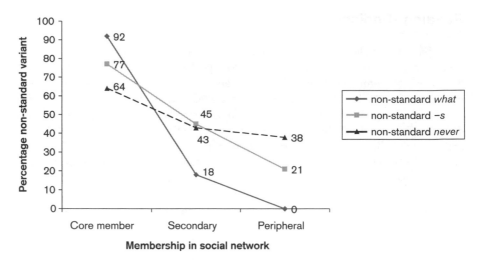

Figure 9.1 Frequency of non-standard variants in the speech of Reading teenagers. (Sources, Cheshire 1982; see also Chambers 2003: 88.)

Belfast, Northern Ireland

James and Lesley Milroy found that trying to do social dialectology in Belfast in the 1970s required rather different methods than the ones employed by Labov in New York City. At that time, Belfast was in the midst of the sectarian violence of the Troubles, and it would have been impossible for a sociolinguist to try and undertake interviews with people identified through random sampling.

Connections with theory

Sociolinguists' methods often have to adapt to the particulars of the histories of the individuals or social groups they want to work with. It is not always possible to control for all the factors that experimental research would control for (and, indeed, controlling for differences would miss the point of a lot of sociolinguistic work). For example, Gafaranga (1998) was working with the exiled Rwandan community in Belgium shortly after the violence of the civil war in the mid-1990s. He could not use the same interviewer/researcher with all members of the community because Rwandans simply would not trust anyone other than a known friend to infiltrate and record their day-to-day lives.

The Milroys therefore adopted a basis for sampling the community that reflected the closeness of some of the communities that they wanted to record in. By always being introduced to new people as 'friends-of-a-friend', and by doing their recordings at someone's kitchen table where their research was open to comment and question by anyone passing by to visit, they built up a sample of speakers that reflected the social networks of three neighbourhoods in Belfast.

Although all three neighbourhoods were working class, they found that there were appreciable differences between the extent to which speakers in the different neighbourhood-based networks had adopted ongoing changes in Belfast English. Fieldwork was undertaken in three areas in Belfast: Ballymacarratt, Clonard and the Hammer. Of these three areas, Ballymacarratt was characterised by the most dense and multiplex social network (Milroy 1987: 81), though within Ballymacarratt there were differences between women and men, with men having the densest networks of all. Milroy (1987) discusses at length the complex interactions between social networks and age (cf. our discussion in Chapter 7) and sex (see Chapter 10), but she notes that overall speakers in Ballymacarratt are significantly more likely to use the highly localised, vernacular variants in six of the variables investigated. For example, Ballymacarratt speakers on average used more backed vowels in *hat* and *man*, and lower vowels in *electric* and *heavy* (polysyllabic words with a stressed DRESS vowel). (Labov subsequently analysed this data using rather different methods and confirmed the correlation between social network and use of vernacular forms with these variables; see Labov 2001: 331.)

The Milroys concluded that one reason for the differences between speakers in the different neighbourhoods was the extent to which the neighbourhood constituted a close-knit or dense network. A more conservative neighbourhood such as Ballymacarratt was typified by dense, multiplex networks. A neighbourhood like the Hammer was characterised by looser social networks.

Chicanos/Chicanas in Los Angeles, USA

Carmen Fought found that the social networks of Chicano/Chicana teenagers in Los Angeles was the best predictor of how likely a speaker was to use sentences with non-standard negative concord. Initially, she had thought that the frequency of negative concord (discussed earlier) might be influenced by the speaker's fluency in Spanish.

When we looked at the historical loss of negative concord in English, we noted that concord is the only grammatical option in a language like Spanish. In fact, it holds within clauses and across clauses as shown in examples (4) and (5). These show that the negative constituent *no* triggers concord throughout the main clause (4), and even into the subodinate clause (5):

(4) a. I did**n't** tell *anybody anything* about *any* of that
         (English: standard without negative concord)
     b. **No** le dije *nada* a *nadie* de *nada* de eso
         (Spanish: standard with negative concord)

(5) a. She better **not** do *anything* to hurt *anybody*.
     b. Mejor ella **no** hace *nada* para dañarle a *nadie*.

Fought hypothesised that if a teenager was more fluent in Spanish, they would be more likely to transfer this kind of pattern into English. If that was the case, then they would be more likely to produce forms like (6) and (7) with negative concord within the same clause (analogous to (4)), and also forms like (8) with negative concord across clauses (analogous to (5)). She thought teenagers fluent in Spanish would do this more often than teenagers whose Spanish was not so good.

(6) I won't do it no more.
(7) They didn't have no car.
(8) I don't like girls that have no tattoos.

In fact, Fought found that four factors significantly affected the rate of negative concord, but that the speaker's competence in Spanish (bilingualism) was the least important factor. In order, the factors were:

Gang status >> syntactic frame >> social class >> bilingualism

The most significant factor was whether or not the speaker was a member of a gang, more loosely affiliated with gang networks, or was a member of some other social network.

Table 9.1   Probability of members of different social networks using negative concord in the English of Chicano/Chicana speakers in Los Angeles. (Data from Fought 1999.)

Gang status	Probability of negative concord
Taggers	0.94
Gang members	0.65
Gang-affiliated	0.47
Non-gang members	0.20

The heaviest users of negative concord were the teenagers whose social networks define them as 'taggers' (i.e., people who draw the bold stylised urban graffiti). If a teenager was a member of a gang, they were also more likely to be a user of negative concord. If a teenager was a peripheral member of a gang network (gang-affiliated), there was a slight indication that they would be less likely to use negative concord, but the effect for this group was pretty minimal. The kids whose networks made them neither taggers, nor gang members were the least likely to use negative concord. The details of Fought's results are shown in Table 9.1, where higher numbers indicate an elevated likelihood of a speaker using negative concord and low numbers indicate that a group of speakers disfavour negative concord. As with previous data showing probabilities, remember that probabilities are not the same as percentage frequencies. They give you an adjusted sense of how likely individuals in each group are to use negative concord – all other things being equal. That is, it takes into account how often taggers and gang members used syntactic frames that favour or disfavour negative concord etc.

NOT ALL NETWORKS ARE EQUAL

These case studies make it clear that the social networks, or the communities of practice in which a person is involved, have an impact on linguistic behaviour. But if people are simultaneously members of many social networks or many communities of practice, how do they interconnect when it comes to accounting for and understanding the way people talk?

This is a very large question (and one which many sociolinguists are actively pursuing). For the purposes of our discussion, and building on the discussion of age in Chapter 7, we could ask whether all networks at all times of an individual's life have equal effect. Intuitively, the answer would be 'no', and work in Catalunya and in Montreal supports this. These studies indicate that a person's childhood networks have a greater impact on some aspects of their speech than the networks they participate in at any other time in their life.

Robert Vann (1998) looked at transfer between Catalan and Spanish in bilingual speakers. He expected to find that there would be more transfer from Catalan into Spanish with speakers whose current social networks were more deeply embedded in the Catalan community. However, he found that this was not a particularly good predictor of transfer. Instead, whether or not a speaker's childhood networks were Catalan seemed to be more important than their adult networks. In addition, there was more transfer with speakers whose mothers had been speakers of Catalan (this showed an effect that was independent of their overall childhood network scores). This indicates that predispositions to the transfer of structures or lexical items from Catalan to Spanish were probably laid down when speakers were quite young. And if they didn't acquire those predispositions then, they were unlikely to acquire them in adulthood, even if their adult social networks were more heavily Catalan than Spanish.

Similarly, a study of how successfully people who grew up in English-speaking households acquired colloquial features of Montreal French found childhood networks to be crucial. Looking at several discourse features (e.g., the equivalent of *well* or *so*), Sankoff *et al.* (1997) found that the degree to which an individual was integrated into the day-to-day activities of French-speaking networks as a child was the best overall predictor of their successful acquisition of these features.

Connections with theory

Saying that a person's childhood networks may be the most important ones doesn't mean that we all talk like we did when we were little children. There are obvious ways in which we don't. Paul Kerswill (1996) suggests that where a change is taking place in a community, children up to the age of about 4 may model their caregivers' speech, but that between 4 and 12 years children move away from their caregivers' speech. We really don't understand how children keep changes in progress moving though, and this is an area that merits further research.

Connections with theory

Both the Catalan and Montreal French findings seem consistent with the widely known fact that children acquire the core grammar and phonology of languages more easily and successfully than adults. But in fact neither involved features that are generally considered part of the core grammar. The Catalan study looked at the production of a mixed variety, and the Montreal study examined the acquisition of discourse variables.

The three network case studies and this very brief discussion of social networks at different ages give some idea about how social networks interact with linguistic variation. They show that systematic linguistic patterns can emerge whether speakers are grouped in larger clusters like socioeconomic classes or in smaller clusters defined in terms of contact and shared goals within a social network. In the remainder of this chapter, I hope to make clear that linguistic analyses based on social networks and those based on social classes can complement each other. The two approaches ask, and therefore answer, different questions about the sources of linguistic variation and the social meaning of linguistic variation. The trick is knowing when it might be more appropriate to use these different levels of analysis.

HOW OCCUPATION INTERACTS WITH SOCIAL NETWORKS

We can illustrate the differences in how network- and class-based approaches analyse language variation by considering how occupation features in both frameworks. We have already seen that occupation is often a key factor in assigning speakers into different socioeconomic classes because occupation has a major impact on an individual's status and life chances. And we have seen that the categorisation system of social class that is largely dependent on occupation can help us to make sense of the ways linguistic variables are stratified in the speech community. In addition, we noted that the lower middle class (or second highest) social group seem more sensitive (in terms of production and perception) to changes in progress than any other social group. Why might this be?

A class-based analysis would suggest that these so-called interior groups tend to be made up of people who are upwardly mobile, so they are especially alert to what's coming in as the norm. Their lead with changes in progress might therefore be a manifestation of a desire to accentuate the positive (Chapter 2). Or we might suggest that because the lower middle class are second from the top they might have a sense of having almost 'made it' – but not quite. As a consequence, they are on the lookout (consciously or unconsciously) for any social markers that will suggest to others that they *have* made it and that they *are* now the ones setting the norms. In this case their lead could be seen more as a desire to eliminate the negative (Chapter 2).

But how would we know if either of these accounts is or is not true? We can't interview everyone in the lower middle class, and even if we could it's unlikely they would be willing or able to articulate these kinds of motives. So accounts like these are necessarily very speculative.

However, another answer to the question might draw on the insights from network analysis. Perhaps the kinds of occupations associated with the interior social classes are also the kinds of occupations that bring people into contact with a wider variety of other speakers, and hence with a wider variety of other speaking styles. Under this approach, the leading role of the lower middle class and upper working class would not necessarily have anything to do with how secure they feel about their place in society. It might simply have more to do with the fact that they are exposed to more opportunities to expand their linguistic repertoire. This expanded input might be what enables them to lead other groups in change. They would both be exposed to more variation and in turn would play a crucial role in brokering the variation to others.

Patricia Nichols (1983) made exactly these sorts of connections between people's occupational patterns and their speech in a study of a Gullah-speaking community in the

United States. On the island where she was working as a teacher, speakers alternated between Gullah (a creole spoken on some of the islands off the south-east coast of the United States) and non-creole, more standard, variants. Her analysis of the variability between speakers highlighted the important role that a person's occupation could make to their social networks, and how these networks in turn alter their opportunity and need to use Standard US English forms.

Figure 9.2 shows the frequency of the non-standard or creole forms in three age groups, older, middle-aged and younger speakers. It divides each age group into male and female speakers (note that there are only two men and two women in each age group). Nichols draws our attention to the way both the older men and two women use creole forms quite often. She also notes the dramatic decrease in the use of these forms among the middle-aged women, and the very high frequency with which they occur in younger men's speech.

Although exposure to Standard US English, through education and travel, plays some part in explaining these differences, it cannot account for them all on its own. Instead, speakers' employment histories provide a more satisfactory explanation. This was particularly clear when she looked at employment trends among the women. Employment opportunities for older women in this community had seldom gone beyond being a household domestic or a farm labourer – jobs that required little in the way of conversation with speakers of Standard English. However, the middle-aged women in her study were typical of their age group on the island. They had begun to take up jobs, such as sales clerk and mail carrier, that require regular interactions with a diverse group of people, many of whom do not speak Gullah. Meanwhile, the employment patterns for men of all ages have stayed relatively constant. Men generally find work in construction crews and these are frequently made up of other family members or other Gullah speakers.

So whereas women's social networks had changed and brought them into increased contact with speakers of mainland varieties of English, men's networks had not. (Nichols's article includes even more detailed discussion of individuals, which enriches this account

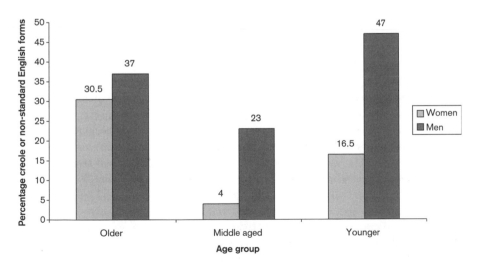

Figure 9.2   Percentage frequency of creole or non-standard English forms in the speech of 12 Gullah speakers – two males and two females in each of three age groups. (Source, Nichols 1983: 60.)

further.) In Chapter 10 we will see that other studies have found that the social networks men and women participate in can have a major impact on the way they talk.

exercise

Language and professional identities

Make a list of five occupations that you think are generally more likely to be held by women and by men. Obviously, all jobs require people to talk or sign to other people, but how central are language skills in fulfilling each of the jobs you have listed? (You might want to rank them as ones where language is integral to the job, and ones where it is necessary but incidental.) Now rank the occupations according to whether they are associated with dense or loose social networks.

Is there a correspondence between the jobs high on the language scale and the networks associated with the jobs?

WHO LEADS?

We have looked at the effect that larger group categorisations, such as socioeconomic class, and smaller, more local groups, such as social networks, have on the distribution of linguistic resources. We have discussed the generalisation that speakers from the interior, or second-highest social class, lead some changes in progress, and we have discussed the generalisation that dense social networks inhibit the transmission of new forms. These generalisations still leave us relatively far from the actual practices of individuals. We might ask who, within those groups (class or network), are the leaders mapping out the trajectory for future developments.

A little bit of work has been done on this subject, and it comes from researchers working within all three frameworks of analysis we have discussed. In his long-term study of the Philadelphia vowel system, Labov has noted that speakers who use the most advanced variants of changes in progress are lower middle-, or upper working-class women who name a number of friends who live outside their immediate neighbourhood. He has also noted that they tend to be the kinds of people who are socially proactive and who become very involved in community 'business'.

This meshes quite neatly with the impressions that the Milroys formed in their Belfast study – namely, that speakers with the most ties outside their networks were more likely to be the **brokers** introducing and leading in the adoption of innovations.

Brokers

The people who introduce innovations into *social networks*.

Other work emphasising communities of practice (whether working explicitly within that framework or not) have noticed the association between extreme variants of changes in progress with speakers who are engaged in more flamboyant and extreme social positioning overall. Again, these are often women or girls, and Penelope Eckert has noted that their flamboyance may be marked not only in their speech but also in their dress, the kinds of social activities they are associated with, and their role as brokers and players in the marketplace of sexual attraction. (We will return to Eckert's work in more detail in Chapter 10.)

The flipside to this is that some of the more extreme users of regionally marked traditional (or conservative) variants are often men who are likewise engaged in occupations that are strongly iconic of older lifestyles. So Walt Wolfram and his associates' work on the

Table 9.2 Fronting of (uw) and (ow) for two groups of California girls. Higher index scores mean more fronted tokens. (Source, Bucholtz 1998.)

Cool girls			Nerd girls		
Speaker	(uw)	(ow)	Speaker	(uw)	(ow)
Erin	136	114	Beth	56	52
Josie	138	145	Bob	48	42
Paige	144	111	Christine	71	42
Sophia	135	138	Fred	125	65
Zoe	69	65	Kate	64	20

small island of Ocracoke found that the more extreme regional variants occurred in the speech of men who were involved in traditional work, such as fishing. As we saw in Chapter 3, one of these men deployed these variants quite consciously at times, using them to emphasise his claim to the social value associated with the traditional practices they were associated with (Schilling-Estes 1998a). In other words, social networks, and an individual's engagement in non-linguistic social practices, can help us define and identify the leaders (and laggers) of a change in progress.

Sometimes, as we saw with the Catalan and the Montreal studies above, an individual's previous networks or earlier participation in a community of practice may be instrumental in understanding how they talk now. A nice example of this can be seen in Mary Bucholtz's work with teenagers in California. Bucholtz compared the extent to which two groups of high school girls ('cool girls' and 'nerd girls') were participating in well-documented sound changes. These involve the fronting of the back vowels /u/ and /o/ – the vowels in GOOSE and GOAT, or the (uw) and (ow) variables (as they are often called in North American dialectology). Table 9.2 shows the index of fronting for five girls in each group.

The fronting of /u/ is an older change in progress in California (and other varieties of) English, while /o/ fronting is more recent. The girl to look at most closely is Fred (two of the nerd girls chose male names as their pseudonyms for the study). Fred leads the other nerd girls in both changes: in particular, her index for /u/ is appreciably higher than the index scores for the other nerd girls. In fact, she seems to be fronting /u/ more like the cool girls do, rather than like the nerds. It turns out that when she was younger Fred used to hang out with Erin, Josie and the other cool girls, and she has only relatively recently moved into the group with the nerd girls. So it seems that the networks she had when she was younger have laid down a relatively stable set of linguistic practices (even if the other social practices she engages in have since changed).

Bucholtz's study illustrates the merit there can be in considering exceptional individuals in our analyses, and the usefulness of complementing our documentation of general trends with detailed ethnographic fieldwork.

CHAPTER SUMMARY

In this chapter we have added two more levels of social categorisation which can be used to analyse language variation and language use: social networks and communities of practice. These nest within social class (discussed in the previous chapter) in terms of how locally they are defined and how much emphasis they place on speakers' attitudes and actions. They complement the discussions of style in Chapter 3, as we could say that style has intensely local meaning – sometimes interpretable only in terms of the relationship between the interlocutors, at that moment, and at that place.

Some sociolinguists find the highly local level at which social network analysis takes place very attractive for practical and theoretical reasons. Many researchers get to know the community they are working in very well, and they are uncomfortable aggregating members into large categories like social class because they see how much internal variability there is within these groups. Moreover, such large groupings often make it very difficult to provide a verifiable analysis of why speakers might be using one variant rather than another. If there is social meaning assigned to different linguistic variants, and if this meaning is ultimately negotiated in face-to-face interaction, then a lot of sociolinguists would argue that we must conduct our analyses at this level of interaction too.

I have suggested that the approaches should not be seen as standing in competition to each other, but rather as complementary. This isn't just a way of having our cake and eating it too – I have tried to show that just as there are layers of social categorisations within a community, there are layers of social meaning for linguistic variables. Being sensitive to the layers of social structure can add to the sensitivity of our analyses.

The next chapter, which examines gender more closely, will continue to build on this fundamental idea. Different social identities contribute differently to the social meaning of language variation and use.

FURTHER READING

In addition to the works referred to in the text, you may also find the following interesting:

Rogers (1995) and Valente (1995) – on social networks and the diffusion of non-linguistic innovations.
Dodsworth (2005) – detailed application of network analysis of linguistic variation.
Mendoza-Denton (1999) – survey of sociolinguistic and anthropological research on Latino speech.
Journal of Sociolinguistics, vol. 9, no. 4 – an exchange of articles on the use of communities of practice in sociolinguistics.

CHAPTER 10

Gender

Key terms introduced in this chapter:

- **sex**
- **gender**
- **exclusive features**
- **preferential features**
- **direct indexing**
- **indirect indexing**
- **indexing**

- **conventional implicature**
- **constitutive**
- **reflexive**
- **performative**
- **laminated**
- **illocutionary force**
- **conversational implicatures**

INTRODUCTION

'What's your research on?' asked the woman at the garden party. 'Language and sex', I replied. 'Whoa-ho', she said, 'You must have them lining up to supervise you.'

In the 1980s, it was not at all unusual for a sociolinguist to describe their interests as being 'language and sex'. However, in the intervening years, the term **sex** has largely been replaced by the term **gender**, and the significance of this change in terminology will become clear in this chapter.

The field of language and gender is one of the most dynamic in sociolinguistics. It is characterised by a lot of discussion about the pros and cons associated with different ways of conceptualising the relationship between language and society. This introductory text has tried to stress that the interplay between language and different social and personal identities is a complex one, and that in order to really understand the social meaning of any instance of language variation we need to start from the particular while simultaneously keeping an eye on the broader context of that variation. There has probably been more work done interrogating these webs of meaning with respect to gender than with respect to any other social category. The vigour of the field has been fed by its close ties to other branches of the social sciences – areas such as feminist theory, philosophy, sociology and anthropology.

As a consequence of the intellectual vitality and diversity of the field, work on language and gender has been conducted within a number of different frameworks and it would be impossible in an introduction to sociolinguistics to cover all of these. Good introductory texts specifically in this area are listed in the 'Further reading' section at the end of the chapter.

Sex

No, not **that** kind of sex. The term is increasingly restricted in sociolinguistics to refer to a biologically or physiologically based distinction between males and females, as opposed to the more social notion of *gender*.

Gender

Not grammatical gender (i.e., different classes of noun that may be called 'masculine', 'feminine'). Not *sex* of speaker which (largely) reflects biological or physiological differences between people. Used increasingly in sociolinguistics to indicate a social identity that emerges or is constructed through social actions. (See also *Constitutive*; *Reflexive*.)

SEX OR GENDER?

What prompted researchers to redefine their interests as being in **gender** rather than **sex**? It wasn't just that the jokes got tiresome. There were more principled reasons for *gender* replacing *sex* in sociolinguistics, and they reflect many changes in the field. Some are changes in the way people think about social identities, and some are changes in the way sociolinguists go about gathering and analysing their data. These changes are interrelated at a deeper level, but their impact is apparent in different areas.

The typical basis for differentiating *sex* and *gender* is that *sex* is a biological category and gender is a social and cultural category. In other words, *sex* is something you have, and it can be defined in terms of objective, scientific criteria — that is, the number of X chromosomes a person has. *Gender*, on the other hand, is a social property: something acquired or constructed through your relationships with others and through an individual's adherence to certain cultural norms and proscriptions. There are many cultural and social assumptions woven into this distinction; for example, the intellectual gulf between the so-called 'hard' sciences and the 'soft' or social sciences. There is some debate over how reliable the supposedly objective biological criteria are as a basis for splitting a population into different sexes (which we will not go into here). Given the cultural assumptions that underlie the sex/gender distinction, there is a good chance that the way we think of and differentiate gender and sex may be transformed again within our lifetimes. But the culture vs biology distinction is still widely used at the moment, and so it will serve our purposes here.

> In some societies, it is quite normal for there to be additional categories breaking down the dichotomy between two sexes that European and North American society takes for granted. Sometimes referred to as 'third sexes' or 'third genders', they include *berdaches* in Native American communities, and *fa'afafine* in Samoa.

Most of the discussion in this chapter is concerned with gender and language, though in the next two sections it would be a good idea to keep the notions of gender and sex in mind, because both play a role in interpreting some of the data we are going to be looking at.

Exclusive and preferential features

An exclusive feature is one associated solely with a particular user or group of users or solely in a particular context. A preferential feature is one that is distributed across speakers or groups, but is used more frequently by some than by others.

EXCLUSIVE GENDER DIFFERENCES

A distinction has sometimes been drawn between gender **exclusive** and gender **preferential** features in a language. So-called exclusive features are those which are only used by (or to) speakers of a particular sex. You can think of some aspects of kinship terminology as being sex-exclusive terms, so for instance the phrase *my Auntie Kath* tells the listener that the person you are referring to is female. Similarly, the terms *grandson* and *niece* respectively tell you the referents are male and female. On the other hand, the term 'cousin' might refer to a male or female. The kinship terms that mark a referent's sex differ even in closely related languages and in cultures that have a lot of mutual contact. For example, in German *Enkel* is gender-neutral, but the English equivalents are the gender-specific terms 'grandson' and 'granddaughter'.

In Māori (the Polynesian language spoken in New Zealand), the words for siblings tell you information about both the referent and the speaker, so the word *teina* tells you that the speaker is referring to a younger sibling that is the same sex as the speaker is (younger brother for a male speaker, younger sister for a female speaker). If a man wants to refer to his sister, he would use a completely different word, *tuahine*, and this could refer to a younger or older sister.

Elinor Ochs has described words like these as being a **direct index** of gender. Direct indexing means that a word has a semantic feature [+female] or [+male] as part of its basic meaning. Pronouns like *he* or *she* directly index gender. That is, words directly **indexing** gender generate a **conventional implicature** that the referent is male or female. Conventional implicatures are rather difficult to cancel. So, while it is technically possible to say,

(1)   My brother has cut herself,

most English-speakers would say that this sentence was bad or even ungrammatical because the [+ female] feature associated with the pronoun *herself* cancels out the [+ male] feature associated with *brother*.

Ochs contrasted the notion of direct indexing of gender with **indirect indexing**, a much more common and complicated relationship mediating language and the way we think about the world. We'll discuss indirect indexing in more detail in the next section.

Some of the earliest work on gender differences in language focused on cases where there were different particles or suffixes that appeared to only be used by men or only by women. Such differences would constitute sex exclusive norms, and non-native speakers sometimes perceived the differences to be so marked and so fundamental that it was said that the communities had separate languages for women and men.

Some examples of the kinds of differences that are supposed to be reliable indexes of the speaker's sex are shown in Table 10.1. There are examples from some Native American languages, an Australian language, and from Japanese.

Table 10.1   Some linguistic features indexing the speaker's sex. (Languages identified by family and location of majority of speakers in 'Ethnologue', accessed December 2004.)

Language	Speaker	Form	Gloss
Yana	Male	*yaa-na*	'person'
(extinct Hokan language, northern California, USA)	Everyone else	*yaa*	'person'
Koasati	Male	*íísks*	'you are saying'
(Muskogean language, Louisiana and Texas, USA)	Female	*íísk*	'you are saying'
Yanyuwa	Child	*buyuka-la*	'at/with the fire'
(Pama-Nyungan, Northern Territory and Queensland, Australia)	Male	*ji-buyuka-la*	'at/with the fire'
	Female	*ki-buyuka-la*	'at/with the fire'
Japanese	Male	*boku*	'I'
(Japanese, Japan)	Female	*atashi*	'I'

Direct and indirect indexing

A relationship of identification. The distinction between direct and indirect indexing was introduced by Elinor Ochs. A linguistic feature *directly indexes* something with social meaning if the social information is a *conventional implicature* (e.g., speaker gender is directly indexed by some forms of some adjectives in French, *je suis* [*prɛ*] (male speaker); *je suis* [*prɛt*] (female speaker). However, most variables associated with, e.g., male vs female speakers only *indirectly index* gender. Their distribution is *sex-preferential* not *sex-exclusive*. They are generally associated with several other social meanings, e.g., casualness and vernacularity with masculinity. Because these other factors help to *constitute* what it means to be 'male' the index between vernacular variants and male speakers/masculinity is indirect.

As you can see, sex-exclusive distinctions occur in many different parts of the grammar and occur in many kinds of phrase: noun phrases and pronouns like 'person' or 'I'; verb phrases like 'you are saying'; and prepositional phrases such as 'at the fire'.

---

exercise

Identifying indexes

Look at the data for 'person' in Yana (Table 10.1). How do you think the group came to be known as the Yana?

Conventional implicature

An inference that arises from the meaning (or semantics) of a word or phrase. This means if you try to cancel the implicature, it sounds bizarre or can't be understood. (See also *Conversational implicature*.)

In the Dravidian language Kuṟux, the morphology of verbs tells us something about both the speaker and the addressee, as is shown in Table 10.2. Some of these differences might cause women's and men's speech to sound very different to a casual observer, but it would be a mistake to say they speak different 'languages', even though such claims have been made, especially for more exotic varieties like those spoken in Australia and North America.

Table 10.2   Kuṟux verb forms marked for sex of the speaker and sex of the addressee. (Source, Fasold 1990.)

Male addressee	Female speaker and addressee	Male speaker, Female addressee	Gloss
barday	bardin	bardi	'you come'
barckay	barckin	barcki	'you came'

---

exercise

Gender effects in lingustic description

Imagine you were writing a dictionary of Yanyuwa or Yana. Which of the forms in Table 10.1 would you list as the main entry and which ones would you list as sub-entries? Is your decision based solely on linguistic facts or does it consider social facts too? How would you justify your decision?

What do you think you would do for Kuṟux (Table 10.2)?

There is one region where it seems that women and men in a community *do* use different languages, and this is the Vaupes, an area on and around the borders between Colombia, Peru and Brazil. The Vaupes is an area of great linguistic diversity, and there is a tradition of marrying outside your father's home language group. Women who move to a new village when they get married maintain their first language, and children usually grow up knowing both their mother's and father's languages. In the past it was customary for people to speak their father's language to their father and his relatives, and their mother's language to their mother and her family. This pattern of language maintenance and multilingualism served a number of useful social functions, including being a good indicator of a person's lineage. However, it is actually debatable whether we would want to call the practice of a woman maintaining her first language an example of sex-exclusive language differences. This is because when men and women in the Vaupes use their first language, they are communicating more than just what their sex is. They are communicating their ties to different villages or communities in the larger region, and ultimately they are also communicating the basis for preferred marriage relations in the Vaupes.

> Among the Tariana in the Vaupes, a person who has 'lost' their father's language is referred to as 'those who speak a borrowed language' – in Tariana *na-sawayā na-sape*, literally 'they borrow they speak' (Aikhenvald 2002: 27).

As we will see repeatedly in this chapter, this example is not atypical. Linguistic differences that correlate with speaker sex may have a lot to say about a much wider range of social dynamics in the community.

Gendered possession

In Anejom̃ (spoken in Vanuatu), speakers refer to a same-sex sibling with a possessive structure known as direct possession, i.e., *etwa-k* ('same.sex.sibling-my'), and an opposite-sex sibling with a subordinate construction, i.e., *nataheñ erak* ('sister-my'), *nataüañ erak* ('brother-my'). Direct possession constructions are generally used with things like body parts ('my hand'), or things over which you have no control ('my spirit'). Subordinate constructions are used with things that can be removed ('my blood', 'its lid').

But there is a surprising asymmetry in how speakers refer to a spouse. A man uses the direct possession construction to refer to his wife, *ega-k* (wife-my), but a woman uses a third construction – active possession – to refer to her husband, *nataüñ uñak* ('husband-my'). Active possession is generally associated with things where the speaker is in active control of the possession ('my house', 'my knife'). (Data from Lynch 2005.)

This data is very limited, but what tentative hypotheses might you draw about how speakers of Anejom̃ understand the gender relations underlying the asymmetry between *ega-k* ('my wife') and *nataüñ uñak* ('my husband')?

exercise

Later in this chapter we will come back to sex-exclusive features (i.e., particles or pronouns etc.) that are said to index the speaker's sex reliably. There, we will see that where researchers have undertaken careful work in the speech communities where such features are attested, it has been found that most indexes of speaker sex can be used creatively and become resources for positioning a speaker in relation to specific community values. This avenue of research is redefining such supposedly sex-exclusive features in terms of gender, showing how they are used to negotiate social positions in and across interactions.

PREFERENTIAL GENDER DIFFERENCES

Linguistic features that directly index sex, or which are exclusively used by one sex rather than another, are quite rare (if, indeed, they exist at all). It is far more common for features to be associated more or less with speakers of one sex rather than speakers of the other.

In the past, sociolinguists often glossed features that occur more in the speech of men as 'male' variants and features that occur more in the speech of women as 'female' variants, but they are less likely to describe them like this now. There are several reasons for this change. One is a greater sensitivity to the fact that any feature that is more likely to be used by women than by men must, by definition, also be used by men, but simply less often. Thus if we were to say that such-and-such a feature is 'male' this overgeneralises enormously, and it violates one of the basic tenets of quantitative sociolinguistics: the need to be accountable to *all* the data, not just the more frequent patterns in the data.

Another reason for the change is that sociolinguists have become more interested in trying to understand what social categories like 'male' and 'female' mean within any given community. Rather than taking the categories to be objectively and pre-culturally determined, they are understood to be culture specific, emerging through conventionalised activities and relationships that individuals enter into throughout their lives. Language can be seen as just one of those conventionalised activities. This means that linguistic features that probabilistically differentiate female and male speakers are seen in a different light.

Constitutive

The view that a correlation between linguistic behaviour and a non-linguistic factor actually helps to bring about and define (i.e., constitute) the meaning of a social category. Often contrasted with an interpretation of variation as reflecting a social category. (See also *Reflexive*.)

For one thing they are seen as being **constitutive** of different group identities rather than merely reflecting them. A speaker uses one variant more than another, not because he *is* male but because in speaking like that he is *constituting* himself as an exemplar of maleness, and constituting that variant as an emblem of masculinity. And we might expect to find uses of that variant to be particularly high or particularly foregrounded in contexts where other, non-linguistic, practices that are constitutive of masculinity are also foregrounded.

It also means that people who would in the past have been seen as atypical – for example, men who predominantly use a variant which is otherwise more frequent in the speech of female speakers – become of particular interest. These speakers become interesting to us because by examining what makes them seem anomalous we can learn a lot about what norms are being reinforced. This in turn means that we understand better what categories like gender actually mean in a particular speech community.

Reflexive

The view that a correlation between linguistic behaviour and a non-linguistic factor is due to the fact that language reflects identification with a social category or a personal stance. Often contrasted with *constitutive* interpretation of variation.

You will remember that Labov defined a speech community as a group of speakers unified by adherence to shared norms and attitudes towards those norms. Early variationist studies focused on trying to document the shared norms (that is, the statistically significant patterns stratifying the community). This encouraged researchers to make generalisations that implied that a social category is directly reflected in speakers' ways of talking – you use [ɑː] in *path* because you are from the north of England; you use negative concord because you are working class, etc. We have called this kind of relationship a **reflexive** one. However, if we understand variation to be not just a mirror that reflects a person's social category memberships, but also a tool by which a person defines their identities, then we would want to call the relationship between language and social categories, like gender, constitutive as well. One advantage in doing this is that our research focuses on all the important aspects that define a speech community. We not only document how speech differences reflect social differences, we also get closer to speakers' attitudes towards normative differences, a point we will develop more in the section 'Gender practices' (pp. 222–7).

The next section will review some of the generalisations that have been made about preferential gender differences in language in the past, and it will lead up to what appears to be a paradox inherent to the generalisations. But in 'Gender practices' (p. 222), we return to the idea that language variation plays a role in constituting the social categories we are interested in, and it will draw together a variety of facts about the preferential distribution of certain variables.

PRINCIPLES OF GENDER AND VARIATION: A HISTORICAL PICTURE

Although many sociolinguists now prefer to go beyond simple generalisations that say men use these forms in a language and women use those forms, it is important to review some of the generalisations that did emerge from the first social dialect studies. Even if we ultimately want to problematise a social category like gender, the generalisations about the preferences of women and men in a speech community may be helpful diagnostics of changes in progress. We will see that in earlier work on language variation and use, the social category 'sex of speaker' was not problematised because the overarching enterprise was to learn more about the way language variation relates to language change, and to better understand what the most important social constraints were on the life-cycle of a change in progress. However, some researchers began to feel dissatisfied with the way in which some of these generalisations were phrased, the apparent contradictions in them, and the way in which:

■   they down-play speakers' agency, and
■   they suggest that a biological category like sex might *determine* the way people talk and behave.

Three generalisations about gender and language variation will be reviewed. These are discussed in more detail in Labov (1990, 2001). The first two identify the circumstances in which women are likely to lead men in the use of a standard-like variant. The last one identifies the circumstances in which women lead men in the use of vernacular variants.

Principle I. Stable sociolinguistic variables: women use the standard more than men

A number of studies have observed that the generalisations for stable linguistic variables are somewhat different from the ones that hold for changes in progress. This is true not only for the way gender correlates with the variable but also with respect to other factors (as we have seen, the correlations with speakers' age differ for changes in progress and stable variables).

For stable sociolinguistic variables, such as the (ing) variable, or the (th) and (dh) variables (the alternation between an initial fricative or stop in words like *thin* and *this*), or negative concord ('I didn't do *nothing ~ anything*'), it has often been noted that women use more of the standard forms than men do overall:

(ing) variable: women [ɪŋ] > men [ɪŋ]
(dh) variable: women [ð] > men [ð]
negative concord: women 'I didn't do anything' > men

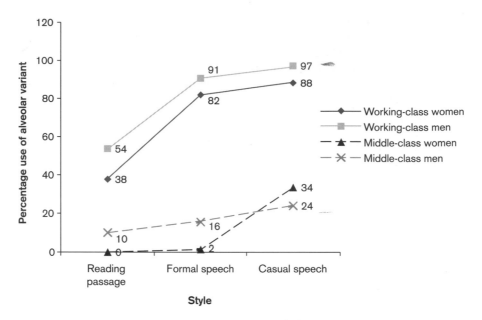

Figure 10.1   Men's and women's use of the alveolar variant [ɪn] in three speech styles and two socio-economic classes in Norwich, England. (Source, Trudgill 1972.)

This generalisation is illustrated in Figure 10.1 which shows the distribution of the alveolar variant [ɪn] in Trudgill's survey of Norwich English. The data for working-class speakers show that in all three speech styles, women use more of the [ɪŋ] variant and men use more of the [ɪn] variant. This pattern largely holds for the middle-class speakers as well, even though their overall rate of [ɪŋ] is much higher than it is for the working class. (Trudgill notes that in casual speech, where the frequency of [ɪŋ] is greater among male speakers than among female speakers, is probably due to the very small number of tokens he happened to elicit from casual conversation with middle-class men.)

The tendency for women to use more of the standard with stable variables has been interpreted in various ways. Very often it is seen as indicating women's greater sensitivity to what is considered standard and non-standard. In the article that Figure 10.1 is based on, Trudgill also pointed out that, at least in Western society, men are evaluated more on what they do and women on how they appear. He suggested that this might make women pay more

---

Negative can *in Tyneside English*

In Tyneside English (spoken in Newcastle, England), two variants realise the negative form of the modal verb *can*: one is *can't* (shared with Standard English); one is the local variant *cannit*. Trousdale's (2000) work showed that this variable is quite stable (younger and older speakers use both variants at about the same rate). The figure below shows the distribution of the variants in men's and women's speech. Is it consistent with Labov's principles? If so, which one(s)?

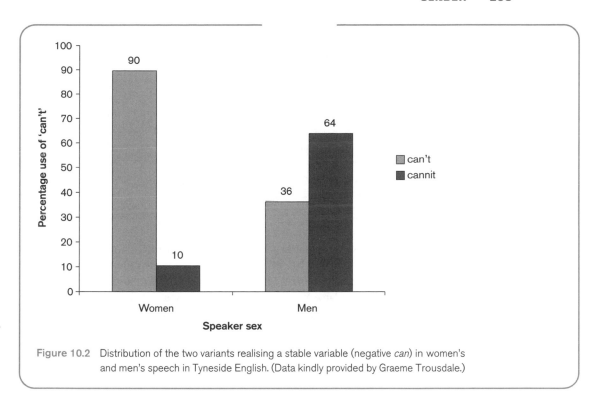

Figure 10.2 Distribution of the two variants realising a stable variable (negative *can*) in women's and men's speech in Tyneside English. (Data kindly provided by Graeme Trousdale.)

attention to stylistic markers in speech. Eckert (2000) develops this argument further and suggests that women generally make greater use of symbolic resources (whether in speech or dress or make-up) to establish their position in and identification with a social group or their opposition to a group.

The idea that women are more aware of what is proscribed and therefore avoid it more than men do is also invoked to explain a related phenomenon in certain kinds of change in progress. This is summarised in Principle Ia.

Principle Ia. Change in progress above the level of awareness: women use the standard more than men

Like Principle I, Principle Ia generalises across variables where women seem to use more of the standard form than men do. However, it deals with cases where speakers are consciously aware of a change in progress, and the incoming variant is positively evaluated in the community ('change from above', Chapter 8). In these cases, women tend to use more of the innovative and positively evaluated variant than men do (cf. 'accentuate the positive', Chapter 2).

We have already examined one of the most famous examples of this kind of variable, the use of (r) in final or pre-consonantal position in New York City. As we saw in Chapters 3 and 8, the shift to r-ful speech is led overall by higher class speakers and it is more frequent in careful speaking styles and when respondents were given tasks like reading aloud. However, Labov also found that within each social class, (r) use was usually more frequently

Connections with theory

The kinds of variables Principle Ia describes are sociolinguistic *markers*, and you will remember that a marker is a variable that people show some awareness of.

One piece of evidence that they have some awareness of is if there is a consistent increase in the frequency of one variant in more careful or marked speech styles. It is often also the variant that members of the speech community will volunteer when they are asked to describe which of two pronunciations or two sentences is 'better'. For these reasons, one variant may be described as being the prestige variant, where the notion of prestige refers to overt recognition of prestige.

in the speech of women than in the speech of men. As a group, working-class women used more tokens of (r) than working class men did as a group, although he noted some individual exceptions to the group patterns as well. In addition to the evidence from style-shifting, it is clear from the way most New Yorkers talked about [r] presence and absence that New Yorkers generally prefer or value r-ful speech more highly than r-less pronunciations.

Sometimes evidence of speakers' awareness of a variant emerges from larger patterns. This is the case for the replacement of oral stops with glottal stops in Newcastle upon Tyne (Milroy *et al.* 1994). In Newcastle, there are several ways in which /t/, for example, is realised in everyday speech. It can be realised as:

- an alveolar stop [t],
- it can be reinforced with a glottal stop [tʔ],
- it can be replaced entirely by a glottal stop [ʔ]

There are also a couple of 'r'-like options, which will not concern us.

So, for instance, a word like *better* can be realised with an oral or glottal stop in the middle of the word: /bɛtə/ or /bɛʔə/. Milroy and his colleagues found that replacement with a glottal stop was more frequent among the girls that they recorded in Newcastle than it was among the boys. The glottal variants also show the kind of decrease that we would expect when you compare conversation and reading styles.

While we don't have explicit information on the Newcastle subjects' attitudes to the glottal stops, there is a lot of evidence that the glottal variant of /t/ is similar to (r) in New York City. Across the United Kingdom as a whole, the replacement of oral stops with glottal stops is gaining ground in the cities. In work on dialect levelling in the cities of Milton Keynes, Hull and Reading, Paul Kerswill and Ann Williams have found evidence that the replacement of /t/ with a glottal stop is one of the few phonological changes in progress in British English that teenagers show some overt awareness of. The following comments were made by a teenage girl (2) and boy (3) from Milton Keynes (Kerswill and Williams 1997: 165):

(2) My mum takes the Micky if I say bu'er. She'll say butter.
(3) My parents don't like me missing letters out, like if I say wa'er.

In New York City, the situation was relatively uncomplicated: the innovative [r] was widely perceived as desirable by individual speakers in the study, and r-less varieties are widely perceived to be non-standard in US society as a whole. However, the comments elicited by Kerswill and Williams in (2) and (3) show that teenagers are aware of the spread of [ʔ] but are also aware that it is considered a non-standard form. In this case, the value or desirability of the glottal variant seems to be tied up with its non-standardness.

Figure 10.3 shows the replacement of [t] with glottal stops in the working-class sample

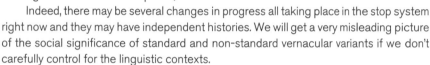

Connections with theory

It is sometimes difficult to get a clear picture of what the distribution of glottal stops for oral stops is in the UK because some studies provide grand summaries of all tokens of glottals in word-final and medial (especially intervocalic) position. Where studies break the environments down more, it seems that the linguistic context plays a fairly big role. These issues are reviewed in Milroy *et al.* (1994). For example, the quality of the glotalling in word-final position is different before a pause than before a vowel, and it may occur across syllable boundaries following a stop but perhaps not following a fricative (see the ranking of constraints in Chapter 3).

Indeed, there may be several changes in progress all taking place in the stop system right now and they may have independent histories. We will get a very misleading picture of the social significance of standard and non-standard vernacular variants if we don't carefully control for the linguistic contexts.

of the Tyneside study. It clearly shows the important role played by the linguistic context. Final (t) behaves very differently from intervocalic (t) in:

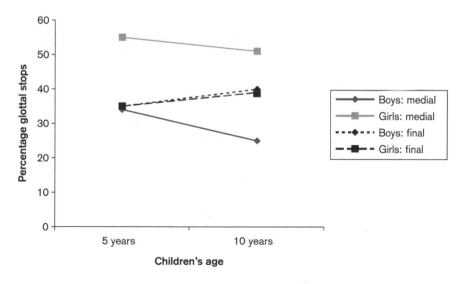

Figure 10.3 Relative frequency of glottal stops for word-medial (t) and word-final (t) in the speech of working class girls and boys in Newcastle upon Tyne. (Source, Milroy *et al.* 1994: 343.)

- its overall frequency,
- its development as the children age,
- its distribution across the sexes.

Both girls and boys decrease the frequency of glottal variants in medial position and increase the frequency of glottal stops in final position between the ages of 5 and 10 years. Figure 10.3 also shows that where girls and boys differ (that is, in the use of glottal stops intervocalically, not in final position), there are consistent and very early differences between boys and girls for intervocalic (t): girls use the glottal variant more than boys at 5 years and this difference is maintained even when both groups decrease the frequency of medial glottals at age 10.

exercise

Spread of glottal stops

Here is some data from interviews with teenagers conducted by Ann Williams and Paul Kerswill (1999). They also investigated the spread of glottal stops where Standard English has [t].

Comment on the distribution of the newer, glottal variants in the speech of the MC teenagers. Is it consistent with Principles I and Ia reviewed above?

Now look at the data for the working class teenagers. Does this also seem consistent with Principles I and Ia?

Can you round out your analysis of the gender variation by drawing on what you know about social class? To what extent is the overall picture consistent with what you have learnt about variation and social class?

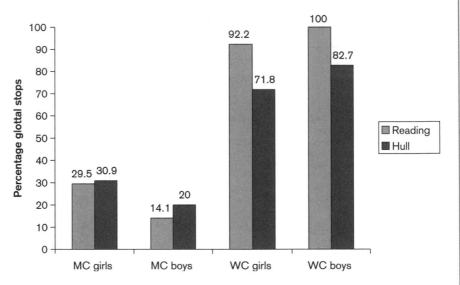

Figure 10.4   Frequency of glottal stops for intervocalic (t) in interviews with 14- and 15-year-olds from Reading (southern England) and Hull (northern England). (Source, Williams and Kerswill 1999: 160.)

Social class, gender and change in Swedish

Figure 10.5 is based on data collected in 1996 in Eskilstuna, Sweden (Nordberg and Sundgren 1998). It shows how strongly men and women from four different social classes are shifting from the use of non-standard, regional vernacular variants to the use of the supra-local, Standard Swedish forms. The two variables shown are the form of the definite neuter article suffix (non-standard -*e* vs Standard -*et*; i.e., *huse* vs *huset* 'the house') and the form of the past participle in Class 1 and Class 4 verbs (non-standard -*a* and -*i* vs Standard -*at* and -*it*; e.g., *sjungi* vs *sjungit* 'sung').

	Non-standard Swedish	*Standard Swedish*
Definite article	-*e*	-*et*
Part participle	-*a*; -*i*	-*at*; -*it*

The social groups along the x-axis in Figure 10.5 are defined largely by how much formal education is required for particular occupations. It is clear that for both variables social class is an important independent variable. However, look at the segments that have been circled. Here, the class stratification is not very sharp; the differences between Mid-high and Mid-low groups are minimal.

Assuming this is analogous to the interior class cross-over effect discussed in Chapter 8, what does this data tell you about the cross-over effect? Who appears to be more likely to cross-over?

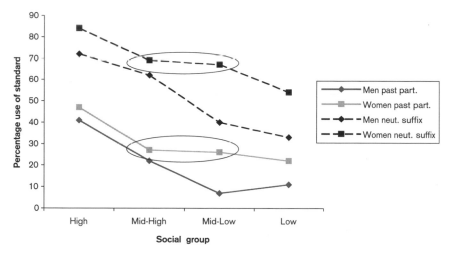

Figure 10.5 Frequency of Standard Swedish variants in the speech of men and women in Eskilstuna, Sweden. Solid lines = past participle in Class 1 and 4 verbs; dashed lines = definite neuter singular suffix on nouns. (Source, Nordberg and Sundgren 1998, tables 9, 20.)

Principle II. Change in progress below the level of awareness: women use more of the incoming variant than men

We now turn to the other kinds of change in progress: change from below the level of conscious awareness. These are variables where there is little or no clear evidence of style-shifting. In these cases, women seem to lead men in the use of the incoming, non-standard variant. Many of the examples of these kinds of variables involve changes to the vowel system.

For instance, in many varieties of English there is laxing of /i/ and /u/ before /l/. The laxing means you end up with a merger between [ɪ] and [i] and between [ʊ] and [u] so that 'still' and 'steel' become homophones (i.e., they sound the same) and 'pull' and 'pool' become homophones. Work on this merger by Marianna Di Paolo (1988, cited in Labov 1994) in Utah and by Guy Bailey and colleagues (1993) in Texas shows that the laxing of [u] to [ʊ] is more advanced in the speech of younger women than it is in the speech of younger men.

Connections with theory

The laxing of [iː] and [uː] to merge with [ɪ] and [ʊ] interacts with the somewhat unusual status of the liquids /l/ and /r/ when they occur in the final (coda) position in a syllable. Work by Lisa Lavoie and Abby Cohn (2003) shows that when [iː] and [uː] occur before a syllable-final [l] in English, this results in what is called a super-heavy syllable. It is unproblematic for English to have heavy syllables (syllables with two moras), but super-heavy syllables with three moras are unusual cross-linguistically. This seems to make such syllables unstable. One way of resolving (or getting rid of) them is for speakers of English to shorten the long vowels [iː] and [uː] to [ɪ] and [ʊ]. This eliminates one mora and makes the syllable less typologically marked.

A second example comes from Penny Eckert's ground-breaking work on language variation and change among Detroit teenagers. Eckert was possibly the first linguist to note the last vowel affected by what is called the Northern Cities Shift. Eckert discovered that the central vowel [ʌ] was backing in some speakers (so *bus* sounds more like *boss* to speakers of other varieties of English). When Eckert was doing her study, this very new change in progress was pretty much restricted to the speech of the group of kids called burnouts, and within this group it was clearly more advanced among the girls than it was among the boys (2000: 118). Notice that this is not *just* a gender-preferential variant: Eckert showed that gender interacts intimately with another social category, the distinction between burnouts and jocks in the high school where she was working.

Many of the changes that linguists have noted happening below the level of community awareness are sound changes, like the complex Northern Cities Chain Shift and the ongoing fronting of back vowels in Southern British English (and the fronting of the GOOSE and GOAT vowels in Midland speakers of US English).

Similarly, New Zealand English is undergoing a merger of the onsets in the diphthongs in NEAR and SQUARE (so that *bear* and *beer* are both realised with a close onset; i.e., something like [biə]). The following data shows how often speakers in Auckland used a close onset for words that are historically in the SQUARE class. The data shown is only from speakers aged 15–54 years because the merger was very infrequent in speakers over 55 years of age.

No, really?

A quick look through any New Zealand Yellow Pages will show that this merger is widely exploited with puns in business names: home brewers can equip themselves at *Beer Essentials*; you can rent sound equipment for your next party from *Musical Cheers DJ and Entertainment Services*; and there are seven hair-dressers in Auckland alone called *The Sharing Shed*. The same kinds of puns can be found in the Yellow Pages in Liverpool, where there is a similar merger (though there the merger is towards the more open onset).

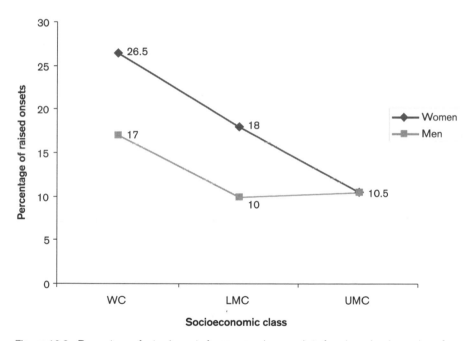

Figure 10.6   Percentage of raised onsets for SQUARE class words in female and male speakers from Auckland, New Zealand, aged 15–54 years. Three social classes: working class (WC), lower middle class (LMC) and upper middle class (UMC). (Source, Batterham 2000: 123–124.)

Figure 10.6 shows that in general female speakers use more of the innovative raised variants than male speakers do. The female lead disappears among the upper middle-class speakers, and this is entirely due to the younger males (15–29 years) suddenly starting to adopt the close onset for SQUARE words. In the 30–54 age group, women still lead men in use of the innovation with 14 per cent vs 9 per cent.

Connections with theory

Researchers have to pay attention to the kinds of tokens they are including in their analysis because there is always the possibility that if one word is particularly common it can skew the results. Similarly, the distinction between function words and content words may be important since function words are seldom given full stress – this, of course, changes the quality of the vowel. So in this case, Batterham analysed the word *really* separately in her analysis (because it is very common as a marker of emphasis), and she analysed words like *they're* and *their* separately because they frequently have reduced vowels.

Using the principles as diagnostics of change

The strength and the utility of generalisations like Principles I, Ia and II lie in the extent to which they hold across a number of different social dialect studies. If there is repeated support for them in independent studies then it means we can go beyond simply describing the patterns and begin to integrate these generalisations into our analysis.

For instance, when Sali Tagliamonte (1998) was studying the non-standard use of *was* and *were* in the English spoken in York (England), she drew on the cumulative insights underlying Principle II to refine her investigation of non-standard *were*. In her analysis of the use of non-standard *were*, she found that men used the *were* variant more often overall in contexts like (4) below, where Standard English would have *was*:

(4) a. Everything *were* going great.
     b. It *weren't* very satisfactory.
     c. Bit before our time, *weren't* it?

The examples show an affirmative utterance (4a), a negative utterance (4b) and a negative tag question (4c).

However, when she looked closely at the different linguistic environments in which non-standard *were* could appear, she found that there was clear evidence of a change in progress taking place in one context. This was where the subject of the clause was *it*. Moreover, she found that this more detailed analysis of the linguistic environment showed that collocations of *it* + *weren't* accounted for virtually all the tokens of non-standard *were* (i.e., the negative and tag contexts illustrated in 4b and 4c above). Speakers under the age of 50 had particularly heightened usage of the variant in these environments.

Because the apparent time data indicated that there was a change in progress, Tagliamonte was able to draw on what we know about the distribution of innovative vernacular variants to push her findings a step further. Principle II holds that women will lead men in changes below the level of conscious awareness, and yet her initial analysis of the data indicated that men generally favoured the use of non-standard *were* in York English. On the face of it, it appeared the York data contradicted Principle II.

But Tagliamonte examined the distribution of the non-standard *were* variants in only the contexts favoured by younger speakers, and she found a startling reversal of her initial

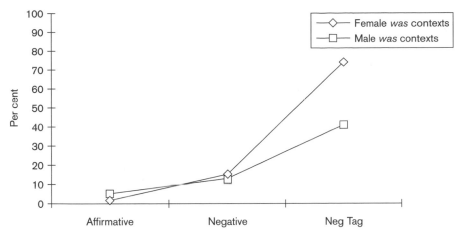

Figure 10.7 Distribution of non-standard *were* in standard *was* contexts according to utterance type and speaker sex. (Source, Tagliamonte 1998: 178.)

findings. It was clear that the spread of non-standard *were* into negative tags (example 4c) was being led by women. As we can see in Figure 10.7, women's rate of the non-standard variant in this innovative context was nearly twice that of men's. (It is important to note that the overall frequency of negative tags in both women and men's speech was very similar, so this difference is very robust.)

Using Labov's Principles as diagnostics

What limits do you suppose there are to using these Principles I, Ia and II as diagnostics of change in progress?

Imagine you were looking at Scots English – historically this is a rhotic (r-ful) dialect of English, whereas Southern British English, especially around London, has been non-rhotic for a long time. Suppose your study found that more women than men are r-less in Scots English. What could you conclude about the (r) variable in Scotland? What more would you want or need to know in order to decide whether the Scots English-speaking community is 'losing' /r/?

Connections with theory

Where do the patterns that give rise to Labov's principles come from? Work on the acquisition of variation is much more sketchy than on the patterns that emerge once a linguistic systems has (largely) been acquired. Some work has explored the impact of caregiver input on the acquisition of gendered patterns of speech, and the findings suggest that, from an early age, mothers (that's all the studies have looked at) provide different models for boys and for girls. That is, the frequency with which they use non-standard variants is greater with boys than with girls (Foulkes *et al.* 1999). However, there is still a lot of work that needs to be done to confirm this and to determine how general it is.

When women don't use more of the standard

Many sociolinguists had been aware of the generalisations underlying Labov's three principles for a long time before he codified them and presented them in this form. In particular, the probabilistic association between female speakers and the use of more overtly prestigious variants had been commented on as one of the most robust findings produced by studies of language variation. However, starting in the 1980s, sociolinguists working in Arabic-speaking communities began to draw attention to equally robust exceptions to this. Over and over, studies of synchronic variation in Arabic seemed to be showing men using more of the overtly prestigious variants associated with Classical Arabic, and women using more of the variants associated with the local colloquial variety of Arabic.

This is shown very clearly in the results of a social dialect survey by Bakir (1986) looking at the distribution of Classicial Arabic variants and local Iraqi Arabic variants.

Figure 10.8 makes it clear that Iraqi women use more of the local variants, and Iraqi men use the Classical Arabic variants more. Similar results were found in studies done in Cairo, Damascus, and Hama (Syria). Since it is clear that Classical Arabic has higher overt prestige

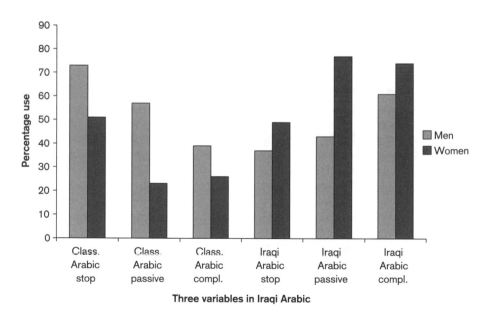

Figure 10.8 Distribution of Classical and Iraqi Arabic variants for a phonological variable ([k] vs [tʃ]), the form used to create the passive (*CuCiC* vs *nCiCaC*), and the complementiser (´*an* vs Ø to introduce a subordinate clause). [Cs in the passive frame indicate the consonants that identify an Arabic verb stem.] (Source, Bakir 1986.)

than local varieties of Arabic, and since the diglossic relationship between Classical Arabic and local varieties is relatively stable throughout the region, these results present a major problem for Principle I.

In order to understand what is happening in the Arabic speech communities it is helpful to consider the social role of women and men. As we saw in Chapter 6, one of the characteristics of a High variety in a diglossic community is that the High code is learnt through formal education; it is not the language children naturally acquire at home. In most of the Arabic communities studied, women are much more likely to be excluded from formal education than men are.

Even where women have been relatively well educated, there continues to be a tendency for men to use more of the Classical Arabic variants than women do (this was the case, for example, with the study in Cairo, in which only middle- or upper-class speakers were interviewed). But even if a Cairene woman is quite well educated in Classical Arabic, her opportunities for participating fully in public life are nonetheless considerably more restricted than a man's. Many of the jobs which involve active use of Classical Arabic are dominated by men (this is very clear in Haeri's (2003) ethnography of the relationship between Classical and Cairene Arabic).

Palatalisation of stops in Cairene Arabic

exercise

Speakers of Arabic in Cairo variably palatalise dental stops (these are /t, d/ and also pharyngealised or 'emphatic' stops, /T, D/). Palatalisation does not occur in Classical Arabic; it is a local innovation. Haeri (1994) discusses the use of palatalised variants of all these stops in the speech of 25 women and 24 men from Cairo. The results for four different speech styles are shown in Figure 10.9 ('response' means speech in direct response to a question).

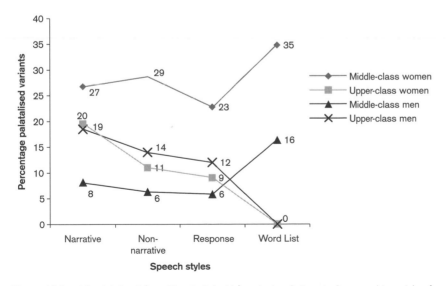

Figure 10.9   All palatalised (non-Classical Arabic) variants of stops in four speaking styles for women and men in Cairo, Egypt. (Source, Haeri 1994: tables 10, 11.)

Comment on the distribution of the local palatalised variants in all four groups of speakers. Are they what you would expect based on Labov's three principles? Pay close attention to the frequency of palatalised variants in the most careful word-list style.

There is relatively little stylistic stratification for this variable. On the basis of this data, say why you would argue palatalisation is a sociolinguistic *indicator, marker* or *stereotype*.

Similar results can be seen in historical sociolinguistic work (Nevalainen and Raumolin-Brunberg 2003). Some of the changes in Early Modern English that came from above the level of conscious awareness were not led by women, presumably because (as with the Arabic variables) the average woman's limited access to education at that time restricted her exposure to and familiarity with the overt prestige forms.

These exceptions to Principles I and Ia are extremely valuable since they encourage us to move beyond simple statements of correlation and force us to consider more carefully what the impact is of speaker's access to linguistic resources. In other words, these results show very clearly that it is not *the fact of being male or female* that causes a speaker to be more or less associated with one set of variants; rather, it is the social role(s) we play and the social networks we enter into *as women or men* that result in the gendered distribution of linguistic variants.

MOVING BEYOND LABOV'S PRINCIPLES

For many years, then, Labov's principles were a descriptive anchor for much of the variationist sociolinguistic work on language and gender. The focus was on splitting the speech community into broad social groupings and seeing whether there were consistent trends in how these groups patterned with respect to different kinds of sociolinguistic variable. Since then, groupings like these have been criticised for being superficial and for masking internal differentiation. Evidence from non-Western and non-urban speech communities also called into question the generalisations in Labov's three principles.

By the end of the 1980s, these criticisms had become particularly trenchant – and a new generation of researchers in language and gender began to reconsider social dialect methods that relied on aggregating speakers and which seemed to assume that how speakers identify as a man or a woman is obvious and straightforward.

The remainder of this chapter will examine their critiques of variationist methods in more detail. One of their criticisms was levelled at the so-called 'gender paradox' that emerges from Labov's Principles I, Ia and II. In the next section we will see how they tackled this head-on.

The 'Gender Paradox'

Generalisations like Principles I, Ia and II are intensely satisfying as summaries of a large body of work. However, social dialectologists quickly noticed that when taken altogether they represented something of a paradox. According to these principles, women are both more likely to use standard forms (Principles I and Ia), and are also more likely to use innovative, vernacular forms (Principle II). Initially, sociolinguistics tried to get around the paradox by saying that these generalisations underlie an even broader and more abstract generalisation. That is, you could say that women's speech demarcates the community targets. So for stable variables and change from above, women's speech conforms more often to the prestige target than men's speech does. For changes taking place below the level of consciousness, women realise the forms that are the vernacular target more often than men's speech does.

However, Eckert (1989) pointed out that the paradox might be ephemeral, and only emerges because of the ways in which we have traditionally grouped large numbers of very different individuals together, solely on the grounds that they happen to be of the same sex. The process of averaging performance across such a wide range of individuals has an important impact on the data in several ways. On the one hand, it essentially erases the atypical outliers within a group. Arguably, this does not appear to be consistent with the sociolinguistic goal of being accountable to all the data. In addition, the practice can easily produce results that seem to be internally inconsistent.

In several papers, Eckert – and her frequent collaborator, Sally McConnell-Ginet – made two points that are of relevance to us here. First, Eckert and McConnell-Ginet (1992, 1999) noted that the gender paradox is only a paradox at all if it can be shown that the women who are leading in the use of non-standard variants are actually the same ones who are using more of the standard variants. However, the social dialectologists' practice of calculating median rates for use of conservative or standard variants and use of innovative or vernacular variants makes it impossible to know whether this is in fact the case. That is, the paradox might be an artefact of the kind of analytic methods that are being used. This point was independently raised in a critique of generalisations about the relationship between language and gender by Aki Uchida (1992).

The second point is more fundamental, and they were joined in making it by other eminent scholars such as Elinor Ochs (1992). Eckert and McConnell-Ginet pointed out that by lumping all women or all men together in an analysis, the researcher is essentially claiming that gender identity is a simplex phenomenon, derived directly from speakers' biological sex. But it has long been recognised in anthropology and other social sciences that this way of thinking about gender is far too limited. The argument here is that because gender is a social identity, it emerges, like all social identities, in the ways we interact with others. Hence, in many respects it is a function of the relationships and responsibilities that are emphasised and valued within the particular communities we are members of.

This work emphasised the importance of understanding gender identity in relation to other identities and other relationships within the wider community. It was argued that there should be a number of advantages to adopting this perspective. One advantage is that our methods now allow us to interpret all of the data we might gather in sociolinguistic research. This has its own benefits. By seeing a social category like gender as being internally complex and encompassing many different instantiations of the categorisation, we won't be troubled by apparent paradoxes or contradictions in the data. This will allow us to come closer to achieving some of the goals sociolinguistics has had from the start: trying to better understand the systematicity and the social patterns underlying the wealth of variation there is in any one speech community.

Another advantage to seeing gender as a socially complex category, and not simply as a reflex of biological sex, is that it makes the question of how gender interacts with other social identities a central concern, rather than a tangential (or side) matter. Researchers advocating this perspective argued that if patterns of language variation and language use are analysed in light of how individuals negotiate their position or place within the communities they belong to, then our analysis of language variation can inform even more than theories of language change. A better understanding of how gender and other social identities interconnect through social practices like language variation will deepen our appreciation of complex social questions, such as who can exercise power in different contexts, and why they might consciously or unconsciously choose different strategies for doing this.

These questions are interesting for many sociolinguists and social anthropologists, but some people would argue that they take us a long way from the linguistic goals that have for a long time played a central role in defining variationist research. However, it is important to note that they are also relevant to the goals of variationist sociolinguistics. We know that change happens when some variant available in the speech community somehow gets reanalysed. It ceases to be heard as some *ad hoc* or idiosyncratic departure from the norm, and acquires the status of an incipient or new change. But how does this happen? The answer to this question cannot lie in the averages of large groups of speakers based on age or social class or gender. It must happen more locally. Consequently, if we want to understand the complex process by which an idiosyncratic token becomes a socially meaningful variant involved in a change in progress, we need to understand how language among many other practices is deployed in the negotiation of social identities first. Then we can address the question of how new variants get transmitted through a speech community.

This necessarily changes the kinds of questions researchers might be asking them-selves. Exactly who are the female speakers leading in the use of non-standard variants? Why do their linguistic practices get picked up by anyone else? How is the social meaning of their linguistic practices reinterpreted or renegotiated as these practices spread more widely and become a feature of ever more diverse kinds of speakers? A text of this kind can't possibly hope to address all of these questions in any depth, but the remainder of this chapter will give you some idea of the methods that are being used to answer them and the directions in which this new approach to studying language and social identity is moving.

GENDER PRACTICES

One very useful way of approaching these questions is to use Ochs's distinction between features that are 'direct' and 'indirect' indexes of social information, and to see them as being related to specific speech events or discourse practices.

Direct and indirect indexing

As we noted in the section on gender-exclusive difference, very few things in language are exclusive markers of either the speaker, the addressee's or the referent's gender. Ochs suggests that when the German word *Onkel* ('uncle') or the Arabic words *bnt* ('girl') or a pronoun like *he* or *she* predictably picks out a male or female referent, we might want to say that we have cases of words that are a direct index of gender. All the other linguistic phenomena we have discussed as being gender-preferential we might consider to be things that are indirect indexes of gender. Ochs's use of the word *index* rather than, say, *marker*, serves several purposes. One useful function of the different terminology is that it means we can reserve the notion of a marker for research conducted within the social dialect paradigm, and index can be used to refer to a more socially situated analysis of variables.

One of the main points in talking about indexing is that it 'puts gender in its place, indicating that it enters into complex constitutive relations with other categories of social meaning' (Ochs 1992: 343).

The reason why most probabilistic variables are indirect rather than direct indexes of gender is that their association with a particular gender is mediated by several factors:

- their use in certain speech acts (such as orders or requests),
- their association with certain stances (such as hesitancy or assertiveness),
- their association with particular social practices or discourse activities (such as making public speeches, or soothing someone who is upset).

Ochs argues that in most cases the best way to understand what it means for a particular linguistic variant or way of talking to be gendered is to understand how those stances, speech acts or discourse activities are more or less associated with different members of the speech community. To the extent that these associations are gender-preferential, the linguistic forms themselves acquire a sense of being 'gendered'.

Here is a specific example from her work. Japanese has a set of sentence-final particles that show the speaker's attitude to (or sometimes certainty) about the larger proposition. These particles have often been described as being gendered. For example, the use of *ze* is considered to be 'male' and the use of *wa* is considered to be 'female'. However, it is clear that this association between *ze* and male speakers is probabilistic only. Not all men use *ze* all the time and women do not always avoid it. Ochs argues that what *ze* actually indexes directly is a stance of assertiveness, and what *wa* directly indexes is a stance of hesitancy. Because the overt expression of assertiveness is conventionally seen as a masculine trait in Japanese society and the overt expression of hesitancy is conventionally seen as a feminine trait, the linguistic forms *ze* and *wa* indirectly index male and female gender respectively. The preferential distribution of *ze* in men's speech arises because of cultural norms governing assertiveness. By and large Japanese men can go on record as being assertive much more readily than women can, and the relative frequency of *ze* in their linguistic repertoire reflects this, not the fact that they are male.

Recent, large-scale surveys of Japanese workplaces found that different workplaces developed their own specific cultures. In some offices, women as well as men predominantly use *ze*, *zo* and other so-called 'masculine' particles, while in other offices, a culture had developed favouring the so-called 'feminine' particles and these were used by both men and women working there (Gendai Nihongo Kenkyukai 1999, 2002, cited in Okamoto 2006). So even though speakers of Japanese and many linguists think about these particles as if they are somehow deterministically linked to a speaker because of their sex – men and women using complementary sets of particles – it is clear that these norms for usage are open to social negotiation, and that they do much more than simply reflect a speaker's sex.

Another example from English illustrates the role that speech acts and discourse activities play in indirectly indexing gender. In a given speech community, it might be the case that there are certain linguistic forms which directly index attention to someone else's wants or needs (positive politeness strategies, as discussed in Chapter 5). These might involve other oriented strategies like question asking, and they might include tag questions. Examples of tag questions are shown in italics in (5) and (6).

(5) Their new house is totally amazing, *isn't it*?
     That was a bit silly, *wasn't it*?

(6) You didn't leave without saying goodbye, *did you*?
     We should treat ourselves to something nice after this, *shouldn't we*?

Tag questions have a number of functions, not all of which can be reviewed here. We can phrase these in terms of Ochs's framework of indexing. An important function that tag questions have is to provide support for the continuation of a conversation. In this case they directly index:

- the speech *act* of asking questions,
- a *stance* of attentiveness,
- the *discourse activity* of eliciting the contributions of others.

They directly index the speech act of asking a question because of their syntactic structure. That's why they are called tag *questions*. They directly index the activity of eliciting contributions because when they are used as in (5) and (6) they are usually followed by an opening for a response from the addressee (though this response can be quite minimal). The content of the questions here also indexes a stance of attentiveness. How can these observations help us in interpreting who uses tag questions of this kind?

Studies based on the occurrence of tag questions in spontaneous speech have found some interesting distributional patterns. They are not uniformly distributed across all groups in the speech community. Teachers, for instance, use tag questions quite often and this can be explained by the fact that in order to fulfil the role of a teacher a person is expected to do all these things: ask questions, be attentive, and elicit contributions from students.

The corpus-based research has also found that the distribution of tag questions is not equal in the spontaneous speech of women and men. When you control for function (that is, separate out challenging or aggressive tags from supportive tags), it has been found that the more supportive tag questions (e.g., those eliciting input from others or mitigating criticism, as in (5) and (6)) occur more often in women's speech than they do in men's.

Early analyses of this correspondence in the linguistic literature offered accounts that essentially treated tags as being a direct index of femaleness. This led to researchers suggesting that this distributional imbalance could be 'explained' because women are more uncertain and seek validation of their opinions or clarification of facts more often than men do. But this account is logically flawed. It conflates the fact that a particular speech act – a question – can be a direct index of uncertainty, with the state of mind of the *users* of that speech act. Moreover, it privileges one function associated with only one type of tag question. Janet Holmes (1982) first noted these problems with such analyses, and she showed that a tag question is generally not used solely to ask for information that the speaker lacks. Instead, it has numerous social functions, some of which I've outlined above.

If we combine Holmes's descriptive insights with Ochs's theoretical distinction between direct and indirect indexing, we get a completely different picture of the correlation between use of supportive tags and female speakers. The correlation between a form and its users is, in Ochs's terms, an indirect index. A tag question has social functions as well as purely linguistic ones. It directly indexes stances and discourse activities, and doesn't just ask for information.

There is a widely held expectation in most English-speaking communities that it is acceptable and desirable for women (like teachers) to be attentive to others, and for them to elicit contributions from others in day-to-day social interaction. (There is also a lot of research showing how these expectations are realised in various different interactional contexts.) Of course men use tag questions, too, but the frequency with which they use them and the contexts in which they use them are constrained by the different social expectations of men and the attributes and characteristics that are associated with being a successful or good man.

Gender performances

Another important development in the study of language and gender since the late 1980s has been an emphasis on the potential for individuals to act agentively in relation to social identities like gender. This is tied in with the rejection of models of language variation and use that talk about correlations between linguistic variants and speakers as if social identities were simple, and deterministic. The alternative view stresses the way gender roles change during an individual's lifespan, and how in a group of men or women an individual's experiences of 'being a man' or 'being a woman' will differ depending on their personal histories. Research in this vein sees speakers as pre-eminently social agents, perhaps constrained by social expectations but certainly always having the potential to engage with them, sometimes conforming and sometimes challenging them.

The idea that individuals might be actively and agentively involved in constructing social positions for themselves has a strong lineage. In the 1970s, for instance, the sociologist Erving Goffman theorised gender (and other social roles) as emerging from our repeated engagement in different activities through which roles like gender took on their meaning. Goffman talked about the way we frame interaction and our footing within those interactions. Framing refers to how we set up an interpretive frame for an interaction or event, while footing is about how we position ourselves and others within the interpretive frame we have established.

Performative/ performativity

Judith Butler argued that gender is performative in the sense that the iteration of actions and ways of talking in a social context acquires *constitutive* force within a community. This underlies the social meaning associated with actions, events or categories.

Connections with theory

The philosopher Judith Butler's analysis of gender casts it as **performative**. This is different from the notion of gender performances in, for example, Goffman. Butler's theory ties in with a longer tradition in the philosophy of language, the idea that some speech acts actually *do* something, hence are called performatives. When you say 'I promise', that is a performative: the saying does the promising. These speech acts acquire their force through their repetition and endorsement as promises in our society. Butler argues that gender is analogous: gendered identities emerging through iterations of acts endorsed as gendered within our society.

The focus on agency in sociolinguistic research has led to a profound shift in the field. Many researchers, especially in the field of language and gender, have taken up the idea that individuals may actively shape their social identities and negotiate them in relation to others' through repeated and shared social practices. Consequently, they explore how ways of talking are integrated with non-linguistic practices – ways of dressing, ways of defining what's cool or desirable, or networks of association. Obviously, this approach has potential relevance to how we think about other social categories. Weber's concept of class, you'll recall, already included a sense of the importance of associated patterns of behaviour (his notion of lifestyle). More recently, too, researchers have turned their attention to the extent to which notions like 'young' and 'elderly' might be more than just labels of chronological age; they might also be socially constituted.

The use of linguistic and non-linguistic practices as complementary sources of data means research methods have to change. There is still a place for social dialect studies that quantify over large numbers of individuals, and there is still a good deal of interest in determining whether there are new generalisations to be made about how performances of gender might affect the path of language change. But there is also a vital branch of research which is not concerned with theorising language change. Instead, it is more interested in undertaking detailed long-term studies of smaller numbers of speakers in an attempt to understand the cross roads where gender, power and language all meet. Researchers argue that the study of communities of practice (introduced in Chapter 9) is particularly important because communities of practice shed light on the very local meanings of categories like *female* or *male*. These local meanings, in turn, provide us with the level of information we need to understand the way gender is part of a larger web (or even hierarchy) of social relations. Let us consider some examples of this kind of approach.

The first example is from Mary Bucholtz's (1998) research in a Bay Area high school. Like Eckert, Bucholtz spent a lot of time getting to know the students in one high school, and recording them as they engaged in a range of activities in and out of school. We looked at some of the results from her study in Chapter 9, where we saw that two different communities of practice were characterised by very different degrees of fronting of /u/ and /o/, the GOOSE and GOAT vowels (we saw this data in Chapter 9). Bucholtz identified the community of practice in which there was limited fronting as the nerd girls. She showed that the nerd girls engaged in many activities that would set them apart from the popular girls. These included their attitudes to and participation in academic life, dating at school, and so forth. She also showed how the nerd girls sometimes went bald on record (see Chapter 5 on politeness) in policing each other's participation in practices associated with their own group norms, and evidence of straying into practices associated with outgroups.

Bucholtz argues that detailed examination of the practices of a small group of girls who largely distance themselves from the more widely accepted norms for femininity in the high school, provides us with telling information about what it means to be a girl or young woman in the wider community. In this case, it also tells us quite a lot about what it means to be trendy or conservative in the wider community, and Bucholtz encourages us to focus on the way in which these social attributes overlap and are layered.

Laminated

Erving Goffman's term to refer to the way aspects of the context or the identity of the participants compound, reinforce and add depth to the meaning of each other.

Connections with theory

Erving Goffman, again, provides an interesting and early argument in favour of the interdependence of different social identities. He talks of social meaning being **laminated**. The metaphor is intended to convey both the idea that the multiplicity of meanings that may be associated with or invoked in a particular interaction relate to each other, and also the idea that when understood together, *en bloc*, they become something distinct, new, and stronger than they are on their own.

The second example of this kind of approach to language and gender can be seen in Natalie Schilling-Estes's analysis of the gender dynamics on Ocracoke island (1998b). Ocracoke, a sea island off the mainland coast of North Carolina in the US, has a small speech community of year-round residents, many of whose families have been on the island for hundreds of years. Schilling-Estes found it illuminating to consider the dynamics of smaller groups of men and women that were readily recognised in the community as a whole. She concluded that an important factor in understanding patterns of linguistic variation on Ocracoke was how much speakers identified with an islander identity, but she also concluded that what people identified with as an 'islander' might differ too.

Schilling-Estes compares the use of a raised and backed onset in PRICE (ay) diphthongs, and the use of a fronted onset and fronted glide in MOUTH (aw) diphthongs. Both are distinctive characteristics of Ocracoke English (known locally as the 'brogue'). However, these two markers of local speech have rather different sociolinguistic histories. The raised and backed PRICE variant ([ʌ^I]) is a widely recognised marker of the brogue and subject to frequent comment and ostentatious performance by both locals and visitors. The fronted MOUTH variant ([ɛ^I]) is much less subject to overt comment or display. She found that among middle-aged speakers on Ocracoke, the raised PRICE variants were most frequent in the speech of a network of poker players (all men) who strongly identified with a particular kind of islander identity – that of the traditional waterman. The frequency of the raised variants among these speakers was even higher than it was among men in the next-older generation. Among their middle-aged peers – women and men who were not part of the poker playing group – the raised variants were much less common. The probability of a raised variant among these speakers was roughly the same as it was among the next-younger generation.

The picture for fronted (aw) variants was rather different. Here, the local variants were favoured most by middle-aged women and middle-aged gay men who were not part of the poker-playing network. Schilling-Estes notes that these speakers also have strong ties to the island, even though they may not share the nostalgia for the traditional macho world associated with making a living from fishing and crabbing. Nevertheless, several of them are actively engaged in work on local history and archaeology. Schilling-Estes argues that these speakers have adopted the fronted (aw) variant as their own marker of an islander identity. Her analysis highlights the usefulness of analysing gender identities in terms of the wider social matrix. It also shows how attention to details in the patterning of linguistic variables can strengthen an analysis which (in this case) calls for a serious reconsideration of the relationship between language and an Ocracoke identity.

In other words, her analysis of the situation is not that there are two ways of speaking – one 'male' and one 'female'. Instead, she uses her knowledge of the community to dig deeper. In doing so, she begins to ask and answer questions that go beyond simple questions like, 'What do men and women do?' Instead, she starts to ask and understand what it means to be an islander on Ocracoke and how that intersects with historical and synchronic practices associated with male and female residents.

STRATEGIC USE OF GENDER DIFFERENCES

Now that we have looked at the way in which sex-preferential differences in language can be analysed if gender is seen as being part of the larger social matrix, we can revisit some of the variables we introduced earlier as being sex-exclusive features of language. With

Connections with theory

You may be wondering why sociolinguists always seem to be studying the PRICE and MOUTH vowels. Both diphthongs usually provide a lengthy stretch of phonetic space for speakers and sociolinguists to focus on. Of course, some varieties of English are characterised by using much shorter glides, and some have monophthongs, but this should only serve to reinforce the point. There's a lot of potential for variation in these vowels, and as a consequence it's perhaps not surprising that they so often acquire or are assigned associations with non-linguistic factors.

these variables, too, the picture becomes fuzzier if gender is seen as being part of a social matrix, and a resource to be negotiated through a range of social practices.

Not so 'exclusive' after all

The Western linguistics canon has often focused on Japanese and some of the Native American languages as exemplars of languages with sex-exclusive differences, and this characterisation of those languages is quite close to the way members of the speech community perceive them.

Sara Trechter is a linguist who has worked for many years on Lakhota (the Teton variety of Sioux) spoken in North Dakota (USA). Sioux languages have a series of sentence-final particles which indicate whether the utterance is a statement, a question, or an order. Native speakers, of course, understand the function these elements have as markers of **illocutionary force**. There is generally more than one variant associated with each function, and native speakers strongly believe that the different variants are 'female' or 'male'. That is, Lakhota speakers will claim 'men say *lo* and women say *le*; men say *yo* and women say *ye*' (Trechter 2003: 432). In Lakhota, *lo* is prototypically used by men to state opinions or show emphasis and *yo* is used to give orders or imperatives. The forms *ye* and *le* are the forms associated with female speakers for expressing the same illocutionary force.

However, Trechter points out that when we talk about these forms as being 'exclusive' what is really meant is that they give a clearly gendered flavour to the speaker's voice. So men can and do use *ye* and *le*, but in doing so they are perceived to be acting in a womanly or maternal way. Likewise, women can and do use *yo* and *lo*, but when they do they may be perceived to be tomboyish (2003: 433). In some cases, the opposition between prototypically male and female forms is breaking down. Trechter's work shows that *le*, the supposed female equivalent to *lo*, is in fact pretty archaic. The women that Trechter spoke to said that they would use *lo* in public speaking simply as a way of emphasising a point or an opinion. In other words, this prototypically male particle is nowadays seen as authoritative (rather than gendered). There may be social reasons why it is more common for men to speak authoritatively in public than for women to do so, and this may give rise to perceived gender differences, but this is an indirect index (in Ochs's terms). If *lo* directly indexes emphasis or authoritativeness and only indirectly indexes gender, then it becomes quite unsurprising to find that both women and men at times use *lo*.

Illocutionary force

The force of a *speech act*. Saying 'I promise' has the illocutionary force of promising if the speaker is geuinely committed to what they utter (and is not lying or hoaxing).

In other words, Trechter's examination of historical recordings of Lakhota and her own more recent fieldwork show that the relationship between speaker sex and use of these particles is far from deterministic. Speakers can and do use these particles as strategic resources for expressing semantic information, such as illocutionary force, and for exploiting the social attributes or characteristics associated with their prototypical users.

Connections with theory

Trechter (2006) has also pointed out that many Native American languages are very endangered, and that even if some members of a community continue to use the language they may not be very fluent speakers. This results in a reduction of stylistic variation which may now mean there is greater regularity (approaching exclusivity) of use of these particles than was previously the case.

Takano (1998) provides an interesting example from Japanese that also illustrates the way speakers appear to use gendered behaviours strategically. Takano was looking at a morphosyntactic change in progress (which seems to be operating below the level of conscious awareness). This variable involves the realisation of the *wa* and *ga* particles that mark a noun as topic or subject in Japanese. In the change in progress, there is a tendency for these particles to be elided in speech, so we find contrasts like those in (7) and (8) (these examples are taken from Takano (1998) with slight modifications to the gloss).

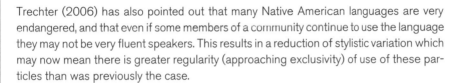

(7) a. *Kuriimu   ga   amain   da.*
         cream   SUBJECT sweet   be
         'The frosting on the cake must be sweet.'
     b. *Kimoti   Ø   warui   toka.*
         feeling   SUBJECT bad   etc.
         'You feel bad, that kind of thing.'

(8) a. *Syusshian   wa   doko   desu   ka.*
         hometown   TOPIC   where   be   Q-word
         'Where are you from?'

(9) b. *Fooku   Ø   arimasu yo   nee.*
         fork   TOPIC   there.is particle particle
         'You have a fork, don't you?'

As with most linguistic variables, the most significant constraint on this variation is another grammatical factor; that is, whether or not the sentence has canonical Japanese SOV word order. However, non-linguistic factors are also relevant.

Previous discussion of these variables had claimed that women delete *ga* and *wa* more than men do. Takano's study did find gender to be an important factor. However, contrary to prior claims, it was not sex or gender *per se* that constrained the variation; rather, it was the context in which women and men were talking. Women talking in single-sex conversations deleted *wa* and *ga* most often, and men in single-sex conversations were most likely consistently to mark NPs with *wa* and *ga*. But when women and men were talking in mixed-sex conversations, the differences between their single-sex styles disappeared entirely. They both seemed to accommodate in the direction of the other group's single-sex norms (see Chapter 4 on accommodation). The result is a remarkable degree of mutual convergence. It will require a good deal more research to determine how much this convergence is a (presumably subconscious) desire to exploit the gendered resources of the speech community, or how much it is a reflex of more interpersonal factors, such as how much the interlocutors like, or want to like, each other. However, Takano's work now provides an excellent benchmark against which such questions can be asked.

exercise

Particle omission in Japanese

Takano notes that in mixed-sex conversation it appears that men and women accommodate somewhat to the other's ingroup norms for *wa* and *ga* use. This helps explain their linguistic behaviour in mixed-sex conversations, but a more complicated question remains? Can you think of any plausible social reason(s) why women might frequently delete *wa* and *ga* in same-sex conversations?

In order to motivate an answer, you will almost certainly have to think about men's tendency to mark subjects and topics with *wa* and *ga* as well as women's tendency not to (as we have done when discussing both the Ocracoke and the Lakhota data).

exercise

Motivating variation

What kind of questions would you ask in order to determine whether or not the effects Takano found are a function of speakers' accommodating to each other to increase mutual liking? What kind of questions would you ask to determine whether women are using the *wa* and *ga* particles strategically (as Trechter discussed with the sentence-final particles in Lakhota)?

It may help to pair up with someone else and try to make their questions as specific as possible by playing devil's advocate.

Connections with theory

You will have noticed that in most of the case studies we have looked at the most important constraints on a variable are linguistic (case marking and word order with *wa* and *ga*; illocutionary force with *lo*), and that social factors account for less of the variation overall. Interestingly, this may be reversed in the early stages of the acquisition of variables (see Roberts 2002 for summary). There is perhaps an even more interesting consequence of the fact that social factors account for relatively little of the constraints on variation. It means that, as social beings, we pay a lot of attention to and ascribe a lot of meaning to constraints which statistically do relatively little work.

Gendered style

In the previous section we looked at ways in which a socially situated view of gender might enrich the analysis of discrete linguistic variables. We have seen that there is evidence that these variables are deployed strategically by speakers in order to draw on attributes or identities that are both directly and indirectly indexed. In this section, we will see that we can apply the same kind of perspective to the analysis of an individual's style-shifting (see Chapter 3).

There has been a considerable amount of work done looking at how gender roles and expectations seem to interact with different interaction styles. Deborah Tannen is one of the best-known researchers in this field, and in her work she has sometimes argued that differences in interactional styles between women and men should be understood in the same way that cross-cultural communication differences are understood (Tannen 1990). Under this framework, for example, a misunderstanding between a woman and a man about whether a complaint about a problem requires a solution (his understanding of the norms for responding to a complaint) or a matching story (her understanding of the norms for responding to a complaint) are similar to the misunderstandings that can arise cross-culturally. For example, if a New Zealander presents her Ni-Vanuatu friend with a gift and her Ni-Vanuatu friend says nothing to acknowledge the gift, she might be offended unless she knows that effusive, public thanks between friends are not normal or expected in informal contexts.

In this section, I am less concerned with trying to generalise about possible differences and similarities between women's and men's interactional styles. Instead, I am more interested in looking at something more subtle: how our ideas about gender may be expressed in interaction and how methods associated more closely with discourse analysis can enrich our understanding of social categories like gender, and complement other methods for interrogating it.

A number of sociolinguists are interested in exploring the extent to which variation between styles can complement detailed linguistic analysis, in order to see how variation in one part of the linguistic system might reinforce the effect of variation in another part (or potentially cancel or mitigate it). This might involve comparing the frequency of the [ɪn] and [ɪŋ] variants at different points in a conversation. Since it is well established that the (ing) variable is socially significant, and since the association of [ɪŋ] with female speakers or speakers of higher socioeconomic class is widely attested, it would be interesting to see how variables like this pattern in different speech styles. Do gendered roles trigger higher frequencies of the tokens that are found most frequently in women's or men's speech at the level of the speech community? Some work suggests that they do (Holmes 1997), but there is still a need for more work in this area. Such research will ultimately move us towards answering the questions posed in Chapters 3 and 8 – namely, how is it that social attributes such as class, attributes like formality of style, and gender come to pattern in consistent ways with respect to each other?

GENDER AND SEXUALITY

A more recent focus in the study of language and gender has been explicitly concerned with the extent to which gender identities and sexuality are linked. Attitudes towards the importance of same-sex and opposite-sex attraction clearly define an important sub-set of the social practices through which gender roles emerge. The gendering of a Mother role, for instance, is something we learn from living in a society where the archetype for parents includes one female and one male. In addition, researchers like Penny Eckert, who want to understand how and when gender identities and gendered ways of talking are acquired, find that for pre-adolescents and adolescents (in the US, at least) the assumed normalness of developing heterosexual desire plays a big role in shaping how kids and adults think about the difference between girls and women, boys and men. Obviously, other practices are important, but participation in (or avoidance of) a heterosexual marketplace becomes just as important as participation in (or avoidance of) the standard language marketplace that we discussed in Chapter 7.

One of the more important early works on language and gender did, in fact, draw readers' attention to the possibility that gendered ways of talking were linked not only to gender identities but also to sexual identities. Robin Lakoff (2004) talked about 'women's language' as being characteristic of not only women but also homosexuals and academics. What Lakoff was trying to point out was that all three groups were in some sense or another marginalised or excluded from institutionalised varieties of male power (see Hall 2003). Researchers in language and gender are increasingly turning their attention not only to describing ways of speaking but to generalising about how individuals in these groups end up lacking in or being excluded from exercising social power.

Deborah Cameron (1997) provides a particularly nice discussion of the ways in which ideologies of gender and sexuality are woven together in discourse. She analyses a short piece of gossip in the conversation of four young Anglo-American men who were watching basketball on TV together one weekend. She argues that the extract in (10) illustrates the way in which their conversation constructs one of their classmates as a social undesirable in terms of his deviance from heterosexual masculine norms. In (10), you can see a short example from a longer exchange along these lines.

(10) The Antithesis of Man

BRYAN: uh you know that really gay guy in our Age of Revolution class who sits in front of us? he wore shorts again, by the way, it's like 42 degrees out he wore shorts again [laughter] [Ed: That guy] it's like a speedo, he wears a speedo to class (.) he's got incredibly skinny legs [Ed: it's worse] you know=

ED: = you know like those shorts women volleyball players wear? it's like those (.) it's l[ike

BRYAN: [you know what's even more ridicu[lous? when
ED: [French cut spandex]

BRYAN: you wear those shorts and like a parka on . . .
(5 lines omitted)

BRYAN: he's either got some condition that he's got to like have his legs exposed at all times or else he's got really good legs=
ED: = he's probably he'[s like
CARL: [he really likes

BRYAN:	= he
ED:	= he's like at home combing his leg hairs=
CARL:	his legs=

| BRYAN: | he doesn't have any leg hair though=   [*yes* and oh |
| ED: | = he *real* [*ly* likes |

| ED: | his legs= |
| AL: | =very long very white and very skinny |

BRYAN:	those ridiculous Reeboks that are always (indeciph)
	and goofy white socks always striped= [tube socks
ED:	= that's [right

| ED: | he's the antithesis of man |

(Cameron 1997: 53–4)

As Cameron points out, there is a certain irony to the fact that in putting this guy down, the four conversationalists themselves draw on precisely the kinds of linguistic strategies that they typify as unmasculine (e.g., concern with the detail of fabric and the cut of clothes). They also use a conversational style which a lot of literature of language and gender has claimed is archetypally feminine, for example, lots of overlapping speech, finishing each other's sentences, etc.

Collaboration or competition?

When Cameron analysed this part of the conversation, she noted that when the participants begin overlapping and finishing each other's sentences, it is hard to tell whether we should see them as being collaborative (jointly constructing the conversation) or competitive (trying to out do each other). How does it read to you? Collaborative co-construction, or competitive verbal duel? Why?

You should probably have the piece read out loud – you can do it alone or get someone else to run through it with you – because it comes across very differently when you read it silently in your head.

Connections with theory

The field of conversation analysis is somewhat divided over what aspects of an interaction an analyst can reliably talk about. Some practitioners argue that you can only talk about gender being relevant in a text when the speakers explicitly use a gendered form of address, for example. Others are more interested in the unspoken assumptions about gender which are implicit in the discourse, and the resonances between and across interactions, and they are interested in talking about them.

The difference in approach is something like the distinction made in semantics and pragmatics between information that is carried by conventional implicatures (i.e., an implication that is part of the word itself) and **conversational implicatures** (i.e., implications that arise from how the word is used).

Conversational implicature

An inference that arises from interlocutors' shared understanding of the norms of conversation. Not part of the semantics or inherent meaning of a word/phrase. Unlike a *conventional implicature*, you can cancel a conversational implicature (e.g., They have two cats *if not more*).

In the previous section, we noted that an interest in stylistic variation and in the analysis of speech interaction isn't necessarily incompatible with detailed analysis of linguistic variables. Rather, in the long run, the goal of understanding the social significance of variation better is most likely to be served by combining these two modes of analysis. Some very interesting results of just this kind have emerged from research comparing the frequency of socially significant variables with an emphasis on the role that sexual identities might play in different speech styles.

Robert Podesva found some interesting differences in a very subtle variable, the duration of the burst when a stop is released. Previous variationist work had argued that longer and more audible releases for a word-final stop (e.g., in *kit* or *kid*) in US English are used by speakers to present a persona that is competent and precise. Podesva (2004) shows how Heath, a gay medical student in California, systematically varies the duration of the release on his stops depending on the context. In a social context among friends, Heath's stops had much longer releases than they did when he was in a professional context, meeting with a patient. So there appears to be an anomaly between what Heath is doing and the meaning for longer released stops that have been forwarded based on earlier studies across the speech community. If a longer release signals competence or precision, we might have expected Heath to use them *more* in a professional setting, when talking to a patient, because we would expect him to be more concerned with conveying competence and precision here than when he is with friends.

On the basis of this, Podesva goes back to his data and reconsiders Heath's linguistic behaviour when he is with his friends in a more holistic way. He notes that Heath makes other phonetic adjustments to the way he speaks in different social situations. In particular, he uses a falsetto voice quality and much wider pitch range when he is socialising with friends as opposed to when he is interacting with a patient. So Podesva considers the possibility that for Heath, released stops convey something slightly different from what they might convey to other speakers of California English. By seeing the longer duration of stop releases as part of a broader stylistic repertoire that marks him as a flamboyant gay man, Podesva concludes that for Heath the longer stop releases signify prissiness rather than precision.

WIDER IMPLICATIONS OF RETHINKING GENDER

This chapter has provided an outline of different methods and perspectives for analysing the relationship between gender and variation in a speech community. One of the clear changes that has taken place over the last few decades is an emphasis on not only analysing how different variants are used by women and men as groups but also on understanding how a social category like gender emerges in more particular, individualised interactions. This may

exercise

Change in progress and developing identities

We know that a lot of changes in progress peak in the speech of adolescents; that is, an innovative variant is more frequent in adolescents' speech than it is in pre-adolescents', or in the speech of people in their twenties. We have also seen that most changes in progress which are taking place below the level of conscious awareness show distinct gender patterning (with women in the lead). How might it help us to better understand the processes underlying these facts if we link the development of both gender and sexual identities in adolescence?

entail more detailed analysis using methods from conversation or discourse analysis, and de-emphasises the role of generalisations across individuals or across interactions.

Many of the reasons that researchers on language and gender want to explore more critically what gender exactly means in a community can be extended to other social categories we have discussed in this book. In the previous chapter, we looked initially at social class and made generalisations across aggregated groups of individuals, and we labelled them as different classes on the basis of their average level of education, their average income and/or where they lived. We then looked in more detail at smaller and more face-to-face groupings such as networks and communities of practice. We saw there that some of the intergroup patterns emerge very locally. In other words, we can problematise categories like social class in the same way that we can problematise categories like gender, and we might want to do so for exactly the same reasons.

By now, we have seen a number of parallels between the way variables pattern with respect to class, gender, age and style: it can be helpful therefore to ask what these categories mean to speakers where their speech community exhibits stratification on all these lines. We are most likely to find the answers to this sort of question by combining analyses that draw on patterns of language use, not only to describe the general outline of a speech community but also to deepen our understanding of the communities speakers inhabit and how variation can come to function as a way of realising very human needs such as avoiding negative stereotypes, fostering a positive image for ourselves and for the groups we identify most closely with (Chapter 2).

Connections with theory

Some recent work on language variation has stressed that linguistic factors are consistently found to be stronger constraints than social factors (Labov 2001; Trudgill 2004). As a result, they claim that social factors are relatively unimportant (even trivial) in determining the outcome of variation and change. This may be strictly true: it might well be the case that social factors never determine how variation will be resolved. But that is only one goal for studying variation in language use. I have tried here to stress that differences in language have the potential to be appropriated and deployed as very subtle but consistent markers of social factors. The subtlety of the non-linguistic effects consequently highlights their potential as objects of enquiry in themselves.

CHAPTER SUMMARY

In this chapter we started out with a review of the traditional way in which the variable of sex or gender has been used in social dialectology and we briefly traced the development of the field from a concern with *sex* to a concern with *gender*. The difference between so-called sex-exclusive and sex-preferential variables was introduced, and it was illustrated with data from several different languages.

We then looked at some of the most robust generalisations that have been made in variationist sociolinguistics about the relationship between language and gender, and we saw that what appears to be a paradox in how variants pattern in the speech of women and men might not really need special explanation. Indeed, what this apparent paradox did was highlight the fact that there were serious problems with the way gender had been operationalised as a variable in earlier social dialect work.

On the basis of this insight we looked more critically at gender in language use, following the lead of researchers such as Eckert and McConnell-Ginet, who introduced the community of practice as an alternative to the speech community as the basis for analysis. We also explored the intersections between gender and other social and linguistic phenomena using Ochs's distinction between direct and indirect indexing.

Having problematised the notion of gender as a monolithic variable in language variation, we returned to the notion of sex-exclusive forms and reconsidered the nature of this supposed exclusivity in the case of gendered sentence particles in Lakhota and case markers in Japanese. We saw that Trechter's detailed analysis of the use of the Lakhota forms showed that speakers of both sexes can and do deploy the gendered meaning of particles to create a particular effect in discourse. We then looked at how the more recent view of gender as an identity that emerges and is negotiated through social interaction has begun to define aspects of the study of language and sexuality.

There is a tension in language and gender studies between work that is highly detailed and particular, and work that continues to quantify over a large number of individuals. The first approach may make researchers reluctant to venture broad generalisations about, for example, the relationship between gender and language variation and change. The second approach continues to be useful in understanding how gender (and other non-linguistic) factors operate as constraints on language variation and change. This chapter has tried to present both approaches and to stress the potential for combining them (as some researchers already do). This suggests the potential for a coherent methodological and theoretical rethinking of our approach to sociolinguistics; but the field is a good way from resolving this tension as yet.

FURTHER READING

In addition to the references provided in this chapter, you may find the following interesting:

Barrett (1998) – on African-American drag queens' use of linguistic variants more frequently found in the speech of white, middle-class American women.

Cameron (2005) – a very important piece of research backed up by considerable data which seeks to integrate facts about gender, age and style.

Cameron and Kulick (2003) – a constructive and critical introduction to the relatively new field of language and sexuality.

Eckert and McConnell-Ginet (2003) – a general introduction to the study of language and gender.

Hall and Bucholtz (1995) – articles emphasising the socially situated nature of gender.

Holmes and Meyerhoff (2003) – major themes, methods and debates in language and gender research.

Schieffelin (1990) – not specifically on gender, but an excellent example of mutually informative analysis of linguistic variables and styles.

CHAPTER 11

Language contact

Key terms in this chapter:

- **dialect levelling**
- **quotative verbs**
- **evidentials**
- **globalisation**
- **lingua franca**
- **pidgin**
- **creole**
- **expanded pidgin**

- **vernacularisation**
- **creolisation**
- **lexifier**
- **substrate**
- **wave model**
- **gravity model**
- **acts of identity**

HOW CONTACT BETWEEN VARIETIES AFFECTS VARIATION AND CHANGE

All variation and change can be viewed as the outcome of some form of contact between different individuals or members of different groups. For example, in New York City the situation could be cast as one in which there was contact between speakers with raised and unraised (oh) and (a). Similarly, the expansion of non-standard *were* into negative tags in York English or the loss of *ne* in French must in some sense be the result of contact between speakers of different ages.

However, as a rule, linguistic studies of contact have been concerned with contact between *languages*, and comparatively few researchers have actively been working on contact between *dialects*. There are a number of approaches to studying language contact – the field has a rich tradition embracing many different theoretical perspectives entirely of its own – and not all of them can be reviewed here (see suggestions in the 'Further reading' section). Here, we will be taking a sociolinguistic perspective on issues in language contact, and in keeping with the rest of this book the focus will be on how the study of variation informs our understanding of the processes implicated in language contact. We will be concerned with the interplay between linguistic, social and interactional constraints and how these seem to affect the structural outcomes of the contact situation. We will see, too, that speakers' perceptions about intergroup relations may play a role in constraining the outcomes of contact.

In Chapter 6 we considered some of the social and political factors relevant to understanding the linguistic situation of multilingual communities, and we saw that code switching and code mixing are linguistic resources available to people who speak more than one language variety. The focus of this chapter is a little different. Here we consider contact between languages or dialects where the outcomes are not bilingualism, bidialectalism or the code-switching skills mentioned in Chapter 6. Here, we are concerned with how varation emerges as a consequence of varieties bumping against each other and how speakers may also use variation as a resource in such contexts.

This chapter will sometimes discuss cases of contact between different languages, and sometimes discuss contact between varieties of one language. Ultimately, it may prove to be the case that the same social and linguistic principles underlie all types of language contact and constrain the outcomes – whether between dialects or languages – but this remains an area in which a lot of research is being carried out today. In the future, it is hoped that we will have a clearer picture of the important commonalities and differences between various situations of language contact.

DIALECT LEVELLING

Dialect levelling refers to the gradual erasure or loss of the differences that have traditionally distinguished very local or highly regionalised varieties of a language. As a rule, the process is the result of new or increased mobility of speakers, and many regional dialectologists and sociolinguists in Europe and Japan are studying the linguistic and social dimensions of the process. Researchers from these parts of the world are interested in dialect levelling because some of the social changes taking place in the twentieth century appear to be having a rapid and marked impact on the degree of local dialect diversity that has characterised these regions for hundreds (if not thousands) of years.

Dialect levelling

Reduction of differences distinguishing regional *dialects* or *accents*. One possible outcome of contact between speakers of different varieties.

In the UK, in Scandinavia, and in Japan, a number of 'New Towns' were built in the decades following the end of the Second World War. A New Town involves the rapid expansion of the existing housing and economic infrastructure in an area which (usually) had formerly been a small village. Residents from all over the country might move in to a New Town in order to take advantage of these opportunities for work or affordable housing. The linguistic result of this is to bring many speakers, drawing on quite different, but mutually intelligible varieties of a language, into close and daily contact with each other.

Ordinarily, if a family moves to a new home outside the parent's own dialect area, the children growing up in the family's new home will acquire the variety that is spoken locally. But in the New Towns, the speakers of the local dialect are dramatically outnumbered by the newcomers, and this disrupts the normal pattern by which children acquire a local variety (and local variation, discussed in Chapter 10). In addition, there is seldom a single group of migrants who are numerically and socially dominant enough for their variety to become the linguistic norm for the New Town. Instead, children growing up in this mixed sociolinguistic context are exposed to a number of different (but comprehensible) models and have to make sense of this in some way.

The immediate outcome is a situation in which there is a good deal of variability within the speech community, but in some New Towns researchers are now able to compare the speech of several generations of children born into the community. What they find is evidence that the native-born children are levelling out the differences between what they hear from their parents, what they hear from their friends' parents, and the traditional local dialect (cf. convergent attunement processes, discussed in Chapter 4).

A particularly detailed study of the linguistic outcomes of a New Town is Paul Kerswill and Anne Williams's (2000) work on Milton Keynes in England. Kerswill and Williams found that in the vowel system, children aged 4–12 years in Milton Keynes were using variants that were closer to those used in London than those used by older speakers in Milton Keynes. This was true for PRICE (ay), MOUTH (aw), THOUGHT (oh) and GOAT (ow). Although migrants from London were not a majority in Milton Keynes, the vast majority of newcomers had come from somewhere in the south-east of England. In Chapter 2, we examined some historical examples of dialect levelling when we looked at what happened when the Fens in south-east England were drained in the seventeenth century. Once the Fens ceased to be a barrier to movement, we saw that contact between local varieties was resolved in various ways. Levelling there resulted in both the reallocation of forms when different dialects came into contact (raised and open onsets for PRICE), as well as the creation of an intermediate form (for the STRUT vowel).

In countries where there was no active programme of developing New Towns, other social trends have created a context in which traditional dialect variation also appears to be levelling out. The migration to and rapid expansion of cities has often subsumed what used to be outlying villages or towns, and this too can lead to the loss of some of the formerly distinctive features of those local dialects.

Sociolinguists in Britain have noted that something like dialect levelling seems to be occurring in geographically dispersed varieties as well. We saw an example of one of these variables in Chapter 10, in the exercise looking at the distribution of glottal stops in Reading and Hull. Intervocalic [ʔ] for [t] (*bu'er* for *butter* as one of the teenagers in the study remarked) is also the more frequent variant in young Milton Keynes speakers, but the Reading and Hull data suggest that this variant is spreading quite rapidly and is becoming entrenched in varieties that have not traditionally had intervocalic glottal stops. One of the striking things about the figure for that exercise is the similar rate with which glottal variants are being used in both Reading and Hull (Williams and Kerswill 1999). The town of Reading is quite close to London, but Hull is not and there is limited evidence that Hull has been affected by immigration from, or contact with, London or other south-east speakers.

Later in this chapter we will consider some sociolinguistic constraints on the outcomes of contact. There we will consider more closely the spread of variants between cities. We will discuss the importance of spatial distance between speakers, and also their perception of social distance between varieties. In the next section, we will examine the apparent spread of variation or levelling of forms internationally. The case study we examine here will consider the question of whether the appearance of the same variants across different varieties can be used to infer that a single linguistic variable has spread from one variety to another.

GLOBAL CONTACT: GLOBAL ENGLISH?

In this section we examine a fairly recent variable – the use of *be like* as a means of introducing reported discourse. This has been spreading rapidly through different varieties of English and just as the creole case studies have shown that a variable may reflect the transfer and/or reallocation of meaning from one language to another, similar principles play a role in the analysis of this variable as it is transmitted across different varieties of English.

The spread of *be like* across varieties of English

Not very long ago, the main way English speakers introduced a quote was by using verbs of speaking – things like *say* (1), *murmur* (2), *call, yell* – or by using the verb *go* (3) (which has probably been an option in English for several hundred years):

(1)   'Donald,' Bech said, 'we would never eat any candy without telling you'. (Updike 1965: 111)
(2)   'Ah well . . . we all do don't we?' murmured Shiva. (Smith 2000: 145)
(3)   I went, you know, 'I don't wanna!' (Schillinger 2004)

There is also the option of using no verb at all to introduce reported speech (shown as Ø in example 4). Although you may think this is mainly a feature of literary English, studies consistently find that it occurs roughly 20–25 per cent of the time in reported spoken discourse:

(4)   I'll come back and she's like, 'So Jason, how are things with Pearl?'
      Ø 'Good.'
      Ø 'Am I still the number one woman in your life.' (Tagliamonte and D'Arcy 2004, ex. 9b)

Because these verbs introduce quoted speech (or present thoughts as if they were speech), they are often referred to as **quotative verbs**. Since the 1970s, two newcomers have made inroads into this general space and in some varieties of English, *be like* and *be all* are now ubiquitous quotatives:

(5)   I'm like, 'Can I please speak with Antonio?'
      And his mom's like, 'Oh no, sorry! He's not home.' (Tagliamonte and D'Arcy 2004, ex. 7b)
(6)   But then I went and drove in L.A. during rush hour and I was all, 'Hmm, Flagstaff traffic's not that bad'.

Individual speakers may have preferences for one quotative or another, but generally the older and the newer forms compete in the speech of a single person. This can be seen in the following quotes from an interview with an aspiring actor, Jaime Pressly. In reporting a conversation she had, Pressly uses the newer variant *be like*, then the older variants *say* and *go*:

(7)   'Lena is **like**, "You haven't done a studio film in a year,"' Pressly grumbled. 'I **said**, "You wanted me to do independent films." And she **said**, "Yeah, but you can't do *all* independent films." So I **go**, "Either way, I am wrong here, Lena." And she **goes**, "No, you have to be part of *all* of it."' (Mead 2003: 97)

It seems fairly clear that both the new variants *be like* and *be all* first appear in spoken US English before they appear in other varieties, and a combination of regional and apparent time data indicates that they probably originated on the West Coast. The speed with which they have been adopted into other varieties is astounding. It possibly reflects the fact that these variables are essentially lexical, and as we discussed earlier (Chapter 7), vocabulary is

Quotative verbs

Verbs introducing reports of discourse, (e.g., direct and indirect speech or thought). They include older, more stable variants such as *say* and *think*, as well as newer ones such as *be like, be all.*

different from core aspects of the grammar, such as phonology and syntax, in that people continue to learn vocabulary throughout their lives.

Recent work in North America shows how well established these new forms are. In particular, *be like* can be used with many functions. It can introduce imitations of sounds, reported or constructed speech (example 5 on p. 241), reported thoughts (example 8), and comments that even in context are ambiguous between the two (example 9). (A number of commentators on quotatives (e.g., Tannen 1986) point out that reported speech or thought is never a completely faithful reproduction of a prior utterance. All reported discourse involves some reimagining or reconstruction, even if it involves your own utterances.)

The following examples illustrate these functions for *be like*:

(8)   There was nothing I could say/I was like 'Whoa, gotta get this girl . . .' (Triple 8, 'Good 2 Go', 2005)

(9)   [speaker is reporting something that happened while she was probably alone] And it's like 'whoops, there goes my chips, OK fine.' (Buchstaller 2004: 49)

Buchstaller's survey of some very large corpora of British and US English recorded during the 1990s found clear evidence of the uptake of *be like* among younger speakers. In an even more recent corpus of three-quarters of a million words of spoken English, Sali Tagliamonte and Alex D'Arcy found that younger Canadians in Toronto used *be like* 60 per cent of the time to introduce reported discourse – that is, reports of either speech or thought (see Figure 11.1). As this figure shows, the increased use of *be like* seems to be at the expense of *say* for the Canadian speakers, while *say* remains a more frequent option in Buchstaller's (slightly earlier) corpora of British and US English.

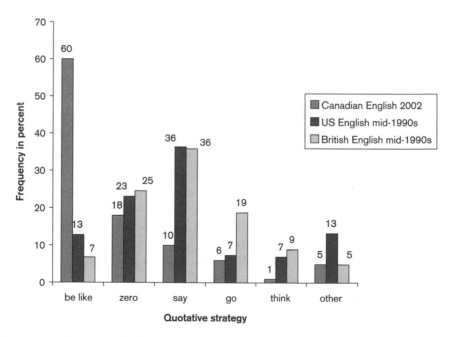

Figure 11.1   Frequency of different strategies for introducing reported speech or thought among speakers of Canadian, British and US English. (Sources, Tagliamonte and D'Arcy 2004; Buchstaller 2004.)

Connections with theory

Notice how important it is to keep track of the quotes that are introduced without any overt verb of quotation. If you were to leave these out (and far too many studies do leave them out, simply because they cannot be searched for automatically), you would have a very skewed picture of the system.

Some people have claimed that *be like* is pushing out the older variants, especially *say* and *go*. However, Buchstaller (2004) looks in some detail at what kind of content is introduced by the new and the old quotatives, and she concludes that even in North American English, where *be like* is very common, the picture is a little more complicated. The introduction of a new quotative *be like* results in the reallocation of quotatives within the whole system (the process of reallocation was introduced in Chapter 2). Different, complementary functions are assigned to different quotatives. As we will see, an analysis that considers the function of these variants in spoken discourse provides a principled means for comparing the development of the variable in varieties of English that are at very different stages of the change.

Buchstaller argues that an important factor constraining the use of the possible quotative variants is how likely a quote was to have been actually uttered. A quote introduced by *be like* was considered a likely actual utterance if there was an identifiable speaker, addressee, time and place for the utterance, and it was pragmatically likely that the speaker would have uttered it. If a number of these elements were missing, it was deemed unlikely that the quote was actually uttered. She also distinguished a fairly large sub-group of quotes which might or might not have been uttered, but occur in discourse as ways of summarising or characterising a situation.

Buchstaller found this was a reliable basis for distinguishing the functions of different quotative verbs in English. Figure 11.2 shows the distribution of the quotative strategies in both US and British English when they are coded in this way. She found that even though the overall frequency of *be like* is much lower in Britain than it is in the US, the functional distribution of each quotative in the two varieties is very similar. A statistical analysis of the variation showed that the differences between the varieties are not significant. That is, what appears to be much greater use of *be like* in contexts where the quote is unlikely to have really been uttered disappears (or becomes non-significant) when you adjust for the low frequency of the form in British English.

Buchstaller argues that *be like* is a 'wild card' quotative in both varieties of English. That is, it can be used to introduce any reported discourse. Unsurprisingly, *say* generally introduces discourse that contextual cues indicate was likely to have been uttered, and *think* introduces discourse that was unlikely to have really been uttered aloud. But *be like* is uncommitted about whether the reported discourse was actually uttered or not.

This makes sense if we think about the semantics of *be like*. Older and more standard uses of *be like* approximate one thing with another. If I say 'That cake is like Sam's birthday cake' I assert that there are (or have been) two cakes in the world. I do not claim that the two cakes are, in fact, the same cake. I assert something weaker: the one we are looking at now resembles – or indeed, may be identical to – the first one. Buchstaller suggests that knowledge of this meaning of *be like* has constrained the way in which speakers have integrated *be like* into the quotative system. The net result of introducing a quotative with an

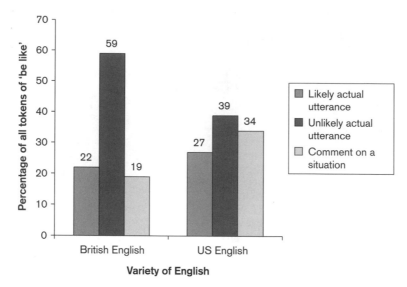

Figure 11.2   Frequency of *be like* as a means of introducing reported discourse in US and British English (mid-1990s) according to the likelihood that the reported discourse was actually uttered. (Source, Buchstaller 2004: 174.)

Evidentials

Forms or structures that provide an indication of how the speaker knows the information being conveyed (e.g., direct experience vs reports from a third party).

approximative meaning is that it allows the system to be more precise. Speakers can use *say* predominantly in domains where there is a stronger claim that something actually was said, and *be like* to hedge on this.

Many languages in the world use some word meaning (BE) LIKE as a means of introducing quotations. In Buang the base form is *be*, in Hiroshima Japanese it is *nanka*, and in Thai it is *baep*. In Bislama it is *olsem*. The semantics of expressing similarity seems to be sufficient for independent innovations of these forms as informal verbs of quotation. We probably don't want to assume that they have all arisen because of the global spread of English and *be like*.

Connections with theory

Many languages require speakers to indicate how they know the information they are passing on: Did they see it? Hear it from someone else? Infer it from physical evidence? These are known as **evidentials** and they are very often realised as different forms of the verb. Buchstaller is proposing that the functional reallocation of quotatives allows English speakers to make some of these distinctions more systematically. This is communicatively useful even if it is marked variably and not categorically.

exercise

Lexical variables and change

Discussion of the notion of apparent time (Chapter 7) rested on the notion that speakers cannot radically restructure their phonological or syntactic systems during their lives. But if a person *can* add to their vocabulary throughout their life, to what extent do you think lexical variables such as *be like* are a problem for the use of apparent time as a method for studying language change?

Sticky places and slippery space: the globalisation of variation?

The spread of *be like* across varieties of English also provides interesting insights into what we might mean by the **globalisation** of English. This can refer to a number of things, including the increased use of English as an international **lingua franca** (i.e., a language used as a means for communicating between native speakers of different languages). I will not go into this aspect of the term here; rather, I will consider the idea that globalisation is resulting in increasing homogeneity across varieties of English. Usually the levelling is seen as being in the direction of US English, which is widely seen as having the most ethnolinguistic vitality (see Chapter 6). However, a number of researchers have noted that the sociolinguistic facts are a little more complicated.

Economists have found that globalisation of services and goods is accompanied by an increased localisation of services. Anne Markusen refers to this as the paradox of 'sticky places in slippery space', by which she means that globalisation makes it easy for an innovation to travel across space – that is, space seems to be more slippery and easy to negotiate. But once an innovation gets to a new locality, the people there tend to customise it – that is, places hold onto the innovation and graft, or stick, local values onto it. An obvious example is McDonald's restaurants, which have a standard, globalised mode for the delivery of fast food, but whose restaurants serve slightly different menus depending on where they are.

The case of *be like* suggests that similar principles may be relevant to understanding the spread of linguistic innovations. The spread of *be like* as a quotative has presumably been facilitated by global aspects of the English-speaking world today. Individuals travel more readily and in greater numbers than at any time in the past so that even if you never leave home yourself, chances are very high that the person answering your call to your bank's service centre or the person serving you your coffee will be from another part of the English-speaking world. For instance, there are between 16,000 and 20,000 Australians and New Zealanders living and working in Edinburgh, the capital of Scotland (Langlands 2002). Many of them are casual workers and they won't settle in Edinburgh, but it does mean that at any one time between 3 and 4 per cent of the total population of the city consists of speakers of varieties of English that even up until the 1970s would have been considered quite exotic.

In addition, the mass media ensures that, even though most Americans don't hold a passport, US English 'travels' in a virtual sense across space and time to other parts of the world. Accents and vocabulary are carried to new locales in television shows and music. So various factors conspire to make the English-speaking world a linguistically slippery space. Sociolinguists need to take this into consideration in their research.

Globalisation

The increased contact between people of different social and linguistic backgrounds across broad swathes of geographical space. Commonly portrayed as a recent phenomenon and strongly associated with (and often attributed to) the new communication technologies (e.g., Internet, mass media, etc.). The dominance of a small number of language varieties (in particular US English) is seen as an important factor decreasing the *ethnolinguistic vitality* of lesser-spoken languages world-wide. It is worth bearing in mind that globalisation has been an issue in some parts of the world at least since the colonial period.

Lingua franca

Language used as a common means of communication among people whose native languages are mutually unintelligible.

Equally, sociolinguists may find it helpful to bear in mind what happens when a variable makes the slippery move across space and ends up sticking in a new environment. Strong local pressures may subtly transform the innovation. This seems to have happened with the quotative verb *be like*. Earlier we saw that the functional distribution of *be like* in British English is similar to its distribution in US English. This justifies considering *be like* to be the same variable in both US and British English. However, some of the first work on this variable in Britain noted that there were subtle differences as well. Macaulay's (2001) study of *be like* in Glasgow found that Scots speakers used *be like* in collocations or structures that US English speakers do not. Buchstaller's work on English English found similar evidence. For instance, she found that while US English speakers quite often introduced reported discourse with the collocation *feel like* (10), the English speakers were more likely to use the collocation *say like* (11) (Buchstaller 2004: 189):

(10) You know I feel like 'oh, I've accomplished something'.
(11) He thought I was mad, he said like 'what are you going on about?'

Arguably, small differences like these (and there are several others) indicate that while the *variable* may have transferred from one variety of English to another, the process of transfer is by no means perfect. Some reanalysis occurs and the variable is transformed, acquiring local colour. This might be the sociolinguistic equivalent of the transformations that occur in the game that is variously known as Chinese Whispers or the Telephone Game (where a whispered message gradually gets transformed by small changes as it goes around a circle). A failure reliably to transmit all the information associated with a variable where it started may be a necessary consequence of the variable moving into the ecology of a very different speech community. Reanalysis and failure to transmit constraints faithfully are perhaps not unrelated, so it is likely that both factors play a part in the phenomenon we can call 'transformation under transfer' (Meyerhoff 2003).

This finding is similar to the position taken by other linguists who have studied English that has been exported to other countries or that is used in post-colonial colonies. As early as the 1960s Braj Kachru (1966) has argued that English in these contexts is gradually and fundamentally nativised so as to express meanings that have local significance. Similarly, it seems that a variable like *be like* may transfer from one variety of English to another but that the transfer may involve some modifications. A new set of speakers tailor the variable to suit the specific social and linguistic needs of the new speech community.

This localisation and nativisation (the 'sticky places' phenomenon) therefore constitutes one constraint on the variation and change that arise from situations of language or dialect contact. In the next section we will look at some further constraints on the transfer of variables from one language variety to another.

CONTACT-INDUCED CHANGE

Now that we have considered contact between different varieties of one language, I turn to examples showing how linguistic variables may arise from contact between speakers of different languages. Both involve pidgins and creoles, the quintessential linguistic by-products of contact, and they clearly tie this study of contact-induced variation to language change.

There are some fundamental similarities between contact-induced borrowing between dialects and the contact-induced change between languages. In this section we will look at two case studies from Pacific creoles. We will see that variability in the languages seems to emerge and be resolved on the basis of a number of social and linguistic factors. The stabilisation of forms cannot be attributed solely to the transfer of features from one or other of the languages that have come into contact with each other. Nor can they be attributed solely to non-language-specific grammatical or communicative constraints. Instead, features from the languages in contact are reanalysed and sometimes reallocated to different parts of the linguistic system in light of speakers' communicative needs, and in light of gaps in the linguistic systems that are in contact.

Pidgins and creoles

Pidgins and **creoles** are languages that emerge out of the contact between the speakers of (usually) more than two different languages. There are usually quite marked social conditions associated with that contact. For example, the speakers may only be in contact in a reduced set of social interactions, such as trading or work. Because of the limited social contact between the speakers, they seldom have extensive access to native speaker models of each other's languages. Moreover, they may not even be particularly motivated to try to acquire native speaker-like skills in the other languages. As a consequence of all these facts, the mode of communication that emerges may be something that owes a little bit to all the sources of input and that also falls back on some features of language learners' speech in general. (There is a whole literature debating how and why pidgins and creoles end up looking the way they do, and further reading is suggested at the end of this chapter. The most widely held view among creolists is that they represent a synthesis of many factors, as I have just suggested.)

Traditionally, linguists distinguish pidgins and creoles on the grounds of how they are learnt, with a pidgin being defined as a contact language that is nobody's first language, and a creole as a contact language that does have native speakers. A community of native speakers can stabilise if there has been widespread language shift to the emerging creole language or if the emerging creole is added to the community repertoire, resulting in bilingualism.

This difference between pidgins and creoles necessarily entails differences in how and where they are used. A pidgin, lacking native speakers, is a contact language that has very restricted social functions within a community, while a creole serves most or all of the functions that any natural human language must serve.

Pidgin

Generally, a language variety that is not very linguistically complex or elaborated and is used in fairly restricted social domains and for limited social or interpersonal functions. Like a *creole*, arises from language contact; often seen as a precursor or early stage to a creole. It is often said that pidgin can be distinguished from a creole in having no native speakers.

Creole

A language variety arising out of a situation of language contact (usually involving more than two languages). A creole can be distinguished from a *pidgin*: (i) on the grounds that it is the first language of some community or group of speakers, or (ii) on the grounds that it is used for the entire range of social functions that a language can be used for. (See also *Creolisation; Vernacularisation*.)

Connections with theory

There is a long tradition in creole studies of looking for structural characteristics that identify creoles and set them apart typologically from other natural languages, and there continues to be considerable debate over how reliable these criteria are. Just as the distinction between pidgin and creole cannot be drawn without mentioning social facts, such as who is using the language and for what purposes, many linguists studying creoles prefer to identify the class of 'creole languages' with reference to social, historical and functional criteria and not solely with reference to formal or structural criteria.

So, for example, if the variety is used solely for business transactions or just within the confines of a workplace then it would be considered a pidgin. This was the case for Russenorsk, the contact language based on Norwegian and Russian used in the Bering Sea between Russian and Norwegian sailors who came into contact with each other only during the fishing season of the northern summer. It is also true for *français tiraillou* ('torn French') which was used in the military in parts of the French colonies in Africa. For a long time, it was also the situation for Fanagalo, the Zulu-based contact language which was used solely in the diamond mines in South Africa. Fanagalo has subsequently become the medium of communication on farms in South Africa and Zimbabwe, and now is sometimes used for more than simply giving orders and organising farm business (that is, it's becoming a fully fledged creole language).

This functional definition of pidgins and creoles means that once a contact variety is used for all the day-to-day needs speakers have – when it becomes the vehicle for telling stories, playing games, arguing over who should have done the shopping, joking, making love, flattering, and so on – then you have a creole. Notice that this does not require that children be monolingual in the creole, though this is implied or required in Derek Bickerton's (1981) well-known theory of creolisation.

Bickerton's work, like that of many other creolists who focus almost exclusively on describing the structural features that typify creoles, allows for variation to have been part of the linguistic input to a creole. Indeed, he presumes that the high degree of interspeaker variability that may have characterised this input is one of the things that motivates children learning the language to fall back on linguistic structures that are inherent to the human language learning faculty.

However, until recently, few creolists have taken this variation in the input seriously and made it the object of systematic study. Even fewer have systematically studied the variability in creoles once they have stabilised as a community language. In the sections that follow, we look at how we might go about doing this.

Connections with theory

Definitions of pidgins and creoles that depend on functions of use and modes of acquisition are not entirely independent of each other. For example, acquiring a first generation of native speakers will entail the functional expansion of a variety; once there has been extensive functional expansion, it is more likely that a variety will be used as the primary medium of a household's daily life, including the socialisation of children.

However, some linguists feel it is important to maintain the strict non-native/native speaker distinction between pidgins and creoles. This is because it is hoped that studying the structure of creoles will tell us a lot about the human language faculty, and the kinds of linguistic structures and relations most basic to natural languages.

One quite well-documented case where a creole has emerged in the context of a fairly abrupt community-wide shift to a new variety is Nicaraguan Sign Language. Judy Kegl and her associates have been studying the emergence of Nicaraguan Sign Language for several decades (Kegl *et al.* 1999). They have documented what happened socially and linguistically when members of the deaf community in Nicaragua came together in one residential school for the deaf after the Sandinista government began a programme of universal education. The deaf community had formerly been socially isolated, and many had developed idiosyncratic varieties of signing at home. The move to a residential school entailed both an increase in the quantity and richness of the input for the young signers and, in many cases, an expansion of the social and functional needs that signing had to serve. The structural outcomes of this change in the sociolinguistic environment of signers have been speedy and profound. They include the innovation of structures such as complex, multi-verb sentences, and also social enrichments and new styles such as ways of gossiping or surreptitiously talking about someone in the same room (Kegl 2004).

In some communities, we can see the social and functional expansion of a creole, even though speakers still acquire it after (or simultaneously with) their acquisition of another vernacular language at home. In this situation, speakers may remain bilingual (or multilingual) throughout their lives, but for some speakers the creole will gradually become their dominant language.

This context of societal, familial and individual multilingualism tends to be the case for the contact languages used in Melanesia. While it is now the case that some children in Vanuatu and Papua New Guinea only hear Bislama or Tok Pisin in the home, many children still only become really fluent in Bislama when they go to school. Some parents I have spoken to in Vanuatu actually say that this is one of the functions they think school has: children will naturally acquire Bislama there – despite the fact that (as we saw in Chapter 6) the official medium of education is French or English, not Bislama! – whereas the local vernacular languages have to be learnt at home. Even though Bislama is not the first language of these children, by the time they are in their late teens or twenties, their sociolinguistic competence in Bislama often greatly outstrips their competence in, say, their parents' vernacular which they may have acquired first. So there are several factors that make it seem reasonable to call Bislama a creole:

- speakers do acquire Bislama from a very early age (and well within the critical period during which native-like acquisition of a variety of language is possible; see Chapter 6),
- it serves the functional depth of any natural language, and
- it shows structural complexity in the shape of inflectional morphology (as we will see shortly).

Expanded pidgin

A term used sometimes instead of *creole* to describe contact varieties that have spent longer as *pidgins* (lacking native speakers) within a community. (See also *Vernacularisation*.)

Vernacularisation

The process by which a contact variety becomes used with the full range of social and personal functions served by a language of the home. Also the linguistic changes associated with the expansion of the variety in this way. (See also *Creolisation*.)

Creolisation

The process by which a *pidgin* becomes the first language of a group of speakers. The linguistic outcomes of the expansion of the pidgin into a wider range of social functions. (See also *Vernacularisation*.)

Connections with theory

Some researchers believe that the term 'creole' should be strictly reserved for varieties acquired as a first language. They do, however, recognise that there is a qualitative difference between functionally restricted pidgins and languages like Bislama and Tok Pisin. One proposal has been to use the term **expanded pidgin** for languages like Bislama or to talk about **vernacularisation** (e.g., of Bislama), as opposed to **creolisation**, of Nicaraguan Sign Language. I will stick to calling Bislama and Tok Pisin creoles until it is clear what specific (socio)linguistic insights and consequences might follow from adopting these other terms.

Although many languages may be part of the contact scenario that gives rise to pidgins and creoles, some languages clearly play a more important part in determining their eventual shape than others. Generally, there is one language that has obviously provided most of the vocabulary in the pidgin/creole. This is known as the **lexifier** because it provides the building blocks of the lexicon (vocabulary). Although other languages may not dominate the surface structure of the pidgin/creole so much, they may still have profound and subtle effects on the way the words are used and how the sentences are structured – that is, on the semantics and syntax. These languages are known as the **substrate**, and their effects show up in underlying structure.

In the case studies that follow, we are going to see how the following factors interact with each other:

- the lexifier,
- the substrate, and
- cognitive principles which are not language-specific.

We will see that all three show up in patterns of structured variation and shape the direction in which a creole develops and changes.

Focus marking in Tok Pisin

The lexifier for Tok Pisin is English (the language name derives from 'talk pidgin'), and it is the first language of an increasing number of people in Papua New Guinea. Although many languages are spoken in Papua New Guinea, careful work by Ulrike Mosel (1980) had established that the Austronesian language Tolai, spoken in New Britain, had a particularly strong influence on the structure of Tok Pisin during the early stages of its development.

Often, once you know what the lexifier form of a word was, you can have a pretty good guess about what its meaning will be in a pidgin or creole. But Gillian Sankoff noticed that in Tok Pisin, the word *yet*, which derives from English (*not*) *yet*, usually means something more like a -*self* pronoun does in English. That is, it emphasises or focuses another noun. This is shown in (12):

(12) *Orait   yu   yet   kilim   pikinini   bilong   mi*
alright 2s focus kill   child   poss   1s
'Alright, you're the one who killed my child.' (i.e., you yourself) (Sankoff 1993)

But it also has three other functions illustrated in the following examples.

(13) *Mi   no   save   tok   yet   mi   nufela   boi*
1s   neg   know   talk   yet   1s   new   boy
'I don't know how to talk [Pidgin] yet; I'm a new boy.' (Chavi, 1920s, cited in Sankoff 1993)

(14) *Bel   bilong   mi   i-hot   yet   i-stap*
belly   poss   1s   hot   still   stay
'I am still angry.' [lit. my belly is still hot] (Chavi, 1920s; Mr Mo in 1960s – both cited in Sankoff 1993)

Lexifier

The language that has provided most of the vocabulary (i.e., lexicon) to a *pidgin* or *creole*.

Substrate

The languages other than the *lexifier* that are present in *pidgin* or *creole* formation. The substrate languages often contribute to the grammatical structure of a creole, or they may constrain the semantics of words that have been taken over from the lexifier – e.g., *han* meaning 'hand' and 'arm' in Bislama (same denotation as equivalent words in the Eastern Oceanic languages of Vanuatu) and not the more restricted sense of English *hand*.

(15) *Mitupela   i-kam   longwe   yet*
    1du.excl   come   far   intensifier
    'The two of us came from very far away.' (Mr T.D., 1970s, cited in Sankoff 1993)

Sankoff noticed that not everyone in the speech community uses *yet* with all four of the meanings equally often. She also noticed that there appeared to have been a change over time. The historical perspective was gained through apparent time inferences based on the frequency of each function in the speech of adults and children recorded in Lai, Papua New Guinea in the 1970s. It was supplemented by real time data from recordings of Tok Pisin made earlier in the twentieth century (apparent time and real time were discussed in Chapter 7). When she combined all her data, she found the patterns shown in Table 11.1 (from Sankoff 1993).

Table 11.1 shows how often *yet* has each of the meanings in examples 12–15. It compares its uses in texts from the 1920s (Chavi), the 1960s, and in the speech of adults and children in the 1970s. The most informative comparison is between the 1920s texts and the 1970s adults (remember that when we analyse children's data there are other, larger, developmental issues involved in their use of language which we may have to take into consideration; these may be reflected in the relatively low overall frequency of *yet* in their texts). In the 1920s text, the principal meaning of *yet* was closer to the meaning of English 'yet', while in the 1970s adults' texts, *yet* is not attested at all with this meaning. Instead, the principal meaning of *yet* has become a means of focusing pronoun subjects. Obviously, the 1970s children's data show that the 'not yet' meaning of *yet* has not disappeared completely, but the overall trend is clear.

Table 11.1 Frequency with which different meanings of Tok Pisin *yet* occur in texts from the twentieth century.

Meaning of yet	1920s	1960s	1970s aults	1970s kids	Total
'not yet'	11	8	0	1	20
'still'	3	10	8	6	27
intensifier	0	3	3	0	6
focus with pronoun	4	8	13	4	29
Total	**18**	**29**	**24**	**11**	**82**

This trend is perhaps even more apparent if we show how often *yet* is used with each of the four meanings as a percentage of its overall frequency at each point in time. This is shown in Figure 11.3. The important thing to focus on is the general trend from the left-hand side of the figure to the right-hand side. The lower shaded band represents how often *yet* is used meaning 'not yet' (example 13 on p. 250), and this band gets thinner and thinner indicating that it accounts for a smaller and smaller proportion of total instances of *yet*. The speckled band at the top of the graph shows how often *yet* is used to focus pronouns (example 12 on p. 250), and this band gets fatter as you move from left to right, indicating that it accounts for a greater proportion of all uses of *yet*. The intensifier meaning of *yet* (example 15 on p. 251) seems to have emerged in the 1960s, and the use of *yet* meaning 'still' (example 14 on p. 250) is relatively steady in the texts from the 1960s onwards.

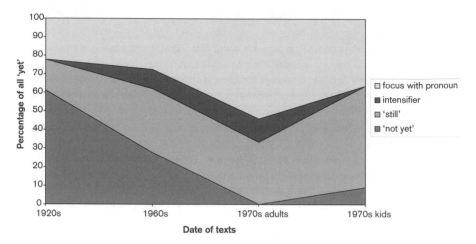

Figure 11.3   Frequency of different meanings of Tok Pisin *yet* shown as a percentage of all uses of *yet* over time. (Source, Sankoff 1993.)

So it appears that the variation we see here involves a change over time. But what kind of change is this when the move appears to be from one meaning to a very different meaning? The uses of *yet* to mean 'not yet' and 'still' are fairly closely related. The first is a negative adverb of time and the second is a positive adverb of time (the second meaning of 'yet' was still widely used in late nineteenth-century English and it lingers in set phrases like 'yet again'). The use of *yet* as a -*self* anaphor is a way of intensifying or focusing conversational attention on the subject, so we can see a semantic link between this meaning and the function as a general intensifier. But the connection between these two sets of meanings are less obvious. One of Sankoff's questions was: how did the now common function in (12) emerge from English 'yet'? An additional puzzle was that she found *yet* was mainly used to focus pronoun subjects, and was seldom used to focus a full noun phrase, like *smol boe* ('small boy').

In order to resolve these puzzles, Sankoff looked to data from the substrate languages, especially Tolai, which had a major impact on early Tok Pisin. She found that Tolai also has a particle that follows subjects as a means of focusing them. In addition, it is only used with pronoun subjects, not full noun phrases, and most remarkably of all the form of this particle is *iat*. This is shown in (16).

(16) Lau **iat**   pa   'au manga nukure mala ra   tianta i   nam ra
       I   particle not I   very   know   well det   story   of   dem det
       tubuan
       tubuan
       'I myself don't know very well the story of that Tubuan.' (Tolai; Sankoff 1993: 136)

She investigated this further and found that Tolai was far from unusual in this respect. Many of the substrate languages have particles that attach primarily or only to pronoun subjects as a way of focusing or emphasising them.

So what seems to have happened in Tok Pisin is that the English adverb 'yet' was initially used to express 'not yet' and 'still'. That is, it had exactly the same meanings that 'yet' had in English during the period when Tok Pisin was stabilising as a language. However, Tolai speakers of Tok Pisin may have heard 'yet' /jɛt/ and made some kind of connection with their own word *iat* /jat/. Having established some kind of equivalency between *yet* and *iat*, they seem to have extended the semantics and syntax of *iat* to *yet*, specifically, its function as a way of focusing a subject pronoun. We can see this stage in the expansion of *yet* as early as the 1920s (Figure 11.3), when 20 per cent of all uses of *yet* in Tok Pisin had this very non-English function. Then, because many non-Tolai speakers also spoke languages that used similar particles for focusing pronoun subjects, those speakers seem to have picked up on this function of *yet* and begun to reinforce its use in their own Tok Pisin. By the time we look at the functions of *yet* in the speech of the adults in the 1970s, the most common function of *yet* is as a focus marker with pronouns.

Creole simplicity

It is very often said that creoles are 'simpler' than either their lexifier or their substrate. Do you think that this is true for Tok Pisin *yet*? What do you understand 'simple' to mean in your answer? In other words, how do you measure it?

exercise

Sankoff's case study of *yet* in Tok Pisin shows us very clearly how socially stratified variation at any point in time may be the outcome of several aspects of the sociolinguistic history of a speech community. Contact between speakers of different languages leads to the creative recycling of resources and the reinforcement of patterns that are consistent with multiple sources. In the case of a creole, like Tok Pisin, where we are dealing with input from very different language varieties (the lexifier and the substrates), it may be especially clear that variation has emerged from the layering of multiple sources. But the principle may apply more widely than to creoles. As we have seen, contact between different dialects of a language can be included in our profiles of language contact. Sankoff's conclusion that contact-induced change favours outcomes that synthesise multiple (sociolinguistic) sources is relevant to more than just Tok Pisin.

The next section looks at another case study of variation and change in a creole. This too highlights the importance of incorporating multiple factors – lexifier, substrate and communicative needs – into our analysis of the source of creole variation and the directions such variation may take.

Subject agreement in Bislama

The second case study I turn to involves the emergence of inflectional morphology in Bislama, another English-based creole, closely related to Tok Pisin. The place of Bislama in the national language policies of Vanuatu was discussed in Chapter 6. Like Tok Pisin, Bislama stabilised, and continues to exist, in a sociolinguistic context characterised by extensive multilingualism. That is, the influence of substrate languages, as well as Standard English, and the history of Bislama itself are all relevant to understanding the shape of the language today.

When Bislama first began to stabilise, there was little or no inflectional morphology in the language at all. That is, unlike English where the distinction between singular and plural is usually marked with the inflectional suffix *-s*, Bislama nouns had the same form in the singular and plural: compare English 'one girl', 'two girls' and Bislama *wan gel, tu gel*. Similarly, there are some distinctions made using inflectional morphology in the substrate languages of Vanuatu which do not show up in Bislama either. These include the classifier system with nouns (you can think of classifiers as a kind of grammatical gender system, like the difference between masculine and feminine nouns in French). We can compare Lolovoli, spoken on Ambae, in (17) and Bislama in (18).

(17) a. *Kenneth u   geni na   ga-na   loli   beno.*
         K.   TENSE eat   ACCUSATIVE   CL.FOOD-3S.POSS   lolly already
         'Kenneth has already eaten her lollies.' (Hyslop 2001: 177, gloss modified)

     b. *Ngire   no-ra   bubusi hate.*
        3.NON-S   CL.GEN-3NON-S.POSS   gun   negative
        'They didn't have guns.' (Hyslop 2001: 180)

(18) a. *Kenneth i   kakae ol loli   blong hem   finis.*
         K.   AGR   eat   PL lolly of   3s   already
         'Kenneth has already eaten her lollies.'

     b. *Olgeta oli   no   gat   masket.*
        3p   AGR   negative have gun
        'They don't have guns.'

In Lolovoli, there are different classifiers for food items (*ga-* glossed CL.FOOD) and for general nouns (*no-* glossed CL.GEN). These attach to the possessive, i.e., *-na* 'her' (glossed as 3S.POSS) in (17a) and *-ra* 'their' (glossed as 3NON-S.POSS) in (17b). Bislama makes no such distinction in the morphology of the noun phrase.

Another grammatical feature common to the substrate languages of Vanuatu is the case of different markings on the verb for different persons and numbers of the subject. English makes only one distinction in this way, marking third-person singular differently from all the other forms of the verb, as in 'I/you/we/they laugh' but 'she/he/it laughs'. Other European languages mark this more consistently on the verb; if you are familiar with Russian or German you will be able to think of some more inflectional differences. In Ni-Vanuatu languages, the marking is usually a prefix rather than the suffixes familiar from European languages. In (19), examples are shown from Tamambo, spoken on Malo, where you see that there is a different pre-verbal particle depending on whether it is third-person singular (3s) or plural (3p). The *mo* and *na* are outside the predicate ('be calm' and 'grow') for the purposes of stress assignment so they can be written as separate words:

(19) a. *Aiente bongi tarusa mo   tamata.*
         some   day   sea   3s   be.calm
         'Some days the sea is calm.' (Jauncey 1997: 313, adapted)

     b. *Dam   na sula ana rango.*
        yams   3p grow on   rango.poles
        'Yams grow along "rango" poles.' (Jauncey 1997: 313)

In the nineteenth century, when Bislama was just stabilising, it had nothing like the system in the substrate languages such as Tamambo, and not even the very limited inflectional morphology of English. As you can see in (20) and (21), the predicate (in these cases, all

People in Vanuatu readily adopt names from other cultures, but they don't always retain the gender-marking associated with the name they borrow. So *Kenneth* (as in 17a) can be a woman's name; *Thierry* (from French) is also often a woman's name.

verbs) stands alone as a bare stem in both the third person singular and plural (I have kept the spelling from the original texts):

(20) *Misi   make   him   bokis   sing.* (1867)
missionary   make   him/it   box   sing
'The missionary made the box sing'. (i.e., played it as a musical instrument)

(21) *Plenty   man   come.* (1867)
plenty   man   come
'Lots of people came/arrived.'

The historical records show us that following the stabilisation of the language from the 1850 to the 1870s, there was variability in how subjects and verbs were related to each other. Specifically, Bislama went through a stage in which there were a lot of sentences that seemed to have a noun subject doubled with a pronoun subject. In (22) and (23), the noun subject is underlined and the pronoun is shown in bold:

(22) <u>*Plenty sugar*</u> **he** *stop.* (1882)
plenty sugar he stop
'There's lots of sugar.'

(23) <u>*Boy*</u> **he** *like go.* (1893)
boy he like go
'The boy wants to go.'

The *he* forms in examples (22) and (23) were probably very often realised as a vowel only; that is [i]. In unstressed function words like the pronoun *he* it's very common for all native speakers of English to drop their *h*'s. This phonetic characteristic of the lexifier would have combined happily with a predisposition to have unstressed, preposed agreement on predicates coming from the substrate. Examples (22) and (23) show that full NPs were 'doubled' with the *(h)e*, but it was also possible to find this doubling with a pronoun subject. However, if a pronoun was doubled, the phonetically stronger object pronoun *him* is used rather than the weaker subject pronoun *he*.

Connections with theory

When we say that English object pronouns are stronger than subject pronouns, this means that they can stand alone more naturally (for most speakers). Part of the reason the vast majority of native speakers answer the question 'Who said that?' with 'Me' or 'Her' (and not 'I' or 'She') is that English subject pronouns are slightly weak and they prefer to attach to a predicate or a compound NP.

By the early twentieth century, the pronoun system in Bislama had undergone some independent changes, which begin to interact with the variability observed in third person singular sentences. These changes indicate that speakers of Bislama were reshaping it,

Table 11.2 The early twentieth-century system of pronouns in Bislama, illustrated using the verb *go* ('go'). (Adapted from Crowley 1990: 231; Jacomb 1914: 96.)

	Singular	*Plural*
First person (exclusive)	mi go	mifala (= 'me fellow') go
First person (inclusive)		yumi (= 'you [and] me') go
Second person	yu go	yufala (= 'you fellow') go
Third person	him he/'e go	olgeta (= 'all together'), all 'e go

making the system fall in line with the Ni-Vanuatu substrate languages. A very clear feature taken from the substrate is a distinction between first-person plural inclusive and exclusive forms ('inclusive' refers to both the speaker and the addressee; 'exclusive' refers to the speaker and someone else, but not the addressee). If we combine these developments in the expression of third person subjects and other pronoun subjects, the system 100 years ago looked something like that shown in Table 11.2.

In the bottom row of Table 11.2 we see that third person singular very often combines *him* and *(h)e*. In the third person plural, a subject pronoun *olgeta* has been formed from English 'all together', and combines with the same *(h)e* form. In the third person plural, this is marked as plural with the word *all* (see also example 18a). Both third person singular and plural predicates now look more like the Tamambo examples, with some form of subject agreement preceding the predicate.

Notice that in Table 11.2 we only find repetitions of the pronoun *(h)e* in the third person. At this point, the variation in the system reflects features that are compatible with the substrate and with the lexifier. Even if the pronouns were beginning to be used in a manner somewhat different from English, *(h)e* appears to have retained some of its lexifier semantics, and is only used when there is a third person subject referent.

But notice, too, that the only way Bislama could even have got to this point was by drawing on the need to topicalise, contrast and focus on different referents, which emerge in the course of normal conversational interaction. Moreover, Bislama uses strategies like subject doubling that are quite common cross-linguistically to realise these needs. So interactional factors, completely unrelated to the specific features of either the substrate or the lexifier languages, also must have played an important role in determining the directions in which Bislama began to develop inflectional morphology.

We do not need to trace exhaustively the continued development of the pronoun and the subject agreement system during the rest of the twentieth century. It is sufficient to say that nowadays it is almost obligatory for third person singular subjects to be marked with, *i* (the reduced form of the erstwhile pronoun), and for third person plural subjects to be marked with *oli* (from 'all he'). These are shown in (24) and (25):

(24) *Wan   man   i   blokem   mi.*
      one   man   i   block   1s
      'A man stopped me.'

(25) *Ol   tija   oli   save   mi.*
      the   teacher oli   know   1s
      'The teachers know me.'

Table 11.3   Bislama pronouns and agreement (in bold) today, illustrated with the verb *laf* ('laugh').

	Singular	Dual	Trial	Plural
First person (exclusive)	mi laf	mitufala **i** laf	mitrifala **i** laf	mifala **i** laf
First person (inclusive)		yumitu laf	yumitri laf	yumi laf
Second person	yu laf	yutufala **i** laf	yutrifala **i** laf	yufala **i** laf
Third person	hem **i** laf	tufala **i** laf	trifala **i** laf	olgeta **oli** laf

In addition, following a further expansion of the pronominal system to include pronouns that explicitly denote two and three referents, use of the agreement marker has spread as well. As Table 11.3 shows, most other non-singular subjects have the agreement marker *i* between the subject and the predicate.

Again, the pattern of this expansion is compatible with aspects of both the substrate and the lexifier. First, it provides a way of expressing semantic distinctions that speakers of many Ni-Vanuatu languages are used to being able to express in their vernacular grammars, such as a distinction between dual (two) and trial (three) referents. Second, the agreement marker *i* still conspicuously occurs in cases where the subject *necessarily* entails the presence of someone other than the speaker and hearer; that is, some third person 'he' or 'she'.

Development of agreement

Look again at the forms in the column headed 'plural' in Table 11.3. We noted that in the third person plural the *i* agreement form seems to have fused with the plural marker *ol* to give *oli* as the third person plural agreement marker.

Why do you think *mifala* and *yufala* have *i* and not *oli*? (You may find it helpful to go back to the glosses for these pronouns in Table 11.2.)

exercise

There are several points to be made from these case studies. First, they illustrate that variation may emerge as a consequence of language contact. In previous chapters, we have looked at variables in different speech communities and treated variation as simply a fact of life. Having looked at these examples from Tok Pisin and Bislama, where the variation clearly emerges because of the contact between different languages, we might want to ask whether the variables we have examined in earlier chapters are also the consequence of linguistic contact. It's possible that the chief difference between Bislama and New Zealand or New York City English would be that in New Zealand or New York the contact is between closely related varieties of one language, while for Bislama the contact is between mutually incomprehensible languages.

The second point to take from these case studies is that where contact results in problematic input (more than one way of saying the same thing), the problem is often resolved through a good deal of creative reallocation of resources. This may be influenced more or less strongly by aspects of the semantics of an individual word (as was the case with Tok Pisin *yet*) or a general property of substrate language grammars (as was the case with subject agreement in Bislama). In the discussion of both these examples, I have tried to show how important it is to understand the syntactic structure and semantics of as many of the most salient languages that are in contact. But in both cases I have also tried to stress that speakers' communicative needs can provide the context that becomes essential for motivating the reanalysis or reallocation of variants.

SOCIOLINGUISTIC CONSTRAINTS ON CONTACT

In the previous sections, we examined several cases where different groups of speakers using different languages have come into contact. Some of these were the situations of contact between a large number of distinct (and often unrelated) languages that are typical of creole language formation. We also looked at *be like*, a variable spreading due to contact between different varieties of English. A new variant is introduced into a relatively stable and elaborate system and (just as in the cases of *yet* and *he*) the semantics of the input seem to constrain how speakers adapt the new variant to the broader communicative and expressive needs of the system. However, we concluded by noting that if *be like* is a contact-induced variable, then our understanding of contact-induced variation needs to allow not only for transfer but also for reanalysis and localisation of a variable when it is transferred. In this section, we consider some constraints on the outcomes of language contact other than the principle of localisation. The first of these constraints also focuses on a slippery aspect of space. The second two are more concerned with speaker attitudes and social factors; that is, speakers' access to their targets and the relative social rigidity in which an innovation is being introduced. These are the more sticky facts of individuals' desires to fit in with others and their desires to be distinctive.

Spatial diffusion by 'gravity'

Wave model

The theory that language change emanates from a single starting point and is gradually incorporated into the speech of the nearest neighbours.

Since the late nineteenth century, the consensus was that linguistic innovations spread like the ripples emanating from a stone dropped into a still pond. This way of thinking about the diffusion of changes has been known as the **wave model**. The idea was that changes start in one environment and then affect successive environments – one wave after another. A corollary of this is that it was believed that changes went to completion first in the environments that favoured them most strongly, that is, where they started first (the first wave). The metaphor of a wave is not a bad one for describing the spread of an innovation over *time*; when looking at the temporal spread of an innovation we can usually infer roughly when it starts, and it then moves slowly and directly through time. But it is not so clear that

Connections with theory

Just as the wave model may not be a particularly good model of changes over space, it is also not clear that it is a good model of how changes progress through different environments. Tony Kroch has argued that even if certain linguistic contexts favour the use of an innovative variant more than other contexts, the change proceeds at a steady rate *within* each of the different contexts, if we use the correct measurements. This postulate is known as the *Constant Rate Hypothesis*.

changes spread in the same way over physical space, and this is where other models become more useful.

The **gravity model** was originally used to describe the diffusion of non-linguistic innovations. Sociologists and economists had observed that innovations, such as the adoption of new brands of cars or the use of new types of seed among farmers, often moved irregularly across physical space. They found that they jumped from cities with the largest populations, gradually moved to smaller cities and towns, and finally took hold in the smaller towns or villages. This meant that even if a small town was close to the starting point of an innovation, the people living there might be relatively late in adopting it. So the 'gravity' that the model refers to is the pull or attraction exerted by the sheer number of people in a given locale.

You can get a rough idea of the gravity effects of major population bases if we consider the spread of a technological innovation. Take, for example, the spread of Hummer vehicles in Pennsylvania. One way to chart their spread is to look for listings of Hummer dealerships in the phone book. The first dealerships opened in Philadelphia and Pittsburgh, the two largest cities in Pennsylvania: Philadelphia is in the far east of the state and Pittsburgh is in the far west of the state. The next opened just outside of Harrisburg, a smaller, more central city, but it is also the state capital. Only after dealerships had opened in these three cities did they begin to appear in smaller towns nearer the starting point of the innovation – Trevose (near Philadelphia), Monroeville (near Pittsburgh) and Emmaus (north of Philadelphia). This is exactly the kind of pattern we would predict from the gravity model, with the innovation appearing first in the main urban centres and then spreading to smaller towns outside the cities.

As a rule, sociolinguists would like the principles accounting for language variation and change to be as general as possible. So it's particularly heartening if principles which apply in other areas of the social sciences apply to some extent in the domain of language use. Peter Trudgill was the sociolinguist who first saw the potential for applying the gravity model to the study of sound changes.

Trudgill examined the spread of innovative phonological variants in Swedish and the spread of uvular 'r' in Europe and he argued that these variables were better explained in terms of population gravity than they were in terms of the spread of a wave from an initial starting point. Trudgill even specified this in terms of quite a precise mathematical formula which he suggested might underlie the effects of population gravity that are felt on the diffusion of innovations. The formula Trudgill applied modelled the influence of one locality upon another as being a result of the relative size of the two localities, and their distance from one another (1974: 235). This was realised in the following way:

(26) $I_{ij} = [(P_i * P_j)/(d_{ij})^2] * [P_i / (P_i + P_j)]$

The formula reads like this. I is the influence of one town 'i' on another town 'j'. We're trying to work out whether this will be strong or weak. P is the population of the towns 'i' and 'j', and d is the distance between them. The bigger town 'i' is compared to town 'j', the greater its influence on 'j'. But the distance between the two towns is still also important, so this is factored in with the variable d. This part of the formula means that, all other things being equal, the influence of town 'i' on another town will be greater if 'i' is closer.

'Distance' can be measured in strictly linear terms (how many kilometres/miles between the two points), or it can be weighted to reflect aspects of the sociolinguistic context of the localities being compared. When Trudgill tested the model on his own data from East Anglia, he weighted distance so that it took into account whether or not the local dialects spoken in

Gravity model

Model of the diffusion of innovations introduced to sociolinguistics by Peter Trudgill. Social innovations (including linguistic innovations) have been observed to 'hop' between large population centres in a (spatially) discontinuous manner. At its simplest, the gravity model predicts that the larger the city/town, the sooner an innovation is likely to show up there. (i.e., the 'gravitational force' is provided by the weight of numbers of people).

Nagy notes that New Hampshire licence plates bear the motto 'Live Free or Die' (ironically, embossed on New Hampshire residents' plates by penal labour). She suggests that the merger of the *father* and *bother* vowels is a sociolinguistic manifestation of their passionate desire not to be swamped or overshadowed by Boston values.

two locations were similar or different, and it may well be necessary to make adjustments like this to the formula as it stands in (26). Studies that have tried to apply Trudgill's gravity model to the distribution of different linguistic variables have not been able to support the details and precise formula he proposed (e.g., Callary 1975; Boberg 2000).

We might also factor in things like ease of movement between two towns (e.g., whether they are connected by highways or minor roads), and the degree of cultural contact (e.g., whether they are served by the same school boards or whether people read the same newspaper). (This would be similar to the way language vitality is measured by a combination of social, demographic and institutional factors; see Chapter 6.)

It is certainly clear that negative attitudes can create a psychological distance that has similar effects to those of geographic distance. Naomi Nagy (2001) found evidence that speakers' attitudes are implicated in accounting for the distribution of pronunciations of *father* and *bother* in smaller townships just outside of Boston. In Boston, and Massachusetts more generally, these words do not rhyme; however, in many other varieties of US English they have the same vowel (that is, they can be said to have merged). Nagy found that younger speakers in southern New Hampshire (close to Boston) were very much more likely to merge the vowels in these words than older speakers in that area were, and even that they were more likely to merge them than New Hampshire speakers who lived further away from Boston did. She linked this pattern to other comments she had observed in southern New Hampshire which suggested that a lot of the locals in that area had a very strong desire to disassociate themselves from the Boston metropolitan values and lifestyle. In other words, even though the geographic distance between southern New Hampshire and Boston was not great, the attitudinal and affective distance was.

Connections with theory

In a similar vein, Britain (2003b) notes that in research on language contact it is useful to distinguish three kinds of 'space': Euclidean space, social space and perceived space. This echoes Montgomery's (2000) observation that 'isolation' can be defined in terms of a number of different physical, social and psychological measures.

Recently, Trudgill (2004) himself has proposed a different account for why innovations jump from city to city. He has suggested that it simply happens because people in cities are more likely to have contact with each other (even if they live some distance apart) than they are with peri-urban or rural dwellers. This recasts the gravity effects as an artefact of contact and face-to-face accommodation (Chapter 4) and transmission of innovation. However, cultural and psychological factors continue to play a large part in other sociolinguists' accounts of the constraints on contact-induced variation and change, and we turn to two of these accounts now.

Access to the codes

The British sociolinguist Robert Le Page is famous for his studies of variation in creole-speaking communities in the Caribbean and Britain. Le Page was intrigued by the number of different styles or registers that were often in play in these communities. Sometimes individuals seemed to have quite extensive linguistic repertoires, and they seemed to draw on different parts of their repertoire to respond creatively to differences in who the person was talking to or where they happened to be. He suggested that a lot of variation should be seen as **acts of identity**. In characterising variation as a series of *acts*, he became one of the first sociolinguists to argue that thinking individuals, with social and personal goals and aspirations, should be at the centre of our models of structured heterogeneity (an idea we have met in a number of earlier chapters).

By focusing on a speaker's desire to sometimes identify more with one social group and sometimes more with another, Le Page injected a sense of rational choice into the discussion of speakers' variability. However, Le Page wanted his framework to be just as good at accounting for speakers who show comparatively little variation as it is at accounting for speakers who exhibit a lot of variation. He pointed out that access to a variety is very important. If you aren't in contact with speakers of a particular variety, it will be very difficult to acquire their style of speaking. We all know that this is true for languages – I can *try* to learn Tongan, even if I never have access to Tongan speakers who I can use the language with, but that's the hard way to learn a language. Le Page argued that this is just as true for the acquisition of mastery of different styles or varieties that are current in a speech community.

He also suggested that even with access to the code, some things are more likely to be acquired because they are simply easier to acquire. We have noted on a number of occasions that new vocabulary is easy to acquire (consider the spread of vocabulary that started out in hip-hop throughout the English-speaking world, and even into other European languages). But phonology may be harder to acquire even if the speaker has access to reliable models. Even some phonological variables may transfer across individuals and groups more readily than others.

Cecilia Cutler undertook a study of a number of white adolescents in New York City who strongly identified with hip-hop culture and used what Cutler calls Hip Hop Speech Style (HHSS), which is derived from African American Vernacular English (AAVE). She found that all the white hip-hoppers she looked at had restructured their linguistic system so that the diphthong /ai/ was realised as a monophthong, [a:], a variant widely perceived as characteristic of AAVE. Most of her subjects had also adopted the low pitch associated with HHSS/AAVE, and most of them had managed to eliminate final and preconsonantal (r) from their speech. But other phonological and prosodic features seemed to be harder to acquire. Few of them had managed to acquire the early rising pitch contour associated with HHSS/AAVE, and only a few had adopted glottal replacement of medial /t/ (e.g., 'getting' as /gɛʔɪn/) (Cutler 2002). Her subjects all love hip-hop, listen to it a lot, and in some cases create it themselves in their own groups. But it appears that this kind of input alone is not sufficient to acquire every aspect of the English that their hip-hop role models use natively. In particular, syntactic variables and some phonological rules don't seem to be able to be acquired with limited access to the code.

Other research in this vein has often found that exposure to a code in childhood through extensive social networks can be particularly important (as we saw in Chapter 9). That is, access to the code has to be when you are relatively young (earlier than the teenagers Cutler looked at); also, that access has to be through really meaningful social networks. Various

Acts of identity

LePage's proposal that *intraspeaker* variation is a result of the speaker's desire to present or foreground a different social identity under different circumstances. Strongly associated with LePage's work on *creole* language speakers who often display extensive variation between consistent use of the *vernacular* norms of a creole and the standard variety of the *lexifier*. Contrasts with *attention to speech* and *accommodation*-based models of style-shifting such as *audience design*.

No, really?

The intersection between perception and production is particularly interesting for people who are 'passing' or 'crossing' (Rampton 1995); that is, speaking in a style associated with another social group. Some speakers can successfully pass as members of a different ethnic group on the basis of speech without having acquired the full set of linguistic features that characterise that group; other people may be able to pass visually, but fail to pass linguistically because they haven't mastered key forms.

attempts to introduce bilingual education programmes have shown that it isn't apparently enough to have access to a code at school. Successful uptake or acquisition of a variety is most likely when a child has access to it through the kinds of social networks associated with the playground or at home.

Rigidity of the social matrix

Even larger aspects of the social and cultural context may act as a constraint on whether features transfer from speaker to speaker. Some time ago, John Gumperz and Robert Wilson (1971) documented the rather unusual linguistic situation in Kupwar, India. In Kupwar, three languages – Hindi, Marathi and Kannada – have been spoken for centuries. Remarkably, given how often people in Kupwar might have to switch between the languages in day-to-day life, the languages have remained distinct codes. That is, it is still always clear when someone is speaking Marathi, when they are speaking Hindi and when they are speaking Kannada. People in Kupwar haven't borrowed lexical items back and forth between the languages, even though (as we have repeatedly noted) vocabulary is usually easily transferred.

And yet, the Hindi, Marathi and Kannada of Kupwar look appreciably different from the standard varieties of each of the languages. This is because there have been some subtle changes to the syntax of the three languages which appear, over the centuries, to have brought them closer in line with each other. You can see this for example in the way that the sentence 'This is your house' is expressed in all three of the main languages spoken in Kupwar:

(27) *Standard Kannada* *idu*   *nim*   **mənə**
     Kupwar Kannada id   nimd   **məni** eti
     Kupwar Marathi he   **tumc-ə** ghər hay
     Kupwar Urdu ye   **tumhar-ə** ghər həy
     this-one your   house is
     'This is your house.'

The data in (27) show that the words for 'house' and 'your' remain very different in Kannada (a Dravidian language), and Marathi and Urdu (Indo-European languages). But the Kupwar variety of Kannada also differs from standard Kannada in fundamental ways. Standard Kannada does not have an overt copula verb 'be' in existential sentences, but the Kannada

Connections with theory

The Kupwar data is often cited as an example of the borrowing of *syntactic structure* from one language to another because of extensive and lengthy contact between speakers of different languages. However, Ruth King (2004) notes that the Kupwar data does not necessarily show that Kupwar Kannada has borrowed syntactic structure from Urdu and Marathi. She argues that the evidence is only that Kupwar Kannada has borrowed a lexical item, *eti*. This characterisation of the data is consistent with lexicalist theories of grammar (where structure is associated with lexical items), such as HPSG.

spoken in Kupwar has created one, *eti*. The result of this is to make it look closer to Hindi and Marathi, which do have a copula, *hay/həy*.

Gumperz and Wilson note that each of the languages spoken in Kupwar are strongly associated with different social castes. As discussed in Chapter 8, a caste system assigns people to different places within the social order at birth, and their caste membership remains with them throughout their life. A person's caste determines to a large extent what an individual can and can't do. However, Gumperz and Wilson tell us that there is enough contact between the castes in Kupwar that people often learn the other languages associated with higher or lower castes. This means there are opportunities for linguistic features to transfer from one group to another.

However, there seems to be a limit on the extent of this contact-induced convergence in Kupwar, and the community maintains clear, superficial distinctions between the languages. This can be partly explained by intergroup factors. There are strong historical and social reasons for maintaining distinctions between the castes in Kupwar. So, because Kannada, Hindi and Marathi are historically linked to specific castes, the caste system provides a strong motivation for keeping the languages divergent in terms of vocabulary, even if there is structural convergence. (But see King's critique – the theory box above.) In other words, the social, historical and cultural context particular to Kupwar acts as a constraint on the ability of certain very salient linguistic features to transfer from one group of speakers to another.

Chapter summary

This chapter has reviewed several case studies of language contact. It has looked at various methods for dealing with contact, from general principles that describe how competing variants may be reanalysed as they are adopted into a new linguistic system through to a very tight formalism such as the gravity model. We have seen the potential for a formalism along the lines of the gravity model, but we have also determined that constraints on the transmission of an innovation through contact cannot be reduced to geographic and demographic factors.

The more general principles which take into account the meaning or semantics of an innovative variant, the language-specific constraints of the varieties in contact, and the communicative needs of the speakers seem to provide a good descriptive basis for understanding the outcomes of language contact. Researchers continue to explore the possibility of turning these descriptive principles into reliable predictive generalisations, and perhaps these lie in the future for sociolinguistic studies of language change.

This chapter has only begun to introduce the richness and rewards associated with studying language contact. I hope that it has made the case for the importance of variation in the study of language contact, and that it has illustrated the connections that are necessary between descriptive and theoretical linguists in a wide range of sub-fields. I have also tried to draw connections between some of the sociolinguistic principles and methods we have looked at in earlier chapters wherever possible to consolidate what we have learnt about variation so far.

In the next, and last, chapter, I continue to try and broaden the lens of our investigation, and consider how what we know about sociolinguistic variation and sociolinguistic variables fits in with linguistic research in other fields.

FURTHER READING

In addition to the references given in this chapter, you might like to look at the following:

Taeldeman (1998) and Hinskens *et al.* (2000) – dialect levelling in northern Europe.
Smith (1983) – more on nativisation of international varieties of English.
Winford (2003) – overview of research and issues in language contact.
Mesthrie *et al.* (2000) – chapters 8 and 9 on language contact and New Englishes.
Trudgill (1983, 2002) – a range of approaches, methods and analytic frames for analysing dialect or language contact.
Britain and Trudgill (forthcoming) – revised edition of the classic work on dialect contact.
Sankoff (1996) – review of several studies illustrating her synthetic approach to the analysis of sources of variation in creoles.
Rickford (1987) and Patrick (1999) – studies of Guyanese and Jamaican creoles that give due emphasis to variation in the languages.

Debates on whether pidgins and creoles can be identified on purely linguistic grounds or whether they require a sociohistorical perspective have a tendency to become quite detailed and sometimes vituperative. Winford (2003) provides a calm overview and represents the main arguments for and against. See also Kouwenberg and Singler (2006).

CHAPTER 12

Looking back and looking ahead

The previous chapter ended with an emphasis on connections and consolidation, and this final chapter continues to focus on these two tasks. It will attempt to consolidate what we have covered in the preceding chapters, and it will also attempt to strengthen the connections that we have made between sociolinguistics and other fields of study. Each of the previous chapters has ended with a detailed summary of its content, so I will not cover that ground again. Instead, I will return to some of the material introduced in Chapter 2. The main points I will be picking up again are:

- the centrality of spontaneous speech as sociolinguistic data,
- the centrality of variation in the way speakers use language to the grammar of a speech community,
- the need for our analyses to draw on non-linguistic factors that are meaningful in the particular communities being studied, and
- the motivations we ascribe to speakers' use of different forms in speech.

As I noted at the start of the book, linguistics is a relatively young field, and sociolinguistics is even younger. There's still a lot of work to be done on the systematicity and meaning of language in use. So as well as restating the material that has gone before, I hope that the chapter will provide the sense of some of the ways in which the field is looking ahead, what some of the trajectories are for future work, and where there might be possibilities for quite significant shifts in how we study language.

THE CENTRALITY OF SPONTANEOUS SPEECH

Throughout this book we have seen that research into language in use is closely tied to and deeply committed to the use of spontaneous data. Moreover, sociolinguistics is committed to the principle of accountability. This means a sociolinguistic analysis takes into account not only the most frequent tokens, or the ones with the most straightforward interpretation, but *all* the tokens of a variable.

As linguists, we still want to be able to draw generalisations about what people 'know' about language, even if we are committed to working with the messiness of spontaneous speech. When the data we are generalising from is drawn from a more restricted data set (e.g., constructed sentences that native speakers have clear intuitions about), this is a more straightforward task than it is when the data set we are using includes differences between and within individuals' speech.

Connections with theory

Different sociolinguists respond to the principle of accountability in different ways. The use of quantitative methods is one way of satisfying the requirement to account for all data. But some sociolinguists would argue that accountability also requires us to scrutinise the details of an individual's use of individual tokens of a variable and not allow them to be subsumed by the majority forms as quantitative methods tend to. This approach is more in tune with the principles and goals of discourse analysis and functional linguistics.

Nevertheless, in this book we have seen several ways in which researchers interested in sociolinguistic questions manage to draw inferences about what people 'know' about language from such heterogeneous data. One approach is to use quantitative methods, because these allow us to get at the patterns of use that are more or less likely in different contexts or with different groups of speakers.

Another approach (discussed in Chapters 10 and 11) is to undertake the kind of close analysis of individual tokens that is typical of conversation and discourse analysis. In this case, the immediate goal is not to make generalisations across different situations or speakers. However, this approach can reveal the ways in which speakers exploit the connections between language and social structure, and indeed how their use of language contributes to building this relationship, in very specific instances. Ultimately, I have suggested, this kind of detailed perspective on the social functions of language use may inform the way in which quantitative patterns may be intepreted by speakers (or sociolinguists).

This willingness to draw on different methodologies has benefited sociolinguistics in a number of ways. A combination of qualitative and quantitative methods can demonstrate plausible routes by which individual or idiosyncratic alternations can be reinterpreted as having more general significance. The willingness to draw probabilistic generalisations from variable data has provided linguists with a means of observing language change in progress. This is particularly clear when variation is viewed through the lens of apparent time (Chapter 7), but, since we have always known that languages change over time, it is gratifying – but in some ways hardly surprising – to find that speakers of different ages in the same community reveal systematic age-based differences in the forms they favour most.

However, one thing we might not have predicted is that the close study of variation can show changes spreading through a community along other forms of social stratification: the patterns of association in social networks or communities of practice (Chapter 8), gender (Chapter 10), speakers' perceptions of shared interests (Chapters 3 and 4). In addition, we can show that exactly the same kinds of factors are important in determining more stable and codified forms of variation in language choice and language use: politeness routines (Chapter 5), conventions for code-switching (Chapter 6) and the use of different speech levels or variants to index social relations (Chapters 6 and 10).

INTERPRETING AND MOTIVATING VARIATION

I suggested in Chapter 2 that it might be helpful to think about what motivates variation in the speech community as falling into four rough categories. As I mentioned then, there are many other ways of characterising speaker motivations, but these four provide us with a useful basis for reviewing some of what we have covered in the book and leading us to some final concluding remarks.

Accentuate the positive

I suggested that speakers do things that have value. At one level, you could say that everything a speaker does has some kind of value to them (otherwise they would have done something different!). However, defining 'value' in such a broad way reduces the usefulness of the term: by describing everything, it ends up explaining nothing. So let us assume that what 'value' refers to here are forms that have local or supra-local prestige.

Some examples of this motivation at play might include the consistent patterns of style-shifting we see according to changes in the addressee or in different kinds of verbal activity. In Chapter 8, we observed a pattern known as the cross-over effect. This can be interpreted as a particularly marked example of a desire to accentuate the positive. In their most careful speech, the interior social classes (either the lower middle class or the upper working class) use more tokens of a variant which the community as a whole responds to as a prestige form than speakers from a higher social class do. This cross-over has often been interpreted as an indication of the high sensitivity that members of this social class have about what linguistic resources have overt prestige in a community. However, we should note that it is simply a more extreme instance of the classic shifting from one favoured variant to another that we observed in all groups of speakers as we moved from one speaking style to another (Chapters 3, 8 and 9).

We also considered examples of code switching in Chapter 6 where we saw that there may be instrumental benefits associated with using one language rather than another (getting better service or a better deal). These might also be considered examples of a desire to accentuate the positive.

While we don't want to define 'value' too loosely, we also don't want to suggest that it is only measured in terms of status or money. We have seen numerous examples of particular variants having value even within very small groups of users (Chapters 9 and 10) and in response to the very idiosyncratic needs of the moment (Chapters 5 and 6).

We noted that the notion of communication accommodation, or attunement, is based on research which shows that where we fundamentally feel positive towards our interlocutor and hope this will be reciprocated, there is often a convergence to our interlocutor's communicative norms. It is possible that as well as providing an account of individual style-shifting (Chapter 3), this might account for the examples of lifespan change that we discussed in Chapter 7.

Eliminate the negative

On the other hand, Chapter 2 also suggested that sometimes what motivates people to use a particular style or variety is a desire to avoid things that carry costs. As we saw in

Chapter 4, Michiganders have such tremendous linguistic security and they seem to believe so strongly that their accent is the norm for Standard American, that they actually filter out regionally marked forms when they are asked to listen to their ingroup speech.

Linked closely at times to the desire to accentuate the positive, a desire to avoid costs might explain why social stratification is maintained. In Chapter 8, when we looked at social class, we did not have space to consider the question of why class differences are maintained. If style-shifting and attitude surveys indicate that speakers throughout the speech community share the same positive evaluations of different forms, you might wonder why working-class speakers don't simply start talking like middle-class speakers (accentuate the positive) and accrue the benefits associated with that.

A common answer has been that many vernacular or working-class norms are valued positively by the speakers (we noted this is sometimes, incorrectly, identified as covert prestige). People may understand that one variant is generally considered better than another, but they may be equally aware that anyone speaking like that would be considered up themselves or just would not fit in (as I said, accentuating the positive and eliminating the negative are often closely tied together). Your mother may disapprove of you saying *bu'er* (Chapters 10 and 11), but you might be more concerned with what your friends will think or say if you use *butter*.

Another possibility is that even if lower class speakers do try and catch up with the norms of the highest class speakers (those who control the linguistic marketplace; see Chapter 7), the middle-class speakers may keep shifting the goal posts. That is, the continuation of some variation within the speech community may be because the groups of speakers who are able (for whatever social reasons) to define the targets, change their norms when other groups get too close. This could perhaps be seen as a social analogue of the phonological principle of maximum differentiation (Chapter 2). An example of this principle of differentiation working on social (rather than purely linguistic grounds) might be the way an ingroup code, like slang, changes quickly if its features (vocabulary, voice quality) start being adopted widely in the community – words or phrases immediately go out of style among the original innovators.

Finally, in Chapter 5 we saw that Brown and Levinson's theory of politeness conceptualises politeness in terms of how much redressive action a speaker decides to take when a face-threatening act occurs. Their assessment is based on a number of factors, one of which – the cost of the imposition – is consistent with the idea that speakers are sometimes motivated to use a particular formulation because they have a desire to minimise costs.

Life's a balancing act

So speakers can find themselves walking the line between wanting to fit in with some people and differentiate themselves from others. The reason you use a raised onset for (ay) might be as much because you *don't* want to sound like a tourist as you *do* want to sound like an old-time Vineyarder (Chapter 2). You may want to identify with the other nerdy girls, but you're going to do that by avoiding the extreme forms of a variable used by cool girls (Chapter 9). The community may uniformly use glide-shortened forms of words in the PRICE and MOUTH sets as indexes of localness, but women, and men who do not identify with the more macho norms of the traditional fishing lifestyle, may use glide-shortened variants of MOUTH and leave the PRICE set as a marker of localness for the more traditional males (Chapter 10).

The idea that speakers might simultaneously be attentive to costs *and* benefits is implicit in other components of politeness theory – social distance and the power differential between speakers. It is also implicit in the very complex manner that speakers compound both positive and negative politeness strategies – attending to both the speaker's and the hearer's face wants in one utterance (Chapter 5).

This balancing act might also be reflected in the patterns we associate with generational change. In Chapter 7 we saw that speakers in different age groups use an incoming or innovative variant at rates that run slightly ahead of the generation above them. This is actually a little mysterious – something we did not talk about in Chapter 7 – and it is not entirely clear how children might learn to use an innovative variant somewhat *more* frequently than their parents do. One possibility is that differentiation between age groups pushes the change on, while commonality with the speech community as a whole provides a check on an abrupt and total shift to the newer form. There may be some support in this by the spike in the use of an incoming variant that has sometimes been observed in teenage speakers (Labov 1994; see also Cameron (2005) who integrates this with data on gender differentiation).

It's a jungle out there

If the first two motivations set the stage for speakers to have to try and manage a sometimes complicated balancing act, then weighing their options and navigating between the desire to accentuate the positive and eliminate the negative means that they are going to have to be ready to formulate and test hypotheses.

For example, I might assume that a particular identity is salient to you at a given point in time, in a particular conversation, and I might try and accommodate to that. But if, as the conversation continues to unfold, you start to use variants that suggest I have misunderstood the situation or mischaracterised you, then I will have to revise my attempts at accommodation accordingly. This kind of face-to-face negotiation of language is somewhat controversial (not all sociolinguists would agree that it is potentially so important), but I take it to be a vital process which enables us to transform and interpret idiosyncratic utterances as socially meaningful variables.

A FINAL WORD: THE TRIUMPH OF MULTIPLE CAUSATION

As I bring this chapter to a close, I realise how often I have written the words *pattern* and *use*, usually stressing their connectedness.

I think I was hoping that something like the Fibonacci sequence would appear for sociolinguistics and language use, and that once I had explained language use in those terms all your questions would be answered. The Fibonacci sequence is the numerical pattern that starts: 0, 1, 1, 2, 3, 5, 8, 13, 21 . . . It turns out to describe all sorts of features in nature, like the whorls of a snail shell and a fern frond. I don't think there is a Fibonacci sequence for sociolinguistics (yet), but there are some very beautiful patterns nonetheless. For me, it is amazing that we find parallelisms between the way a variable is distributed across an individual speaker's styles, and the way it is distributed across social categories like class, age or gender, since these social categories are quite far removed from the way individuals actually use and experience language. It is almost as wonderful as finding out that there is a mathematics to the way a fern unfolds.

The fact that we can use language, be creative with it and manipulate it so that it mediates our relationships with others in meaningful ways is, in my opinion, quite a beautiful and fabulous thing. Whatever else this book has done, I hope it has communicated my sense of that to you.

It's tempting to try and find a silver bullet or some grand unified theory that will deal with all the data and provide all the answers. But if variables are part of the grammar, and if there is inherent variability in linguistic systems, there will always be an element of indeterminacy in outcomes. It would be rather odd – notwithstanding our emphasis on patterns and systematicity – if a complex social tool, such as language, lent itself to simple, unidimensional explanations.

Life isn't like that, and we live our lives in and through language. It makes sense that what drives and motivates patterns of language in use should be at least as complicated, as least as laminated, and at least as interdependent on each other, as the other attributes that make us social beings.

Notes on the exercises

The following notes on the exercises included in the text are intended to help structure discussion of the material in the exercises, suggest connections between topics covered in different parts of the book and help readers ask their own sociolinguistically informed research questions. They are *not* intended as answers.

In some cases, the exercise asks readers to reflect on their opinions, or argue a position. Obviously, there is no single answer to these kinds of exercises. In other cases, several interpretations of the data in a figure are possible. I have provided the interpretation that I drew from the data provided and which seemed to me to best address the issues that are being discussed in the immediately surrounding text. However, thoughtful readers will generally be able to see connections between different exercises, e.g., ways in which the data in the chapter on social networks reminds them of issues discussed in the section on mutlilingualism. I would encourage those sorts of connections and I hope people using this book as a course text will take each exercise as the starting point for a critical synthesis of the ideas that may have been introduced in the text or in tutorials and sections, and not as an end in itself.

CHAPTER 2

Identifying variables and variants (p. 9)

I can express the idea that someone has died in lots of ways: 'she died', 'she karked it', 'she passed away', 'she is no longer with us', and many more. Some people switch into a different language to express the idea. We could talk about a (die) variable that is realised by all these different variants.

The form I use will depend on factors like how well I knew the person I'm talking about, how well the person I am speaking to knew the person we're talking about, how formal the situation is (whether I'm mentioning it in a formal report at a board meeting or while gossiping over a coffee with friends), and so on.

We will see lots of examples of words or sets of words that people pronounce differently as this book unfolds. And some of the same factors just mentioned will resurface as important constraints on pronunciation. You may find it easier to talk about the factors influencing your use of *die* vs *karked it* than it is to talk about factors influencing use of different pronunciations. A lot of what we do in pronunciation occurs below our level of conscious awareness (as we will discuss further in later chapters).

Our awareness of the different linguistic forms we use (p. 12)

If you are a native speaker of any variety of English, chances are that you use both of the alternatives, but you may not be aware of using the first alternative in each of these pairs. The duplication of 'is' in constructions like *The problem is, is* . . . is a grammatical variable, while the others are phonological variables.

The fact that speakers are very often unaware of the range of forms they use is part of the reason sociolinguists use recordings of spontaneous conversation to collect their data.

Calculating index scores (p. 19)

You will calculate your index scores for use of the newer assibilated variant like this:

Flora $(24 \div 80) \times 100 = 30$ per cent or index of 0.30
Pablo $(3 \div 20) \times 100 = \dots$ etc.

You will calculate scores for each generation like this:

Gen. I (Flora + Pablo + Luis + Carmen) = ??

and then divide that total by the number of speakers to get the group average. In this case: $(30 + 15 + 2 + 40) = 87 \div 4 = 22$.

Identifying relevant non-linguistic factors in a community (p. 21)

Some of the factors you might discuss include: where you live (is it a large city or a small town?), who you associate with (do you have a wide circle of acquaintances or a close-knit circle of friends?), what kind of education you had (did you go to a private or state school?), how stable the population in your area is (are there newcomers as well as old-time residents?). Sometimes differences in educational background only become relevant or important considerations when you move away from home or go on to higher education. Certain ways of talking may be considered 'posh' or 'nice' (depending on your perspective). In some communities, people are very aware of some of these differences and can talk quite explicitly about differences in pronunciation or vocabulary different groups of people in the community use. But sometimes people aren't aware of pronunciation differences.

CHAPTER 3

Designing materials for a social dialect survey (p. 31)

Labov (1972a: 82) gives one of the reading passages used in the New York City social dialect survey. Here is part of the reading passage used in the social dialect survey in Porirua (New Zealand, Holmes *et al.* 1991). In New Zealand English, syllabic or coda /l/ may be vocalised and a coda /l/ often effects the phonetic realisation of the preceding vowel. You'll notice lots of tokens of /l/ in the reading passage:

> Last summer we went touring around the East Cape in our old van. We towed our boat behind us. One day we stopped at a small bay for a bite to eat . . . I decided to sail around a little island . . . The breeze which had blown me out was getting stronger. I pulled in the sail tight . . . I howled till my voice gave up, but it was a waste of time. I was wearing only shorts and a T-shirt and the wind was cruel. The swell grew bigger but I tried not to panic. I said to myself 'Carl knows I'm out here. He'll get help' . . .

The effect of topic on style (p. 36)

I would not be terribly surprised if I found that a speaker seemed to be using less casual styles when talking about education, how things have gone to ruin 'compared to when I was a child', or politics. Similarly, I wouldn't be surprised if their speech seemed somehow more casual when telling a funny story, or retelling local gossip.

Integrating topic shifts in audience design (p. 46)

It's possible that speaking about a topic like education might make speakers imagine they are talking in an educational context and therefore they will speak like they are talking to a teacher. This shift may be completely subconscious, and not available for them to reconstruct or explain afterwards. That makes it somewhat difficult to determine whether an 'imagined addressee' is a better or worse account of their behaviour than attention to speech.

'Attention to speech' vs 'audience design'? (p. 46)

Labov's model of style-shifting as attention to speech, and the research methods associated with it in social dialect surveys, dominated sociolinguistics for many years. One of the attractions of audience design (and the accommodation processes it is assumed to be based on) is the fact that it puts the *relationship* between speaker and hearer(s) in centre stage. It therefore allows researchers to consider style-shifting as something that happens between particular individuals and at particular moments in an interaction. The perspective on style may draw on more qualitative methods of analysis (e.g., close analysis of conversational turns), rather than on the quantitative methods of the social dialect tradition. So there are clear differences in both theory and method between the two approaches to style.

But it is easy to set up this kind of opposition. What's harder, but more interesting, is to consider the ways in which the approaches can be brought closer together, and perhaps be seen as complementary perspectives along the same dimension. This is why you are encouraged to try thinking of audience design in terms of attention to a (real or imagined) listener.

Testing assumptions about topic-induced shift (p. 49)

Suraratdecha suggested that because the students she recorded had mostly only travelled for university, and their university experience was now in English in the US, they considered these topics 'English' ones. Stories about the supernatural, however, generally draw on experiences back in Thailand, so they were 'Thai' topics.

Frequently people who have studied at university in a foreign language find that they feel strange talking about the subjects they have studied in their native language (sometimes they even lack the vocabulary to do so).

CHAPTER 4

Semantic derogation (p. 57)

In answering this question, you might find it helpful to distinguish between words that are widely known or recognised and words which might only be used by you and a close group of friends. The word *rake*, which is offered as an explicit contrast to *slut*, is archaic or quaint in many dialects of English. Moreover, even for people who know and might use the term, it generally has carefree or 'laddish' connotations that *slut* seldom (if ever) does.

Attitudes and context of use (p. 57)

Some younger British women have reported that *minx* is not entirely negative to them and can be used affectionately (meaning something like 'mischievous woman') between friends (or from mother to daughter). Similarly, describing a stranger as 'dressed like a tart' seems far more negatively judgemental than describing a friend's outfit that way. With close friends we often find a suspension of politeness norms (more on this in Chapter 5). Because we presume we must be joking or affectionate, we can be less careful in how we speak.

Pretty nice? (p. 58)

Even though *pretty* is generally a positive way of describing something, for many people it also trivialises a little what it describes. Because *pretty* can imply that what it describes is harmless or insignificant, many artists would be quite offended if you suggested that their work was *pretty*.

Generic reference terms (p. 62)

In addition to the suggestions in the text, you could:

- consider the age at which children seem to become aware of the potential for generic reference;

■ see how long people take to respond to a sequence of sentences where a generic term is followed by male or female pronuns – for example, *A police officer . . . she . . .* vs *A police officer . . . he . . .*;

■ see if word frequency seems to matter more than morphology to people's judgements.

For example, is a high-frequency occupation term without morphological gender marking (e.g., *nurse*) more or less likely to resist generic interpretation than one with overt gender marking (e.g., *fireman* or *seamstress*)? Or you could consider relative frequency within either category (e.g., compare *fireman* and *linesman*).

Address and reference (p. 62)

These exercises are quite detailed and your analysis will depend very much on the kind of data you end up collecting. Generally, address terms encode a lot of social information and go far beyond the basic need to pick someone out as the addressee of an utterance. Some (nick)names or endearments mark intimacy, and some people find it quite inappropriate for non-intimates to use them. Some address terms are asymmetrical: in some varieties of English *love* can be used as an address term even between non-intimates, but it is more usually used to address women than men. It is also more usually used to address someone younger than the speaker. It is interesting to see how factors like intimacy, age and sex interact in patterns of use.

Reclaiming negative words (p. 65)

An interesting word to discuss in this context is *nigga*, which is acceptable as a term of ingroup reference among Blacks and which (especially with the final -*a* spelling) announces strong identification with hip-hop norms. The use of the term by Whites or to describe Whites is somewhat contentious.

It is also possible that you might want to distinguish between the intergroup effects and the ways in which individual members of a group experience attempts to reclaim and revalorise words.

CHAPTER 5

Intuitive notions of politeness (p. 82)

These are some of my answers. Yours will undoubtedly differ.

Polite: Holding the door open for someone coming behind you; introducing yourself when you meet someone for the first time; saying you can't come to someone's place for dinner because you're too busy (not because you find them too boring); chewing with your mouth closed; softening criticism with comments about something good.

Impolite: Talking too long about something you are interested in but others aren't; pushing ahead of people in a line; not acknowledging someone when they arrive; spitting; not acknowledging a mistake.

My lists seem to focus a lot on our responsibilities with respect to other people's physical or talking space and making people feel valued and welcome.

Speech levels or respect in English vocabulary (p. 83)

This should be pretty straightforward. You may notice parallels between what you have been doing and the classic jokes that go along the lines: *I am determined, You are stubborn, S/he is pig-headed*; or *Ladies glow, Gentlemen perspire, Horses sweat.*

Orienting to different kinds of politeness (p. 87)

People who grow up in communities that are more oriented to negative face wants and negative politeness may find that they are perceived as aloof or cold if they move somewhere where positive politeness is emphasised more. They may also mistake some of the conventionalised positive politeness routines as being expressions of 'genuine' friendship or closeness (I put this in quotes because obviously there is a difference in how different parties evaluate genuineness). Conversely, people accustomed to paying attention to positive face wants and using positive politeness strategies may find that they come across as unsophisticated or vulgar if they find themselves in a community that is more oriented to negative face wants.

Costs of an imposition (p. 88)

You will probably find that the greater the cost, the more elaborate and longer your request is. You may also notice that the ways you imagine formulating your request include both negative and positive politeness for higher-cost impositions.

Untangling face threats (p. 90)

Your answers to all three scenarios will probably depend on how close you are to the person you are asking to do this. If the distance and/or power between you is relatively small the cost will usually be lower.

For me, these three requests are increasingly costly impositions. Assuming the person I am asking lives fairly close to me (e.g., a neighbour), then the first requires minimal time and effort on their part. The second requires them to spend more time and effort, while the third involves them investing a good deal of time and exercising their judgement on your behalf. The last request is sufficiently costly (for me) that I would be reluctant to ask anyone to do this unless I knew them very well; that is, unless the social distance between us was so small that it would offset the cost of the imposition.

Linguistic features expressing attention to face wants (p. 94)

These notes should enable you to identify and discuss more features. You might comment on:

- Attention to negative face wants

  - the use of a question/request, which the hearer can choose to accommodate or refuse;
  - the use of the conditional (*could*), suggesting the hearer can opt out on the grounds of lack of ability;
  - going on record with the debt about to be incurred (*do me a favour*), and acknowledging potential imposition (*sorry*).

- Attention to positive face wants

  - the use of inclusive pronoun (*should we*), suggesting speaker's and hearer's wants and desires are the same;
  - (apparent) attention to hearer's needs (*you look . . .*);
  - suggestion that hearer's and speaker's wants might converge (*a favour*).

Notice some features have overlapping functions (whether you evaluate them from the speaker's perspective or the hearer's perspective will make a difference).

Manipulating cost of an imposition (p. 94)

Generally, you will find use of negative politeness strategies increases as cost of imposition increases. An exception to this may be if you imagine making the request of a very close friend, in which case positive politeness strategies may increase as well as or instead of negative politeness strategies.

Translating politeness (p. 97)

Your results will determine your discussion. When people undertake surveys or research in this manner, they often notice other factors that enter into politeness (intersecting with P and D especially); for example, gender or attraction. Many people find refusing an invitation requires more politeness work if they are attracted to the other person (or suspect the other person is attracted to them).

CHAPTER 6

Language choice in education (p. 105)

Afrikaans was identified as the language of apartheid and this made it a very loaded choice of code in any circumstances. Many people considered being forced to learn it as a medium of education to be adding insult to injury. At the time, the alternative favoured instead of Afrikaans was English (also a colonial language, but not identified with the apartheid regime). Now, as you have seen, South Africa recognises a number of indigenous languages which could (in theory) be used at least at elementary/primary school level.

The situation with Ebonics in the US was a little different, since Ebonics (one name given to African American English) is not currently recognised as the official medium of education or public business anywhere in the US. However, you might perceive some analogies with the resistance to Afrikaans, since the calls to recognise Ebonics in schools in Oakland, California, was also a step towards (re)claiming the classroom as a domain for pupils' vernacular language.

Enjoyment of language (p. 105)

In the weakest sense of 'enjoy', this clause simply says all official languages must have the benefits of equal esteem etc.

I find 'enjoy' an interesting choice of word here because it always implies that the object is a source of pleasure. So even though the *speakers* of the languages are not explicitly mentioned in this clause, it seems to me that this phrasing sneaks their needs and preferences back into the overall considerations. You can imagine a situation in the future where interpretations of whether this clause in the constitution has been met (or not) might depend on how speakers of different languages feel about their status within society.

Switching styles and languages (p. 116)

Using Pidgin sounds more 'Local'. It may seem more appropriate in a very 'local' situation like the store, and it may also imply a shared identity that will get him help more quickly. In theory, there might be times when it is helpful to use Pidgin in his legal work, but it's more likely to be when talking to clients outside of court than when presenting argument (though some Local lawyers will switch into Pidgin for special effect!).

Mapping your language choices (pp. 119–120)

The trees in Figures 6.2 and 6.3 went through a lot of revision to get them as clear as they are. Often people started with questions about domain ('Where am I?'), but notice that in Figure 6.2 this almost immediately gets reinterpreted in terms of *who* you are talking to. So you might find it makes more sense to start by asking 'Who am I with/talking to?' Your choice of language (or style) might depend more on your intuitive understanding of what it means for a situation to be 'formal' or 'informal'. However, you should be able to unpack what you understand 'formal' to mean if you start from a decision like that.

Borrowing or co-opting? (p. 122)

All languages borrow words here and there when speakers come into contact with a new thing or a new concept that they have no words for in their native language. But some people find it patronising or insincere if a speaker borrows easily translatable terms from a language, especially if they don't fluently speak that language.

On the other hand, there is a long tradition of comics strategically using highly stereo-typed features of language either to create a sense of their 'outsiderness' (which can allow them to say or do things that are otherwise sanctioned) or to evoke the very rich mental schemas we associate with different accents or ways of talking (we discussed some of this in Chapter 2; you might also want to connect this discussion on co-optation with the discussion of Whites' using *nigga* in the exercise 'Reclaiming negative words' on p. 65).

Cross-over between speech levels in Sasak (p. 124)

The important difference between the two clauses is that one has a first-person subject (*aku/tiang* 'I') and the other has a second-person subject (*kamu/side/pelinggih* 'you'). A *mènak* using *alus* humbles themself (as it were) with their choice of the verb 'to eat'. Since Sasak has its different speech levels as widely recognised resources for showing attention to caste, the resources of *jamaq* and *madie* are available for *mènak* to draw on in order to indicate humility.

CHAPTER 7

Projecting variation into the future (p. 129)

With a couple of exceptions, Hoban reduces a final consonant cluster in monomorphemic words, but doesn't reduce it when it is the marker of past tense. Perhaps he sees this as going along with the regularisation of [t] as the marker of past: where our contemporary English has *stared* and *unbarred* with final [d], Riddley Walker uses [t].

Hoban's pattern is interesting for variationist linguists because there is a sound basis for it in the distribution of these reduced cluster forms. Many studies find that speakers reduce the cluster more often in monomorphemic words than they do when it is a marker of the past. Researchers have proposed a number of reasons for why they might do this. They are reviewed in Labov's (1994) discussion of 'functional' motivations for variation.

Two variables or one? (p. 136)

There are a number of things you might say about these two figures. If you look only at the women's use of non-standard *was* in existentials (*There was these three people* . . .) and their use of non-standard *were* in negative tags (*Loads of fun, weren't it?*), you might be struck by the apparent parallel in frequencies and in the stratification between the different age groups. You might want to argue, therefore, that the variables seem to be related or connected (an increase in one non-standard variant is matched by the increase in another). You might also argue that this link is strengthened by the fact that the same verb, BE, is involved – perhaps young women in York are taking the most irregular English verb in the system and imposing a regularity on the distribution of the forms.

On the other hand, you might be reluctant to analyse a variable that is almost entirely restricted to negative contexts (non-standard *were*) as being linked to a variable that occurs in affirmative sentences (non-standard existential *was*). Another, purely linguistic, reason for being cautious about linking them is that both variables concern agreement (or an apparent mismatch in English agreement). In both existential sentences and tag questions, there can be problems deciding what the 'real' subject is, and whether the verb is close enough to agree with it. Where there is a problem in identifying how agreement should be resolved, we typically find some default form of agreement emerging. We would expect a language to have one default form (if the variation is structurally motivated): here we see two different forms being defaulted to.

Puerto Rican reported discourse (p. 138)

The preference for *y NP* strategies is very marked for pre-teen and teenage girls. Although you don't have the data for men and boys, a comparison between the women's data and the community overall in Figure 7.4 (p. 137) would lead us to conclude that men and boys cannot be using *y NP* very much.

In addition, the data for girls in their teens shows that they slightly disfavour use of the freestanding quote variant and strongly disfavour the canonical verbs. But among all teenagers, the freestanding quote is somewhat favoured and the canonical verbs are not so markedly disfavoured. This suggests that teenage boys are using one innovative variant (freestanding quote) and perhaps holding on to the canonical variants, while girls are using another innovative variant (*y NP*). So it would be too simplistic to claim there is an across-the-board shift towards use of *y NP* forms.

CHAPTER 8

New York vowels (p. 166)

Speakers from the three lowest SEC are using more of the raised variants with short (a). There seems to be a monotonic relationship between short (a) raising and SEC, with progressively less raising as you move through higher SECs. This steady pattern is not replicated with (oh) raising, where there is not a consistent trend across speakers from different social classes. There also doesn't seem to be a consistent style effect for short (oh) raising: the index scores for reading and spontaneous speech overlap (or virtually do so) for speakers in six SECs (0–5).

Which group leads and which group follows for changes in progress is affected by factors such as the extent to which a variable is stigmatised or the subject of overt and prescriptive evaluations.

The lower middle-class leaders in change (p. 174)

Weber defined social class in terms of aspirations (chances) and lifestyles. It might be that speakers from the lower middle class, being nearly at the 'top' of the SEC scale, are eager to identity (and use, cf. the cross-over effect) any social and linguistic resources that might blur the line between them and social classes whose life chances afford them more status already. Sensitivity to a variable (identifying its social value) is presumably a precursor to using it to try and establish or assert one's aspirations (cf. the cross-over effect).

Use of (r) in North Carolina (p. 175)

As we have noted, level of education is often a good indicator of social class. Surprisingly, here, the speakers with college or university education and speakers who didn't go beyond grade (primary) school pattern are alike. The speakers who graduated from high school (but didn't go on to university) use more of the constricted [r] than anyone else. This is especially clear in word-list style. The high school graduates might turn out (in this community) to be the people who are the second highest social class (analogous to the lower middle class). In that case, their behaviour is consistent with what we have seen so far.

Notice, though, that there is another cross-over: speakers who didn't go beyond grade school appear to favour the constricted [r] variant somewhat more than speakers with some high school education. However, since this cross-over is only clear in the sentence-reading task, we would want to be cautious about how we interpret it.

CHAPTER 9

Identifying social networks (pp. 186–7)

Katie and Corbin are less central to the network when it is based on reciprocal naming. Independent observation of the children's interactions with each other would tell us whether this is in fact the case.

Dense or loose networks? (p. 187)

The network based on reciprocal naming is denser than the one which is not. The smaller network made up of Sam, Leah and Corbin is maximally dense; they all reciprocally name each other.

Multiplex ties within networks (p. 188)

Multiplexity means people know each other in a number of different roles or capacities, so communities where people work in the family business and also know their sibling as co-worker (or boss) increases the mutiplexity of that network. In places where there is a large gap between the prices of accommodation at the low end of the market and the high end of the market, people who work in the same kinds of jobs (and have the same kinds of salary) will end up buying close to each other, so they may know their neighbours as co-workers as well. The greater mobility of the middle class (for work and, before that, higher education) means it is less likely that middle-class people will maintain or develop multiplex ties like these.

The importance of individual variation (p. 190)

For several reasons, we might want to keep a closer eye on the individuals who are well in advance or well behind the group averages. These people may provide crucial evidence about what kind of social meaning the group as a whole understands a particular variant to have. This information may emerge more clearly in the ways (or contexts) in which some speakers avoid or actively use a variant. Detailed attention to these so-called 'outliers' can also provide clues about directions and rates of change. As yet, I'm not aware of anyone trying to use this kind of data to ask questions about *rate* of change (and indeed, sociolinguists usually stay clear of making predictions about this), but it seems that this is a possible avenue for further work.

Language and professional identities (p. 198)

Some examples of professions in which language is a key part of the job are: receptionist, teacher, lawyer/barrister, call-centre worker. In these professions, a person's verbal skills contribute a great deal to how good they are considered to be in them. How you communicate is considered less central in defining success in other jobs: parking warden, bus driver. You might want to reframe your answer to this question in terms of the linguistic marketplace.

CHAPTER 10

Identifying indexes (p. 204)

Perhaps someone asked a man, 'Who are you?' or 'What do you people call yourselves?' and he replied something to the effect of, 'We call ourselves "people"'. We can assume they asked an adult male, rather than a woman or a boy because they would have answered 'Yaa'.

Gender effects in lingustic description (p. 204)

A linguistic decision might choose the form that all others can be derived from most economically (i.e., with the fewest rules and exceptions to rules). An argument taking social factors into account might argue for considering the basic form to be the one that refers to or denotes more people.

Gendered possession (p. 205)

At the very least, the terms suggest that for a man, his relationship with a wife (like with his brothers) is seen as similar to a part–whole relationship (as hands are to a body). However, women's use of the active possession construction and men's use of direct possession may historically have something to do with traditional preferences for marrying within the extended family, where same-sex cousins are referred to with the same term as same-sex siblings.

Negative *can* in Tyneside English (pp. 208–9)

This distribution is consistent with Principle I. You have been told the variable is stable, so it is not surprising to find that women use more of the variant shared with Standard English while men use more of the local variant. You might like to consider these Tyneside results alongside the data on glottaling among children in Newcastle that follows on p. 211.

Spread of glottal stops (p. 212)

The glottal stop variant is clearly one that there is some awareness of. Is it the 'standard' form though? This illustrates problems with the notion of 'standard' as a principle in variation and a diagnostic of change. It is certainly not the conservative form used in more formal contexts by most speakers. But it is spreading so quickly in British English that it would be a major over-simplification to call it 'non-standard'. If something is ubiquitous in everyday speech, when does it become the 'standard'? Attitudes may enter into the analysis as early as the process of simply describing variants.

The pattern for MC teenagers in Figure 10.4 looks more like a change from below the level of consciousness (discussed on pp. 170–3). The much greater use of glottal stops in WC boys and girls would also support this. It does not look like a pattern predicted by Principles I and Ia, where we would expect girls to use more of the standard (i.e., alevolar stops [t]) than boys. This distribution is only found among the WC adolescents in Hull. (The differences in overall frequency shown in Figure 10.4 – without weighted adjustments for the distribution of tokens in more or less favourable contexts – mean the differences between the WC teenagers are unlikely to be statistically significant.)

Social class, gender and change in Swedish (p. 213)

The social-class stratification is more consistent among men for both variables. It appears there is something like the cross-over effect among women. It has been suggested that the prime leaders in change are *women* from the interior social classes – and specifically lower middle-class or upper working-class women with the broadest and least dense social networks. This might result in focusing of the cross-over effect in a speech community among women.

Using Labov's Principles as diagnostics (p. 217)

You need to know more about either the social evaluation of the two variants in Scotland or their distribution among women and men of different ages before you can draw any conclusions about likely directions of change. This pattern might reflect Principle I effects, but only if it is clear that women and men are both orienting to r-less pronunciation in more careful or outgroup speech (independent evidence of shared evaluations) and if it is easy to elicit negative comments about r-ful accents (independent evidence of change from above).

Palatalisation of stops in Cairene Arabic (pp. 219–20)

A pattern in which women from the second-highest social class are leading the community in a change is one we would associate with a change occurring below the level of conscious awareness (Principle II). However, it is hard to reconcile this with the fact that middle-class and upper-class women (who will have had access and exposure to Classical Arabic) must be aware of the overt prestige associated with Classical Arabic. The fact that all groups of speakers show a marked shift either *towards* or *away from* palatalised variants in their most careful word-list style adds to the complexity. Middle-class speakers' increased use of palatalisation in this style would suggest they perceive it as a prestige variant, while the complete avoidance of palatalisation among upper-class speakers in this style suggests that they perceive non-palatalised stops to be the prestige variants.

We might be able to unravel this if there were clear overall trends across styles in all four groups of speakers. However, in all groups, the frequency of palatalised variants remains fairly uniform across the other three styles. This 'flat' pattern, where there is intergroup differentiation without stylistic stratification within the group, is typical of a sociolinguistic indicator. The absence of style-shifting is generally taken to indicate a lack of awareness, yet we cannot ignore the shifts occurring in word-list style. It is possible that (i) palatalisation is on the verge of moving from being an indicator to a marker, or that (ii) the distinction between indicators and markers may be less helpful in describing variation and change in Arabic speech communities since the indicator/marker distinction is based on speakers' degree of conscious awareness, and this is clearly complicated by the contrast between a naturally acquired Low and a learnt High variety.

Particle omission in Japanese (p. 230)

Explaining the patterns in mixed-sex conversations in terms of convergence focuses on speakers' desires to be liked (or be perceived as being *alike*). But people may also want to differentiate themselves from groups with whom they might be compared (remember the notion of divergence).

Motivating variation (p. 230)

'Who uses *wa* and *ga*?' 'When?' 'When can *you* omit them?' 'When would you omit them?' 'Is it more "polite" to use *ga* and *wa*?' 'Does it sound more "friendly" or "casual" if you leave them out?' 'Who would you want to sound "friendly" (like this) with?'

You can think of more . . .

Collaboration or competition? (p. 233)

Your first reaction may be that (like 'art'), you can't define competition and collaboration, but you know it when you see it. You can try to pin down your intuitions a little by asking whether a laughing or smiling voice is compatible with the delivery, how long pauses might be, whether challenges for the floor would be strange or acceptable.

Change in progress and developing identities (p. 235)

Factors you might like to consider include: the extent to which gender polarisation or complementarity of social roles (including sexual identities) are expected; the kinds of social networks or the strength of participation in different communities of practice in teen years.

Cameron (2005) attempts to make connections between age and gender in a variationist paradigm, drawing both on Labov's principles and social constructionist views of gender.

CHAPTER 11

Lexical variables and change (p. 245)

It will be difficult to infer change over time from the distribution of lexical or vocabulary items in older and younger speakers if older speakers can learn new words and start using them along with younger speakers. However, some lexical items are more closely tied into the grammatical system than others, and for these it is probably reasonable to draw apparent time inferences with caution. For example, speakers of all ages may learn new words in open grammatical classes, like nouns or verbs (*an **email** message; to **text** someone*). But where a word like *like* is being extended to new syntactic slots from older, more established grammatical functions, then we may see differences between older and younger speakers' use of the term in its new grammatical function.

Creole simplicity (p. 253)

'Simple' can be defined in all sorts of ways. It could be measured in terms of the size of vocabulary, range and type of syntactic structures available to speakers, the extent to which there is productive inflectional morphology (like agreement) or derivational morphology (like word compounding). You might consider how straightforward or difficult it is to find comparable data for comparing across languages in this way.

One measure that is seldom considered in measures of 'simplicity' or 'complexity' is how variable rules or probabilistic tendencies play into defining the grammar.

Development of agreement (p. 257)

No one can know this for sure. One possible explanation is that the pronouns *mifala* and *yufala* already have something marking plurality in them (i.e., the suffix *-fala*). As a consequence, the plural marking inherent in *oli* may be redundant. Look again at the pronouns in Table 11.3 and decide whether you think this argument is consistent with all the data.

Glossary

Accent Where speakers differ (or vary) at the level of pronunciation only (phonetics and/or phonology), they have different accents. Their grammar may be wholly or largely the same. Accents can *index* a speaker's regional/geographic origin, or social factors such as level and type of education, or even their attitude.

Accommodation The process by which speakers *attune* or adapt their linguistic behaviour in light of their interlocutors' behaviour and their attitudes towards their interlocutors (may be a conscious or unconcious process). Encompasses both *convergence* with or *divergence* from interlocutors' norms. (See also *Social identity theory.*)

Acquiring (language) It is sometimes useful to distinguish between the natural acquisition of a language variety (e.g., a mother tongue) and learning of a language variety (e.g., in the classroom).

Active knowledge Knowledge of a linguistic *variety* that includes the ability to produce and use that variety, and not only understand it. (See also *Passive knowledge.*)

Acts of identity LePage's proposal that *intraspeaker* variation is a result of the speaker's desire to present or foreground a different social identity under different circumstances. Strongly associated with LePage's work on *creole* language speakers who often display extensive variation between consistent use of the *vernacular* norms of a creole and the standard variety of the *lexifier*. Contrasts with *attention to*

speech and *accommodation*-based models of style-shifting such as *audience design*.

Age-grading If, as a rule, all speakers of a community use more tokens of one variant at a certain age and more tokens of another variant at another age, the variable is said to be age-graded.

Ageing deficits Changes in individuals' performance in later stages of their lifespan. 'Deficits' refers to impaired performance on tasks or activities compared with younger speakers (e.g., recall, hearing). Focused on more than improvements that are associated with increased age (e.g., narrative skill, vocabulary).

Apparent time The apparent passage of time is measured by comparing speakers of different ages in a single-speech community at a single time. If younger speakers behave differently from older speakers, it is assumed that change has taken place within the community. The apparent time construct relies on the assumption that speakers only minimally change the way they speak after the *critical period* or in adulthood. A useful method where *real time* data is absent.

Attention to speech Labov proposed that the different distribution of forms in different *styles* was motivated by the amount of attention the speaker was paying to the act of speaking. In activities, such as reading aloud, reading word lists or minimal pairs, Labov argued that speakers are paying more attention to their speech than they are in interviews and in interviews they paid more attention than when conversing with friends and family. Contrasts with *accommodation*-based accounts of style-shifting such as *audience design*. Also contrasts with more agentive theories of style-shifting such as *acts of identity*.

Attunement A term sometimes preferred over *accommodation* because of the strong (but incorrect) association of the specific strategy *convergence* with the more general phenomenon of *accommodation*. Just as instruments in an orchestra have to be in tune with each other, speakers attune their behaviour to the situation and in relation to the way their interlocutors are behaving.

Audience design Derived from *accommodation* theory. Proposal that *intraspeaker variation* arises because speakers are paying attention to who they are addressing or who might be listening to or overhearing them, and modify their speech accordingly.

Bald, on record A technical term in Brown and Levinson's theory of *politeness*. Refers to an *inherently face-threatening act* made without any softening through *positive* or *negative politeness strategies*. Notice they do not call this 'impolite'.

Broad stratification A distribution of variants – for example, across groups of speakers in different styles – which shows each group of speakers patterning markedly differently from each other in each style. Shows up as a big gap between *trend* lines on a line graph.

Brokers The people who introduce innovations into *social networks*.

Caste systems Relatively fixed social groups. A person is usually born into a particular caste and the possibilities for movement out of it are limited. (See also *Social class*.)

Change from above Changes taking place in a *speech community* above the level of individuals' conscious awareness. Able

to be commented on. One *variant* is clearly standard or has clear *overt prestige*. It does **not** refer to changes led by higher social classes (though this may often be the case). (See also *Change from below*.)

Change from below Changes taking place in a *speech community* below the level of conscious awareness. Not the subject of overt comment. It does **not** refer to changes led by lower social classes. (See also *Change from above*.)

Code mixing Generally refers to alternations between varieties, or codes, within a clause or phrase. Often elicits more strongly negative evaluations than alternations or *code switching* across clauses.

Code switching In its most specific sense, the alternation between varieties, or codes, across sentences or clause boundaries. Often used as a cover term including *code mixing* as well.

Collectivist A collectivist society emphasises the relationships and interdependence of the individuals it is comprised of (cf. *individualistic*). (See also *Wakimae*.)

Communication accommodation The full term for *accommodation* in which accommodation between individuals' linguistic behaviour is seen as only one way in which individuals may *converge* or *diverge* from each other.

Community of practice Unit of analysis introduced to sociolinguistics by Penelope Eckert and Sally McConnell-Ginet in their research on language and gender. A smaller unit than a *social network*. Co-membership is defined on three criteria: mutual engagement, a jointly negotiated enterprise, and a shared repertoire. Associated with analyses of variation that emphasise speakers' agency. (See also *Acts of identity; Speaker design*.)

Community-wide change An entire group or community switch to use of a new *variant* at about the same time.

Competence and performance A distinction drawn by Chomsky. Competence is identified primarily with *grammatical competence* and is understood as the underlying or innate principle from which the structure of all natural languages derive. Performance, or what speakers do with their competence replete with errors and infelicities, is not seen as the primary interest of linguistics. (See also *Pragmatic competence; Sociolinguistic competence*.)

Constitutive The view that a correlation between linguistic behaviour and a non-linguistic factor actually helps to bring about and define (i.e., constitute) the meaning of a social category. Often contrasted with an interpretation of variation as reflecting a social category. (See also *Reflexive*.)

Constrain/constraints If the distribution of *variants* is neither random nor *free*, and instead shows systematic correlations with *independent factors*, those factors can be said to constrain the variation, or to be the constraints on the *variable*.

Contrastive analysis An approach to second-language acquisition that focuses on points of similarity and difference in two varieties. The assumption is that where they differ, learners will have most difficulty.

Conventional implicature An inference that arises from the meaning (or semantics) of a word or phrase. This means if you try to cancel the implicature, it sounds bizarre or can't be understood. (See also *Conversational implicature*.)

Convergence *Accommodation* towards the speech of one's interlocutors. Accentuates similarities between interlocutors' speech styles, and/or makes the speaker sound more like their interlocutor. It is assumed to be triggered by conscious or unconcious desires to emphasise similarity with interlocutors we like, and to increase attraction. (See also *Divergence; Social identity theory*.)

Conversational implicature An infer-ence that arises from interlocutors' shared understanding of the norms of conversation. Not part of the semantics or inherent meaning of a word/phrase. Unlike a *conventional implicature*, you can cancel a conversational implicature (e.g., They have two cats *if not more*.)

Core network member Term used by Jenny Cheshire to describe the members centrally involved and actively participating in a friendship *network*. Distinguished from peripheral and secondary members who were progressively less involved.

Cost of imposition Modified term from Brown and Levinson's *politeness* theory. A scalar measure of how serious a *face-threatening act* is in a particular society, and given the *power* and *distance* difference between speaker and hearer.

Covert prestige A norm or target that is oriented to without the speaker even being aware that they are orienting to it. Evidence of covert prestige can be found in mismatches between speakers' self-report of using one *variant* and actual use of another variant. Often used (wrongly) to refer to the value associated with non-standard or *vernacular* varieties.

Creole A language variety arising out of a situation of language contact (usually involving more than two languages). A creole can be distinguished from a *pidgin*: (i) on the grounds that it is the first language of some community or group of speakers, or (ii) on the grounds that it is used for the entire range of social functions that a language can be used for. (See also *Creolisation; Vernacularisation*.)

Creolisation The process by which a *pidgin* becomes the first language of a group of speakers. The linguistic outcomes of the expansion of the pidgin into a wider range of social functions. (See also *Vernacularisation*.)

Critical period The period during which language learning seems to be easiest;

that is, in childhood and for some people going into early adolescence. Exposure to language outside the critical period usually results in less than native-like acquisition. Some researchers believe the critical period is an artefact of (i) developmental changes in the brain, or (ii) changes in the receptiveness or attitudes of language learners, or (iii) a mixture of physiological and social factors.

Cross-over effect The cross-over effect emerges at the intersection of style and class. Typically it refers to the breakdown in the most careful speech styles of clear *stratification* between speakers of different *social classes*. For example, when reading word lists, speakers from the **second** highest social class will suddenly produce more tokens of an incoming or prestige form than speakers in the **highest** social class do, instead of producing slightly fewer tokens as they do in their conversation or interview styles (cf. *Hypercorrection*).

Dense and loose networks Dense networks are characterised by everyone within the network knowing each other. In loose *social networks* not all members know each other.

Determinism/deterministic The idea that there is a strong causal relationship between two factors (i.e., one determines how the other will be). The idea that if you know the value for one factor, you can automatically and reliably predict the value for another. (See also *Linguistic relativism*.)

Diachronic change Change realised over chronological time.

Dialect A term widely applied to what are considered sub-varieties of a single language. Generally, dialect and *accent* are distinguished by how much of the linguistic system differs. Dialects differ on more than just pronunciation, i.e., on the basis of morphosyntactic structure and/or how semantic relations are mapped into the syntax. (See also *Variety*.)

Dialect levelling Reduction of differences distinguishing regional *dialects or accents*. One possible outcome of contact between speakers of different varieties.

Diglossia Classically defined as a situation where two closely related languages are used in a speech community. One for *High (H)* functions (e.g., church, newspapers) and one for *Low* (L) functions (e.g., in the home, or market). The situation is supposed to be relatively stable and the languages/varieties remain distinct (cf. *creole* outcomes of language contact). Now often extended to refer to any two languages (even typologically unrelated ones) that have this kind of social and functional distribution.

Direct and indirect indexing A relationship of identification. The distinction between direct and indirect indexing was introduced by Elinor Ochs. A linguistic feature *directly indexes* something with social meaning if the social information is a *conventional implicature* (e.g., speaker gender is directly indexed by some forms of some adjectives in French, *je suis* [prɛ] (male speaker); *je suis* [prɛt] (female speaker). However, most variables associated with, e.g., male vs female speakers only *indirectly index* gender. Their distribution is *sex-preferential* not *sex-exclusive*. They are generally associated with several other social meanings, e.g., casualness and vernacularity with masculinity. Because these other factors help to *constitute* what it means to be 'male' the index between vernacular variants and male speakers/masculinity is indirect.

Distance Social distance is a component of Brown and Levinson's *politeness* theory. It refers to horizontal differences between people (cf. *power*). Also spatial distance e.g., between cities in the diffusion of an innovation.

Divergence *Accommodation* away from the speech of one's interlocutors. Accentuates differences between interlocutors' speech styles, and/or makes the speaker sound less like their interlocutor. It is assumed convergence is triggered by conscious or unconcious desires to emphasise difference and increase social distance. (See also *Convergence; Social identity theory.*)

Domain The social and physical setting in which speakers find themselves.

Envelope of variation All, and only, the contexts in which a *variable* occurs.

Evidentials Forms or structures that provide an indication of how the speaker knows the information being conveyed (e.g., direct experience vs reports from a third party).

Exclusive and preferential features An exclusive feature is one associated solely with a particular user or group of users or solely in a particular context. A preferential feature is one that is distributed across speakers or groups, but is used more frequently by some than by others.

Expanded pidgin A term used sometimes instead of *creole* to describe contact varieties that have spent longer as *pidgins* (lacking native speakers) within a community. (See also *Vernacularisation.*)

Face and face wants Erving Goffman's notion of face, our social persona, adopted into politeness theory. Face wants are the desire to protect our *positive face* and *negative face* from threat or damage.

Fine stratification A distribution of variants e.g., across groups of speakers in different styles, which shows each group of speakers patterning minimally differently from each other in each style. Shows up as small gaps between *trend* lines on a line graph.

Free variation The idea that some *variants* alternate with each other without any reliable *constraints* on their occurrence in a particular context or by particular speakers.

Gender Not grammatical gender (i.e., different classes of noun that may be called 'masculine', 'feminine'). Not *sex* of speaker which (largely) reflects biological or physiological differences between people. Used increasingly in sociolinguistics to indicate a social identity that emerges or is constructed through social actions. (See also *Constitutive; Reflexive.*)

Generational change Each generation in a community shows progressively more and more frequent use of a *variant.* A change that can be inferred to be taking place on the basis of *apparent time* evidence is a generational change.

Globalisation The increased contact between people of different social and linguistic backgrounds across broad swathes of geographical space. Commonly portrayed as a recent phenomenon and strongly associated with (and often attributed to) the new communication technologies (e.g., Internet, mass media, etc.). The dominance of a small number of language varieties (in particular US English) is seen as an important factor decreasing the *ethnolinguistic vitality* of lesser-spoken languages worldwide. It is worth bearing in mind that globalisation has been an issue in some parts of the world at least since the colonial period.

Grammatical competence See *Competence and performance.*

Gravity model Model of the diffusion of innovations introduced to sociolinguistics by Peter Trudgill. Social innovations (including linguistic innovations) have been observed to 'hop' between large population centres in a (spatially) discontinuous manner. At its simplest, the gravity model predicts that the larger the city/town, the sooner an innovation is likely to show up there. (i.e., the 'gravitational force' is provided by the weight of numbers of people).

Group differentiation A hypothesised function for language variation. Social (in which we can include regional) varieties *index* group boundaries. In some theories of social psychology differentiation between groups is argued to be an important basis for forming positive self-image.

High (H) variety See *Diglossia*.

Hypercorrection The production of a form which never occurs in a native variety on the basis of the speaker's misanalysis of the input (cf. *Cross-over effect*).

Illocutionary force The force of a *speech act*. Saying 'I promise' has the illocutionary force of promising if the speaker is geuinely committed to what they utter (and is not lying or hoaxing).

Independent factors Many things may correlate with or predict the distribution of different linguistic variants. These factors are *independent* if they have an autonomous effect on the variable. Some factors are *interdependent* and don't exert an independent effect. (See also *Significant/significance*.)

Index score A means by which scalar *variables* like raising of a vowel can be converted into quantifable data. For example, very low *variants* can be assigned a score of 0, and very raised ones a score of 3 with two intermediate levels. Aggregate scores across all tokens allow the researcher to identify some speakers or groups of speakers as more or less conservative/innovative than others.

Indexing See *Direct and indirect indexing*.

Indicator A linguistic *variable* which shows limited or no *style-shifting*. Stratified principally between groups.

Indirect index See *Direct and indirect indexing*.

Individual agency Recent approaches to sociolinguistics have tried to emphasise individuals' freedom of choice in their analyses. Analysts argue that speakers are social actors or agents, (re)defining themselves through linguistic and other social behaviour. (See also *Acts of identity; Community of practice*.)

Individualistic A society that emphasises and celebrates the individual over relationships (cf. *Collectivist*).

Inherent variability A way of modelling variation as a property of the grammar. Contrasts with a model of variation as speakers' (or a speaker's) alternation between different sound or grammar systems (see *code switching*). Also contrasts with the notion of *free variation*. Inherent variability unifies *interspeaker* and *intraspeaker* variation in ways that the other two approaches do not.

Inherently face-threatening acts *Speech acts* which necessarily threaten the speaker's and/or hearer's *positive face* and/or *negative face*. In Brown and Levison's framework, they require the speaker to decide whether or not to mitigate the threat and which *politeness strategies* to use.

Interlocutor The people who are talking together are each other's interlocutors.

Interdependent factors Many things may correlate with or predict the distribution of different linguistic variants. Some factors bundle together and can be said to be interdependent. This means that for every possible combination of the factors may not actually be attested, only a sub-set of combinations. As a consequence you can predict or rule out some factors if you know another factor. For example, the linguistic factors place and manner of articulation are interdependent, so for English if you know you are dealing with an initial nasal, you can predict that it will be either /m/ or /n/ and will not be /ŋ/.

Intermediate forms Forms emerging following contact between closely related varieties that fall in between the various input forms.

Interspeaker variation Differences and variation that is measured between different speakers (individuals or social groups).

Intraspeaker variation Differences in the way a single person speaks at different times, or with different *interlocutors*, or even within a sentence. Intraspeaker variation is a necessary corollary of *inherent variability* in grammars.

Laminated Erving Goffman's term to refer to the way aspects of the context or the identity of the participants compound, reinforce and add depth to the meaning of each other.

Language attitudes The study of what people think about different linguistic varieties and how those perceptions about language relate to perceptions of attitudes about different users of language.

Learning (language) See *Acquiring (language)*.

Lexifier The language that has provided most of the vocabulary (i.e., lexicon) to a *pidgin* or *creole*.

Lifespan change A term introduced to the study of language variation and change by Gillian Sankoff. A change to a speaker's pronunciation or grammar that takes place after the *critical period* can be described as a lifespan change. Lifespan changes in pronunciation appear to be severely restricted in their form: they generally only move in the direction of the community overall (see also *Generational change*) and they may also be *constrained* to certain input or starting points for a speaker. On the other hand, lifespan change is well-attested for vocabulary.

Lingua franca Language used as a common means of communication among people whose native languages are mutually unintelligible.

Linguistic and non-linguistic factors Sometimes referred to as 'internal' and 'external' factors respectively. The distribution of the *variants* of a *variable* may be *constrained* by or depend on other factors in the linguistic system. (For example: Is the subject a pronoun or a full NP? Is the following phonological segment coronal or velar?) The distribution may also be constrained by factors that lie outside of the grammar or core linguistic system. (For example: Is the speaker talking to a close friend or a stranger? Is there a lot of background noise?)

Linguistic insecurity Speakers' feeling that the variety they use is somehow inferior, ugly or bad. Negative attitudes to one's own variety expressed in aesthetic or moral terms.

Linguistic marketplace A way of talking about the extent to which an occupation or activity is associated with use of the standard language.

Linguistic relativism Weaker position than *determinism*. Holds that the value of one factor is not wholly independent of the value of another factor, but instead is somehow *constrained* by it. Associated with the Sapir–Whorf hypothesis which suggests that the way we perceive the world around us is in some way reflected in the way we talk. (See also *Reflexive*.)

Loose networks See *Dense and loose networks*.

Low (L) variety See *Diglossia*.

Marker A *variable* that speakers are less aware of than a *stereotype*, but which shows consistent style effects. (See also *Indicator*.)

Monotonic A steady increase or decrease in a feature along the x-axis of a graph. (See also *Trend*.)

Motivation Some linguists believe there are social or psychological factors which drive or motivate variation. Speakers of a language may be able to talk about the different goals, intentions or motivations that are served by using one *variant* rather than another, but some motivations may be subconscious and not available for such comment.

Multiplex and uniplex ties Individuals in a social network can be linked through a single social relationship (a uniplex tie; e.g., mother~daughter) or through several social relationships (multiplex ties; e.g., cousins~co-workers~neighbours).

National language A linguistic *variety* that has been chosen by a nation as the language expressing or representing national identity.

Negative concord A language where a negative element/constituent in a sentence requires all other indefinites to also be negative has a rule of negative concord.

Negative face The want of every competent adult member of a community that their actions be unimpeded by others. 'Don't tread on me.'

Negative politeness strategy An action, phrase or utterance that indicates attention is being paid to the *negative face wants* of an *interlocutor*. Often achieved through shows of deference. One type of action available to mitigate an *inherently face-threatening act*. (See also *Positive politeness strategy*.)

Observer's paradox The double-bind researchers find themselves in when what they are interested in knowing is how people behave when they are not being observed, but the only way to find out how they behave is to observe them.

Official language A linguistic *variety* that has been designated as the medium for all official, government business. There is usually a right to have all legal and public services provided in an official language, and an obligation on state or regional authorities to satisfy this right.

Overt prestige The prestige associated with a *variant* that speakers are aware of and can talk about in terms of standardness, or aesthetic and moral evaluations like being 'nicer' or 'better'. (See also *Covert prestige*.)

Panel studies Studies of variation across *real time* when the participants are held constant. (cf. *Trend studies*.)

Participant observation The practice of spending longer periods of time with speakers observing how they use language, react to others' use of it, and how language interacts with and is embedded in other social practices and ideologies. A means of gathering qualitative data rather than quantitative data.

Passive knowledge The ability to understand, but not speak, a language. (See also *Active knowledge*.)

Perceptual dialectology The study of people's subjectively held beliefs about different dialects or linguistic varieties. The focus on lay perceptions about language complements the regional dialectologists' more objective focus on the way people are recorded as speaking.

Performative/performativity Judith Butler argued that gender is performative in the sense that the iteration of actions and ways of talking in a social context acquires *constitutive* force within a community. This underlies the social meaning associated with actions, events or categories.

Peripheral network members See *Core network members*.

Pidgin Generally, a language variety that is not very linguistically complex or elaborated and is used in fairly restricted social domains and for limited social or interpersonal functions. Like a *creole*, arises from language contact; often seen as a precursor or early stage to a creole. It is often said that pidgin can be distinguished from a creole in having no native speakers.

Politeness The actions taken by competent speakers in a community in order to attend to possible social or interpersonal disturbance. (See also *Wakamae*.)

Positive face The want of every competent adult member of a community that their wants be desirable to at least some others. 'Love me, love my dog.'

Positive politeness strategies An action, phrase or utterance that indicates attention is being paid to the *positive face wants* of an *interlocutor*. Often achieved through shows of friendliness. One type of action available to mitigate an *inherently face-threatening act*. (See also *Negative politeness strategy*.)

Power A vertical relationship between speaker and hearer in Brown and Levinson's theory of *politeness*. Along with *distance* and *cost of imposition*, power determines how much and what kind of redressive action the speaker might take with a face-threatening act.

Pragmatic competence The ability of a well-socialised speaker to know when certain speech acts are required, appropriate or inappropriate. A competence required over and above *grammatical competence* in order to successfully participate as a member of a speech community. (See also *Sociolinguistic competence*.)

Preferential differences If a feature or variant is found only in the speech of some speakers, it is exclusively associated with them. If it is found more or less frequently in the speech of any member of the community, but occurs more often in the speech of some group of speakers, it is preferentially associated with them. (See also *Direct and indirect indexing; Exclusive differences*.)

Principle of accountability Refers to accountability to accurately represent our data. All tokens must be included in a linguistic analysis, rather than focusing solely on the most typical uses, or only on examples that require very subtle, decontextualised judgements.

Principle of maximum differentiation An idea that there may be functional *constraints* on phonological variation preventing the realisations of one phoneme overlapping or encroaching too much on the realisations of another.

Probability/probabilistic The likelihood with which a *variant* will occur in a given context, subject to the linguistic and non-linguistic *constraints*. An adjustment on raw frequencies of forms.

Quotative verbs Verbs introducing reports of discourse (e.g., direct and indirect speech or thought). They include older, more stable variants such as *say* and *think*, as well as newer ones such as *be like, be all*.

Rapid and anonymous study A questionnaire used to gather data quickly in the public domain. (See also *Sociolinguistic interview; Triangulation*.)

Real time Augustinian time. The passing of years, hours, minutes and seconds that we measure with calendars and clocks and that we think we understand until we really think about it.

Reallocate/reallocation Reassignment or reanalysis of forms in contact in a systematic way, e.g., as allophonically distributed *variants* of a phoneme.

Reflexive The view that a correlation between linguistic behaviour and a non-linguistic factor is due to the fact that language reflects identification with a social category or a personal stance. Often contrasted with *constitutive* interpretation of variation.

Regional dialectology The identification and mapping of boundaries between different varieties on the basis of clusters of similar and different features in particular regions, towns or villages.

Salient/salience A maddeningly under-defined term when used in sociolinguistics. Sometimes refers to how readily a particular variant is perceived/heard (this may be due to physiological factors affecting perception, or social and psychological factors that affect prime speakers and make them attend to a form). Sometimes refers to a non-linguistic factor that the context or participants appear to have foregrounded in discourse.

Secondary network members See *Core network members*.

Semantic derogation *Semantic shift* that results in a word acquiring more negative associations or meanings.

Semantic shift Incremental changes to the meaning of a word or phrase. Sometimes included within the scope of grammaticalisation (or grammaticisation) theory, but unlike classic grammaticalisation, semantic shift need not entail structural reanalysis of the word/phrase. That is, a verb might stay a verb but its meaning might be severely weakened or altered over time.

Sex No, not **that** kind of sex. The term is increasingly restricted in sociolinguistics to refer to a biologically or physiologically based distinction between males and females, as opposed to the more social notion of *gender*.

Shibboleth A linguistic feature that is used to differentiate between groups.

Significant/significance Significance has a technical sense, in which it is a statistical measure. The distribution of a variant is said to be statistically significant if it is unlikely to have arisen just by chance. Sociolinguists generally follow normal social science practice and require that tests show there is less than a 5 per cent chance that the distribution of a variable in relation to other factors might be simply a coincidence before they will claim there is a significant correlation or patterning between the variant and some independent factor.

Situation(al) A more idiosyncratic and personalised view of the context or situation of language use (cf. *domain*). In this text, used to describe one of the motivations for *code switching*.

Social class A measure of *status* which is often based on occupation, income and wealth, but also can be measured in terms of aspirations and mobility. These factors can then be used to group individuals scoring similarly on these factors into socioeconomic classes.

Social dialectology The study of linguistic variation in relation to speakers' participation or membership in social groups, or in relation to other *non-linguistic factors*.

Social distance See *Distance*.

Social identity theory A social psychological theory holding that people identify with multiple identities, some of which are more personal and idiosyncratic and some of which are group identifications. Experimental work in this framework suggests that people readily see contrasts between groups in terms of competition, and seek to find means of favouring the co-members of the group they identify with over others.

Social meaning Inferences about speakers or the *variety* they use and the interpretations we draw about how those speakers are positioned in *social space* because of this.

Social networks Introduced to sociolinguistics by Jim and Lesley Milroy. Social networks provide an alternative basis for studying the systematic variation of language to the *speech community*. Networks are defined by contact between members; however, not all members may know each other, the network connections may be distributive (*dense and loose networks*) and some members may know each other in a different capacity from others (*multiplex and uniplex ties*).

Social space How a community perceives boundaries between established or emergent groups within it, and individuals' (externally or internally perceived) position in relation to those groups. Questions like 'Where does a person come from?', 'What kind of education have they had?', 'How much have they moved around in their youth?' help locate a person in social space.

Sociolinguistic competence The skills and resources speakers need to deploy in order to be competent members of a speech community using language, not only grammatically but appropriately in different contexts, *domains* or with different *interlocutors*. (See also *Grammatical competence; Pragmatic competence*.)

Sociolinguistic interview An interview, usually one on one, in which different tasks or activities are used to elicit different styles of speech. (You will sometimes hear it used simply to refer to a one-on-one interview lasting at least an hour covering a range of topics.)

Sociolinguistics The study of language in use, language in society. The field of sociolinguistics is a big tent: it can encompass work done in discourse analysis, studies of interaction, sociology, anthropology, cultural studies, feminism, etc. It can also be used much more restrictively to only refer to variationist studies in the Labovian tradition. For this reason, when you come across the term, it is worth stopping long enough to work out how the writer/speaker is using it.

Speaker design A further approach to analysing *style-shifting*. Stresses the speaker's desire to represent her/himself in certain ways. (See also *Acts of identity*.)

Speech acts Utterances which, in saying, do something.

Speech community Variously defined on subjective or objective criteria. Objective criteria would group speakers together in a speech community if the distribution of a variable was consistent with respect to other factors (e.g., style). Subjective criteria would group speakers as a speech community if they shared a sense of and belief in co-membership.

Speech levels Replacement of vocabulary with sometimes radically different forms in the different styles associated with different social groups or *castes*.

Stable variable If there is no evidence (e.g., from *generational change*) that one variant is pushing out another variant, the variable can be considered stable. A classic example is the alternation between the alveolar and velar nasals in the word-final *-ing* which has existed for centuries and shows no signs of disappearing at present. Stable variables may exhibit *age-grading* (i.e., avoidance of a stigmatised variant in adulthood).

Status Max Weber's theory of *social class* held that it was based on a person's status, measured in terms of their lifestyle and life choices in addition to measures of wealth and occupation (as per Marx).

Stereotype A linguistic feature that is widely recognised and is very often the subject of (not always strictly accurate!) dialect performances and impersonations.

Stratified The systematic and consistent patterning of a variant with respect to some independent factor, e.g., style, age, class. See *Broad* and *Fine stratification*.

Style-shifting Variation in an individual's speech correlating with differences in addressee, social context, personal goals or externally imposed task.

Subjective and objective measures A speaker's perceptions of their own performance and their performance evaluated by some external measure.

Substrate The languages other than the *lexifier* that are present in *pidgin* or *creole* formation. The substrate languages often contribute to the grammatical structure of a creole, or they may constrain the semantics of words that have been taken over from the lexifier – e.g., *han* meaning 'hand' and 'arm' in Bislama (same denotation as equivalent words in the Eastern Oceanic languages of Vanuatu) and not the more restricted sense of English *hand*.

Symmetric and asymmetric accommodation *Symmetric accommodation* means both interlocutors converge or diverge.

Asymmetric means one interlocutor converges while the other diverges (can be motivated by mismatch in how interlocutors perceive the interaction).

Synchronic variation Variation occurring now.

Trend Steady increase or decrease in the frequency of a form across a scale or set of measures. (See also *Monotonic.*)

Trend studies A trend study involves comparing speech from members of the same community at different points in time. (See also *Panel studies; Real time.*)

Triangulation A researcher's use of several independent tests to confirm their results and aid in the interpretation of their results. For example, use of data from *sociolinguistic interviews* and a *rapid and anonymous study.*

Uniplex tie A network tie between individuals that expresses one role or basis for contact and interaction. (See also *Multiplex tie.*)

Variable In this text, principally an abstract representation of the source of variation. Realised by two or more *variants.*

Variant The actual realisation of a *variable.* Analogous to the phonetic realisations of a phoneme.

Variationist sociolinguistics The study of language in use with a focus on describing and explaining the distribution of *variables.* An approach strongly associated with quantitative methods in the tradition established by William Labov.

Variety Relatively neutral term used to refer to languages and dialects. Avoids the problem of drawing a distinction between the two, and avoids negative attitudes often attached to the term *dialect.*

Vernacular In this text, usually used to refer neutrally to the linguistic *variety* used by a speaker or a community as the medium for everyday and home interaction. In some linguistic work the term may be associated with the notion of non-standard norms.

Vernacularisation The process by which a contact variety becomes used with the full range of social and personal functions served by a language of the home. Also the linguistic changes associated with the expansion of the variety in this way. (See also *Creolisation.*)

Vitality ethnolinguistic A measure of the strength and liveliness of a language, usually a good indicator of the likelihood that it will gradually die out or continue to be used as the living language of a community. Measured in terms of demographic, social and institutional support.

Wakimae A Japanese term introduced to the study of *politeness* by Sachiko Ide. Refers to the attention paid to people's interdependence and to the reciprocity of relationships, and, specifically, the discernment of appropriate behaviour based on this.

Wave model The theory that language change emanates from a single starting point and is gradually incorporated into the speech of the nearest neighbours.

Weighting An adjustment that can be made to raw frequencies of a *variant* so as to take into account any biases or skewing of its overall distribution. Expresses the *probability* or likelihood with which a variant will occur in a given linguistic environment or with a given non-linguistic factor.

Bibliography

Aberle, David F. (1966) *The Peyote Religion among the Navaho.* New York: Wenner-Gren Foundation for Anthropological Research.

Aikhenvald, Alexandra Y. (2002) *Language Contact in Amazonia.* Oxford: Oxford University Press.

Aikhenvald, Alexandra Y. (2003) Multilingualism and ethnic stereotypes: the Tariana of northwest Amazonia. *Language and Society* 32: 1–21.

Ammon, Ulrich, Norbert Dittmar, Klaus J. Mattheier and Peter Trudgill (eds) (2005) *Sociolinguistics/Soziolinguistik: An International Handbook of the Science of Language and Society/Ein internationales Handbuch zur Wissenschaft von Sprache und Gesellschaft.* Berlin: de Gruyter.

Ash, Sharon (2002) Social class. In J.K. Chambers, Peter Trudgill and Natalie Schilling-Estes (eds) *The Handbook of Language Variation and Change.* Oxford: Blackwell, 402–422.

Auer, Peter (ed.) (1998) *Code-switching in Conversation: Language, Interaction and Identity.* London/New York: Routledge.

Bailey, Guy (2002) Real and apparent time. In J.K. Chambers, Peter Trudgill and Natalie Schilling-Estes (eds) *The Handbook of Language Variation and Change.* Oxford: Blackwell, 312–332.

Bailey, Guy, Tom Wilke, Jan Tillery and Lori Sand (1993) Some patterns of linguistic diffusion. *Language Variation and Change* 5: 359–390.

Bakir, Murtadha (1986) Sex differences in the approximation to Standard Arabic: a case study. *Anthropological Linguistics* 28: 1.

Barker, Valerie, Howard Giles, Kimberly Noels, Julie Duck and Michael Hecht (2001) The English-only movement: a communication analysis of changing perceptions of language vitality. *Journal of Communication* 51: 3–37.

Barrett, Rusty (1998) Markedness and style-switching in performances by African American drag queens. In Carol Myers-Scotton (ed.) *Codes and Consequences: Choosing Linguistic Varieties.* New York/Oxford: Oxford University Press, 139–161.

Batterham, Margaret (2000) The apparent merger of the front centering diphthongs – EAR and AIR – in New Zealand English. In Allan Bell and Koenraad Kuiper (eds) *New Zealand English.* Wellington: Victoria University Press, 111–145.

Baugh, John (1979) Linguistic style-shifting in Black English. Unpublished Ph.D. dissertation, University of Pennsylvania.

Baugh, John (2000) Racial identification by speech. *American Speech* 75: 362–364.

Beebe, Leslie M. (1981) Social and situational factors affecting the communicative strategy of dialect code-switching. *International Journal of the Sociology of Language* 32: 139–149.

Bell, Allan (1984) Language style as audience design. *Language in Society* 13: 145–204.

Bell, Allan (1990) Audience and referee design in New Zealand media language. In Allan Bell and Janet Holmes (eds) *New Zealand Ways of Speaking English*. Wellington: Victoria University Press, 165–194.

Bell, Allan (1991) *The Language of News Media*. Oxford: Blackwell.

Bell, Allan (2000) Maori and Pakeha English: a case study. In Allan Bell and Koenraad Kuiper (eds) *New Zealand English*. Wellington: Victoria University Press/Amsterdam: John Benjamins, 221–248.

Bender, Emily M. (2001) Syntactic variation and linguistic competence: the case of AAVE copula absence. Unpublished Ph.D. dissertation, Stanford University.

Besnier, Niko (2003) Crossing gender, mixing languages: the linguistics construction of transgenderism in Tonga. In Janet Holmes and Miriam Meyerhoff (eds) *Handbook of Language and Gender*. Oxford: Blackwell, 279–301.

Biber, Douglas (1995) *Dimensions of Register Variation: A Cross-linguistic Comparison*. Cambridge: Cambridge University Press.

Bickerton, Derek (1981) *Roots of Language*. Ann Arbor, Mich.: Karoma.

Billig, Michael (1995) *Banal Nationalism*. London: Sage.

Blake, Renée and Meredith Josey (2003) The /ay/ diphthong in a Martha's Vineyard community. *Language in Society* 32: 451–485.

Blondeau, Hélène, Gillian Sankoff and Anne Charity (2003) Parcours individuels et changements linguistiques en cours dans la communaté francophone montréalaise. *Revue Québécoise de Linguistique* 31: 13–38.

Bloomfield, Leonard (1933) *Language*. New York: Holt, Reinhart & Winston.

Blum-Kulka, Shoshana (1997) Dinner talk : cultural patterns of sociability and socialization in family discourse. Mahwah, N.J./London: Lawrence Erlbaum.

Boberg, Charles (2000) Geolinguistic diffusion and the U.S.–Canada border. *Language Variation and Change* 12: 1–24.

Bourdieu, Pierre (1990) *Language and Symbolic Power*. Cambridge: Polity Press (in association with Blackwell).

Britain, David (1997) Dialect contact, focusing and phonological rule complexity: the koineisation of Fenland English. *Penn Working Papers in Linguistics: A selection of papers from NWAVE 25*, 4: 141–169.

Britain, David (2003a) Exploring the importance of the outlier in sociolinguistic dialectology. In David Britain and Jenny Cheshire (eds) *Social Dialectology: In Honour of Peter Trudgill*. Amsterdam/Philadelphia: John Benjamins, 191–208.

Britain, David (2003b) Space and spatial diffusion. In J.K. Chambers, Peter Trudgill and Natalie Schilling-Estes (eds) *The Handbook of Language Variation and Change*. Oxford: Blackwell, 603–637.

Britain, David and Peter Trudgill (forthcoming) *Dialects in Contact* (2nd edn). Oxford: Blackwell.

Brown, Penelope and Stephen Levinson (1987) *Politeness: Some Universals in Language Use*. Cambridge: Cambridge University Press.

Bucholtz, Mary (1998) Social categories and local identities in the California vowel shift. Paper presented at NWAVE 27, October, Athens, Ga.

Buchstaller, Isabelle (2004) The sociolinguistic constraints on the quotative system: British English and US English compared. Unpublished Ph.D. dissertation, University of Edinburgh.

Burchfield, Robert (ed.) (1986) *The New Zealand Pocket Oxford Dictionary*. Auckland: Oxford University Press.

Bynon, Theodora (1977) *Historical Linguistics*. Cambridge: Cambridge University Press.

Callary, R.E. (1975) Phonological change and the development of an urban dialect in Illinois. *Language in Society* 4: 155–170.

Cameron, Deborah (1997) Performing gender identity: young men's talk and the construction of heterosexual masculinity. In Sally Johnson and Ulrike Hana Meinhof (eds) *Language and Masculinity*. Oxford: Blackwell, 47–64.

Cameron, Deborah (2000) *Good to Talk: Living and Working in a Communication Culture*. London: Sage Publications.

Cameron, Deborah and Don Kulick (2003) *Language and Sexuality*. Cambridge: Cambridge University Press.

Cameron, Richard (1998) A variable syntax of speech, gesture, and sound effect: direct quotations in Spanish. *Language Variation and Change* 10: 43–83.

Cameron, Richard (2005) Aging and gendering. *Language in Society* 34: 23–61.

Carroll, Lewis (1970) *The Annotated Alice: Alice's Adventures in Wonderland and Through the Looking Glass*. Introduction and notes by Martin Gardner (rev. edn). Harmondsworth: Penguin.

Cassell, Justine (1994) The role of beliefs about gender stereotypes in the acquisition of gendered words. *Noga*. (No other information available, even from author.)

Chambers, J.K. (2003) *Sociolinguistic Theory* (2nd edn). Oxford/New York: Blackwell.

Chambers, J.K. and Peter Trudgill (1998) *Dialectology* (2nd edn). Cambridge: Cambridge University Press.

Chambers, J.K., Peter Trudgill and Natalie Schilling-Estes (2001) *The Handbook of Language Variation and Change*. Oxford: Blackwell.

Cheshire, Jenny (1982) *Variations in an English Dialect: A Sociolinguistic Study*. Cambridge: Cambridge University Press.

Cornips, Leonie and Karen Corrigan (2005) *Syntax and Variation: Reconciling the Biological and the Social*. Amsterdam/Philadelphia: John Benjamins.

Coulmas, Florian (1997) *The Handbook of Sociolinguistics*. Oxford: Blackwell.

Coupland, Nikolas (1984) Accommodation at work: some phonological data and their implications. *International Journal of the Sociology of Language* 46: 49–70.

Coupland, Nikolas (2001) Language, situation, and the relational self: theorizing dialect-style in sociolinguistics. In Penelope Eckert and John R. Rickford (eds) *Style and Sociolinguistic Variation*. Cambridge: Cambridge University Press, 185–210.

Coupland, Nikolas, Justine Coupland, Howard Giles, Karen Henwood and John Wiemann (1988) Elderly self-disclosure: interactional and intergroup issues. *Language and Communication* 8: 108–133.

Crowley, Terry (1990) *From Beach-la-Mar to Bislama: The Emergence of a National Language*. Oxford: Oxford University Press.

Cukor-Avila, Patricia and Guy Bailey (2001) The effects of the race of the interviewer on sociolinguistic fieldwork. *Journal of Sociolinguistics* 5: 254–270.

Cutler, Cecilia (2002) The authentic speaker revisited: a look at ethnic perception data from white hip hoppers. Paper presented at NWAV 31, October, Stanford University.

Di Paolo, Marianna (1988) Pronunciation and categorization in sound change. In Kathleen Ferrara *et al.* (eds) *Linguistic Change and Contact: NWAV-XVI*. Austin: Department of Linguistics, University of Texas, 84–92.

Dodsworth, Robin (2005) Atrribute networking: a technique for modeling social perceptions. *Journal of Sociolinguistics* 9: 225–253.

Early, Robert (1999) Double trouble, and three is a crowd: languages in education and official languages in Vanuatu. *Journal of Multilingual and Multicultural Development* 20: 13–33.

Eckert, Penelope (1989) The whole woman: sex and gender differences in variation. *Language Variation and Change* 1: 245–267.

Eckert, Penelope (2000) *Linguistic Variation as Social Practice*. Oxford: Blackwell.

Eckert, Penelope and Sally McConnell-Ginet (1992) Think practically and look locally: language and gender as community-based practice. *Annual Review of Anthropology* 21: 461–490.

Eckert, Penelope and Sally McConnell-Ginet (1999) New generalizations and explanations in language and gender research. *Language in Society* 28, 2: 185–201.

Eckert, Penelope and Sally McConnell-Ginet (2003) *Language and Gender*. Cambridge: Cambridge University Press.

Eckert, Penelope and John R. Rickford (eds) (2001) *Style and Sociolinguistic Variation*. Cambridge: Cambridge University Press.

Edwards, John (ed.) (1998) *Language in Canada*. Cambridge: Cambridge University Press.

Eelen, Gino (2001) *A Critique of Politeness Theories*. Manchester: St Jerome.

Ethnologue: Languages of the world. <http://www.ethnologue.com/>

Fasold, Ralph (1990) *Sociolinguistics of Language*. Oxford: Blackwell.

Ferguson, Charles (1959) Diglossia. *Word* 15: 325–340. (Reprinted in Dell Hymes (ed.) (1964) *Language in Culture and Society*. New York: Harper&Row, 429–437.)

Fought, Carmen (1999) I'm not from nowhere: negative concord in Chicano English. Paper presented at NWAVE 28, October, York University/University of Toronto.

Foulkes, Paul, Gerry Docherty and Dominic Watt (1999) Tracking the emergence of structured variation: realisations of (t) by Newcastle children. *Leeds Working Papers in Linguistics and Phonetics* 7: 1–25.

Francis, W.N. (1983) *Dialectology: An Introduction*. London/New York: Longman.

Gafaranga, Joseph (1998) Elements of order in bilingual talk: Kinyarwanda-French language alternation. Unpublished Ph.D. dissertation. Lancaster University.

Gallois, Cynthia, Howard Giles, Elizabeth Jones, Aaron C. Cargile and Hiroshi Ota (1995) Accommodating intercultural encounters: elaborations and extensions. In Richard L. Wiseman (ed.) *Intercultural Communication Theory*. Thousand Oaks/London/New Delhi: Sage Publications, 115–147.

Gauchat, Louis (1905) L'unité phonétique dans le patois d'une commune. In *Aus Romanischen Sprachen und Literaturen: Festschrift Henrich Mort*. Halle: Max Niemeyer, 175–232.

Gendai Nihongo Kenkyukai (ed.) (1999) *Josee no kotoba: Shokuba-hen* [Women's language: at work place]. Tokyo: Hitsuji-shobo.

Gendai Nihongo Kenkyukai (ed.) (2002) *Dansee no kotoba: Shokuba-hen* [Men's language: at work place]. Tokyo: Hitsuji-shobo.

Giles, Howard (1973) Accent mobility: a model and some data. *Anthropological Linguistics* 15: 87–105.

Giles, Howard and Nikolas Coupland (1991) *Language: Contexts and Consequences*. Pacific Grove, Calif.: Brooks/Cole.

Giles, Howard, Richard Y. Bourhis and D.M. Taylor (1977) Towards a theory of language in ethnic group relations. In Howard Giles (ed.) *Language, Ethnicity and Intergroup Relations*. London/New York: Academic Press, 307–348.

Goffman, Erving (1981) *Forms of Talk*. Philadelphia: University of Pennsylvania Press.

Gordon, Elizabeth (1997) Sex, speech, and stereotypes: why women use prestige forms more than men. *Language in Society* 26: 47–63.

Gordon, Elizabeth, Lyle Campbell, Jennifer Hay, Margaret Maclagan, Andrea Sudbury and Peter Trudgill (2004) *New Zealand English: Its Origins and Evolution.* Cambridge: Cambridge University Press.

Gumperz, John J. and Robert Wilson (1971) Convergence and creolization: a case study from the Aryan/Dravidian border in India. In Dell Hymes (ed.) *Pidginization and Creolization of Languages.* Cambridge: Cambridge University Press, 151–167.

Guy, Gregory R. (1988) Language and social class. In Frederick Newmeyer (ed.) *Language: The Socio-cultural Context.* Cambridge: Press Syndicate of the University of Cambridge, 37–63.

Guy, Gregory (1997) Violable is variable: optimality theory and linguistic variation. *Language Variation and Change* 9: 333–347.

Hachimi, Atiqa (2001) Shifting sands: language and gender in Moroccan Arabic. In Marlis Hellinger and Hadumod Bussman (eds) *Gender Across Languages: The Linguistic Representation of Women and Men,* Vol. 1. Amsterdam/Philadelphia: John Benjamins, 27–51.

Haeri, Niloofar (1994) A linguistic innovation of women in Cairo. *Language Variation and Change* 6: 87–112.

Haeri, Niloofar (2003) *Sacred Language, Ordinary People: Dilemmas of Culture and Politics in Egypt.* New York/Basingstoke: Palgrave Macmillan.

Hall, Kira (2003) Exceptional speakers: contested and problematized gender identities. In Janet Holmes and Miriam Meyerhoff (eds) *The Handbook of Language and Gender.* Oxford: Blackwell, 353–380.

Hall, Kira and Mary Bucholtz (eds) (1995) *Gender Articulated: Language and the Socially Constructed Self.* New York: Routledge.

Harwood, Jake (2006) Aging and language. In Keith Brown (ed.) *Encyclopedia of Language and Linguistics* (2nd edn). Oxford: Elsevier, 116–119.

Hay, Jennifer, Stefanie Jannedy and Norma Mendoza-Denton (1999) Oprah and /ay/: lexical frequency, referee design and style. In *Proceedings of the 14th International Congress of Phonetic Sciences, 1999.* Berkeley: University of California.

Hellinger, Marlis and Hadumod Bussmann (eds) (2001–2003) *Gender Across Languages,* Vols 1–3. Amsterdam/Philadelphia: John Benjamins.

Henderson, Anita (2001) Is your money where your mouth is? Hiring managers' attitudes toward African-American Vernacular English. Unpublished Ph.D. dissertation, University of Pennsylvania.

Henderson, Anita (2003) What's in a slur? *American Speech* 78: 52–74.

Hermann, M.E. (1929) Lautveränderungen in der Individualsprache einer Mundart. *Nachrichten der Gesellschaft der Wissenshaften zu Göttingen, Philosophisch-historische Klasse* 11: 195–214.

Hinskens, Frans, Jeffrey L. Kallen and Johan Taeldeman (2000) Merging and drifting apart: convergence and divergence of dialects across political borders. *International Journal of the Sociology of Language* 145: 1–28.

Hoban, Russell (1980) *Riddley Walker.* London: Picador.

Hockett, Charles (1958) *A Course in Theoretical Linguistics.* New York: Macmillan.

Hofstede, Geert (1980) *Culture's Consequences: International Differences in Work-related Values.* Beverly Hills, Calif.: Sage Publications.

Holmes, Janet (1982) The functions of tag questions. *English Language Research Journal* 3: 40–65.

Holmes, Janet (1995) Two for /t/: flapping and glottal stops in New Zealand English. *Te Reo* 38: 53–72.

Holmes, Janet (1997) Maori and Pakeha English: some New Zealand social dialect data. *Language in Society* 26: 65–101.

Holmes, Janet (2001) *An Introduction to Sociolinguistics*. London: Longman.

Holmes, Janet and Miriam Meyerhoff (2003) *The Handbook of Language and Gender*. Oxford/New York: Blackwell.

Holmes, Janet, Allan Bell and Mary Boyce (1991) *Variation and Change in New Zealand English: A Social Dialect Investigation*. Report to the Social Sciences Committee of the Foundation for Research, Science and Technology (NZ).

Holmes, Janet and Maria Stubbe (2003) *Power and Politeness in the Workplace: A Sociolinguistic Analysis of Talk at Work*. London: Longman.

Houston, Ann (1985) Continuity and change in English morphology: the variable (ING). Unpublished Ph.D. dissertation, University of Pennsylvania.

Hymes, Dell (1974) *Foundations in Sociolinguistics: An Ethnographic Approach*. Philadelphia: University of Pennsylvania Press.

Hyslop, Catriona (2001) *The Lolovoli Dialect of the North-east Ambae Language, Vanuatu*. Canberra: Pacific Linguistics.

Ide, Sachiko (1989) Formal forms and discernment: two neglected aspects of universals of linguistic politeness. *Multilingua* 8: 223–248.

Jackendoff, Ray (2002) *Foundations of Language: Brain, Meaning, Grammar, Evolution*. Oxford: Oxford University Press.

Jacomb, Edward (1914) *The English and the French in the New Hebrides*. Melbourne: George Robertson.

Jauncey, Dorothy (1997) A grammar of Tamambo: the language of western Malo, Vanuatu. Unpublished Ph.D. dissertation, Australian National University.

Jaworski, Adam (1993) *The Power of Silence: Social and Pragmatic Perspectives*. Newbury Park, Calif.: Sage Publications.

Johnstone, Barbara (2000) *Qualitative Methods in Sociolinguistics*. Oxford/New York: Oxford University Press.

Joseph, John E. (2004) *Language and Identity: National, Ethnic, Religious*. Houndmills/New York: Palgrave Macmillan.

Kachru, Braj (1966) Indian English: a study in contextualization. In C.E. Bazell, J.C. Catford, M.A.K. Halliday and R.H. Robins (eds) *In Memory of J.R. Firth*. London/New York: Longman, 224–287.

Kasper, Gabriele and Shoshana Blum-Kulka (eds) (1993) *Interlanguage Pragmatics*. New York/Oxford: Oxford University Press.

Kearns, Kate (2000) *Semantics*. Basingstoke: Macmillan.

Kegl, Judy (2004) Language predispositions that persist beyond critical periods for language acquisition. Plenary address, LSA 2004, Boston, Mass.

Kegl, Judy, Ann Senghas and Marie Coppola (1999) Creation through contact: sign language emergence and sign language change in Nicaragua. In Michel DeGraff (ed.) *Language Creation and Language Change: Creolization, Diachrony, and Development*. Cambridge, Mass./London: MIT Press, 179–237.

Kerswill, Paul (1996) Milton Keynes and dialect levelling in south-eastern British English. In David Graddol, Dick Leith and Joan Swann (eds) *English: History, Diversity and Change*. London/New York: Routledge, 292–300.

Kerswill, Paul and Ann Williams (1997) Investigating social and linguistic identity in three

British schools. In Ulla-Brit Kostinas, Ann-Brit Stenström and Anna-Malin Karlsson (eds) *Ungdomsspråk i Norden.* Stockholm: Meddelanden från Institutionen för nordiska språk vid Stockhoms universitet (MINS 43) [Working Papers of the Institute for Nordic Languages, Stockholm University], 159–176.

Kerswill, Paul and Ann Williams (2000) Creating a new town koine: children and language change in Milton Keynes. *Language in Society* 29: 65–115.

King, Ruth (2000) *The Lexical Basis of Grammatical Borrowing: A Prince Edward Island French Case Study.* Amsterdam/Philadelphia: John Benjamins.

King, Ruth (2004) Language contact and linguistic structure. Plenary address. New Ways of Analyzing Variation in English conference, University of Pennsylvania, Philadelphia.

Kouwenberg, Silvia and John V. Singler (2006) *The Handbook of Pidgin and Creole Studies.* Oxford: Blackwell.

Kroch, Anthony S. (2001) Syntactic change. In Mark Baltin and Chris Collins (eds) *The Handbook of Contemporary Syntactic Theory.* Oxford: Blackwell, 699–729.

Krosnar, Katka (2005) Prague mayor goes underground to end kafkaesque nightmare of taxi rip-offs. *Independent,* 15 January, p. 35.

Labov, William (1966) *The Social Stratification of English in New York City.* Washington, DC: Center for Applied Linguistics.

Labov, William (1972a) *Sociolinguistic Patterns.* Philadelphia: University of Pennsylvania Press.

Labov, William (1972b) *Language in the Inner City.* Philadelphia: University of Pennsylvania Press.

Labov, William (1990) The intersection of sex and social class in the course of linguistics change. *Language Variation and Change* 2: 205–254.

Labov, William (1994) *Principles of Linguistic Change: Internal Factors.* Oxford: Blackwell.

Labov, William (1995) The two futures of linguistics. In Ik-Hwan Lee (ed.) *Linguistics in the Morning Calm 3: Selected Papers from SICOL-1992.* Seoul: Hanshin Publishing.

Labov, William (2001) *Principles of Linguistic Change: Social Factors.* Oxford: Blackwell.

Labov, William ([1985] 2005) Some observations on the foundations of linguistics. <www.ling.upenn.edu/~wlabov/Papers/Foundations.html> Sampled November 2004, January 2005.

Lakoff, Robin (2004) *Language and Woman's Place: Text and Commentaries.* (Revised and expanded edition, edited by Mary Bucholtz.) New York/Oxford: Oxford University Press.

Landry, Rodrigue and Richard Y. Bourhis (1997) Linguistic landscape and ethnolinguistic vitality: an empirical study. *Journal of Language and Social Psychology* 16: 23–49.

Langlands, Eva (2002) Staff wanted: only Aussies need apply. *Sunday Herald,* 4 August, p. 9.

Lass, Roger (2002) South African English. In Rajend Mesthrie (ed.) *Language in South Africa.* Cambridge: Cambridge University Press, 104–126.

Lave, Jean and Etineene Wenger (1991) *Situated Learning: Legitimate Peripheral Participation.* Cambridge: Cambridge University Press.

Laver, John (1981) Linguistic routines and politeness in greeting and parting. In Florian Coulmas (ed.) *Conversational Routine.* The Hague: Mouton de Gruyter, 289–304.

Lavoie, Lisa and Abigail Cohn (2003) Sesquisyllables of English: the structure of vowel-liquid sequences. *14th International Congress of Phonetic Sciences Proceedings,* 109–112.

Lear, Edward ([1877] 1969) *The Quangle Wangle's Hat.* Illustrated by Helen Oxenbury. London: Heinemann.

Leech, Geoffrey (1980) *Explorations in Semantics and Pragmatics.* Amsterdam/Philadelphia: Benjamins.

Lenneberg, Eric H. (1967) *Biological Foundations of Language.* New York: Wiley.

Le Page, R.B. and Andrée Tabouret-Keller (1985) *Acts of Identity: Creole-based Approaches to Language and Ethnicity.* Cambridge: Cambridge University Press.

Lippi-Green, Rosina (1997) *English with an Accent: Language, Ideology, and Discrimination in the United States.* London/New York: Routledge.

Lucy, John (1992) *Language Diversity and Thought: A Reformulation of the Linguistic Relativity Hypothesis.* Cambridge: Cambridge University Press.

Lynch, John (2005) The odd couple: an unusual kin term in Aneityum. In Claudia Gross, Harriet D. Lyons and Dorothy A. Counts (eds) *A Polymath Anthropologist: Essays in Honour of Ann Chowning.* Department of Anthropology, University of Auckland: Research in Anthropology and Linguistics, 191–196.

Macaulay, Ronald (2001) *You're like 'why not?'* The quotative expressions of Glasgow adolescents. *Journal of Sociolinguistics* 5: 3–21.

McConnell-Ginet, Sally (2003) 'What's in a name?' Social labeling and gender practices. In Janet Holmes and Miriam Meyerhoff (eds) *The Handbook of Language and Gender.* Oxford/New York: Blackwell, 69–97.

McCormick, Kay (2002) *Language in Cape Town's District Six.* Oxford: Oxford University Press.

Mahootian, Shahrzad (2006) Code switching and mixing. In Keith Brown (ed.) *Encyclopedia of Languages and Linguistics.* Oxford: Elsevier, vol. 2, 511–527.

Mahootian, Shahrzad and Beatrice Santorini (1996) Code-switching and the complement/adjunct distinction. *Linguistic Inquiry* 27: 464–479.

Makihara, Miki (2001) Modern Rapa Nui adaptation of Spanish elements. *Oceanic Linguistics* 40: 191–223.

Makihara, Miki (2004) Linguistic syncretism and language ideologies: transforming sociolinguistic hierarchy on Rapa Nui (Easter Island). *American Anthropologist* 106: 529–540.

Makihara, Miki (2005) Being Rapa Nui, speaking Spanish: children's voices on Easter Island. *Anthropological Theory* 5: 117–134.

Martyna, Wendy (1980) The psychology of the generic masculine. In Sally McConnell-Ginet, Ruth Borker and Nelly Furman (eds) *Women and Language in Literature and Society.* New York: Praeger Publishers, 69–78.

Matus-Mendoza, Maríadelaluz (2004). Assibilation of /-r/ and migration among Mexicans. *Language Variation and Change* 16: 17–30.

Mead, Rebecca (2003) The Almost It Girl. *New Yorker,* 20 October, pp. 96–104.

Melancon, Megan E. (2000) The sociolinguistic situation of Creoles in south Louisiana: identity, characteristics, attitudes. Unpublished Ph.D. dissertation, Louisiana State University.

Mendoza-Denton, Norma (1999) Sociolinguistic and linguistic anthropology of US Latinos. *Annual Review of Anthropology* 28: 375–395.

Mesthrie, Rajend (ed.) (2001) *Concise Encyclopedia of Sociolinguistics.* Amsterdam/Oxford: Elsevier.

Mesthrie, Rajend (ed.) (2002) *Language in South Africa.* Cambridge: Cambridge University Press.

Mesthrie, Rajend, Joan Swann, Andrea Deumert and William L. Leap (2000) *Introducing Sociolinguistics.* Edinburgh: Edinburgh University Press.

Meyerhoff, Miriam (2000) The emergence of creole subject–verb agreement and the licensing of null subjects. *Language Variation and Change* 12, 2: 203–230.

Meyerhoff, Miriam (2001) Dynamics of differentiation: on social psychology and cases of language variation. In Nikolas Coupland, Christopher Candlin and Srikant Sarangi (eds) *Sociolinguistics and Social Theory*. London: Longman, 61–87.

Meyerhoff, Miriam (2003) Formal and cultural constraints on optional objects in Bislama. *Language Variation and Change* 14, 3: 323–346.

Mills, Sara (2003) *Gender and Politeness* (Studies in Interactional Sociolinguistics). Cambridge: Cambridge University Press.

Milroy, James (1992) *Linguistic Variation and Change*. Oxford/Cambridge, Mass.: Blackwell.

Milroy, James and Lesley Milroy (1991) *Authority in Language: Investigating Language Prescription and Standardisation* (2nd edn). London: Routledge.

Milroy, James, Lesley Milroy, Sue Hartley and David Walshaw (1994) Glottal stops and Tyneside glottalization: competing patterns of variation and change in British English. *Language Variation and Change* 6, 3: 327–357.

Milroy, Lesley (1987) *Language and Social Networks* (2nd edn). Oxford: Blackwell.

Milroy, Lesley and Matthew Gordon (2003) *Sociolinguistics: Method and Interpretation*. Oxford: Blackwell.

Montgomery, Michael (2000) Isolation as a linguistic construct. *Southern Journal of Linguistics* 24: 41–53.

Morales, J. Francisco, Mercedes López-Sáez and Laura Vega (1998) Discrimination and beliefs on discrimination in individualists and collectivists. In Stephen Worchel, J. Francisco Morales, Darío Páez and Jean-Claude Deschamps (eds) *Social Identity International Perspectives*. London/Thousand Oaks (Calif.)/New Delhi: Sage Publications, 199–210.

Mosel, Ulrike (1980) *Tolai and Tok Pisin: The Influence of the Substratum on the Development of New Guinea Pidgin*. Canberra: Pacific Linguistics (Research School of Pacific Studies, Australian National University).

Mufwene, Salikoko (1996) The Founder Principle in creole genesis. *Diachronica* 13: 81–134.

Mugglestone, Lynda (2003) *Talking Proper: The Rise of Accent as a Social Symbol* (2nd edn). Oxford: Oxford University Press.

Myers-Scotton, Carol (1993a) *Duelling Languages: Grammatical Structure in Code-switching*. Oxford: Clarendon Press.

Myers-Scotton, Carol (1993b) *Social Motivations for Code-switching: Evidence from Africa*. Oxford: Clarendon Press.

Nagy, Naomi (2001) 'Live free or die' as a linguistic principle. *American Speech* 70: 30–41.

Nagy, Naomi and Bill Reynolds (1997) Optimality theory and variable word-final deletion in Faetar. *Language Variation and Change* 9: 37–55.

Nahkola, Kari and Marja Saanilahti (2004) Mapping language changes in real time: a panel study on Finnish. *Language Variation and Change* 16: 75–92.

Nevalainen, Terttu (1999) Making the best of 'bad' data. *Neuphilologische Mitteilungen* 100: 499–533.

Nevalainen, Terttu and Helena Raumolin-Brunberg (2003) *Historical Sociolinguistics: Language Change in Tudor and Stuart England*. London: Longman.

Newmeyer, Frederick J. (ed.) (1988) *Linguistics: The Cambridge Survey*. Vol. 4: *Language: The Socio-cultural Context*. Cambridge: Cambridge University Press.

Nicholl, Katie (2003) If I'm the second Queen of England, why not Spain too? *Scottish Mail on Sunday*, 9 November, p. 35.

Nichols, Patricia C. (1983) Linguistic options and choices for Black women in the rural South. In Barrie Thorne, Cheris Kramarae and Nancy Henley (eds) *Language, Gender and Society*. Cambridge, Mass.: Newbury House, 54–68.

Niedzielski, Nancy (1997) The effect of social information on phonetic perception. Unpublished doctoral dissertation, University of California, Santa Barbara.

Niedzielski, Nancy (1999) The effect of social information on the perception of sociolinguistic variables. *Journal of Language and Social Psychology* 18: 62–85.

Niedzielski, Nancy and Dennis R. Preston (2000) *Folk Linguistics*. Berlin: de Gruyter.

Nordberg, Bengt and Eva Sundgren (1998) *On Observing Language Change: A Swedish Case Study*. FUMS Rapport nr. 190. Institutionen för nordiska språk vid Uppsala Universitet.

Nothofer, Bernd (2000) A preliminary analysis of the history of Sasak language levels. In Peter K. Austin (ed.) *Working Papers in Sasak*, Vol. 2. University of Melbourne, 57–84.

Ochs, Elinor (1992) Indexing gender. In Alessandro Duranti and Charles Goodwin (eds) *Rethinking Context: Language as an Interactive Phenomenon*. Cambridge: Cambridge University Press, 335–358.

Okamoto, Shigeko (2006) Variability in Japanese (Discourse). In Keith Brown (ed.) *Encyclopedia of Language and Linguistics* (2nd edn). Oxford: Elsevier, vol. 13, 319–326.

Orton, Harold *et al.* (1962) *Survey of English Dialects*. Leeds: E.J. Arnold & Son Ltd, for University of Leeds.

Patrick, Peter L. (1999) *Urban Jamaican Creole: Variation in the Mesolect*. Amsterdam/Philadelphia: John Benjamins.

Pauwels, Anne (1998) *Women Changing Language*. London/New York: Longman.

Podesva, Robert J. (2004) The significance of phonetic detail in the construction of social meaning. Paper presented at the Linguistic Society of America, annual meeting, Boston, Mass.

Pope, Jennifer (2002) The social history of a sound change on the island of Martha's Vineyard, Massachusetts: forty years after Labov. Unpublished MA dissertation, Department of Theoretical and Applied Linguistics, University of Edinburgh.

Poplack, Shana (1980) Sometimes I'll start a sentence in Spanish y termino en español: towards a typology of code-switching. *Linguistics* 18: 581–618.

Poplack, Shana and Douglas Walker (1986) Going through (L) in Canadian French. In David Sankoff (ed.) *Diversity and Diachrony*. Philadelphia/Amsterdam: John Benjamins, 173–198.

Preston, Dennis R. (1989) *Perceptual Dialectology*. Dordrecht: Foris Publications.

Preston, Dennis R. (1991) Sorting out the variables in sociolinguistic theory. *American Speech* 66: 33–56.

Preston, Dennis R. (1994) Sociolinguistics. In R.A. Asher (ed.) *Encyclopedia of Language and Linguistics*. Oxford: Pergamon, 180–184.

Preston, Dennis R. and Daniel Long (eds) (1999) *Handbook of Perceptual Dialectology*. Amsterdam/Philadelphia: John Benjamins.

Purnell, Thomas, William Idsardi and John Baugh (1999) Perceptual and phonetic experiments on American English dialect identification. *Journal of Language and Social Psychology* 18: 10–30.

Queen, Robin (2004) '*Du hast jar keene Ahnung*': African American English dubbed into German. *Journal of Sociolinguistics* 8: 515–537.

Rajah-Carrim, Aaliya (2003) A discussion of language tables from the 2000 population census of Mauritius. *Edinburgh Working Papers in Applied Linguistics* 12: 64–75.

Rampton, Ben (1995) *Crossing: Language and Ethnicity among Adolescents*. London: Longman.

Rampton, Ben (1998) Language crossing and the redefinition of reality. In Peter Auer (ed.) *Code-switching in Conversation: Language, Interaction and Identity*. London/New York: Routledge, 290–317.

Rickford, John R. (1987) *Dimensions of a Creole Continuum: History, Texts, and Linguistic Analysis of Guyanese Creole*. Stanford: Stanford University Press.

Rickford, John R. and Faye McNair-Knox (1994) Addressee- and topic-influenced style shift. In Douglas Biber and Edward Finegan (eds) *Sociolinguistic Perspectives on Register*. Oxford/New York: Oxford University Press, 235–276.

Roberts, Julie (2002) Child language variation. In J.K. Chambers, Peter Trudgill and Natalie Schilling-Estes (eds) *The Handbook of Language Variation and Change*. Oxford/New York: Blackwell, 333–348.

Rogers, Everett M. (1995) *Diffusion of Innovations* (4th edn). New York/London: Free Press.

Sachdev, Itesh (1998) Language use and attitudes among the Fisher River Cree in Manitoba. *Canadian Journal of Native Education* 22: 108–119.

Sankoff, David and Suzanne Laberge (1978) The linguistic market and the statistical explanation of variability. In David Sankoff (ed.) *Linguistic Variation: Models and Methods*. New York: Academic Press, 239–250.

Sankoff, Gillian (1980) *The Social Life of Language*. Philadelphia: University of Pennsylvania Press.

Sankoff, Gillian (1993) Focus in Tok Pisin. In Francis Byrne and Donald Winford (eds) *Focus and Grammatical Relations in Creole Languages*. Amsterdam/Philadelphia: John Benjamins, 117–140.

Sankoff, Gillian (1996) The Oceanic substrate in Melanesian pidgin/creole revisited: a tribute to Roger Keesing. In John Lynch and Fa'afo Pat (eds) *Oceanic Studies: Proceedings of the First International Conference on Oceanic Linguistics*. Canberra: Pacific Linguistics (Research School of Pacific Studies, Australian National University), 421–450.

Sankoff, Gillian (2004) Adolescents, young adults and the critical period: two case studies from *Seven Up*. In Carmen Fought (ed.) *Sociolinguistic Variation: Critical Reflections*. Oxford/New York: Oxford University Press, 121–139.

Sankoff, Gillian (2006) Apparent time and real time. In Keith Brown (ed.) *Encyclopedia of Language and Linguistics* (2nd edn). Oxford: Elsevier, vol. 1, 110–116.

Sankoff, Gillian (2005) Cross-sectional and longitudinal studies in sociolinguistics. In Ulrich Ammon *et al.* (eds) *Sociolinguistics/Soziolinguistik: An International Handbook of the Science of Language and Society/Ein internationales Handbuch zur Wissenschaft von Sprache und Gesellschaft*. Berlin: de Gruyter.

Sankoff, Gillian, Pierrette Thibault, Naomi Nagy, Hélène Blondeau, Marie-Odile Fonollosa and Lucie Gagnon (1997) Variation in the use of discourse markers in a language contact situation. *Language Variation and Change* 9: 191–217.

Schieffelin, Bambi B. (1990) *The Give and Take of Everyday Life: Language Socialization of Kaluli Children*. Cambridge: Cambridge University Press.

Schiffrin, Deborah, Deborah Tannen and Heidi E. Hamilton (eds) (2001) *The Handbook of Discourse Analysis*. Oxford: Blackwell.

Schilling-Estes, Natalie (1998a) Investigating 'self-conscious' speech: the performance register in Ocracoke English. *Language in Society* 27: 53–83.

Schilling-Estes, Natalie (1998b) Reshaping economies, reshaping identities: gender-based patterns of language variation in Ocracoke English. In Suzanne Wertheim, Ashlee C. Bailey and Monica Corston-Oliver (eds) *Engendering Communication: Proceedings from the Fifth Berkeley Women and Language Conference*, 509–520.

Schillinger, Liesl (2004) The boards: more. *New Yorker*, 8 March, p. 8.

Schultz, Muriel R. (1978) The semantic derogation of woman. In Barrie Thorne and Nancy Henley (eds) *Language and Sex: Difference and Dominance*. Rowley, Mass.: Newbury House, 64–75.

Schütz, Albert J. (1994) *The Voices of Eden: A History of Hawaiian Language Studies*. Honolulu: University of Hawai'i Press.

Shenk, Dena, Boyd Davis, James R. Peacock and Linda Moore (2002) Narratives and self-identity in later life: two rural American older women. *Journal of Aging Studies* 16: 401–413.

Simons, Gary F. (1982) Word taboo and comparative Austronesian linguistics. In Amran Halim, Lois Carrington and S.A. Wurm (eds) *Papers from the Third International Conference on Austronesian Linguistics*. Canberra: Pacific Linguistics C-76, 157–226.

Smith, Larry (1983) *Readings in English as an International Language*. Oxford: Pergamon.

Smith, Zadie (2000) *White Teeth*. London: Hamish Hamilton.

Taeldeman, Johan (1998) Levelling phenomena in the Flemish dialects: some observations on their teleology. *Folia Linguistica* 32: 11–22.

Tagliamonte, Sali (1998) *Was/were* variation across the generations: view from the city of York. *Language Variation and Change* 10: 153–191.

Tagliamonte, Sali and Alex D'Arcy (2004) *He's like, she's like*: the quotative system in Canadian youth. *Journal of Sociolinguistics* 8: 493–514.

Tajfel, Henri (1978) Interindividual behaviour and intergroup behaviour. In Henri Tajfel (ed.) *Differentiation between Social Groups: Studies in the Social Psychology of Intergroup Relations*. London/New York: Academic Press, 27–60.

Takano, Shoji (1998) A quantitative study of gender differences in the ellipsis of the Japanese postpositional particles -wa and -ga: gender composition as a constraint on variability. *Language Variation and Change* 10: 289–323.

Tamata, Apolonia (2004) *Taivosa*: a case of deliberate language shift. Paper presented at the Sixth Conference on Oceanic Languages, Port Villa, Vanuatu.

Tannen, Deborah (1986) Introducing constructed dialogue in Greek and American conversational and literary narrative. In Florian Coulmas (ed.) *Direct and Indirect Speech*. Amsterdam: de Gruyter, 311–332.

Tannen, Deborah (1990) *You Just Don't Understand: Women and Men in Conversation*. New York: Morrow/London: Virago.

Thackeray, William Makepeace (1968) *Vanity Fair: A Novel Without a Hero*. Harmondsworth: Penguin (edited with introduction by J.I.M. Stewart).

Thakerar, Jitendra N., Howard Giles and Jenny Cheshire (1982) Psychological and linguistic parameters of speech accommodation theory. In Colin Fraser and Klaus R. Scherer (eds) *Advances in the Social Psychology of Language*. Cambridge: Cambridge University Press, 205–255.

Ting-Toomey, Stella (1988) Intercultural conflict styles: a face-negotiation theory. In Young Yun Kim and Willam B. Gudykunst (eds) *Theories in Intercultural Communication*. Newbury Park (Calif.)/London/Delhi: Sage Publications, 213–235.

Ting-Toomey, Stella (ed.) (1994) *The Challenge of Facework: Cross-cultural and Interpersonal Issues*. Albany: State University of New York Press.

Trechter, Sara (2003) A marked man: the contexts of gender and ethnicity. In Janet Holmes and Miriam Meyerhoff (eds) *The Handbook of Language and Gender*. Oxford/New York: Blackwell, 423–443.

Trechter, Sarah (2006) Variation in native languages of North America. In Keith Brown (ed.) *Encyclopedia of Languages and Linguistics* (2nd edn). Oxford: Elsevier, vol. 13, 370–377.

Trousdale, Graeme (2000) Variation and (socio)linguistic theory: a case study of Tyneside English. Unpublished Ph.D. dissertation, University of Edinburgh.

Trousdale, Graeme (2005) The social context of Kentish raising: issues in Old English sociolinguistics. *International Journal of English Studies* 5: 59–76.

Trudgill, Peter (1972) Sex, covert prestige and linguistic change in urban British English. *Language in Society* 1: 179–195.

Trudgill, Peter (1974) Linguistic change and diffusion: description and explanation in sociolinguistic dialect geography. *Language in Society* 3: 215–246.

Trudgill, Peter (1983) Acts of conflicting identity: the sociolinguistics of British pop-song pronunciation. In Peter Trudgill, *On Dialect: Social and Geographical Perspectives*. Oxford: Blackwell, 141–160.

Trudgill, Peter (1986) *Dialects in Contact*. Oxford: Blackwell.

Trudgill, Peter (2002) *Sociolinguistic Variation and Change*. Edinburgh: Edinburgh University Press/Georgetown: Georgetown University Press.

Trudgill, Peter (2004) *New-Dialect Formation: The Inevitability of Colonial Englishes*. Edinburgh: Edinburgh University Press/Georgetown: Georgetown University Press.

Trudgill, Peter and Jean Hannah (2002) *International English: A Guide to the Varieties of Standard English* (4th edn). London: Arnold.

Tsujimura, Natsuko (1996) *An Introduction to Japanese Linguistics*. Oxford: Blackwell.

Turner, John (1996) Introduction. In W. Peter Robinson (ed.) *Social Groups and Identities: Developing the Legacy of Henri Tajfel*. Oxford: Butterworth-Heinemann.

Uchida, Aki (1992) When 'difference' is 'dominance': a critique of the 'anti-power-based' cultural approach to sex differences. *Language in Society* 21: 547–568.

Uhlenbeck, E.M. (1970) The use of respect forms in Javanese. In S.A. Wurm and D.C. Laycock (eds) *Pacific Linguistic Studies in Honour of Arthur Capell*. Canberra: Pacific Linguistics (Research School of Pacific Studies, Australian National University), 441–466.

Updike, John (1965) *Bech: A Book*. Greenwich, Conn.: Fawcett Publications.

Valente, Thomas W. (1995) *Network Models of the Diffusion of Innovations*. Cresskill, N.J.: Hampton Press.

Van de Velde, Hans, Marinel Gerritsen and Roeland van Hout (1996) The devoicing of fricatives in Standard Dutch: a real-time study based on radio recordings. *Language Variation and Change* 8: 149–175.

Vann, Robert E. (1998) Aspects of Spanish deictic expressions in Barcelona: a quantitative examination. *Language Variation and Change* 10: 263–288.

Warner, Sam L. No'eau (1999) *Kuleana*: the right, responsibility, and authority of indigenous peoples to speak and make decisions for themselves in language and cultural revitalization. *Anthropology and Education Quarterly* 30: 68–93.

Watts, Richard (2003) *Politeness*. Cambridge: Cambridge University Press.

Wells, J.C. (1982) *Accents of English*. Cambridge: Cambridge University Press.

Wenger, Etienne (1998) *Communities of Practice: Learning, Meaning and Identity*. Cambridge: Cambridge University Press.

Wetherell, Margaret and Jonathan Potter (1992) *Mapping the Language of Racism: Discourse and the Legitimation of Exploitation*. New York/London: Harvester Wheatsheaf.

White, L. and F. Genesee (1996) How native is near-native? The issue of ultimate attainment in adult second language acquisition. *Second Language Research* 12: 233–265.

Williams, Ann and Paul Kerswill (1999) Dialect levelling: continuity vs change in Milton Keynes, Reading and Hull. In Paul Foulkes and Gerry Docherty (eds) *Urban Voices*. London: Arnold, 141–162.

Williams, Colin H. (2000) *Language Revitalization: Policy and Planning in Wales*. Cardiff: University of Wales Press.

Winford, Donald (2003) *An Introduction to Contact Linguistics*. Malden, Mass./Oxford: Blackwell.

Wodak, Ruth and Martin Reisigl (2001) *Discourse and Discrimination: Rhetoric of Racism and Antisemitism*. London: Routledge.

Wolfram, Walt (1981) Varieties of American English. In Charles A. Ferguson and Shirley Brice Heath (eds) *Language in the USA*. Cambridge: Cambridge University Press, 44–68.

Wolfram, Walt (2006) Variation and language: an overview. In E.K. Brown (ed.) *Encyclopedia of Language and Linguistics*. Oxford: Elsevier.

Wolfram, Walt and Natalie Schilling-Estes (2005) *American English: Dialects and Variation* (2nd edn) Oxford: Blackwell.

Woolard, Kathryn A. (1998) Introduction: language ideology as a field of enquiry. In Bambi B. Schieffelin *et al.* (eds) *Language Ideologies: Practice and Theory*. New York/Oxford: Oxford University Press, 3–47.

Wucker, Michele (1999) *Why the Cocks Fight: Dominicans, Haitians and the Struggle for Hispaniola*. New York: Hill & Wang.

Index

Related titles from Routledge

The Language and Sexuality Reader

Deborah Cameron and Don Kulick

The Language and Sexuality Reader is the first of its kind to bring together material from the fields of anthropology, communication studies, linguistics, medicine and psychology in an examination of the role of sexuality in written and spoken language. The text begins by guiding students through early study in the field from the 1940s to the 1980s, where the focus is homosexual language, and its difference from the heterosexual mainstream. The second part of the reader widens the focus: moving away from the generic labels of 'homosexual' and 'heterosexual', it explores the diversity of linguistic and sexual practices as documented and debated among scholars from the mid-1990s to the present.

Organised into thematic sections, the reader addresses:

*   Early documentation of vocabulary used by male homosexuals; including Gershon Legman's glossary of 1941, and later work on the existence of a discourse style signifying gay identity
*   The use of language by individuals to present themselves as sexual and gendered subjects
*   The way language reflects, reinforces or challenges cultural norms defining what is 'natural' and desirable in the sphere of sex
*   The verbal communication of sexual desire in different settings, genres and media

Contributors include:

Hideko Abe, Laura Ahearn, Rusty Barrett, Deborah Cameron, Kathryn Campbell-Kibler, Donald W. Cory, Justine Coupland, Louie Crew, James Darsey, Penelope Eckert, Susan Ehrlich, Joseph J. Hayes, Scott Kiesling, Celia Kitzinger, Don Kulick, William L. Leap, Gershon Legman, Momoko Nakamura, Sally McConnell-Ginet, Julia Penelope, Robert J. Podesva, June Machover Reinisch, Sarah J. Roberts, Stephanie A. Sanders, David Sonenschein, David Valentine.

Deborah Cameron is a sociolinguist, and currently holds the Ruppert Murdoch Chair of Language and Communication at Oxford University. Her previous publications include *Verbal Hygiene* (1995) and *The Feminist Critique of Language* (1998).

Don Kulick is Professor of Anthropology and director of the Center for the Study of Gender and Sexuality at New York University. His books include *Travesti* (1998) and the co-edited *Fat*

Together, Deborah Cameron and Don Kulick are the authors of *Language and Sexuality* (2003)

ISBN10: 0–415–36308–X (HB)
0–415–36307–1 (PB)
ISBN13: 978–0–415–363082 (HB)
978–0–415–36307–5 (PB)

Available at all good bookshops
For ordering and further information please visit:
www.routledge.com

Related titles from Routledge

Language and Gender: An advanced resource book

Jane Sunderland

'This book marks a timely intervention in the field of language and gender research and provides students and researchers alike with essential primary materials. The book contains articles from a very wide range of disciplines; if you think that this book will contain all of the usual suspects, then prepare to be surprised – there are extracts on masculinity, corpus linguistics, post-structuralist linguistics, fairy tales, ELT textbooks, queer theory, and social networks. This would make an ideal textbook for gender and language courses.'
Sara Mills, Sheffield Hallam University, UK

Routledge Applied Linguistics is a series of comprehensive resource books, providing students and researchers with the support they need for advanced study in the core areas of English language and Applied Linguistics.

Language and Gender:

- Presents an up-to-date introduction to language and gender
- Includes diverse work from a range of cultural, including non-Western, contexts, and represents a range of methodological approaches
- gathers together influential readings from key names in the discipline, including: Deborah Cameron, Mary Haas and Deborah Tannen

Written by an experienced teacher and researcher in the field, Language and Gender is an essential resource for students and researchers of Applied Linguistics.

ISBN10: 0–415–31104–7 (pbk)
ISBN10: 0–415–31103–9 (hbk)
ISBN10: 0–20345649–1 (ebook)

ISBN13:978–0–41531104–5 (pbk)
ISBN13:978–0–41531103–8 (hbk)
ISBN13: 978–0–203-45649–1(ebook)

Available at all good bookshops
For ordering and further information please visit:
www.routledge.com

Related titles from Routledge

Reading Images: The Grammar of Visual Design
2nd Edition

Gunther Kress and Theo van Leeuwen

Praise for the first edition

'Reading Images is the most important book in visual communication since Jacques Bertin's Semiology of Information Graphics. It is both thorough and thought-provoking; a remarkable breakthrough.'
Kevin G. Barnhurst, Syracuse University, USA

This second edition of the landmark textbook *Reading Images* builds on its reputation as the first systematic and comprehensive account of the grammar of visual design. Drawing on an enormous range of examples from children's drawings to textbook illustrations, photo-journalism to fine art, as well as three-dimensional forms such as sculpture and toys, the authors examine the ways in which images communicate meaning.

Features of this fully updated second edition include:

*   new material on moving images and on colour

*   a discussion of how images and their uses have changed through time websites and web-based images

*   ideas on the future of visual communication.

Reading Images focuses on the structures or 'grammar' of visual design - colour, perspective, framing and composition - provides the reader with an invaluable 'tool-kit' for reading images and makes it a must for anyone interested in communication, the media and the arts.

ISBN10: 0–415–31914–5 (HBK)
ISBN10: 0–415–31915–3 (PBK)

ISBN13: 978–0–415–31914–0 (HBK)
ISBN13: 978–0–415–31915–7 (PBK)

Available at all good bookshops
For ordering and further information please visit:
www.routledge.com

Related titles from Routledge

The Routledge Companion to Sociolinguistics

Edited by
Carmen Llamas, Louise Mullany and Peter Stockwell

Have you ever noticed an accent or puzzled over a dialect phrase? Language can be a powerful tool with which one can create a persona; it can be a common ground between people or can be used as a divide between social groups. This companion is for anyone who is interested in how and why people speak and write with such diversity.

The Routledge Companion to Sociolinguistics includes articles by leading scholars in the field on:

- Methods of Observation and Analysis
- Social Correlates
- Socio-Psychological Factors
- Socio-Political Factors
- Language Change.

This is followed by a Glossary of terms with References and an Index. *The Routledge Companion to Sociolinguistics* opens up this discipline for the newcomer and provides a useful reference guide for the more advance sociolinguist.

0–415–33850–6
978–0415–33850–9

Available at all good bookshops
For ordering and further information please visit
www.routledge.com